Media in Hong Kong

This book examines the Hong Kong media over a 40 year period, focusing in particular on how its newspapers and TV stations have struggled for press freedom under the colonial British administration, as well as Chinese rule. Making full use of newly declassified material, extensive interviews and specific case-studies, it provides an illuminating analysis of the dynamics of political power and its relationship with media censorship. It reveals how the British colonial government repressed the Hong Kong media during the 1960s, and that despite the subsequent acquisition of greater independence and pluralism, press freedom has come under assault once again from Beijing since 1997. Consideration of the changes that took place around the handover of sovereignty includes detailed case-studies of press treatment of the case of a Hong Kong journalist jailed in China, and the coverage of the sensitive topic of the Taiwan presidential election of 2000. Nonetheless, despite the tremendous pressure to conform to the parameters of the new political climate in the wake of regime change, the case is made that not only has the Hong Kong media retained the capacity to exert the democratising influence of non-profit advocacy journalism, but it has succeeded in preserving traits largely lost in British and American journalism with the growth of media consumerism and capitalism. Overall, this book is an impressive discussion of the evolving face of the Hong Kong media, and is an important contribution to theoretical debates on the relationship between political power, economics, identity and journalism.

Carol P. Lai is Assistant Professor at the Department of Communication, University of Macau. She is a veteran journalist who has travelled extensively from the mid-1980s to the late 1990s to cover mainland China news. Elected as the chairperson of the professional trade union, Hong Kong Journalists Association, in 1997, she played a leading role in lobbying for press freedom internationally and in raising public awareness about free speech in the 1990s. She has also written book chapters and articles on journalism, media independence and the importance of pluralism in Hong Kong politics.

Routledge media, culture and social change in Asia
Series Editor Stephanie Hemelryk Donald
Institute for International Studies, University of Technology, Sydney

Editorial Board Devleena Ghosh, University of Technology, Sydney; Yingjie Guo, University of Technology, Sydney; K. P. Jayasankar, Unit for Media and Communications, Tata Institute of Social Sciences, Bombay; Vera Mackie, University of Melbourne; Anjali Monteiro, Unit for Media and Communications, Tata Institute of Social Sciences, Bombay; Gary Rawnsley, University of Nottingham; Ming-yeh Rawnsley, University of Nottingham; Jing Wang (MIT)

The aim of this series is to publish original, high-quality work by both new and established scholars in the West and the East, on all aspects of media, culture and social change in Asia.

Media in Hong Kong

Press freedom and political change, 1967–2005

Carol P. Lai

Routledge
Taylor & Francis Group

LONDON AND NEW YORK

First published 2007
by Routledge
2 Park Square, Milton Park, Abingdon, Oxon, OX14 4RN

Simultaneously published in the USA and Canada
by Routledge
270 Madison Ave, New York NY 10016

Routledge is an imprint of the Taylor & Francis Group, an informa business

Transferred to Digital Printing 2009

© 2007 Carol P. Lai

Typeset in Times by Wearset Ltd, Boldon, Tyne and Wear

British Library Cataloguing in Publication Data
A catalogue record for this book is available from the British Library

Library of Congress Cataloging in Publication Data
A catalog record for this book has been requested

ISBN10: 0-415-40121-6 (hbk)
ISBN10: 0-415-54421-1 (pbk)
ISBN10: 0-203-28047-4 (ebk)

ISBN13: 978-0-415-40121-0 (hbk)
ISBN13: 978-0-415-54421-4 (pbk)
ISBN13: 978-0-203-28047-8 (ebk)

In memory of
my father, Lai Yat, my father-in-law, Wong On, and my
mother-in-law, Au Lai-sang

Contents

Foreword

James Curran

Much theorising about the media draws upon a limited range of countries (mostly in north America and western Europe) but has the presumption to present itself in the form of universalistic generalisation. The patent absurdity of this ethnocentrism is beginning to dawn on western and other media researchers, which is why many are seeking out media books that relate to Asia, Latin America, the Middle East and Africa. This is one reason why Carol Lai's book on the media in Hong Kong will be of interest to media specialists around the world.

Another reason is that Carol Lai examines the development of Hong Kong's media in a rapidly changing political context. This enables her to draw attention to the complex interaction, and also changing nature, of the forces that made and remade the Hong Kong media. She begins her narrative with an account of the way in the British government suspended pro-Beijing newspapers, and jailed opponents of its colonial regime during the later 1960s. She then shows how the Hong Kong press became more critically independent and also professionally oriented during the 1990s in response to pressure from media staff, the growth of civil society and the ebbing away of colonial power. Her narrative concludes with the re-imposition of strong official pressures in the 2000s, following the reversion of Hong Kong to Chinese rule in 1997. These were reinforced by new media owners, a politicised distribution of advertising, and the siren call of Chinese nationalism and Confucian tradition. But there were also countervailing influences that prevented a complete subordination of the Hong Kong media to the new regime: most notably, the professional concerns of journalists, consumer pressure and the institutions of a still vibrant civil society. This produced a media landscape in which there were servile papers responding to pressure to be more independent, and critical papers that reined in criticism out of pragmatic caution ('no breaking news on China' commanded one outspoken publisher).

Part of the interest of this book stems from the rich sources that the author has skilfully mined: recently declassified public records in London, extensive interviews with people at different levels within media organisations, and careful textual analysis. This brings to life a complex and rich understanding of the forces influencing Hong Kong's media, with wider theoretical implications for the study of the media in general. Just one example must suffice. It has become commonplace within one western tradition for the market to be viewed as a system of public empowerment: the voice of the public is heard through the media, it is claimed, because the sovereign consumer demands it. It is commonplace within another opposed tradition to see the market as a system of control in which millionaire media owners impose their views. What Carol Lai reveals is a complex situation which conforms to neither theory. On the one hand, she documents the way in which conglomerate media businesses act as proxy censors imposing internal editorial controls in order to ingratiate themselves, and reap economic advantage from the Chinese government. One the other hand, she also shows the way in the market encourages and rewards populist independence (as in the case of *Apple Daily*). These contradictory pressures are overlaid by other influences which also leave their mark, and give rise to a differentiated media system.

Another feature of this book is that the author is herself critically independent. She deflates western humbug, revealing the way in which the British government proclaimed in the 1960s the virtues of freedom and democracy, while suppressing Communist papers, jailing critics and blocking democracy. But she is also critical of attempts to impose unjustified controls on contemporary Hong Kong media. Carol Lai is a lecturer in journalism in a Chinese university, and is part of one of the fastest growing areas of media studies in the world. If this is an indication of what is to come, China will become a major international centre of critical media research.

Acknowledgements

Journalism is my first love. I worked in the profession for more than a decade and was involved in campaigning for Hong Kong press freedom. This book is in many ways a continuation of that process. The works of Cliff Bale, To Yiu-Ming, Willy Lam, Albert Cheng, Daisy Li, Charles Goddard and Fong So remain my major sources of inspiration. They demonstrate enormous courage, determination and professionalism in support of their own cause. I salute their efforts and contributions to the field.

It is no exaggeration, however much a commonplace among authors, to say that this book could not have been written without the counsel and cooperation of many individuals. Acknowledgement is due, and gladly made, to those journalists who have granted me interviews. A full list of their names appears in the appendix. Some of them not only generously shared their time and thoughts, but they also provided me with insider information and insights during my field work in Hong Kong and, in other instances, while they were in London.

I am also grateful for the information and assistance which I have received from Theresa Leung, Joyce Nip, Anne Cheung, Grace Leung and Richard Wu, Adrian and Regina Cheung, Shum Yee-Lan, Sze Li-Yee, Winnie Tam, Leung Yiu-Wing, Fan Cheuk-Wan, Mak Tung-Wing, Chan Wai-Fong, Chiu Hsiang-Chung, Wong Kit-Gi, Jack Li, Andy Ho, Chris Yeung, Magdelena Wong, Virginia Ng, Man Cheuk-Fei, Liu Mei-Heung, Liu Kin-Ming, Allegro Poon, Ada Yeung, Ida Leung, Lau Suk-Fan, Teresa Ng, Pauline Mok, Eric Ma, Joseph Man Chan and Clement So.

Various friends and colleagues read and criticised draft chapters. Monika Metykova, Maurice Walsh and Lee Chin-Chuan provided me with helpful comments on an early draft, whilst Cliff Bale and To Yiu-ming helped immensely by reading and updating me with the latest developments concerning my final draft. The entire manuscript was read by Lui Tai-Lok, Gren Manuel, Sidney Rennert, Faizel Ismail and Sarah Blair, each of whom made valuable comments. I owe a particular debt of gratitude to my copy editor, Sarah Blair whose careful reading and suggestions helped me to clarify while giving free expression to my opinions. Thanks are also due to Stephen Ng, Bill and Katy Blair for their many kindnesses throughout our sojourn in London.

I also enjoyed inspiring lectures, stimulating conversation in London. I want to thank Dave Morley, Kevin Robins, Hugo de Burgh and Des Freedman, Angela Cockett, Brenda Ludlow, Zehra Arabadji, Aeron Davis, Casper Melville, Louise Chambers, Hyunju Park, Andre Luis Favilla, Maria Fernanda Maio Dias Veloso, Jonathan Grey, Jonathan Hardy, Masashi Iwasa, Carmen Sammut, Bong-soo Lee, Colin Sparks. I am also grateful to the staff of Goldsmiths media and communications department and library, the British Library, the Kew Public Record Office and the School of Oriental and African Studies library for facilitating the use of research materials and books. Special thanks to Routledge's editor Peter Sowden and his assistant Tom Bates, and the two anonymous reviewers who have given me useful comments and kind words. Thanks also due to the Research Committee, University of Macau for funding the second leg of this study, which will see its fruition in the next book.

For their continual personal support, my love and thanks to Kan Tai, Raymond and Cathy, Bo and Ken Yum, Ivy Wong and Philip Lo and Wong Kwan-You. Finally, I will always be grateful to James Curran, my guide and mentor during this project. A combination of thoughtful insights, kind words, tough deadlines, publishing and teaching advice and friendship all played a part in getting me to the finish line.

Abbreviations

CCP	Chinese Communist Party
CNS	The semi-official *China News Service*
CPPCC	Chinese People's Political Consultative Conference
DAB	Democratic Alliance for the Betterment of Hong Kong
DP	Democratic Party (Hong Kong)
DPP	Democratic Progressive Party (Taiwan)
HKEJ	*Hong Kong Economic Journal*
HKJA	Hong Kong Journalists Association
KMT	Nationalist Kuomingtang/Guomindang
LP	Liberal Party
Leftist	'Leftist' has a specific definition in the context of Hong Kong. It is usually used to denote those who adopt a friendly position to the Chinese authorities or who form some kind of alliance with the Chinese Government.
MPDN	*Ming Pao Daily News*
NCNA	*New China News Agency*, Hong Kong Branch. Before 1997, as well as its function of supplying news, the Agency acted as the de facto Chinese embassy. After 1997, its political office was renamed 'The Liaison Office of the Central People's Government in Hong Kong'.
NPC	National People's Congress
ODN	*Oriental Daily News*
HKSAR	Hong Kong Special Administrative Region
SCMP	*South China Morning Post*
UD	United Democrats, the leading opposition party in Hong Kong. It was later renamed the Democratic Party (DP).
Xinhua	*Xinhua News Agency*, alias for NCNA

1 Introduction

In this chapter, the two political economy approaches to media analysis, the radical and the liberal tradition, will be examined, and a brief summary of the major components concerning the relationship between the media and the power structure within Hong Kong society is set out. The chapter also provides a critical evaluation of Hong Kong scholarly work concerning the media, and a short outline of the Hong Kong context.

Radical tradition

Radical political economists tend to view capitalist society as being class dominated. The media are seen as part of an ideological arena in which various class ideas are contested. Although dominated by certain classes, ultimate control is increasingly concentrated in the monopoly of capital. Analysts of this tradition are concerned that the increasing concentration of media power coincides with dominant political and economic power interests.[1] Media professionals, while enjoying some measure of autonomy, are believed to be socialised into, and internalise the norms of, the dominant culture. Taken as a whole, the interpretive framework relayed by the media coincides with the interests of the dominant classes. Although it is acknowledged that audiences sometimes negotiate and contest these frameworks, in fact they lack access to alternative meaning systems that would enable them to reject the framework suggested by the media.[2]

One of the major propositions of this tradition is that the news product reflects the dominant ideology. News is said to carry dominant ideas, and is a construct, omitting items which do not conform to the dominant view. Textual dominance can be achieved by constructing news texts in an interpretive framework consonant with the dominant meaning systems. News is produced and organised in such a way that the frame of reference is biased in favour of the establishment.[3] It is also argued that the media promote the values of capitalism. Capitalism and consumerism emerge largely uncontested.[4] However, it is not only the message carried by the media that is problematic; it is the media themselves, as they become increasingly conglomerated and transnational.[5] News as a 'construct' illustrates the dominant patriarchal culture; female roles are depicted in a biased way.[6] Similarly, in reporting ideologically sensitive issues, such as industrial disputes, dominant discourses are relayed using credible sources such as elites, experts and officials, whereas opposing views are marginalised by the use of less credible personalities or the man/woman in the street.[7]

Apart from the use of sources, textual dominance can also be achieved by omission. Consistent patterns of omission have been found in news and current affairs where there are imbalances of media attention, concentrating on individuals rather than on corporations, and policy operations are separated from the underlying relationship to the political and economic power.[8] Oppositional and alternative views are only presented occasionally in order to maintain the legitimacy and credibility of news organisations. In fact, limitations can be put in place to block the elaboration of alternative views.

Analysts working within this tradition note that part of the press, or certain news items, might contest the dominant ideology. But taken as a whole, the news product is set within the dominant ideology framework, and alternative viewpoints are either left out or well contained. The dominant ideology reflected in news texts is largely a result of direct or indirect influence exerted on the media by the dominant groups. In capitalist societies most media institutions are privately owned. The degree of the dominant groups' influence on the media, and the degree of autonomy the journalists exercise against the constraints imposed by media organisations, serve as opposing forces, and the interaction between the two results in various levels of control over the media.

From the perspective of political economy, there is a significant amount of research investigating the effects of media ownership on the ideology of news output. Despite the proliferation of news media, there are growing trends towards media concentration, cross-ownership, networking with non-media operations, and ties between media and government officials.[9] There is substantial evidence of power concentration in media institutions. Newspaper owners are generally closely affiliated with, and share the interests of, the economic and political establishment. The overall effect is the tendency of media conglomerates to limit the range of information made available, and to protect their related commercial interests.

According to this perspective, the commercial aims of owners or advertisers have a bearing on news operations and news content. The media serve to enhance the economic interests of the newspaper's proprietor, and in consequence pressure is exercised over editorial coverage to serve the needs of major advertisers. It is argued that the delegation of power from owners to managerial elites provides partial freedom in the daily operation of the media, but dispersion of ownership at the managerial level does not necessarily loosen the control of owners on the organisational orientation and editorial culture.[10] The fact that the news media owners can control the allocation of resources and the operation of the newsroom limits the 'managerial-revolution'.[11] There are largely two forms of control that owners and managerial executives can exert – at the level of allocation and at the operational level. Allocative control involves setting overall policy, making decisions such as senior appointments, allocation of resources, dictation of editorial lines and investment, and control of overall distribution of profits. Capital concentration sets broad boundaries for exercising allocative control in the larger media environment, which may, in turn, influence how specific media organisations implement operational control within that environment. Budget cuts represent one strategy used to force journalists to suit the needs of advertisers and owners. This kind of self-censorship is regarded as being hard to detect because it involves internalised organisational values. Moreover, journalists are obliged to report favourably on the owners' economic ventures and investment. In fact, a number of authors have provided evidence of an owner's interference that affected operational control to a great extent.[12]

Despite claims of autonomy, news content is generally found to be in accordance with the owner's ideology in liberal democratic societies. Some media moguls have explicit political commitments that filter into the media output of their organisation.[13] Not all owners are politically oriented, but few of them are politically indifferent. Within the organisation, journalists usually internalise the organisational norms and understand the boundaries of the ideological spectrum. The ultimate power of hiring and firing senior journalists serves as a deterrent to transgression. Routine compliance is the result of this subtle mechanism of self-censorship and the interpretation of corporate norms.[14] Thus, the strength of this control process lies in the education and training of journalists, the in-built penalties and rewards within media organisations, and in direct intrusion from the management. But the most useful control mechanism is the internalisation of values.[15]

It has been argued that the problem with journalism is primarily its professionalism.[16] According to this theory, the professional code that aims to achieve objectivity and neutrality has undermined the authority of journalists who, in turn, need to seek official sources as authoritative or legitimate sources of information. The news agenda is then set according to official demands. As a consequence, the news media cannot antagonise their sources (such as government officials, powerful individuals), as they have to rely on them to obtain news information or insider information. Eventually this results in a mainstream bias, the so-called 'official stenography' or expert opinion, which largely coincides with the mainstream opinion of the dominant power.[17]

It is also argued that journalists tend to avoid describing the background to a story. This omission of contextualisation results in news becoming an event-oriented item, usually shaped by public relations people who, in turn, play a major role in promoting de-politicisation.

In addition, there are indirect influences on the media at work. For instance, there are situations where owners do not have any ideological interests or connection with the dominant groups. The problem of control in these ambiguous situations remains significant. Critical analysts propose three main types of indirect influence on the media by the dominant groups: market influences, cultural links and indirect links with the government. Irrespective of ideological orientation, all owners of media corporations have a vital interest in increasing the profitability of their enterprise.[18] The profit motive in turn affects the range and ideological spectrum of the media organisation. 'The enormous resource commanded by these conglomerates, their large economy of scale, and extensive dominance of linked markets, have undermined the functionary of the market as a free and open contest.'[19] According to Curran, the commercial media do not create a free market place of ideas as they promise; instead market forces can distort the free exchange of ideas, for instance, high entry costs effectively prohibit ordinary people from setting up a newspaper. Indeed, because of the mainstreaming effect of the commercial market, along with the need to generate advertisement and subscription revenues, the proliferation of media choices does not result in substantial expansion of the media's ideological range.[20]

Apart from the market link, there is usually indirect political influence from the government. In different periods in the past, the ruling classes restrained and regulated the shape and boundaries of the media by setting up a wide range of media legislation including censorship, libel laws, taxation, licensing and official secrets acts.[21] In addition, the connection between the media and the dominant cultural patterns is more subtly pervasive than legal repression and market influence. Due to the nature of journalistic work, news workers (under constant pressure in respect of deadlines and circulation) are prompted to produce news content that reflects the dominant culture and ideology. In the routine of news production, journalists find it easier to produce content using widely familiar meaning systems and frames of reference.[22]

While some Marxist media scholars are criticised for being instrumentalists/ functionalists,[23] many others maintain a critical edge in non-reductive ways.[24] An essential argument is that the media play a functional role in legitimating capitalism in most industrial societies.[25] However, the strength of the radical political economy approach is its analysis of the relationship between the media and the power structure of society, and its examination of whether the media are particularly sensitive to the realignment of power structures and power relationships in society. By analysing political and economic pressure from dominant power blocks and its direct and indirect influence on the media, many writers (despite notable differences) have developed important insights into the media's substantial, albeit not total, dependence on the power structure. However, the approach may overlook the part that market forces play. The profession not only has a role in supporting state legitimacy, it also has to maintain its own legitimacy in a market economy. The media are not only responsive to political and economic pressure from the dominant power, they also define issues, help to draw public attention to issues, and manifest the scope and extent of social debate. The next section looks at the counter-argument to the radical political economy approach.

Liberal pluralist tradition

According to the liberal tradition, the media respond to, and reflect, the views and values of the public, thus ensuring consumer control. The liberal theorists' view differs from the radical tradition in that, while the radical approach emphasises media censorship, the liberal approach emphasises the market that enables consumers to exercise control over the media. The latter's argument is formulated around the concept of the sovereign consumer. The central idea is that the general shape and nature of the press is ultimately determined by its readers because of the hidden hand of the free market.[26] It is argued that media owners in a market-based system have to provide people with what they want if they are to stay in business and prosper. This ensures that the media as a whole represent the views and values of their audience, and act as a mouthpiece for the public. The press, it is argued, are managed by executives who seek to maximise sales, rather than to advance their political aspirations. This then establishes the consumer as the ultimate controller of the press, which in turn means the media reflect public opinion rather than the views of organised political interests. The argument goes further to celebrate a market-based media system that liberates the media even from those who run it. The main motivation for this ultimate liberation is, supposedly, the drive to maximise profits.

Furthermore, it is argued that the free market not only ensures that the media express the public's views, but it also enhances the informational role of the media. This is portrayed as facilitating public rationality and enabling a collective expression of opinion. Thus it is claimed that the free market system should, in theory, allow people to air whatever opinions they wish, and ensure that all significant viewpoints are published and that a wide range of information is made available. Hence, intellectual resources of information are mobilised from varied and diverse sources. Significantly, a free market place of ideas should have a tendency to correct errors and biases during the course of interaction. Thus the market system is hailed as the best possible mechanism for facilitating self-governance. It will help keep open channels of communication between government and governed, and among the various interest groups in society. Because the free market produces a media system that responds to, and expresses, the people's views, market processes enhance, and are central to, the exercise of democracy.

The liberal tradition also emphasises the importance of state control, and argues that the removal of state control would lead to the liberation of the media.[27] This is because liberals view the media as having a more autonomous role with respect to the dominant power structure in practice. Overall, the liberal tradition's emphasis on the media's greater independence from the power structure within a free society is largely what distinguishes it from the radical tradition. That said, a number of liberalists have got one foot inside and one foot outside the liberal tradition.[28] In essence, although they believe that the media have more independence from the power structure than do their radical colleagues, they do not fully sign up to the key tenets of liberal tradition.

Dissenting liberal views

While radical analysts emphasise media control by owners and advertisers, liberal sociologists, such as Michael Schudson, stress the autonomy of professional journalism in resisting external and internal pressures. While it is doubtless true that members of the media have some autonomy and authority to depict the world according to liberal ideals, in his essay on objectivity as a journalistic norm, Schudson argues that journalistic professionalism as a norm serves as a kind of social control and plays a role in constructing a social identity. As a norm, the professionalism of journalism has to establish, above all, a self-conscious pursuit of internal group solidarity and, moreover, articulate ideals of social practice. This involves, for example, exercising control over subordinates and passing on group culture to the next generation.[29] Hence, 'objectivity' is a moral ideal, a set of reporting and editing practices, and an observable pattern of news writing.

> What is clear is that the moral norm American journalists live by in their professional lives, use as a means of social control and social identity, and accept as the most legitimate grounds for attributing praise and blame is a norm that took root first, and most deeply, in this journalism and not in others across the Atlantic.[30]

It is the media's concern with public legitimacy that helps to shield them from big business manipulation.[31]

In connection with professionalism, Hallin puts forward another important argument, saying that the relation of contemporary American journalism to political authority is ambivalent.[32] He argues that there is a closer relation developing between journalists and the state. Journalists are used to borrowing the authority of the state. Thus, they are more inclined to use sources of dominant power, 'para-journalists', namely government officials, public relations agents, powerful and wealthy people.[33] Hence, the behaviour of the media attempts to reflect a societal consensus. The media have moved towards the ideal type of differentiated media that are 'structurally free from inhibiting economic, political, solidary and cultural entanglement'.[34]

On the one hand, structurally, the American news is both highly autonomous from direct political control and, on the other hand, through the routine of the news-gathering process, deeply intertwined in the actual operation of government and becomes a sort of 'fourth branch of government'. This part of the informal constitution of the political system in turn makes the media accept certain standards of 'responsible behaviour'. These standards involve not only the renunciation of the right to exercise partisan criticism of political authority, but also the granting of certain positive rights of access to news, and the acceptance, for the most part, of the agenda and perspective of the establishment.

Elaborating his argument further, Hallin points out that the behaviour of the media is nonetheless closely tied to the degree of consensus among political elites:

> [W]hen consensus is strong, the media play a relatively passive role and generally reinforce official power to manage public opinion; when political elites are divided, on the other hand, the media become more active, more diverse in the points of view they represent, and more difficult to manage.[35]

According to Hallin, American news media are structurally autonomous from economic and political control. He refers back to historical developments, the displacement of power, when nationalism replaced liberalism, and the suspicion of power. Currently journalists have more autonomy in relation to government, and it tends to be equally true that professional journalists have more autonomy within news organisations.

Thus, liberal analysts tend to see society as a complex of competing groups and interests, none of them predominant all of the time. Media organisations, in general, are seen as systems that enjoy a significant level of autonomy from the state, political parties and institutions. Control of the media is said to be in the hands of an autonomous managerial elite who allow media professionals a considerable degree of flexibility. Media audiences are seen as capable of manipulating the media in a variety of ways in accordance with their needs and demands.[36]

It is frequently argued that the concentration of power in a small number of profit-making news organisations would restrict the free-flow of expression. However, as a consequence of the separation of press from political parties and political movements, commercial considerations become more influential, and the press becomes increasingly organised by a set of self-governing professional norms and practices.

Undoubtedly, one of the major propositions of this tradition is that the media function as a mirror, and reflect reality.[37] Liberal analysts, in general, define journalism as the business or practice of producing and disseminating information about contemporary affairs of general public interest and importance. Schudson echoes the view that the function of journalism is to promote communication and social coordination of individuals and groups through shared symbols and meanings.[38]

Despite these developments, the norms and institutions differ from country to country; indeed, commercialisation and professionalism vary across nations. Yet Schudson acknowledges that the problem with news lies largely in political cynicism and cultural infotainment, the complexities of issues linked with journalism having largely to do with profit matters. Despite that, he argues that some scholars[39] write as if corporate ownership and commercial organisations necessarily compromise the democratic promise of public communication. However, from a global perspective, the worst-case scenarios involve the absence of commercial organisations, or their total domination by the state.

Indeed, Latin America serves as an example in this context for this tradition, as Latin American governments benefit more from state-controlled media that are subject to censorship and manipulation.[40] Also in China, the news media are both market-dominated and state-dominated, though this distinction is not easy to make.[41] In China a self-censorship system is at work, and its formation is largely due to external pressures and structural effects, thus party control and rapid commercialisation both occur at the same time.[42] While Schudson acknowledges that there is reason to worry that not just the state but also the market can threaten press freedom, he argues that it does not follow from this that capitalism is necessarily the enemy of free expression. News reports are basically 'constructed reality',[43] and verification of facts is both a political and a professional accomplishment.

Although radical and pluralist traditions have co-existed in tension, some critical theorists argue that the two traditions are not so far apart as is usually supposed.[44] There are variations within, and convergence between, the two camps. Attempts have been made to develop a 'midway' in media theory.[45] Similarly, I shall argue that the dominant ideology and liberal market theses both have their merits as well as shortcomings in analysing a changing society. At a time of political change, journalists apparently need to restructure their news net in order to respond to the new configuration of authority.[46] The case of Hong Kong as part of China, in particular whether it deviates from the western model of media organisation or whether it could bring some insight to the traditional model of political economy, is the major concern of this book. In the next section I attempt to trace the evolution of the Hong Kong press and critique Hong Kong scholarly work concerning the media from the perspective of this tradition.

Evolution of the Hong Kong press

The Hong Kong press can be traced back to the mid nineteenth century when Hong Kong was ceded to Britain. From then on, the Hong Kong press served largely as a meeting place between China and the West, and as a contested space for Chinese political parties. Hong Kong was first acquired in 1842, but territorial expansion was not Britain's primary goal.[47] Instead, the main goal was to secure a naval base, and an entrepot to protect and expand British economic interests in the Far East. At the time of cession, Hong Kong was a barren island with an estimated indigenous population of 5,000 inhabitants, mainly fishermen, whereas British residents were largely traders.[48]

In the early days, the colonial authorities were anxious to curb any opposing voices, whether British or indigenous. For example, between 1857 and 1859, William Tarrant of *Friend of China* was imprisoned for 12 months for libel for accusing the Colonial Secretary of corruption.[49] George Ryder of the *Daily Press* faced similar punishment when he exposed the possibly corrupt acts of English officials in Hong Kong. He was found guilty of criminal libel and sentenced to six months in jail.[50]

However, these incidents involving the English press did not deter the Chinese from setting up their own anti-authority Chinese press. In the 1840s, Hong Kong was a haven for political dissidents escaping persecution from the imperial Chinese government in mainland China. Revolutionaries came to Hong Kong to advocate the overthrow of the last imperial government of China, and to seek to mobilise people to this end.[51]

In 1847 Wang Tao set up the first Chinese-language newspaper, *Tsun Wan Daily News* (*Circulation Daily*).[52] Wang was generally regarded as the father of Chinese journalism.

In 1858, Wu Ting-fang, a former Chinese foreign minister who had received a western education, started *Chung Wei Hsin Pao* (*Sino Foreign Daily News)*, which backed the reform movement in China. However, the paper was prosecuted by the British government for sedition, and was fined $101 for opposing Chinese participation in the First World War.[53]

While the Chinese press in general were marked by their concern in China politics, the early Chinese press in particular were steadfast nationalist. They were largely seen, and used, as a mobilising force for enlightenment, anti-colonialist social reform and political revolution.[54]

Despite the fact that the Chinese newspapers were concerned primarily with overthrowing the imperial Chinese regime of the Qing dynasty, and later with civil unrest in China, the British had reason to fear that such nationalistic sentiments might easily spill across the border and be transformed into anti-colonial sentiment. Partly out of fear that Hong Kong might become a centre for sedition and social instability, and partly as a gesture to appease China, the Seditious Publication Ordinance was enacted in 1907.[55] After the end of the Qing dynasty in 1911, China entered into a period of contending warlords, and Hong Kong resumed its role as a propaganda and information base. The colonial government was very cautious and sensitive in this period of turmoil. In 1914, the Seditious Publication Ordinance barred publication of material containing content that might damage the colony or the mainland's law and order or political stability, and it prohibited importation of publications that contained such material.[56] In 1927, the Printers and Publication Ordinance was enacted to deter attacks on the British establishment.[57]

Though the concept of a free press had been well entrenched in Britain as early as 1695, the colonial government did not implement the liberal ideology in Hong Kong.[58] After the Second World War, Hong Kong became a shelter for Chinese refugees.

In 1948, the Chinese Communist Party launched *Ta Kung Pao* and *Wen Wei Po* in Hong Kong, and a year later the Nationalists launched the *Hong Kong Times*.[59] With the Communist take-over of mainland China, the ideological war in Hong Kong became critical.

In this political atmosphere there was a growing fear that the spread of nationalism might lead to instability and the possible overthrow of the colonial regime, so two ordinances were enacted to curb the possible spread of nationalistic sentiment. In 1949, the Emergency Regulations (Amendment) Ordinance[60] granted the Governor extensive powers to deal with an emergency, including censorship, and the control and suppression of publications and other means of communication. In 1951, the Control of Publication (Consolidation) Ordinance[61] was passed to punish the publication of 'false' news.[62]

While the early Hong Kong press was closely tied to the colonial and business elite, sections of it later turned to serve as propagandists for Chinese parties and interests.[63] Between 1925 and 1952, various Chinese newspapers were established, some of which have survived to the present day.[64] In contrast to the partisan press, the primary concern of these commercial papers was to provide the public with information about local affairs and daily entertainment, albeit some retained a strong political inclination towards Taiwan, and others adopted an 'anti-communist' attitude. Still, they can be distinguished from the partisan press that was owned and controlled by political parties and regimes.[65] Hong Kong became an ideological battleground for Chinese nationalism/patriotism.[66]

The decline of partisan papers, and the rise of the commercial press, was most noticeable during the decades from the late 1970s and early 1980s, respectively, to the present. According to mainstream scholarly views, one of the major factors that accounted for this phenomenon was demography. The proportion of the locally born population increased as the overall population expanded.[67] In the 1950s, many citizens were refugees from mainland China, with a large proportion of them viewing Hong Kong as their temporary shelter. The change in demography and later localisation tended to foster the commercial press and affect the development of the partisan press.[68] The second major reason for the expansion of the commercial press was the growth of the advertising industry.[69] As early as the late 1940s, rich people from cosmopolitan Shanghai fled to Hong Kong together with their business skills and capital.[70] Hence, the growth in the local-born population and increasing business opportunities all contributed to the rise of a commercial press.

Likewise, with the commercial press dominating the market, the partisan newspapers were marginalised, serving only as the mouthpiece for either the Chinese Communist Party or the Nationalist Taiwan Kuomintang. Their circulation was so low that they were not included in the annual Hong Kong Media Index (as shown in Table 1 of the appendix).[71] With financial backing from Beijing, the pro-Chinese Communist Party newspapers maintained a presence in Hong Kong, but in recent years they were forced to make adjustments because of keen market competition.[72] Traditionally, the 'centrist press' meant those newspapers not taking a clear position on either the politics of the Chinese Communist Party or the Nationalist Taiwan Kuomintang. They expressed more or less independent views on the issues of Chinese politics, and focused mainly on making profits. Their involvement in local political affairs was limited, but less constrained than in the case of Chinese politics. Even when local issues were commented upon, they tried to avoid clashes with the Hong Kong government. During the political transition, the centrist newspapers became increasingly pro-Hong Kong, especially in the case of the mass press. Despite that, they refrained from opposing dominant power ideas and avoided presenting alternative viewpoints.

In sum, under colonial rule, the majority of the mainstream press reflected the dominant power interests, although at one time a radical press emerged that struggled against the state and ownership control. Apart from the radical press backed by the People's Republic of China, political journals flourished briefly in the late 1970s and early 1980s as shown in Table 1 of the appendix. However, not many were able to survive to become popular and influential. British colonial political suppression was usually not that explicit. One strategy was to allow at least an appearance of balance that in fact amounted to a policy of divide-and-rule. Thus they allowed the pro-Nationalist groups to survive and gave some room to anti-colonial political forces. So at least until the riot of 1967, the communist group were left relatively free to do what they wanted (as a means of balancing the pro-Nationalist group).[73] However, the restrictive measures (such as legal instruments) were in place, to be used if needed. The costly licensing fee also prevented the less advantaged from entering the public arena by opening a newspaper.

Contemporary media[74]

A former British colony, Hong Kong following the political reunification with China serves as a test case for the 'one country, two systems' concept where a capitalist economy interacts with a socialist system. The Hong Kong press is part and parcel of a hybridised city full of contradictions and ambivalence, where traditional and western values, and a capitalist economy and an authoritarian bureaucratic rule, exist at the same time. In the late 1990s, with a population of about 6.6 million, Hong Kong had a diversified and dynamic news media. They included: 50 daily newspapers (with 14 comprehensive dailies), more than 600 periodicals, two commercial terrestrial TV companies, one cable TV service, a regional satellite TV service, one public broadcaster and two commercial radio stations. The political spectrum of the press has become narrower, with a major shift towards the new regime (pro-communist and pro-establishment), and a cleavage between a pro-Hong Kong and a pro-China political orientation.[75] The media also cover a range of tastes from the elitist to the more commercial and trivial. Paradoxically, the limited democratic development of Hong Kong indirectly helps to reinforce the role of the media as a contentious forum for various interest groups and the public.

Journalism and power

Hong Kong was a British colony for 156 years. It was a relatively free society in the early 1990s, albeit an undemocratic one, but then became subject to the rule of an authoritarian regime that pledged a high degree of autonomy in 1997.[76] In the last century, Hong Kong was transformed from a lone barren fishing port to a prosperous city state that is home to more than seven million (mainly Chinese) residents. Situated at the tip of southern China, this island had long depended on the mainland for food and water. During the Cold War, the former British colony served China as a port of entry and a window to the western world. During the long history of precarious arrangements and political negotiations between Britain and China, Hong Kong developed into a leading financial, trading and communication centre in Asia.[77] Yet, after the change of political regime in 1997, the fate of civil liberties in this highly sophisticated capitalist city, with an established rule of law and a dynamic and diversified news media, remained uncertain.[78] This is the political background in which the situation of the contemporary Hong Kong press should be explored. I provide a more detailed discussion on the socio-political and economic context when dealing with the period in question in further chapters. The following section includes my critical review of scholarly work on the Hong Kong media that focuses on the transition and the post-handover period, although I shall also comment on media studies research since the late 1960s. I examine journalism from a historical point of view in three broad periods: under colonial rule in the late 1960s; in the 'power vacuum' of the political transition; and under Chinese rule in the post-handover period.

First stage – the late 1960s

The mass media usually form a very significant component of the political system of a society. As a result of their size and diversity, coupled with the opportunities offered by an unrepresentative bureaucratic administration, the mass media in Hong Kong should arguably have taken up a bigger role in the political process.[79] According to Hong Kong political scientists, however, past developments in Hong Kong suggest this was not the case. The growth of the mass media has neither contributed to the development of democracy nor to an independence movement. Kuan and Lau argue that the experience of Hong Kong is a result of the minimal integration of the political and mass media systems: 'Hong Kong [is] a minimally-integrated media-political system wherein interactions between the mass media and local political institutions have until recently [the late 1980s] been restricted.'[80]

Kuan and Lau believe that, first of all, no integration of the media and the political elite occurred in the case of Hong Kong. The media elite (especially the owners of the Chinese press) and the high-ranking officials (the British expatriates) were two distinct types of people. Moreover, the structural linkage between press and political institutions was also weak. All press institutions were privately owned. The colonial government passed legislation to secure ultimate control over the mass media institutions by means of registration, franchise conditions, prohibitions and emergency powers. During the past century, the Hong Kong press was intensively involved in Chinese rather than Hong Kong politics. At the time, there was no local party in Hong Kong. Media partisanship still existed, but basically with an external reference. Party papers were externally controlled from Beijing or Taipei, and had an overseas orientation. Political ideology was divided along the China–Taiwan continuum, not on issues relevant to Hong Kong. Furthermore, the press/party parallelism grew not out of local politics but was 'a residual extension of modern Chinese politics'.[81] The Chinese orientation of the press in Hong Kong had thus significantly reduced its relevance to the local political system. It is argued that the press in Hong Kong had, unlike its counterparts in many other colonies, contributed only minimally to changes in the political system of which it was a part.[82]

Under colonial rule, the news media were said to be 'apolitical and apathetic'.[83] They did not provide much coverage of local affairs, but rather concentrated on events outside the territory, namely mainland China and Taiwan. The reason behind this was said to be the 'refugee mentality' that meant Hong Kong was a 'borrowed place' at a 'borrowed time'.[84] The relationship between the Hong Kong news media and the colonial regime was in general characterised as cordial and harmonious, provided the former worked within the boundaries set by the colonial administration. Research by Mitchell published in 1969 shows that there was not much emphasis on colonial policy in the news, let alone critical commentary and editorial.[85] In his study of papers published between 1951 and 1966, Mitchell found that editorials critical of the Hong Kong government were indeed rare. The indifference of the press to local politics left the Hong Kong government without any serious challenger, thus it could afford to grant the press a substantial degree of freedom of expression, which it mostly exercised with reference to Chinese politics. The press in turn buttressed the colonial status quo of Hong Kong.

Apart from the leftist (communist) press, the press in general did not criticise the colonial regime. Rather, they focused on Chinese party politics, which were considered to be extra-territorial politics and so relatively safe, tolerated by the British as long as the reports and commentary did not violate British sovereignty. Therefore, some scholars have characterised the Hong Kong press tradition as indifferent, apolitical and apathetic. According to some, this is the result of a rivalry between 'party-press' and 'partisan press', i.e. the tension between, and indeed the contradictory emphasis of, the leftist (Chinese Communist Party (CCP)-funded press) and the rightist press (the Kuomintang (KMT)-funded press which was pro-KMT, the nationalist Taiwanese party).

The argument, however, is not so straightforward, as in fact the Hong Kong news media did not give up their political role entirely. The fact is rather that many of the media chose to comment more extensively on issues that concerned them most, namely Chinese politics. Also, one can argue that the commercial press, independent of the two Chinese parties, was in fact a pro-establishment (local administration) press. This became evident when a significant sociopolitical crisis occurred in 1967. It revealed that the radical/leftist press played a significant role in terms of advocating, provoking and engaging in a so-called 'psychological warfare' with the local administration to protest against repressive colonial policy over labour issues, while the rightist and centrist press was supportive of the violent crackdown authorised by the British Hong Kong administration.

In her study of newspaper coverage of the disturbances in 1967, Alice Lee argues that press partisanship dictated the paradigm.[86] The leftist press supported the disturbance, and the rightist and centrist supported the government and helped to create a superficial scenario of stability. Arguably, one explanation for the decline of the radical press is that they did not report 'objectively' on the disturbances, and provided one-sided, anecdotal stories. Thus the circulation of the leftist press dropped because of 'biased' reporting. However, one can argue that, at the time, journalism's norms such as 'objectivity' were not yet generally adopted. It was after classified exchanges and official records were declassified in the early years of the twenty-first century that other explanations, such as the role of the Chinese authorities, and indeed the British government, in the event became clearer.[87] Because of state oppression, the communist press was financially non-viable and shifted to a milder stance. (This actually did not occur under the influence of advertising, since once they were actively sponsored, the leftist press 'flourished' in the 1990s.)[88]

At the end of the confrontation between the radical press and the British Hong Kong administration, the British and the Chinese reached reconciliation. Although the radical press failed in its struggle to remove the colonial regime, the British Hong Kong administration had a difficult lesson to learn.[89] In the wake of the confrontation, the British administration apparently admitted the failure of their policy on Hong Kong. After that, the Hong Kong administration largely reviewed its policy, which involved a series of social reforms.[90] I shall argue in the Chapter 2 that the British local administration introduced measures to crack down on the pro-PRC press in the face of a threat to its rule. As a result of this, the radical press, a progressive force and one-time advocate of social justice, went underground and largely disappeared, though some of the titles remained.

Second stage – transition period

While the colonial administration used the Government Information Services and government officials acting as a source of information as a means of coercion, the Chinese authorities adopted a policy of co-optation and united front work[91] to gain support from, and build up links with, local news media.[92] Co-optation was achieved through *Xinhua News Agency* (the de facto Chinese Embassy under British rule), and other politicians, agents and sources of information, by bestowing honours and material rewards on key media people. The British Hong Kong administration also used co-optation by granting special honours, such as appointments to the legislature, to news media proprietors and senior journalists. In the case of the Chinese, co-optation measures included granting trips to China and invitations to insider briefings, offered mainly to proprietors and the heads of news desks.[93] This strategy continued until the political transition period when Hong Kong underwent huge structural and institutional changes, and at the same time the policy of China towards Hong Kong seemingly shifted to become more hard line.[94] There are, however, questions that remain to be dealt with. How do these developments affect the organisation of news, professionalism, internal mediation of news, and external control over the press? How has the relationship between power structures (political and economic) and the media changed? How did the news media restructure and reposition themselves in anticipation of the political handover?

During the political transition period, there occurred a power vacuum, as the decreasing influence of the British regime coincided with the lack of authority of the Chinese regime. During this period, the Chinese regime apparently adopted both a soft-handed and heavy-handed policy simultaneously. For instance, the united front or lobby strategy remained in place, but a more heavy-handed policy was visible, as shown by the case of the jailed Hong Kong reporter Xi

Yang and others.[95] The profession faced grim prospects. The consequence was self-censorship. But the root of this self-censorship was unclear: why did Hong Kong journalists censor their own stories in the first place? How did it happen? Did they resist interference?

In this connection, the first across-the-board industrial survey provides some interesting insights.[96] According to this study, in theory, journalists maintained the outlook and ideal of journalism's norms such as objectivity, impartiality and accuracy. In practice, however, they perceived a lot of self-censorship going on, but usually affecting other people and other organisations. This pioneer survey was conducted into the industry in general to find out detailed characteristics of the journalistic profession including age, education, professionalism, journalism's norms and ideals, job satisfaction and security, democratic aspirations and nationalist inclinations, perspectives and envisaged problems, and, above all, threats to press freedom. Within the category of journalistic outlook are listed: attitudes towards China, the profession, the future, political orientation, and emigration to other countries. The survey depicts a bleak picture, but many issues remain to be clarified. These include: What makes journalists self-censor their copy and how does it happen? Is there any internal mediation or is journalism controlled externally? Is it exposed to external pressure? How did media content change? How did journalism fare in the transition? Although the survey was illuminating at the time, as it gathered basic information on journalists in transition, overall research on the Hong Kong media only began two decades ago and is regarded as newly established.[97] Further studies on various areas are needed in order to explore and clarify the implications for Hong Kong journalism in transition in general, and its relationship with society and the Chinese authoritarian regime in particular.

Third stage – the post-colonial era

Lee's study of the political economy of the Hong Kong news media, drawing empirical data mainly from news reports and the annual reports of Hong Kong Journalists Association, remains until now the most illuminating and comprehensive piece of research which traces the evolution of Hong Kong news media as well as related issues such as the prospects for press freedom.[98] However, Lee's study does not pay much attention to the news process itself and the implications of actual interactions. The extent to which the wider environment (namely the culture, civil society and public opinion) influences Hong Kong journalism remains largely unexplored. In addition to that, it also appears to be politically deterministic in its conclusion that the fate of Hong Kong press freedom remains in the hands of China: 'The ultimate guarantee of press freedom in Hong Kong lies in China – in China's continued liberalization and its determination to carry out faithfully the "one country, two systems" policy.'[99] Notwithstanding that, he notes that Beijing's influence on Hong Kong is not necessarily 'unidirectional', and the policy of 'one country, two systems' is imbued with tensions and contradictions.

A crisis implies an opportunity. These tensions and contradictions will be a fertile ground for the struggle against state control, while the glaring incongruity between Beijing's public commitment to Hong Kong and its vacillating policy whims will provide leakage in ideological control. China cannot, in the final analysis, fully close off the public space from liberal struggle in Hong Kong.[100]

While Lee convincingly uses the liberal approach in his analysis of the struggle against authoritarian rule, Lee and Chu by contrast argue that due to the news media's co-optation under the British, and their dependence on the British under colonial rule, the political determinants would continue to prevail.[101] In this respect they offer a static model to account for the dynamic interplay between political and economic factors that is particularly inadequate for a period during which the Hong Kong news media underwent rapid structural changes. Their extensive emphasis on political determinants results in the neglect of economic logic and civil society as potential countervailing checks on state power.

In conclusion

It may be that the liberal interpretation, with its emphasis on professional norms, market influence and the civil society, is key to understanding the changes reshaping the Hong Kong press. Alternatively, it may be that the radical tradition, with its emphasis on the role of owners, the state and advertisers, and its belief in the subordination of journalists to the dominant ideology, offers the key to understanding. Or, indeed, we may find both interpretations are useful in seeking to understand the changes that took place. The next chapter includes a case study examining British policy towards the Hong Kong communist press, illuminating the role of a liberal democracy in the late 1960s.

2 British policy and the Hong Kong communist press, 1967–1970

Introduction

Although the British government during the period 1967 to 1970 proclaimed the importance of a free press and press freedom as a foundation for liberty, in practice, the regime was consistently repressive. Its main concern was to nip any threat to public order in the bud. While the general public was concerned about infringements of freedom, the British priority was to maintain their authority rather than press freedom. However, a tension developed between an illiberal tradition of imperial rule in Hong Kong and the more liberal approach that was emerging in London. The situation was further complicated by the fact that Britain was caught up in Cold War politics and was also adjusting its foreign policy as regards the Far East towards one of decolonisation and a phasing out of imperial rule.

This chapter attempts to investigate the relationship between the British regime and the radical Hong Kong press (i.e. the communist-funded newspapers), by examining the disturbances that occurred in 1967. I first look at the available British official archive, such as the declassified files of the Colonial Office and the Foreign and Commonwealth Office between 1967 and 1970. Second, I examine British foreign policy as it applied to Hong Kong and China. Third, I look at the elite and public opinion at the time by examining three newspapers, the independent English Daily *South China Morning Post* with a pro-establishment position, the liberal *Far Eastern Economic Review* and the English edition of the Beijing-funded daily, *Ta Kung Po*, between May and December 1967, during which period the disturbances took place. The chapter focuses on the regime's attitude towards the dissenting and opposition voice (largely represented by the communist press), and examines the British strategy of coercion conducted through the Hong Kong administration. It also looks at the parts played by China and the British liberal faction, and local domestic considerations.

The British imperial retreat and Chinese politics

Britain's policy towards China and Hong Kong

According to historians, British post-war colonial policy was both complicated and inconsistent. On the one hand, Britain was committed to colonial withdrawal from South Asia; on the other hand, there was an uncompromising re-assertion of colonial rule in Hong Kong.[102] The situation has to be understood in the context that Britain, with its limited resources, found it extremely difficult to be a serious rival to either the United States or the Soviet Union as a major power in the increasingly polarised world. However, the end of the British Empire did not mean the end of the aspirations of British political leaders for Britain to continue to play an important role in international politics. The contradictory attitude of the British towards their empire was demonstrated in their changes in policy towards Hong Kong in the face of the rise of communism in the early post-1945 period as the communists took power in China. Hong Kong, a symbol of British imperialism and a centre of commercial activities in south China, presented a complex problem in Sino-British relations as the Cold War intensified. The British, however, were unwilling to return Hong Kong to China after the Second World War; initially because they wished to maintain the empire, and later because of their aspiration to remain a global power.

The rise of the Chinese Communist Party and its subsequent take-over of China presented a dilemma for British officials. On the one hand they had to demonstrate solidarity with the USA, which was at the forefront of the conflict with the communist bloc. On the other hand, they also needed to protect British interests in China. Thus, British and Chinese officials were caught in the dilemma of an ideological divide and a clash between their respective countries' interests. An important outpost in the far east of the British Empire, Hong Kong was a valuable trade centre for British commercial activities in Asia. However, in the eyes of the Chinese, the colony was a symbol of western imperial domination. As one Hong Kong governor noted, the fundamental political problem of Hong Kong was its relationship with China and not the advancement to self-government and independence, as in the case of most British colonies.[103]

Thus, Hong Kong's political status was inevitably linked with Britain's policy towards China. The outbreak of the Second World War and Japan's occupation of Hong Kong ended British administration of the colony. Before the end of the war, the Chinese government had pressed for the return of Hong Kong to Chinese sovereignty. Britain initially reluctantly accepted. That attitude changed, however, towards the end of the war. Increasingly, the retention of British Far Eastern territory was seen as a matter of prestige that was crucial to the British Empire.[104] Concurrently, the Chinese leaders' desire to recover Hong Kong was not particularly strong.[105] Thus, Hong Kong did not at this time create any real difficulty in Sino-British relations. The Labour government came to power in Britain in 1945, but did not fundamentally change Britain's stance towards Hong Kong's status. Although the Labour government was willing to allow self-government and to introduce constitutional reforms in British colonial territories, it had no intention of giving up British colonial rule to China. The fact that there was no possibility of decolonisation without giving the territory to China[106] also made Hong Kong's status complicated and unique.

Thus, the implications of the communist victory for British interests in China and Hong Kong depended on whether the communists found the existence of a British port convenient for their trade with the outside world.[107] The assessment of the British policy-makers at that time was: even if the communists agreed to use Hong Kong for trading purposes, Hong Kong would be 'living on the edge of a volcano' because of a vast refugee problem.[108] While Hong Kong's political position would depend very much on Britain's relationship with the Chinese communists, Cold War politics made Britain's attempt to adopt a pragmatic policy towards China difficult. After the communist take-over of China, the British government eventually accorded diplomatic recognition to the People's Republic of China in January 1950. However, with the outbreak of the Korean War in 1950, Britain's policy towards China and Hong Kong took another turn, with far-reaching consequences. Sino-British relations entered their most difficult period, though the countries did not terminate their informal diplomatic links. With the imposition of the embargo,[109] Hong Kong's 'life-blood',[110] its trade with China, was cut down. Also, a massive influx of refugees arrived in Hong Kong on a daily basis. Paradoxically, this massive inflow of Chinese refugees, bringing both capital and labour, enabled Hong Kong to shift from an entrepot to a manufacturing and industrial city.

The extent of the decline of British power became fully evident after the Korean War. In other British territories in East Asia, the process of decolonisation had already begun. Malaysia was to become independent in 1957. The British Prime Minister, Harold Wilson, continued to insist that Britain intended to play a world role by maintaining a military presence east of Suez. Political and economic realities showed the opposite: London announced in early 1968 that British forces would be phased out from the Far East and the Persian Gulf by the end of 1971. In contrast to Britain's gradual military retreat from Asia, the Hong Kong garrison was not only maintained, but naval and air forces in the colony were actually strengthened. This reflected Britain's policy of continuing to use Hong Kong's unique position as an outpost to maintain its influence and interests in the Far East.

Although Peking's official stance towards the British presence in Hong Kong has been described as one of 'virulent opposition',[111] the Chinese government avoided confronting the British authorities in Hong Kong directly, even when pro-Peking elements in the colony became involved in the 'anti-colonial' movement. Although Sino-British relations suffered when radical politics swept through China during the Cultural Revolution in the 1960s, they improved rapidly in the 1970s following the Sino-U.S. rapprochement. Hence, Hong Kong remained important to British trading interests in East Asia and to Cold War politics from the end of the Second World War onwards. The retention of Hong Kong was first justified in the name of empire and later as part of the struggle against communist aggression. This attitude must be seen in the context of the general decline of British power and prestige in post-war East Asia.

Chinese politics and Hong Kong as a British Chinese colony

Apart from British foreign policy on China and Hong Kong, the emergence of Hong Kong as a British Colony but with a Chinese society was the other significant factor shaping the British-Hong Kong relationship in the late 1960s. As mentioned in Chapter 1, Hong Kong was acquired by the British as a colony, primarily serving as a base for free trade in the Far East. Chinese people came to Hong Kong to subject themselves voluntarily to the rule of an alien colonial administration rather than to oppose it. From the very beginning, the development of Hong Kong was based on a kind of partnership between the British and the Chinese with a common goal of economic gain, even though this was an unequal partnership in the political sense.[112]

As mentioned earlier, in the mid twentieth century, most countries in East and Southeast Asia had suffered major political upheavals. Throughout this period Hong Kong continued to run its affairs in accordance with a constitution that was effectively the same as it was in the nineteenth century. Power was concentrated in the hands of a London-appointed governor, advised by a nominated legislative council in which he could command a majority of votes, just as was the case when the British first acquired Hong Kong by force.[113] The reason the colony continued to exist while its larger neighbours had undergone far-reaching changes was because it suited the interests of Britain, China and the Hong Kong people. In fact, any one of these three could have initiated a change in the status quo, but each apparently refrained from making any move.

According to sociologists, the unique circumstances of Hong Kong, in particular, the bureaucratic polity and the Hong Kong Chinese society had helped to preserve the status quo. While Britain allowed its other dependent territories and colonies to become independent, it retained its colonial rule over Hong Kong for economic, strategic and moral reasons.[114] Although Britain had an adverse balance on visible trade, it was compensated for this by a surplus on invisible transactions, including such items as the pensions paid to retired Hong Kong civil servants in Britain, consultancy fees and payments for insurance, shipping and other commercial facilities arranged through London. Furthermore, from 1941 to 1972 Hong Kong was obliged to keep her external reserves in sterling because the colony had been compulsorily enrolled as a member of the sterling area by Britain.[115] As mentioned earlier, the British wanted to retain Hong Kong for the sake of its business interests and as an outpost in the Far East.

In addition, the cultural system in Hong Kong was heterogeneous, with a division between the western and Chinese cultures. Even among the Chinese themselves, variations in dialects, customs and styles of living ensured the division of Hong Kong society into antagonistic fragments. In terms of political orientation, ideological identities ran from the extreme right to the extreme left. This cultural heterogeneity and range of political identities were potentially destabilising. The Chinese in Hong Kong zealously preserved their customs, habits, lifestyles and modes of social organisation that constituted the cultural and social heritage of the Chinese people. But Chinese nationalism, to the extent it existed at all in Hong Kong, was cultural rather than political.[116] Furthermore, the staggering inequality in the distribution of income in Hong Kong in the period concerned had the potential to generate class conflict and industrial hostilities, which it could ill afford to have. These potential conflicts finally blew up in the late 1960s.

Myth of the free press

Conventionally historians have assumed that Hong Kong's success had much to do with the British legacy. In connection with this, the British-instituted Hong Kong press was often hailed as one of the pillars of this success. However, recent research has begun to challenge this British legacy[117] in general, and the myth of the 'free press' in particular.[118] It has questioned whether the tradition of the Hong Kong free press, to the extent it existed, was indebted to British colonial rule. Instead, it has argued that the 'free press' was established as a result of its own long struggle against colonial suppression.[119] But, had there actually been any press freedom back in the 1960s? The 1967 disturbances should be seen in the light of British foreign policy, Chinese politics and Hong Kong's special situation. I shall now discuss what actually happened, in particular, the role of the communist press during this turbulent period that posed the most serious threat to British rule.

From labour dispute to anti-colonial disturbance 1967–1970[120]

The 1967 disturbances seem to constitute a forgotten issue, in the sense that neither the Chinese government nor the present Hong Kong administration is interested in reviewing the official record.[121] More importantly, there are no official law reports documenting this carefully planned prosecution of newspapermen and women, and unprecedented suppression of the radical press.[122] There is no lack of academic analysis of this period of history, but explanations for what happened are derived from the perspective of the excesses of the communist proletariat revolution in mainland China. However, when we dig into the once-classified British files, a different story emerges: for example, the disturbances, which stretched from the summer of 1967 to 1970, resulted in a death toll of more than 50,[123] and detention and imprisonment for over 1,000 ethnic Chinese, were, in fact, provoked by the British. Furthermore, the communist press was suppressed at this time. Out of several dozens of journalist detainees and prisoners, five were senior communist newspaper officials. A total of 99 charges related to the three independently owned and pro-communist papers, which were suspended and later suppressed for six months.[124]

In this section I focus on British action against the communist press and the latter's resistance during a most violent confrontation between the two sides in

1967. The first part of this section analyses different phases of action against the communist press. The second part scrutinises the strategies of, and differences within, the British government, and other factors working against British control.

British suppression of the radical (communist) press

According to the British Foreign and Commonwealth Office, Hong Kong in 1970 resembled England in 1870 in many ways.

> The industrial revolution, pushed on its way by private venture with the spur of quick profits; a hypocritical attitude towards sex and gambling; low rates of tax with extremes of wealth and poverty – all this is true of Hong Kong now as it was of England then.... Add to that, that the structure of the Hong Kong government is necessarily colonial, with all that that implies, and the picture is complete. Power in Hong Kong today lies in the hands of a few rich men, and the glory in an OBE or an invitation to Government House.[125]

Although economic development had raised the standard of living of people in general, many of the poorest families still lived in appalling conditions of urban squalor, and there seemed to be a 'growing desire among the post-war generation for a greater say in the conduct of government business'. But 'the policies of the government were designed primarily to further the interests of the wealthy industrialists.'[126] On the political front, different departments of the British government reached a consensus that it was not in British interests to see the rivalry between Peking and Taipei intensified.[127] Hong Kong was regarded in some ways as being in a permanent Cold War situation, and the same standards could not always apply to it as were possible in countries less delicately situated. However, there were differences among British government offices as regards ways of improving Sino-British relations, with Hong Kong as the central issue.

There was a gulf between rich and poor in Hong Kong, but no official channel for the working class to air their grievances. Neither were they represented politically. Domestically, the acute ideological rivalry between the two Chinese parties – the Chinese Communist Party (CCP) and the Taiwan Nationalist Kuomintang (KMT) Party – had prompted violent conflicts. In the incident of 10 October 1956,[128] the Hong Kong government was alleged to have shown biased treatment in favour of the right-wing press.[129] Earlier, the Hong Kong government had passed The Control of Publication Consolidation Ordinance 1951, which stipulated that the press had to apply for registration of publications, and that the governor had the power to accept, reserve or cancel a publication's registration depending on its social effect. Also, the ordinance regulated the media and forbade them to incite others to commit criminal offences, including publishing provocative statements, participating in political organisations outside Hong Kong and publishing fabricated news to disturb public order.[130]

In the late 1960s, the Hong Kong government faced an unprecedented challenge from the pro-communist community in general and the leftist press in particular. Unlike previous rioting, the protest, which turned into a major disturbance, had explicit, anti-colonial objectives. Historians have traced its origins to the Cultural Revolution in China.[131] According to this argument, the militant Red Guards and other local dissidents, who symbolised the movement, wanted immediate solutions to what they regarded as long-standing problems, i.e. Hong Kong's return to Chinese sovereignty. Indeed, in December 1966, Red Guards in Macau rendered the government there virtually impotent and essentially achieved their goal of control in January 1967. So it was suggested that in March 1967, communists in Hong Kong had begun to attempt the same thing.[132]

According to historians, the background to the demonstrations and riots in Hong Kong were largely pro-CCP labour disputes, which started in March 1967, in a shipping company, four taxi companies, a textile factory, a cement factory and the Hong Kong artificial flower works.[133] All the companies concerned had a substantial number of communist supporters in the workforce. The unions that took up their cause were all members of the Federation of Trade Unions, which had strong links with Peking. However, the disturbances have not been analysed by looking, in particular, at British foreign policy, which might throw some light on the role the British played in provoking those involved and intensifying the situation.

According to British analysis, this protest-turned-disturbance was not instigated by Peking, but by local communists. It was this assessment of the level of Chinese involvement that largely guided the decisions of the Hong Kong Government. With regards to the situation in early 1967, the Hong Kong governor's preliminary assessment was that it was 'simply a ferment of the cultural revolution'.[134] He regarded Hong Kong as being in a state of psychological warfare in which the main weapon of the left was their sustained press campaign aimed at undermining the morale of the police, as well as discrediting the government and destroying public confidence in its will and capacity to resist.[135] On 13 May 1967, there was serious rioting in Kowloon. Buses were set alight, government offices were looted and there were other arson cases. On the same day, the Hong Kong Governor, David Trench, considered that 'the tone of the left-wing press, in particular the Chinese People's Government (CPG)-controlled semi-official dailies, the *Ta Kung Pao* and the *Wen Wei Po*, has steadily deteriorated over the past week ... [reaching] the level of vituperation of yesterday's editorials.'[136] He considered there were grounds for prosecution of both papers, either for seditious publication under section 4 of the Sedition Ordinance, or for attempts to cause disaffection in the police under section 62 of the Police Force Ordinance, or both.

However, there were concerns that prosecutions might fail to prove an adequate deterrent or achieve any real improvement, even if they resulted in convictions. The risk was that the prosecutions would be strongly contested, and provide undesirable opportunities for political propaganda. The incident of 1952 confirmed this worry.[137] In that case, the Hong Kong government used the stringent 1951 ordinance to prosecute the publisher and the editor of *Ta Kung Pao*. The paper was then suspended for six months. The paper was fined after the appeal, but later all the charges were dropped following the intervention of the Chinese Premier, Chou En-lai. Thus, the Hong Kong government envisaged that any attempt to prosecute or to suppress those left-wing papers in 1967 would result in similar formal protests from Peking, even though there was no evidence at that time to suggest that the CPG had changed its policy towards Hong Kong or desired to 'rock the boat'. The Hong Kong Governor, David Trench, wrote to the Secretary of State:

> I am reluctant to take overt action against the left-wing press, if it can be avoided, since it would involve a direct confrontation from which retreat on either side would be very difficult. Equally there are limits to what can be tolerated without risk of an irretrievable loss of public confidence and abdication of authority on Macau lines.[138]

The governor was worried that the situation would in effect put them in pawn to the Chinese, and turn Hong Kong into a second Macau, where the communists had made the Portuguese government impotent after disturbances in late 1966. In the meantime, Trench continued to make use of intermediaries and face-saving tactics in an attempt to de-escalate the situation. However, their discussions with left-wing contacts had not yielded any progress towards an acceptable settlement. By late May the situation had deteriorated to such a degree that the Hong Kong governor considered various new measures. On 22 May, people tried to demonstrate outside Government House. They were thwarted by the police, and serious clashes occurred between police and demonstrators in Garden Road. On 1 June, Emergency Regulations were introduced forbidding the display of wall posters that were largely anti-colonial slogans. According to the FCO exchanges,

> An important feature has been the continuous broadcasting from the Bank of China of incitements to violence against government and Europeans generally, including such slogans as 'Kill Trench', 'Police turn your weapons (i.e. against your officers)'. The pro-communist press is giving full and approving accounts of violent action by demonstrators and calling for their extension.[139]

The key to the situation, according to the Hong Kong governor, was the maintenance of public confidence and especially police morale. He observed that there were signs that unless 'we are seen to take effective action to control the situation, instead of simply acting to block individual communist initiatives, public confidence will slip. A landslide could quickly follow.'[140] In the face of an escalating challenge to colonial rule, various new measures were considered by the governor to deal with the situation.[141] First, it was suggested that a selection of the known leaders of the present left-wing campaign should be picked up and if possible deported, failing which they should be detained for up to 24 hours. The disruption of the leadership was regarded as a distinct and positive gain, at least in the short term.

Second, action to neutralise several of the buildings from which the campaign was being directed (notably the Bank of China, the Communist-controlled Federation of Trade Union headquarters, and the Workers' Club) was proposed. This could be achieved, for instance, by declaring 24-hour curfews in areas around the buildings, or possibly declaring them closed areas under the Public Order Ordinances. It was envisaged that that would seriously hamper the communist leadership in their control and development of anti-government operations, as they would be bottled up in their existing headquarters and cut off from outside contacts. At the very least, it was foreseen that it would disrupt their communications, because government could pick up all their couriers. Thus the communist leaders might eventually have to move to other premises where it would be easier for government to keep them under closer surveillance.

Third, the British official also considered taking action against the *Wen Wei Po*, the official CPG organ in Hong Kong, for either sedition or inciting the police to disaffection. This course was abandoned because it might provoke the Chinese authorities. However, to the British, the worrying thing about not taking action against these 'worst offenders' among the communist press was that the paper was daily in breach of the law. If the Hong Kong authorities continued to ignore this, it might well be taken as a sign of weakness. Furthermore, there were eight other communist newspapers that could all continue the campaign unless similar action was taken against them.

Fourth, it was suggested that the commando ship BULWARK should be brought on a visit to Hong Kong. Though it would take three and a half days for BULWARK to reach Hong Kong, it was envisaged that her presence there would strengthen public and police morale. The concern was that if there were a prolonged crisis, the worst of all possible situations for Hong Kong would be that 'morale would tend to deteriorate rapidly, capital would depart, and the effect on the economy could be irreparable'.[142] In order to avoid this situation, Governor Trench suggested there was a choice between accepting a substantial loss of face and authority on the part of the British Hong Kong government, on the one hand, and taking initiatives against the left-wing on the other. For instance, he suggested taking legal action against the communist newspaper, arresting key left-wing leaders and deporting them to China. Although the Governor foresaw that that would likely provoke China and an 'all-out confrontation' would result, he preferred to use repressive measures.

However, the Secretary of State adopted a different opinion to that of the governor on this matter. While the Secretary of State endorsed the paramount need to maintain internal security, he cautioned against involving the CPG:[143]

It would be wiser to avoid action against their 'officials' in the New China News Agency [the de facto Chinese Embassy in Hong Kong], Bank of China [the official finance institute] and China Resources Company [mainly in charge of the export of staple food to Hong Kong] if at all possible, since this would make it the more difficult for them to disengage from a policy of all-out confrontation.[144]

By July 1967, the Hong Kong police had taken offensive actions against communists, raiding premises, seizing weapons and detaining suspects.[145] Among those detainees, there were journalists from the left-wing press.[146] The aim was to use them as 'political pawns' to be exchanged with China for British hostages such as Anthony Grey, Reuter's Peking correspondent. Ironically, Grey was put under house arrest by the Chinese authorities in retaliation for the sentencing of Hsueh Ping, a New China News Agency reporter, to two years' imprisonment in Hong Kong. While the Hong Kong governor returned to London on sick leave and to discuss important matters concerning Hong Kong, a team of four senior officials was set up to administer Hong Kong from late June to September 1967.[147]

In the meantime, the Acting Governor in Hong Kong, Michael Gass, continued his action against the communist press. In order to silence dissenting voices, a substantial fine was imposed for breaching a ban on inflammatory articles printed in a communist broadsheet. It was aimed at putting this 'mosquito [broadsheet] out of business and sow seeds of doubt in the minds of other editors'.[148] In late July, as the stringent measures failed to stop the protest, and there was a flood of criticism and challenge from the communist press, the Acting Governor started lobbying London to give him more power to take further action against the communist press. 'The press is now one of the communists' few remaining weapons still intact ... the main driving force behind the confrontation.'[149]

The Acting Governor admitted that there were risks in acting against the press, so he proposed refraining from acting against the three leading papers with an aggregate circulation of 140,000 that were to all intents and purposes CPG-owned. Instead, he suggested that it would be possible to act initially against only the six independently-owned and pro-communist newspapers with an aggregate circulation of 270,000. The Acting Governor was of the firm view that, provided the official New China News Agency were not touched, it seemed possible that Peking might not be provoked into any retaliation against Hong Kong. He considered that the first move should be made against selected independent papers. This should reduce the chances of Peking reaction and might curb the activities of the leading communist newspapers.[150] Officials in London were not only doubtful about the tactics, but also reluctant to virtually turn off the 'safety valve' that the communist press represented. Yet, after a vigorous exchange and negotiation, the Acting Governor had his way. The Secretary of State finally issued a go-ahead note on 4 August 1967: 'Your proposal to proceed against selected independent communist papers under existing law is approved.'[151]

That was the beginning of a clampdown on the communist press. As a result, the three Chinese-language newspapers – *Tin Fung Daily News, Hong Kong*

Evening News and *Afternoon News* – were ordered to suspend publication pending court proceedings against five of their publishers, printers and editors who were arrested on 9 August 1967. The five were charged with alleged violation of laws against sedition, inflammatory reports and spread of false reports. In the meantime, the 'defiant edition', a combined edition of the three papers that was handed free to morning rush-hour passers-by, demanded the immediate release of the five men. Other pro-Peking newspapers also carried a joint statement issued by fourteen communist publications and printing houses condemning the suspension order and demanding its immediate withdrawal.

The above action by the Hong Kong authorities led to the delivery of a note by the CPG to the British Chargé-d'Affaires' Office in Peking on 20 August 1967. This note demanded that the British authorities should, within 48 hours, cancel the ban on the three suspended papers; declare all those arrested innocent and set them free; and call off the lawsuits against the other newspapers involved.[152] But the British paid no heed to this note. More and more journalists were detained and arrested in Hong Kong, and some British officials feared that the deterioration of the situation in Hong Kong would adversely affect the Peking office and Anthony Grey, Reuter's correspondent in Peking. Indeed, the deterioration of the Hong Kong situation had in the past triggered Chinese retaliation against the British missions in Shanghai and Peking. Following the suspension of the three newspapers, single sheet pamphlets started to appear, totalling 150 different titles, reproducing items from the main newspapers. They were widely distributed free, including a large number by post to government officers. The Hong Kong authorities at first attached little importance to these new style 'Mosquito' broadsheets as lacking authority and being of limited distribution and appeal, and so a rather poor substitute for suppressed papers. However, on 28 August 1967 at least one named six prominent personalities as targets for assassination. After that, the Hong Kong authorities decided that their use as a means of indicating assassination targets and issuing terrorist warnings changed the situation.

Although those suspended newspapers were regarded as having been carefully selected for the purpose as being minor and independently-owned papers (i.e. not CPG-owned or funded) and as being less likely therefore to provoke reaction from Peking, the suspension of the three papers led directly to the sacking of the British Mission in Peking on 22 August 1967. British diplomats and their families in Peking were intimidated, and their personal security and movement were restricted. Therefore, in late August, the Hong Kong Acting Governor changed his mind and reported to London: 'We are, as you know, steering clear for as long as we are able, of taking action to suspend any of the main Communist papers for fear of reprisals in Peking.'[153]

However, when the Hong Kong Governor, David Trench, returned from London to resume office, he did not wait too long to start another round of action against the press. In October 1967, the Hong Kong government sought London's approval to take action against the *Youth Garden Weekly*. With a circulation estimated to be in the region of 1,500, this independently owned youth weekly was alleged to be 'urging its readers to fight against the police, attempting to stir up hatred to those who support the government and generally inciting to disaffection.'[154] The Hong Kong government was prepared to arrest the publisher and also a proprietor of the printing company and charged both with several counts of sedition. An interim closure of the printing press was also sought.[155]

Divergence of opinion within the British Government

As mentioned earlier, Hong Kong was the central issue in relations between Britain and China. However, there had always been a divergence of opinion within the British government as to how to better the Sino-British relationship in general and as regards to solving the 1967 disturbances. As early as mid-May of 1967, the Commonwealth Office had suggested that it seemed clear that the trouble was not instigated by the CPG, but derived, partly at least, from management-labour relations at the plastic flower plants involved. Also, since the Hong Kong Governor had described the situation as one of psychological warfare, the British officials in London wondered whether it would be possible to present the affair as having the 'character and proportions of a normal trade dispute' rather than a political matter by arranging for a London official to fly to Hong Kong to assist the Hong Kong labour commissioner.[156] The Commonwealth Office hoped that might give the left wing a face-saving excuse for turning the pressure off and generally de-escalating.[157] In the meantime, a former Junior Minister at the Trade Ministry made a similar point after paying a visit to Hong Kong, 'the Hong Kong government, without any question, should set up a strong labour department with some people who are trusted by both sides.'[158]

Moreover, when the acting Hong Kong Governor telegrammed London for approval to take action against the communist press, officials based in London disagreed with this approach:

> As the acting governor says, the press is now one of the communists' few remaining weapons left intact, it could be argued that it provides a safety valve and that if this safety valve were turned off, it might well cause communist elements to turn to even more extreme measures than they have so far adopted.[159]

Another doubted whether moving first against selected independently owned newspapers would curb the activities of leading Communist papers because

> a dangerous situation would arise if the leading communist press were to continue to publish virulent and inflammatory material with apparent impunity.... If we start action against the communist press now we shall almost certainly have to be prepared to act equally firmly, and soon, against CPG-owned press, or face possible humiliating setback.[160]

However, the Acting Governor argued: 'There is just a chance that action against the lesser papers might provide the bigger ones with an acceptable excuse for moderating their tone if the alternative were likely to be suppression.'[161] Since the Acting Governor was determined that the time had come to clamp down on the press, the Colonial Secretary could only accept his urgent proposals.

Yet, after half a year of head-on confrontation a British official in Hong Kong finally admitted that the escalation of the 1967 disturbances was largely due to British suppression of the press. Tony Elliot, in the political adviser's office in Hong Kong, said: 'The experience of the last six months has shown that interference with the press produces more violent reactions than anything else, from the moderate as well as the militants.'[162] Also, according to the report compiled by the Special Branch of the Hong Kong Police on the pros and cons of moving against the communist press, there was still a divergence of opinion locally regarding the measures against the communist press. Two days later, however, and contrary to the Special Branch's recommendation, Governor David Trench reasserted his position that further action needed to be taken against the three remaining non-CPG owned but pro-communist newspapers.[163] This time, because of enormous external pressure and the sharp reaction by China to the closure of the three newspapers in August, the Commonwealth Office objected to the governor's proposal, saying

> if action [against the Communist schools] were to be taken in conjunction with action against the press, China would be certain to regard this as a two-pronged attack on the propagation of communist ideological thought and react violently.[164]

In fact, there was an on-going negotiation on whether further action should be taken against the communist press. It was felt that simultaneous action against all six remaining papers would achieve the maximum effect, but could be expected to draw the strongest reaction from China. Therefore Special Branch recommended the prosecution of those responsible for publishing, printing and editing the other three non-CPG owned papers, i.e. *Ching Po*, *Hong Kong Commercial Daily* and *Cheng Wu Pao*, with a view to obtaining the closure of these journals.[165] In the end, this proposal was abandoned because of lack of support from London, as well as out of concern for British hostages and the London Mission in Peking.

Indeed, the British Mission in Peking continued to urge the Hong Kong government to consider adopting flexibility in granting detainees' remission so as to secure the freedom of British subjects. One year after the disturbances in Hong Kong, the strained relations between the British and the Chinese continued to cause problems in Peking. Reuters' Peking correspondent, Anthony Grey, was still under house arrest and the free movement of members of the office of the Chargé d'Affaires and their families was restricted. Sir Donald Hopson in the Peking Office wrote to the London office: 'I hope that consideration will be given to amending rules to allow greater remission. This ... may be the only means of ensuring Grey's release before September 1969 ... [and] to facilitate a return to normal working relations with China.'[166] Yet, the Hong Kong Governor was more concerned that the Chinese might take advantage of any adverse publicity that accompanied remission. 'A major difficulty about releasing prisoners to China [is that such a course is] heavily dependent on Chinese good faith. If any prisoners were released prematurely they would be almost certain to publicise the facts ... [and claim a public victory],' the Governor said.[167]

This dispute also attracted intervention from British officials stationed elsewhere. As Anthony Grey would expect to regain his freedom when the last of the news workers imprisoned in Hong Kong in 1967 had been released, a British diplomat based in America suggested: 'Would it be a good idea to ... encourage the [Hong Kong] Governor ... [to authorise] a premature release if it could be regarded as a gesture of accommodation rather than an act of weakness.'[168] This discrepancy of views between British officials based in London and Hong Kong continued until more and more public pressure emerged from both home and the colony.

The China factor

China's attitude was also instrumental in shaping changing Sino-British relations. The Chinese People's Government (CPG) was established in 1949, and the British Government accorded recognition to the CPG on 6 January 1950. However, since the British had representatives in Tamsui in Taiwan, they could not have official ties with China. Therefore, the British and Chinese maintained minimal contact except on issues concerning Hong Kong. 'Hong Kong was, and always had been, a natural place for the Chinese to make difficulties for HMG [Her Majesty's Government] whenever they felt like it.'[169]

The imposition of immigration controls, which had begun as early as May 1950, triggered incessant border disputes between the Hong Kong police and Chinese people on the border with China. Some of the incidents were politically motivated. For instance, demonstrations by mainland Chinese were organised on the Chinese side of the frontier at Lowu, Man Kam To and Sha Tau Kok, following British and American intervention in the Middle East.[170] A few incidents, in fact, were due to misunderstandings; others were simply due to ignorance. For instance, in the 'blackboard' incident, British soldiers took away a blackboard from a Chinese. The Chinese were infuriated because Chairman Mao Tse-tung was referred to on the blackboard. Local Chinese reacted fiercely and demanded the return of the blackboard, and this turned into a border conflict. British officials in London later reviewed this incident and concluded that the border soldier should have been more sensitive. If the blackboard had been returned earlier, then one major dispute between the Chinese and the British could have been avoided.[171] With regards to Chinese protests against border control on the British frontier, public opinion within the colony was manipulated by the press. The British arguments were, first, that restrictions on border movement were not new – they had been imposed between 1950 and 1952; second, the limited space of Hong Kong's physical environment was emphasised and it was said that border controls were necessary to ensure the health, safety and welfare of local people.[172]

Apart from these escalating tensions and conflicts on the frontier, the Hong Kong government also felt that communist influence on Hong Kong ideology had been accelerating. From the British perspective, the Chinese government was exerting its influence through cultural exchanges, communist-run schools, the left-wing press, films and movies, trade unions and by helping the poor by giving out free rice, for example.[173] While Chinese officials sent diplomatic notes to the British government regarding border incidents, the British protested against intimidation of, and restrictions on, her diplomats and subjects. However, even when relations were at their worst, neither side terminated their diplomatic links, which, as stated above, were based on mutual interests.

For the same reason, a Hong Kong government official tried to persuade the Americans to lift their ban on communist cinemas on the grounds that letting communist-controlled cinemas run United States movies would have an anti-communist effect on local culture. The political adviser of the Hong Kong authorities noted:

I feel that the more American, British, French and other non-Communist films that are shown in the Colony the better, and if an owner with strong Communist connections, like Ho Yin,[174] is prepared to show them, he should not be prevented. In practice, if not by design, the showing of non-communist films in Hong Kong is a joint propaganda effort – even if the films are punk they keep out communist ones.[175]

Indeed, American policy was so restrictive towards the communists that even the American news agencies were forbidden to provide news to the Chinese government-funded newspaper in Hong Kong. 'The question of the supply of A.P. [Associated Press] and U.P. [United Press] material to the Communist newspapers in Hong Kong had been decided on similar grounds' – that was, 'to enforce Treasury rules on designated persons, who must be given no gratuitous chances to earn U.S. dollars'.[176]

Furthermore, theatrical productions, for example, from mainland China were regarded as 'offensives'. The Hong Kong government was worried that they would have such a cumulative effect on the Hong Kong people that these kinds of 'cultural manifestations' were limited to two groups per year. The policy was so restrictive that even London was alarmed and questioned whether Hong Kong was doing the right thing.

A policy quite so limiting and inflexible as you propose ... [is] reminiscent of the most severe 'cold war measures' ... A precise annual limitation (and to such a low number as two) strikes precisely the same uncompromising attitude as we object to in the CPG's handling of cultural relations with the West.[177]

Thus, the Hong Kong government was asked by London to consider a softening of policy. However, a Hong Kong official rejected this request arguing that Hong Kong was a special case and politically sensitive:

> It is not in our interests that the CPG should have things all their own way in this field, nor do we wish to see rivalry in it between Peking and Taipei intensified ... Hong Kong is in some ways in a permanent cold war situation and cannot always apply the same standards as is possible in countries less delicately situated.[178]

Tension thus developed between London and Hong Kong over censorship of communist cultural material. Furthermore, British film censors in the period 1957–1959 banned 72 Chinese films and censored 27, including one in which the sentence 'Now the country [China] has been liberated everyone can have a free life' was deleted.[179] The Association of Chinese Cinema workers protested that this was 'discriminating' against Chinese films, while 'Hong Kong British authorities permitted to be shown many United States films and newsreels which slandered and were hostile towards China'.[180]

In addition, the Hong Kong government used legislation and other measures to curb the CPG's influence through education. For example, they introduced Education Ordinances, which gave the Hong Kong government the right to ban political activities in schools. Communist-run schools were not allowed to display Chairman Mao Tse-tung's pictures, and no communist teaching was allowed in schools.[181] In the late 1960s, the number of communist-run schools as a proportion of the total number of middle schools in Hong Kong was only 2.5 per cent. However, the total number of students studying in these schools had reached the highest level so far.[182] When Chung Wah Middle School was ordered to shut down, 33 communist schools closed for a day in protest against the Hong Kong government's suppression, affecting 10,000 pupils in total.[183]

The fact that the communists were exerting influence through schools alarmed London, which demanded that the Hong Kong government change this situation. One issue they suggested should be exploited is reflected in the following question: 'Are we right in thinking that the low standard of academic achievement at these schools is generally well-known and is being well-exploited by Government Information Services whenever opportunity offers?'[184] A. F. Maddocks, from the political adviser's office in Hong Kong, replied that he could assure the Foreign Office that their publicity machine was very conscious of the advantage of exploiting the poor academic achievement of the communist schools, though he did not have the impression that their publicity efforts had much success with communist parents.[185] In connection with this, it was recommended that more government or government-subsidised schools should be built in order to encourage communist sympathiser parents to send their children to government-funded schools. Activities that might have political implications, such as communist-flag flying, were to be banned in communist-run schools.[186] The Hong Kong Government was determined that the law should be enforced. For example, there had been a number of incidents that resulted in the banishment of Parker To, the Principal of Pui Kiu Middle School. The Government also withdrew aid from the Nairn Road Workers' Children's school for persistent breaches of the regulations. They cancelled the registration of the society of Plantation, and closed many unregistered schools operated by the communists. Other examples of law enforcement included the prohibition of a mass physical education display, and the prosecution of a number of schools for offences under the Building Ordinance.[187]

Unsurprisingly, British officials were also critical of Hong Kong's handling of communist educators. With regards to the decision to allow Ng Hon Man, another communist follower and teacher, to succeed Parker To as Principal of Pui Kiu Middle School, a London official said: 'Ng Hon Man is now thought to be a more important figure in the communist hierarchy than Parker To, yet it would be more difficult to remove him from his post as Principal now than it would have been to prevent his appointment in the first place.'[188] Under Section 28A(2) of the Education Ordinance, 'the director may withhold his approval if he is not satisfied that the person recommended is a fit and proper person to act as Principal for the purposes of the Ordinance.'[189] Despite the disagreement amongst British officials, Ng continued to act as Principal of Pui Kiu Middle School, since he had been approved in the first place.

In another incident, the Hong Kong authorities escalated their clampdown on communist influence by evacuating students of Chung Wah Middle School, a communist-run school, and pulled it down after the School had an explosion in their laboratory. Although the School was allowed to re-open, and students were re-allocated to a new school building, the demolition of a communist-run school provoked vigorous resistance from communist sympathisers. For instance, the *Far Eastern Economic Review* published articles criticising the Hong Kong government for closing down the school.[190]

In addition, at the peak of the confrontation in 1967, in order to curb communist influence, the Hong Kong government adopted a series of measures to manipulate public opinion and in turn to contain the CPG's influence on ideological grounds. A Hong Kong working group was set up in London, whose expertise could be drawn upon, while a publicity office was established specifically to coordinate press briefings and surveillance by sending regular press releases, making publicity films and pamphlets. They also helped to record violent activities by left-wing camps, and organised cooperative action with the administrative secretary at a district level.[191] In this connection, an obscure organisation – the LIC – used intelligence surveillance on the movement of left-wing leaders and scrutinised the activities of communist schools and organisations. For instance, Fei Yi-man, the publisher of the CPG-owned daily, *Ta Kung Pao*, was identified as an active member of the prestigious Country Club, apparently leading a capitalist lifestyle that was contrary to his claim to be a socialist. This press leak was meant to expose Fei's scandalous behaviour.[192]

Apart from using severe measures to clamp down on ideological influences, the Hong Kong government adopted coercive measures to threaten Communist

followers and sympathisers. For instance, the Hong Kong government considered restricting the free movement of left-wing leaders. One idea under
consideration at that time was either: '1) To refuse to allow selected *New China
News Agency* and newspaper officials now in China to return; or 2) to refuse to
renew the visas of some of those here when they run out.'[193] The type of person
against whom this action might be contemplated included Li Tze-chung, the
managing director of the Communist-run daily, Hong Kong *Wen Wei Po*, and Li
Chung, the editor-in-chief of *New China News Agency*. According to British
intelligence, both of them had gone back to the mainland for some time. The
intention behind taking such action was to discourage other communists from
making short trips to China and from going to Shenzhen, the Special Economic
Zone neighbouring Hong Kong, to telephone Canton (Guangzhou) for instruction from the communist leadership.[194]

In other cases, the Hong Kong government quietly sent back unwelcome
Chinese to the mainland. The Hong Kong government saw the latter measure as
being less provocative than political deportation, because it would probably help
Chinese 'face-saving'.[195] In the summer of 1967, the unprecedented anti-colonial
disturbances broke out. The Hong Kong governor concluded that the communist
press was the provocative force behind the disturbances, and he needed to take
action against this enemy. A purge of newspapers and journalists began.

Differences among British offices

Although British policy on China and Hong Kong was generally consistent, at
times there existed a more liberal faction that helped to weaken the illiberal
policy in Hong Kong. In fact, differences of opinion within the British offices
concerning how to deal with China can be traced back to the early twentieth
century when there was a revolutionary movement going on in China. Hong
Kong at that time was left to deal directly with the Canton government, which
was controlled by the nationalist Kuomintang (KMT) party, on a daily basis.
Apart from practicality, the unique circumstances of the Colonial Office also
enhanced the autonomy of the Hong Kong government. For instance, the position of Secretary of State was usually a stepping-stone for diplomatic officials.
During the first half of the twentieth century, therefore, many Secretaries of
State worked less than eighteenth months and very few completed the term of
three years.[196] Therefore, by tradition and the very nature of the job, the Hong
Kong Governor had in general a lot of autonomy in carrying out his duties in
Hong Kong.

The Hong Kong Government was able to maintain a kind of precarious
balance, partly because of an understanding that China's long-term policy was to
make use of Hong Kong as a trading port.[197] So the British need not worry that
China was in any hurry to reclaim Hong Kong. For example, the Chinese attitude was conveyed to the Hong Kong public through an official meeting with
communist supporters. When a delegation of Hong Kong ethnic Chinese representatives went to visit Peking in the early 1960s, they received instructions

from the Chinese government through Liu Shing Chi, Chairman of the CPG Overseas Chinese Affairs Commission. 'The present status of Hong Kong is to our benefit,' Liu told them, 'through Hong Kong we can trade and contact people of other countries and obtain materials we badly need. For this reason, we have hitherto made no demand for the return of Hong Kong. We want to get back Hong Kong in a good state and not in a state of ruin.'[198] However, from the perspective of the Hong Kong authorities, the story was rather different. According to Murray MacLehose, an official in the political adviser's office of the Hong Kong government:[199]

> I found it hard to consider Chinese policy on Hong Kong in isolation, and I should have thought that present calm could easily be disturbed, and disturbed quickly, if there was any overall change in Chinese external policy, or even a change in their assessment of the usefulness of the role HMG is playing in international affairs.[200]

Differences between the British Trade Commission and the Hong Kong Government

These differences between British offices added another dimension to the maintenance of Hong Kong's political stability. Hegemonic control sometimes got split between Hong Kong and London and British officials in Peking. Control of dissent within Hong Kong could not be relaxed even though this course of action might act against British policy towards China. While the Hong Kong authorities' primary concern was law and order within the colony, the concern of trade officials was economically oriented, and they were sensitive to anything that might damage Sino-British trade.[201] The Foreign Office in London believed the tension between officials representing London interests and those representing Hong Kong interests was due to the fundamental structure and strains inherent in a highly sophisticated and flourishing economy governed by a colonial constitution.[202] The tension between the British Trade Commission and the local government was apparent on the many occasions when trade officials were approached by left-wing organisations such as the Chinese Chamber of Commerce and the Marco Polo Club, which were formed by Chinese communist lawyers and businessmen, who either did business with China or were Communist followers themselves. Trade officials assessed invitations from the Chinese side, from a diplomatic point of view, as representing to some extent a thaw in their relations with the Chinese in the aftermath of the 1967 disturbances. For instance, a trade officer in Hong Kong noted:

> To turn them down would be tantamount to a rebuff and be altogether unhelpful if our policy is to try to improve relations. On the other hand, I have been given clearly to understand by the Hong Kong government, at the highest levels, that my presence at such crypto-communist functions would be viewed very unfavourably.[203]

The main reason for that attitude was that the Chinese government had been under the impression that there was a dichotomy of policy towards China as between the British government and the Hong Kong government. In view of the fact that the Chinese authorities appeared to be determined to cultivate the Trade Commission, the Senior Commissioner wrote to seek clarification whether 'the British Government felt that in the general interest of better UK relations with China [these] approaches should be encouraged or whether in the context of special conditions of Hong Kong they should be refused.'[204] After several exchanges, and negotiation between London and Hong Kong, it was agreed that the Trade Commission was free to develop contacts. Still, Maddocks, the political adviser to the Hong Kong Government, raised a series of questions as to what could be done to improve Hong Kong/London relations: whether the Trade Commission in Hong Kong should become more visible with bigger quasi-diplomatic missions, or whether there should be an exercise of restraint over time.[205] An official of the Hong Kong Department, Foreign and Commonwealth Office (FCO), replied: 'More visits could certainly help to paper over the cracks ... but if this (quasi-diplomatic mission) is a reference to the British Trade Commissioner's office in Hong Kong, then I would almost certainly not support the idea.' The reason was:

> [The] relation between that office and the Hong Kong Government would hardly be described as cordial. The strained relations between Hong Kong and London are, I suggest, due to the fundamental structure and strains inherent in a situation where a highly sophisticated and economically flourishing territory has to be governed under a Crown Colony Constitution. Hong Kong is a contradiction in terms.[206]

Thus, the Hong Kong government's repressive efforts were sometimes weakened by the more liberal factions within the British government, with whom the Chinese government could negotiate.

Tension amongst British officials

Apart from differences between London representatives and the Hong Kong authorities, British officials based in Peking also tended to have their own views on China, which might not be agreeable to the Hong Kong government. This was because in case of a Sino-British dispute, British representatives would, at best, be summoned to, and reprimanded by, the Ministry of Foreign Affairs; and, at worst, be the first casualty in the frontline. For instance, the Chargé d'Affaires' office in Peking was sacked on 22 August 1967 by the Chinese Red Guard in retaliation for Hong Kong's suppression of the communist press. Besides, the British official mission in China was to enhance British trade.

> I was surprised to learn ... that the Colonial Secretary had warned Kenneth Blackwell [the Senior British Trade Commissioner in Hong Kong] ... I find

it hard to believe that any damage would be done to the interests of Hong Kong by commercial contacts of this sort ... I should be glad if in due course you could let us know whether you have been able to remedy this seemingly absurd situation which is damaging to Sino/British trade.[207]

In another incident, the Peking Office complained that, as front-line officers, they had not been furnished with sufficient political news concerning events such as the death of a Hong Kong trade union leader in prison, and the subsequent line adopted by local communists. They believed their task in Peking had been made difficult by their ignorance of these facts. The officer said: 'This is a serious case and has an obvious bearing on the position of detained British subjects: I must therefore repeat my request that in matters of this sort I should be left fully and promptly informed.'[208]

This showed that differences existed within the British offices that later on intensified because each office represented different interests. These differences, however, also served as a restraining force, counterbalancing some of the illiberal acts of the Hong Kong government. It was in this context that the British representatives in Peking came to the conclusion that 'Hong Kong is the prime element in Sino-British relations'.[209] Thus they tended to press for de-escalation and an easing-off of the strained relations between China and Hong Kong and urged that there should be a continuous review of sentences of prisoners convicted in the 1967 disturbances. For this reason, they repeatedly urged London to 'steer the Hong Kong Governor away from injudicious policies' during the late 1960s to early 1970s.[210] Another reason was simply personal. During the peak of the confrontation, the movement of diplomatic officers and their families from both sides was restricted. Because of this, British officials in Peking recommended that London should take initiatives to untangle events in Peking from the separate problem of Hong Kong.

This rigid policy, though occasionally countered by more liberal notions, was getting nowhere, but it continued for more than two years. Thus, a Foreign Office representative put the blame on the stubbornness of the Foreign Secretary, which had served to worsen Sino-British relations. Percy Cradock, the former acting Chargé d'Affaires at the Peking office, noted:

By jibbing over the NCNA [*New China News Agency*, the de facto Chinese embassy in Hong Kong] visas, London had missed the point ... then in April there came an intervention from on high, George Brown resigned and was replaced as Foreign Secretary by Michael Stewart ... our recommendations on tactics were approved ... I fear that officials were also to blame: he [George Brown] was wrong-headed, but also wrongly advised.[211]

According to Michael Stewart, the then Foreign Secretary: Britain's long-term view towards China was behind the decision not to give concessions and release political detainees prematurely 'purely because of [the situation in] Hong Kong'.[212]

Elite and public opinion

Elite and local public opinion also acted as opposing forces to colonial control, although some of the quality newspapers, such as *Ming Pao Daily News* and *South China Morning Post*, maintained either an anti-communist or a pro-British position regarding the industrial dispute and later the disturbances in 1967. Alastair Hetherington, editor of the British newspaper, the *Guardian*, described Hong Kong's system of Government as 'an anachronism' after a brief visit there. He also advocated the introduction of representative government. *South China Morning Post* (*SCMP*) quoted him as saying 'the fact that you have a situation where 4m [million] people enjoy virtually no rights as regards representation in Government is a bad reflection on Britain.'[213] While admitting that the question of self-government in Hong Kong was beset with difficulties, he stressed that 'it is important to avoid anything that will bring to a crisis the tensions between pro-Communist and pro-Nationalist elements among the Chinese people here, and to avoid anything that could give rise to racial or political disturbances, but one cannot get away from the fact that it is time representative government was evolved.'[214] The criticism, in fact, came immediately before the major industrial dispute of early May 1967, which later triggered territory-wide disturbances.

SCMP, however, disagreed with the British editor's opinion. They argued that Hong Kong politics were different from British politics. Their editorial argued that the 'anachronism' in Hong Kong in fact worked. This stance largely reflected the fact that at that time the English-language paper was rather pro-British rule, and satisfied with the status quo.

> To many thinking Chinese (who of course constitute the great majority of the population) it is moreover preferable to the introduction of the kind of politics of which we have just had a taste at various factory entrances. . . . Chinese politics is not a matter of polite hair splitting between the policies of a Liberal, Labour or Conservative Party. It is totally polarised between Peking and Taiwan and there is no halfway house other than the system of government now in force in Hongkong [sic] where by preserving the polite fiction that politics does not exist at all, people of widely varying races, religions, and political creeds are enabled to live and work together in reasonable amity and to enjoy standards which may not measure up to those of the most fully developed Western nations but are certainly high by comparison with most of the rest of Asia.[215]

With the escalation of the labour dispute to a large-scale anti-colonial movement, the Hong Kong government charged five newspaper executives with sedition. They were Wu Di-chau, director of *New Afternoon News* Limited, Chak Nuen-fai, Lee Siu-hung, director of the Nam Cheong printing company (printer of *New Afternoon News*, *Hong Kong Evening News* and *Tin Fung Daily News*), Poon Wai-wai, editor of *Tin Fung Daily News*, and Chan Yim-kuen, publisher of *Tin*

Fung Daily News.[216] In the meantime, a Government official, speaking in a private capacity, pressed for a further clampdown on the communist press. I. D. McGregor, assistant Director to the Commerce and Industry department, said he felt that the Government had been too tolerant towards the left-wing press. 'It says a great deal for the Hong Kong government that it has permitted, for instance, certain newspapers to go on day after day pouring out seditious material and making damaging accusations against those who oppose the leftist[s],' he added.[217]

This rhetoric appeared to have prepared the way for more severe measures against the opposition. Two days later, the Hong Kong court issued an order against red publications, and three communist newspapers were suspended following an application from the Director of Public Prosecutions. The three papers were *Tin Fung Daily News*, *Hong Kong Evening News*, and *New Afternoon News*. The publisher and printer of one of the papers faced court proceedings for an alleged violation of laws against sedition, inflammatory reports and the spreading of false reports.[218]

Unsurprisingly, *SCMP* was at the frontline in support of British action against the pro-communist press. While the implementation of the Emergency Regulations came under criticism from not only the communist press, but also law lecturers,[219] the *SCMP* used the 'rule of law' argument to defend British repression.

> Absolutism about the rule of law is perhaps too much to hope for in turbulent times. 'Freedom of the press', for instance, is a popular topic just now though no one, apparently, has attempted to homologise the two totally different concepts of this principle now current in the two halves of the existing world. This contradiction lies at the root of one of Hong Kong's current confusions. While newspapers which know and respect the law do not comment on matters which are 'sub judice', other papers which know it but do not respect it have no hesitation in so doing. . . . To put this in another way, if this newspaper were to describe some action taken by the legal authorities as, say, 'sinful persecution' it would not expect to make such comment unscathed.[220]

SCMP increasingly justified actions against the Communist press on the grounds of its 'constant excesses of language'.

> The question is, then, whether the rule of law, as it exists here and now, can be split up in such a way as to permit constant excesses of language and menacing to go scot free in some cases when in others they would undoubtedly be subject to the full and deserved rigours of legal actions.[221]

These newspapers clearly supported continuing British colonial rule rather than the return of Hong Kong to Chinese rule. One of the most revealing statements appeared in another, so-called independent,[222] Chinese-language newspaper, *Ming Pao Daily News*. In a long essay on the current situation *Ming Pao Daily News* made the point that

> [T]he local people were not concerned with how the British authorities gov-
> erned Hong Kong – the most important thing was that citizens could breathe
> the air of freedom here. . . . Even if the Hong Kong British authorities were
> ten times worse, plus many more times unpopular, citizens would choose
> colonial freedom rather than Hong Kong Communist domination.[223]

Their assumption was that colonial freedom was better than communist rule, but
the paper did not go on to discuss whose freedom it was talking about.

In contrast to *SCMP*, *Far Eastern Economic Review* (*FEER*) printed quite a
few articles and commentaries criticising the Hong Kong government's mal-
treatment of communists in the first place, and its unnecessary 'provocation'
which did not help to resolve the incident later. For instance, the Hong Kong
government was criticised for not taking a more positive approach to: the question of the release of the detainees; the re-employment of the sacked strikers;
and a reappraisal of the sentences imposed by the court. It added,

> What is incomprehensible to the outside observer in the present situation is
> that the Hong Kong Government appears ready to escalate the struggle. One
> of the firmest planks of Hong Kong's policy vis-à-vis China has been the
> guarantee that Communist schools should be allowed to function and that
> the Thoughts of Mao could be studied without official interference. . . . Why
> therefore after 8 months did the Hong Kong authorities find it necessary to
> de-register the Chung Wah Middle School, which was closed after a bomb
> had exploded in its laboratory in November last year [1967]?[224]

FEER queried how much forethought the Hong Kong Government had given to
the political implications of its unexpected initiative against this school. The
Hong Kong government had made it clear that the school could reopen again as
a communist school (with the name and the staff changed), so the journal wondered what political advantage could have been gained by this move.[225] *FEER*
further demonstrated the dilemmas inherent in the situation:

> Sir David Trench naturally keeps his eyes fixed most firmly on what he
> judges to be the requirements of the local political and security situation
> while Britain must be concerned to convince Peking that British policy
> towards China does not exclude the possibility of conciliation.[226]

Moreover, *FEER* argued that what was more perturbing to those who opposed
deregistration was the construction that Peking would put on the closure of
Chung Wah Middle School. The deregistration of the School was announced on
the same day that Sir Donald Hopson, Britain's most senior diplomat in Beijing,
was allowed to leave China. While an exit visa was no more than a right to
which any diplomat was entitled, the journal argued that 'Peking's permission to
allow Sir Donald to leave the country must be seen as a significant gesture of
conciliation towards Britain by the strange standards which Chinese diplomacy
has had to adopt in the Cultural Revolution.'[227]

Furthermore, *FEER* criticised the Hong Kong government for choosing to ignore the findings of its own Commission of Enquiry into the 1966 riots (i.e., before the 1967 disturbances). In its report, the Commission commented on the public's worries about the economy and fears of inflation, and on the room for improvement in labour conditions and wages. It recommended legislation to improve working conditions, allied with an effort to win 'the active cooperation of young people'. But

> [T]he government made no discernable effort to accomplish this. Similarly, the Commission's conclusion on social conditions in paragraph 502 and 503 were ignored; these pointed to deficiencies and defects in housing, environment, education and community spirit which fed the undercurrent of suppressed frustrations and resentments.[228]

Thus, *FEER* demonstrated itself to be one of the rare critical voices, apart from the communist press, by advocating reform. It also made no secret of the fact that it was not particularly supportive of having the incumbent governor, David Trench, carry on for another year or term and stated: 'It is not known how long the Governor will remain in Hong Kong to preside over the process of strengthening the community's ability to withstand troublemakers. The colony has certainly proved its economic resilience once again; the effort now must be made to bring other sectors – the social and political ones – up to a level of development which can balance its economic sophistication.'[229]

Public opinion and the emergency regulations

Furthermore, 18 months after the disturbances in Hong Kong, there was correspondence in *The Times* and in Hong Kong newspapers centering on the justification and need for keeping the Emergency Regulations in force. This correspondence sparked off parliamentary interest, as questions were put down for reply centering largely on the power of detention and the position of the remaining detainees.[230] At a Hong Kong press conference, Percy Cradock, the Acting British Chargé d'Affaires in Peking, complained about the Chinese treatment of Anthony Grey. John Rear, a law lecturer at the Hong Kong University Extramural Department, wrote a letter to the London *Times*, suggesting Percy Cradock's remark was 'pure hypocrisy' because some 30 to 40 local Chinese communists were still in detention following their arrest during the disturbances. The Emergency Regulation in force in Hong Kong empowered Hong Kong's Colonial Secretary to direct any person he named to be detained, without trial, for up to one year. The Colonial Secretary needed to give no reason for ordering a particular person's detention, and there was nothing to prevent re-arrest and further detention.[231]

Rear was not alone in his criticism, but was supported by the legal community. After the Hong Kong government had refuted the charge, Henry Litton, secretary of the Hong Kong Bar Association, wrote to defend and support his colleagues:

The Hong Kong government has at present totalitarian powers over the people of Hong Kong in the form of Emergency Regulation. And in particular regulation 31 of the Emergency (Principal) Regulation which permits the Colonial Secretary to detain any person for a period of up to one year without trial.[232]

There were also articles in English periodicals analysing the situation. One of the strongest counter-government arguments concerning the 1967 disturbances was put forward in a well-researched article written by Andrew Kwok-nang Li,[233] a reporter from *Far Eastern Economic Review*, who had examined the records of 100 political prisoners, many of whom he had interviewed.[234] Li made a critical analysis of the nature of the disturbances and referred to one interviewee's opinion:

If the labour dispute had been dealt with fairly and justly by the Labour Department, everything would have been fine. Instead the Hong Kong British sent in the police to deal with a labour dispute, and they beat up fellow Chinese. The Hilton or Garden Road incident marked a turning point. Fellow Chinese went to stage an orderly demonstration but they were beaten up by the cunning police. After this, it became a radical and political struggle.[235]

Besides tracing the roots of the unrest, which pointed to social inequality, the article also examined the disillusionment of Hong Kong youngsters in the colony. Andrew Li cited the history of one student, with a brilliant academic record in an outstanding missionary school, so as to throw some light on the question why young people were attracted to the communist party's ranks. This 20-year-old was a science student in the lower 6th when he was arrested on a charge of putting up and distributing inflammatory posters on the school premises.[236] He had printed the material himself, and the posters called on the students to love their country, China, and rise up in struggle. He said he came from an ordinary lower middle-class background.

He had always been aware of the injustices in Hong Kong society. He recalled one incident: a policeman overturned a hawker's tomatoes and then stamped on them ... he has examined things for himself and concluded that Hong Kong is decadent, a city in which everyone makes money as fast as they can. Sickened by his view of the colony, he opted for communism and an anti-government movement.[237]

Aftermath

As a result of the disturbances in 1967, the left wing press suffered a heavy blow.[238] The communist press, apart from suffering from constant harassment, detainment and imprisonment, found that circulation had plunged after a brief surge at the beginning of the disturbances. After three independently owned but pro-communist newspapers had been suspended for six months, circulation dropped even further. The circulation of the communist press after that never achieved the pre-1967 figures. The communists' strategy of establishing a few independent papers was undermined by the exposure of the nature of all nine pro-communist newspapers during the crisis.[239] The once popular communist papers lost their readership as well as the image they had constructed for themselves because first, they exposed their ideological link with the Chinese Communist Party and, second, their business operations suffered in the aftermath of the disturbances.

In 1969, approximately 250 prisoners were still serving sentences in respect of alleged offences committed during the disturbances of 1967. Of these, approximately 130 were sentenced to terms of imprisonment of four years or more.[240] Yet, regulation 31 of the Emergency (Principal) Regulation, which conferred the power of detention, was discontinued on 20 June 1969, together with a number of other regulations.

However, despite enormous pressure from both London and Hong Kong, the Hong Kong government refused to grant the premature release of 13 Hong Kong left-wing journalists in exchange for Anthony Grey, who had been kept in house arrest for two years, on the grounds that this might be seen as a sign of weakness. After Grey was released, he asked the then Foreign Secretary, Michael Stewart, if the British Government had believed that the 13 news workers were themselves likely to instigate fresh rioting. Stewart replied that they were all 'skilful propagandists' and it was felt they would possibly have caused new riots if released.[241] Grey then asked what had led to the release of Wong Chak, a left-wing journalist in Hong Kong, two years early. The Minister said it was thought at that time it could be done 'without risk to the situation'. However, the British Government had not publicly admitted that Wong's release was connected with Grey. In response to a campaign urging the British Government to release the Chinese prisoners in Hong Kong to secure Grey's freedom, a printed letter was sent out in May 1969 explaining the reasons why nothing like that was being done. The Foreign Office letter set out succinctly the official attitude and its dilemma. It said,

> [T]here had been no clear guarantee from the Chinese side. Even if such a guarantee had been given ... there are also serious objections to arranging an exchange of this kind.... The well-being of Hong Kong and the welfare of its people are dependent on continued confidence that the British Government will maintain law and order there so that people can go about their legitimate business unmolested and without fear. If it appeared that by holding British subjects as hostages the Chinese could influence British action and policy in Hong Kong, this confidence could well be undermined.[242]

However, in the aftermath, the Hong Kong government realised that there was a need for social and economic reform. There were several calls for change. For example, Elsie Elliot, a Hong Kong Urban Councillor, proposed that Chinese should be the second official language;[243] and the media and senior figures advocated one day off per week for workers.[244] Better communication channels between the government and ordinary people were set up in the form of district offices at municipal level; and a new department of Census and Statistics was set up to assess Hong Kong's progress.[245]

Analysis

The anti-colonial movement never succeeded because apparently it was neither in the Chinese interests nor those of the British. Macau having been brought under Communist control by force in January 1967, the British were very aware of the risk that they would lose Hong Kong in a similar fashion. However, British judgement at the time was that local communists did not have the full support of the Chinese central government, though at times local communists in Hong Kong were allegedly subsidised by Beijing.[246] Despite the fact that Beijing was unhappy with 'British atrocities towards Chinese compatriots', there was no call for a return of Hong Kong even at the worst time. Nevertheless, the Hong Kong administration, having finally understood that they were following the wrong strategy, adopted a series of social and economic reforms in the aftermath of the disturbances in order to rule Hong Kong in a relatively civilised manner, though without democratic representation.

Conclusion

In short, the 1967 disturbances fully demonstrated that the so-called free press of Hong Kong was not in fact autonomous. On the one hand, the British government acted in a repressive fashion during the late 1960s. Its policy on China and Hong Kong was largely guided by its general foreign policy, which at the time was intended to retain British imperial influence while simultaneously following a policy of decolonisation. On the other hand, British policy-makers had to take into account the effect of Chinese reaction, trying to avoid a head-on confrontation while launching a purge on the Hong Kong communist press. British attempts to control dissenting voices were further obstructed by differences existing within the British government, and also by liberal elite and public opinion, although these formed a minority view in the colony. However, this case study illustrates the significance of political influences on the development of the Hong Kong press. Three decades were to pass until a critical press emerged in the space created by an apparent political vacuum. Next we shall look at how the press fared during the political transition of the 1990s.

3 Reporting on a jailed journalist
A textual analysis during the transition period, 1993–1997

Introduction

Hong Kong underwent what has been called 'de-colonization without independence' in anticipation of 1997.[247] Unlike other British colonies, the option of national independence was not open to Hong Kong.[248] Due to historical and political restrictions, Hong Kong was not given a chance to decide on its own future. The findings of a number of opinion polls conducted at that time showed that the vast majority preferred the status quo of British rule, and the return of the territory to Chinese sovereignty and administration was the least preferred option. Yet Hong Kong people were neither given the chance to participate in the Sino-British negotiations, nor was the Sino-British Joint Declaration[249] agreement submitted to a referendum of the Hong Kong people.[250] Political negotiations between Britain and PRC began in the late 1970s and ended in 1984. From then on, Hong Kong entered a transition period with two political regimes attempting to assert their authority over an island where six million people lived.[251]

In the 1990s, Hong Kong society was occupied with all sorts of political issues emanating from the Sino-British negotiations, the 1989 Tiananmen crackdown,[252] and the disagreements between the Chinese and British governments regarding the pace of democratic development in Hong Kong.[253] On a personal and family level, Hong Kong people pondered their own future, notwithstanding the fact that they had no say in deciding Hong Kong's future. The phrase 'decide to leave, decide to stay, decide not to decide'[254] vividly depicted their confusion in terms of what was the best solution. In the face of an uncertain political future,[255] many opted for emigration, if their wealth or skills permitted or they had good connections in their future home country.

At this historical juncture, when political leadership was vague and shifting, and democracy was remote,[256] the media were perceived as shouldering the emerging role of watchdog.[257] The media were expected to monitor the many promises that the way of life of Hong Kong's people would be maintained.[258] At this time, Xu Jiatun, the former head of Hong Kong *Xinhua News Agency* (de facto Chinese Embassy), remarked that Hong Kong was a sensitive city[259] and the media were in a particularly sensitive position. The media were very diverse and would not be easily controlled by the Chinese Communist Party (CCP) either before or after 1997.[260]

Similarly, Chris Patten, the last Hong Kong Governor, stressed the importance of preserving the British legacy of press freedom and suggested a set of 16 benchmarks that could be used to check whether Hong Kong continued to enjoy a relative degree of civil liberties. One of the crucial questions he reminded Hong Kong people to pose after the handover was: 'Is the HK [Hong Kong] press still free, with uninhibited coverage of China and of issues on which China has strong views?'[261]

On the media front, there was both scepticism and optimism concerning the future of press freedom. On the one hand, certain foreign media predicted that Hong Kong would roll back drastically after 1997;[262] on the other hand, local journalists were hopeful about the future, since they believed that, provided Hong Kong could sustain its market economy, market forces might help sustain the diversity of the media.[263] Scholarly opinion held the view that press freedom would be more or less contingent upon continuing variations in PRC's reform policy,[264] or that, after the handover, 'the press will continue to legitimate the new master without feeling great discomfort because of its power-dependent nature'.[265] Which of these views was held was largely dependent on the researcher's individual position and personal perspective.

Yet, it was during this period of political transition that the Hong Kong press consolidated its position and organised a protest against Chinese coercion.[266] The case of Xi Yang is intriguing, as it constituted one of the most significant events in the fight for press freedom. Hundreds of local journalists, in an unprecedented move, took to the streets to protest against the detention, secret trial and imprisonment of Xi Yang, a Hong Kong journalist, by the Chinese government. It is also crucial to look at what happened in the pre-handover period to see what might have affected the development of the media in the run-up to 1997, before discussing the post-1997 situation. During the transition period, the key questions remained: Was the press independent or subordinate to the Chinese state? Did market forces help to counter both governmental and proprietary intervention? What was the unfolding scenario for the media?

The first section of this chapter examines political developments, paying special attention to power distribution in the political transition and how it may have affected the wider context in which the media were situated. The second section discusses the choice of newspaper samples for news analysis. The third section discusses the reasons for choosing particular cases, and their significance. The focus is on the newspaper coverage of the case, which not only raised great concerns within the profession, but also brought out fear and anxiety in the minds of Hong Kong people.

The key questions are then as follows. How independent was the press during the transition? Did its defiance have anything to do with the shift in the power structure and the wider social context? What were the public and journalistic perceptions of press freedom? Was this clash between the Hong Kong press and the Chinese state inevitable during the transition?

Influence of the two powers

For most of the 150 years of British colonial rule, Hong Kong politics was generally regarded as premised upon a consensus supportive to the British regime.[267] Political parties did not exist. However, after the Sino-British Declarations, a number of political groups emerged seeking to influence government policies through the mechanisms afforded by district and municipal, and legislative council elections. Although these elected groups had no executionary power, owing to the restrictions imposed by both the British and the Chinese governments, they were nevertheless increasingly influential in affecting public policy: partial direct elections allowed political parties to play an increasingly significant role. With voters' support, they consistently pressed for a faster pace of democracy, and adopted a more confrontational approach towards the central government over various issues, such as the promotion of democracy in Hong Kong and the mainland, and the protection of civil liberties and human rights.[268] Compared with colonial days when there was minimal political opposition, the administrative state had become more political. Although the attitude of the Hong Kong population towards democratic reform had in the past been somewhat indifferent, there was now a significant change in public attitudes towards political participation.

As the handover of Hong Kong approached, the political scene shifted as the Hong Kong Chinese elite, fragmented in their allegiances, became disunited in their political alignment.[269] At the same time as the economy of Hong Kong prospered in the 1970s and 1980s, there rose a new middle class, which identified with the values of fair competition and self-improvement, and based their identity on hard work, material well-being and the acquisition of credentials.[270] This new middle class made their way up the social ladder by means of education.[271] However, they were disorganised politically, or political apathetic.[272] (Some have even argued that this new middle class in fact withered under the blow of economic recession in the first few years after the handover.)[273] Thus, their potential as an organised force against the state was in doubt. They appeared to be unprepared, if not totally unreliable.

Owing to the unique decolonisation process in Hong Kong, where independence was never an option, the elite was fragmented, while the middle class became cynical and distrustful of political authority. When it came to the final days of British rule, it has been argued that the political situation in Hong Kong did not involve a class struggle, but rather a difference in political orientation: for example, political orientations ranged from pro-China to pro-democracy, and in the final British days from pro-Patten to pro-Hong Kong. Under such circumstances, an awareness of how remote democracy was, and a lack of political leadership, further perplexed the people of Hong Kong. In this context, the press helped to create a space/forum for public debate.

British policy

The development of the Hong Kong press had in many ways been facilitated by the relaxation of colonial rule during its final days. Reform mainly involved the relaxation or repeal of draconian laws that might have an enduring effect on press freedom.[274] In addition, the government also underwent structural changes in order to appear to be more open and accountable, as well as transparent. All the measures adopted by senior Hong Kong officials, including the British governor (for instance, the holding of regular press conferences and efforts to develop a closer relationship with the public), were supposed to lay down yardsticks with which the Hong Kong people could measure the new regime after the changeover.[275]

Chinese policy

Unlike its British counterpart, the Chinese government was extremely sensitive about the Hong Kong media's development. The question that concerned it most was whether or not the British would successfully turn Hong Kong into a 'subversive base'[276] before their departure. With this in mind, any last minute changes to Hong Kong's social and political system were regarded by the Chinese as a conspiracy, and so an attempt to maintain Hong Kong as a postcolonial British outpost.[277]

Yet it was China's long-standing policy to 'make use of Hong Kong'[278] to gain revenue,[279] as well as status in the international community. At the end of the Sino-British talks over Hong Kong's future, it was commonly argued that China would honour the terms of the Joint Declaration agreement because it needed a prosperous Hong Kong to contribute to China's own economy. It was also commonly believed that between 30 to 40 per cent of China's foreign exchange earnings came from trade with and through Hong Kong. Moreover, 70 per cent of the foreign investment in China came from companies based in Hong Kong, and in the southern Guangdong province alone more than two million Chinese workers were employed by Hong Kong-owned enterprises.[280] Another argument was that China would leave Hong Kong alone because they needed to persuade the Taiwanese people that they had nothing to fear if they abandoned their independent stance and reunited with China. However, in the early 1990s, it seemed that none of these considerations had any weight in the determination of China's policy towards Hong Kong.[281] The PRC had long maintained that the western model of liberal democracy was neither applicable to, nor suitable for, Hong Kong.

The Hong Kong media during the transition

As mentioned in Chapters 1 and 2, from the end of the First World War until the mid-twentieth century, most of the Hong Kong newspapers were not partisan. During the 1950s and 1960s when Hong Kong was seen to be 'neither like mainland China, nor Taiwan', most of the mainstream papers claimed not to be strongly political in orientation; but the press in fact manifested a political spectrum from leftist to rightist.[282] In the late 1960s, an anti-British protest developed into major disturbances. The Hong Kong government used the disturbances as an excuse to repress the communist press, and this had a bearing on the development of the Hong Kong press as a whole.[283]

As Hong Kong changed rapidly from an entrepot to one of the most important trading, commercial and financial centres, there was a dramatic change in the Hong Kong press during the 1970s and the 1980s. In the 1970s, *Ming Pao Daily News* gained public attention: during the ten-year Chinese Cultural Revolution it reported extensively on, and provided critical analysis of, the development of the CCP. It sold up to around 120,000 issues, and so ranked as the third or fourth best-selling Chinese-language newspaper in Hong Kong. *Oriental Daily News*, was also set up during this period. The paper's proclaimed aim was to speak out for the lower classes, and it sold up to 400,000 copies and reached a readership of a million people. That is, almost one-sixth of Hong Kong people read this mass circulation paper, as Hong Kong's population reached six million in the early 1990s.

On the other hand, *South China Morning Post* was a traditional English-language newspaper. It was regarded as liberal in the western sense, but at times upheld a pro-British policy, especially during the colonial era, including the transition period from the early 1980s onwards.

As Hong Kong entered the political transition of the 1990s, most of the Hong Kong press developed the characteristics of a 'social and economic press',[284] that is, they emphasised local social and economic affairs, and proclaimed the papers' 'objectivity and neutrality'. At the time, the ten most popular newspapers were not party-affiliated papers. Many of them had more than one-third of their editorials concentrating on domestic affairs.[285] After the signing of the agreement between the Chinese and British concerning Hong Kong's future, the Hong Kong press was critical of the deal.[286] This criticism, however, was spread among individual columns or letters to the editor, rather than resulting from an organised effort in the papers' editorials. In other words, the Hong Kong press appeared to have developed tactics in order to play the role of watchdog, without directly approaching highly sensitive political issues such as the case of the jailed reporter, Xi Yang.

Summary

The role of the Hong Kong media as watchdog during the period before the take-over by the Chinese was complicated by a number of issues. These included the confusion prevalent in the everyday lives of Hong Kong people regarding their future, the constitution of a new middle class, and further fragmentation of the Hong Kong political scene as a result of the complex Sino-British relations. In respect of the future freedom of the Hong Kong press, the most significant clash appeared to be between the British efforts to establish lasting arrangements for press freedom, and the Chinese attempts to maintain the strict rules for Hong Kong journalists reporting on China. It was in this context that the most significant case of Chinese intervention in Hong Kong reporting occurred.

Textual analysis: reporting on a jailed journalist

Introduction

Xi Yang, a trained reporter, was born in mainland China and emigrated to Hong Kong in the early 1990s. He worked for *Ming Pao Daily News* (*MPDN*), an elitist broadsheet Chinese-language newspaper, with a shifting editorial position.[287] Xi Yang was arrested in China on 7 October 1993 and sentenced to 12 years' imprisonment and two years' deprivation of political rights for reporting on China's financial and economic news. According to the Chinese authorities Xi had engaged in 'spying and stealing of state secrets' which resulted in serious economic loss to the Chinese government.[288]

In response to the heavy sentence an outcry ensued; it triggered a series of petitions (including signatory letters), an early release campaign, lobbying, and other protests including a hunger strike. More than a hundred reporters on the China beat published a signed statement condemning the Chinese authority's heavy sentence on Xi Yang, and stating that they would stop covering any official promotional functions in China for a month as a protest.[289] This group of reporters later suffered retaliation from China; for instance, those who had put their names on protest documents against China were forbidden to cover a tragic accident that happened in Hangzhou, a famous tourist city near the coastal city of Shanghai.

There was strong criticism, both local and foreign, of the Chinese conviction of Xi Yang, and not just from local journalists. This heavy-handed approach by the Chinese reflected the fatal drawbacks of the illiberal system, and represented a deliberate attempt by the CCP to suppress the Hong Kong press in order to exercise total control.

However, the case was more complicated and complex than this, and involved a struggle between various power factions. Hong Kong officials were accused of adopting a passive and ambivalent attitude by locally elected politicians, though the move seemed to backfire on China. Hundreds of Hong Kong journalists took to the streets and pressed for publication of the full text of the verdict.[290] The organiser of the protest reportedly said it was 'an encouraging turnout . . . [and expressed] fear over the "unjustifiable" measures by Beijing to control [the] local press.'[291] The momentum appeared to gather pace and there was a series of concerted actions, for example, a 72-hour relay hunger strike initiated by the three most senior editors of *MPDN*, and 15 members of the faculty of journalism issued a statement expressing their anger and lending their support to Xi Yang. After Xi Yang lost his appeal case, more than 2,000 people took to the streets to support him.

In a 'free Xi' rally, a Hong Kong Journalists Association (HKJA) representative remarked that Xi Yang had become a scapegoat for the differences between the two systems, the mainland socialist system and the Hong Kong capitalist system. Daisy Li, the chairperson of the HKJA, said that although she had anticipated that there would be a contraction in press freedom after 1997, she had never expected that the Hong Kong press would need to contend with the Chinese government for 12 years because of one reporter.[292]

The appeal, protest and petitions were to no avail. Xi Yang was sent to jail. He emerged from prison after three years, and later departed for Canada. The significance of the Xi Yang case lies in the complex set of circumstances prevailing at the time. Hong Kong had come to the final stage of British rule, and was entering the second half of the political transition. Xi's heavy sentence came as a shock to Hong Kong people, as many could visualise what the future held for them. It was understood that at best the controversy arose from the discrepancy between the two systems, and at worst from Chinese authoritarian rule. The Chinese authorities insisted that Xi's case was an individual incident that involved criminal activity rather than regular journalistic work.

At this time, Chinese influence was increasingly impinging on various aspects of Hong Kong's affairs.[293] It also had an enduring effect on local newspaper proprietors, the majority of whom wishing to explore business opportunities in China, both media and non-media. The position of the reporter's company, for this reason, was seen as shifting and controversial. *MPDN* first rejected Chinese allegations categorically, stressing that its reporter was only carrying out reporting duties. The company later changed its stance, however, and admitted its reporter's crime on his behalf in order to bargain for a no strings-attached release. After the Chinese conviction and sentencing, the paper reverted to a vigorous protest against this heavy-handed Chinese measure. When Xi got an early release in early 1997, however, *MPDN* shifted its position again to an appeasement strategy by praising Chinese leniency and sincerity.

In short, this incident triggered doubts, fears and grievances in relation to reporting in China, the prospects for Hong Kong press freedom, and above all confidence in Hong Kong's future after the political changeover. The Xi case was chosen not only because it was highly significant, but also because the relevant events took place over the period from 1993 to 1997,[294] so that it highlights the shifting position of the press during these crucial years.[295]

Selection of newspapers for analysis

This research attempts to study empirically the mainstream newspaper coverage of the events surrounding the arrest and detention of the journalist, Xi Yang, prior to Hong Kong's political changeover. Surprisingly little empirical research has been completed on newspaper representations of the media themselves; still fewer studies combine such research with that on the conduct of journalists and their working practices. The majority of work so far completed has used selective anecdotal evidence to illustrate biases in media coverage.[296] There are even fewer studies on the relationship between the state and the media. This study is informed by a political economy perspective, which views journalistic discourse as being conditioned by both internal and external constraints, and in particular as being influenced by the wider social context.

This research focuses mainly on broadsheet papers for several reasons: first, the traditional stress the broadsheet press places on objectivity and balanced reporting, as opposed to the tendency towards sensationalism and overt partisanship of the tabloid papers. Second, the readership profile of broadsheet papers is heavily biased in favour of Hong Kong society's more powerful middle and upper classes, although, as suggested earlier, Hong Kong is less a class-based society than a politically oriented one. The audiences of broadsheet papers are predominantly educated, professional, economically independent individuals and groups.

The research focuses on the content, editorial stance, reporting style and agenda of three daily broadsheet papers in Hong Kong: *South China Morning Post* (*SCMP*), a leading independent English-language daily newspaper; *MPDN*, a well-respected Chinese-language daily newspaper that can be classified as liberal shifting to conservative-leftist;[297] and Chinese-language *Oriental Daily News* (*ODN*), which can be classified as critical and independent in terms of its political reporting, with a mix of tabloid-style reporting and sensationalism in its social news.[298] As the best-selling daily from the late 1980s until the present day, *ODN* was especially influential with middle to lower-class readers. The choice of papers was also guided by a wish to compare reporting in an English-language title with that of its Chinese-language counterparts.

The papers selected for case study: context and reasons for choice

Hong Kong has 16 major daily newspapers, ranging from highbrow papers that aspire to be world class to those devoted almost entirely to pornography or horseracing.[299] The three papers chosen for this case study represent positions ranging from relatively independent to relatively patriotic.

ODN is a mass-circulation Chinese-language broadsheet and the highest-selling paper in Hong Kong, with a daily circulation of over half a million.[300] In the early 2000s, it was a relatively independent tabloid in style and content.

MPDN is the highest-selling Chinese quality daily, with a daily circulation of 120,000 copies,[301] and is tightly bound up with Hong Kong's cultural identity. It used to be anti-Chinese Communist, and critical of mainland policy. However, it started to change from the late 1980s with a change in ownership. In 2000, a Malaysian Chinese businessman, Tiong Hiew-king, owned it. The editorial position of the paper was sympathetic to China or pro-China in respect of the Sino-Hong Kong controversy. Its proprietor wanted the paper to become the 'Chinese people's paper'.[302]

SCMP, with a daily circulation of slightly over 100,000 copies,[303] was a leading English-language newspaper, which used to be pro-British and critical of Chinese policy. It represents in its purest form the western liberal newspaper tradition that is a constant force in the Hong Kong press. However, in the early 1990s, it was sold to Rupert Murdoch and then subsequently to a Malaysian Chinese businessman, Robert Kuok, after which the editorial position of the paper became less critical of the Chinese government.

Additionally, it was important to ensure that the sample of papers should span the political spectrum expressed in Hong Kong broadsheet newspapers. This seemed to be best achieved by choosing *MPDN* and *ODN*. When deciding upon the dates for the sample period, the length of the case and its starting date were taken into account. A sample covering the unfolding of the whole incident will be discussed, that is, the detention, official arrest, sentencing, appeal and release of the journalist in question.

The analysis of the coverage was largely guided by the events. Thus it covers the output of the relevant papers from September 1993 to May 1994, and January 1997, over ten months in total. The selected time-span also enables the analysis of the major significant events and the observation of any change in editorial position over time. The most representative stories published by these newspapers relating to the Xi Yang case were selected, as these were best suited to making inferences about how the papers presented the case. In this study, the analysis mainly focuses on editorial formats such as news reports, columns, letter to the editors, feature writing, editorials, advertisements, cartoons, photographs and so on. The case is covered in three main phases: arrest, conviction and release.

Case study

South China Morning Post

The ordeal of Xi Yang largely reflected the precarious political environment in which the Hong Kong press was situated. This balance of sources reveals the unusual juggling between the two powers, namely the British and the Chinese. This daily tended to give more weight to the sources of the Chinese camp in respect of this specific case.

Throughout Xi Yang's ordeal, information about him was announced through Chinese official propaganda instruments. *South China Morning Post* (*SCMP*) when relaying information about Xi Yang's alleged crime used the official *Xinhua News Agency's* press releases, and other semi-official sources such as *Chinese News Services*, as authoritative sources of information.

Back in Hong Kong, *SCMP* could turn to top mainland Chinese officials for comments on, and explanation of, the trial. For instance, Zhang Junsheng, vice-director of *Xinhua News Agency* (*New China News Agency*), the de facto Chinese embassy in Hong Kong, remarked that Hong Kong reporters should be able to make a judgement as to whether Xi Yang's conduct was against the law or not.[304]

At the same time, *SCMP* tried to get immediate reactions from the British side, for instance, from Sir Robin McLaren, British Ambassador to Beijing, and from the Hong Kong governor, Chris Patten. Sometimes it was unsuccessful in this, because the former refused to give specific assistance to the reporter, and the latter declined to comment. At least, the paper managed to get some official British Hong Kong reaction from the Hong Kong Financial Secretary in Washington, Hamish Macleod said he could sense the tension and uneasiness prevailing in the press.

The paper also revealed the emerging role, which was still relatively weak, of the Hong Kong Chinese elite. For instance, all the mainstream political parties voiced their differing levels of disagreement with Beijing's coercive action towards this Hong Kong journalist. The business-oriented Liberal Party, the United Democrat Party (the largest opposition party, which was later rebranded as the Democratic Party), other pressure groups and independent legislative councillors, Hong Kong Chinese academics and mainland Chinese legal experts who were based in Hong Kong, all voiced their disagreement concerning the jailing of Xi Yang.

After Xi Yang was granted an early release on parole, while most of the Hong Kong press hailed this as showing Chinese leniency, *SCMP* printed the 'cautious welcome' of a senior U.S. official in Washington, who remarked that the release 'doesn't change our view that how he (Xi Yang) was arrested in the first place was unjustified. At this stage, it's difficult to know what this means in the larger scheme of things [in China].'[305] This stance differed from the uneasy harmony most of the local media attempted to portray.

Conversely, *SCMP* refrained from analytical reportage on the politically sensitive relationship between the Hong Kong, British and Chinese governments. The British showed a distinct unwillingness to support his cause actively. The excuse they gave for this attitude was the ongoing Sino-British tensions over conflicts between the governments on constitutional reform in Hong Kong. On some occasions, however, the last governor appeared to be critical and demanded an explanation from China.

Unsurprisingly, *SCMP* reports showed the reporter's family and the newspaper management and proprietor rejecting any help from the British or the Hong Kong government. The daily did not, however, explain that this reluctance to seek help resulted from pressure from the Chinese authorities.

It was only when the British and Hong Kong governments were widely criticised for not lending any help that the daily reported this explicitly. For instance, the United Democrat Party criticised the Hong Kong government for lacking a stronger position when one of its citizens was sentenced to 12 years' imprisonment in China. The Hong Kong legislative council also pressed the British Foreign Secretary, Douglas Hurd, to summon the Chinese ambassador to London, and issued a protest.[306] Despite an earlier warning by the Chinese not to meddle, the Hong Kong governor, Chris Patten, remarked that 'in particular people in Hong Kong deserve straightforward answers to straightforward questions'.[307] However, when Patten was called on for help, he said his 'main concern [was] to avoid [making] his (Xi Yang's) very difficult position even more difficult.'[308]

Nature of news coverage: Xi Yang's case as a yardstick for coverage of relations with China

The news coverage of *SCMP* underlined the fact that Xi Yang did not receive an open, fair and just trial. The paper's approach was mainly factual, but also critical of China's handling of the Xi case in the beginning. At first, the paper's coverage of Xi's case was dotted with sympathetic stories, and largely appeared to support the campaign for his release. This was demonstrated by the many news reports, with prominent pictures of Xi Yang, about the demonstrations and hunger strikes organised by his colleagues and supporters. The ordeal's strain on the reporter was vividly depicted by showing his fresh looks before imprisonment in sharp contrast to his grey-haired appearance after three and a half years' imprisonment.

The coercive violence applied by the Chinese authorities was criticised indirectly by, for example, a political cartoon depicting a bloody human ear.[309] Another cartoon showed a reporter putting his/her microphone across the mouth of a gun.[310] Both of these featured on protest placards, which in turn were photographed and the photographs printed with news stories.

The headlines pointed out that an unexpected consequence of a piece of journalistic work was that the reporter was sentenced to 12 years in jail. The paper used strong words, such as 'shock', 'harsh sentence', 'clear warning' (to Hong Kong) and 'outrageous verdict'.

The handling of Chinese official statements reflected the acute tension between the Chinese and British governments, for instance, 'Keep your nose out'[311] was a warning issued by the vice-director of *Xinhua News Agency* to the Hong Kong governor, Chris Patten. The general reaction to the Chinese authorities was reflected in headlines too, such as 'Heat in Beijing over Xi's jailing',[312] and 'The politics of injustice'.[313] On the other hand, China's counter-argument was published alongside. For instance, a Chinese official rejected criticisms by saying that Xi Yang's jail term was considered light, as the maximum sentence for his alleged crime was life imprisonment.

Sometimes, the headlines were simply descriptive, for instance, 'Zhu [Rongji, the Chinese Premier], Qian [Qichen, the deputy Chinese Premier] deny role',[314] indicating a denial of the involvement of Chinese top leaders. However, the official Chinese position that the trial was non-political was countered by an accompanying picture showing an ordinary Hong Kong person supporting Xi's release by launching a hunger strike. This sent out the message that the reporter was being unreasonably suppressed.

Another headline appeared to press for more information: 'full text of verdict demanded'.[315] In addition to the political story, *SCMP* also printed a human interest story entitled 'Father sees little hope in appeal',[316] in which Xi's father was shown as having little expectation of fairness in a secret trial. On another occasion, an unnamed spokesman from *China News Services*, under pressure from both the Chinese authorities' friends and enemies to release further details, provided information that was published in an article in *South China Morning Post* entitled 'China gives details of Xi allegation'.

One can identify changes in the editorial line as the case developed. During the initial period, the tone of the editorials was cautiously optimistic, although *SCMP* already anticipated that Xi might be treated more harshly because he was a mainlander. In one of its early editorials entitled 'Arrest reason unclear', it said: 'there is [a] worrying aspect ... no one feels confident ... Xi, [a] recent immigrant treated as ... a mainland resident, must not be subject to arbitrary imprisonment.'[317] Apart from issuing a warning, *SCMP* reported that Xi was praised as a hardworking 'man of few words'[318] by his colleagues, which illustrated that the paper was willing to lend support to the detained journalist. Then the official announcement of the arrest occurred.[319] *Xinhua News Agency* announced that his crime was obtaining information about a possible increase in interest rates and a rumour about Chinese gold sales. It said that the behaviour of Xi and Tian (a senior official in the Bank of China) 'was quite different from the normal work of a journalist'. The story was, however, balanced by another source saying he 'believes Xi innocent'.

During this period, *SCMP* stressed the political element by highlighting tension between the British and Chinese. The Chinese authorities also tried to manipulate the press. For example, some pro-China politicians gave out information that provided false hope about Xi's situation, and this information was summarised in the paper as 'journalist arrested but not charged'.[320] *MPDN* was advised by pro-China politicians to adopt a low-key approach. The Hong Kong governor, Chris Patten, was also warned by a Chinese official in Hong Kong to keep his nose out of the Xi case.[321]

A further dramatic twist occurred during this period when Xi's proprietor, Yu Pun-hoi of *MPDN*, together with the paper's senior editors, decided that the paper would offer apologies to the Chinese authorities in the hope of securing Xi's release. To the surprise of many journalists, Yu also admitted that Xi might have committed criminal activities in the course of reporting in China.[322] *SCMP* criticised *MPDN*'s handling of the case pointing out the sharp contrast with its previous position: 'Arrested reporter may have broken law, says *Ming Pao Daily News*'. It further quoted *MPDN* as saying we now have 'reason to believe he (Xi) might have broken [the] law – [this is a] purely "criminal" case, nothing to do with the British Hong Kong government.'[323]

The coverage of *SCMP* reflected a gloomy outlook for the future. When Xi Yang was sentenced to 12 years' imprisonment and a two-year deprivation of political rights, the verdict was conveyed to Hong Kong through *Xinhua News Agency*. 'Shock at Xi's 12-year term – harsh sentence a "threat to press freedom after 1997"'[324] was *SCMP*'s headline. It also quoted the chairperson of the Hong Kong Journalists Association as saying the 'low profile [of *Ming Pao Daily News*] resulted in a heavy sentence',[325] thus pointing out the outcome of *MPDN*'s misguided concession to China. *SCMP* also described the serious consequences of the verdict with the headline, '*Ming Pao Daily News*: hamper news organization, shake faith, harm Chinese image'.[326] However, the story was balanced with a quote from a senior Hong Kong government official describing the verdict as 'disappointing', and another, from a top Chinese official in charge of

Hong Kong affairs, saying it was 'not [a] heavy sentence'. Although the reportage largely maintained a matter of fact approach, the editorial headline, 'Verdict Outrageous', was more upfront. The editorial questioned the prospects for press freedom after 1997, and foresaw that there was a limit to how much the British could help.

The remarkable differences between the interests of the journalists and the proprietor were graphically shown here. The paper's proprietor, Yu Pun-hoi, was quoted as saying that he believed the Xi case would not affect the group's business in the mainland.[327] On the other hand, surprisingly, the business-oriented Liberal Party was quoted as saying, 'it was legitimate for the Hong Kong government to stand up' to the Chinese authorities.[328] This position, however, was probably more linked to a desire for a secure environment for investment than support for freedom of the press. At least it appears to be like that in the *SCMP* presentation.

Following Xi's conviction and sentencing, the paper reflected feelings of disbelief, shock, anger and disappointment. Both *MPDN* and Xi's colleagues were reported as feeling cheated because they followed Chinese advice. They looked forward to Xi's release on the basis of seemingly good news dispatched by the Chinese Judicial Minister and other Chinese allies[329] who claimed that they were well-connected and informed. The situation was made harder to bear, because in addition to the absurdity of these empty promises was the fact that neither the current regime in Hong Kong nor the journalists' profession itself could alter the outcome.

SCMP also conveyed the general mood of Hong Kong society, which was a bit confused. For instance, *MPDN*'s editors, while fasting in protest, admitted that they had adopted the wrong approach: 'it was thought to be a matter only between *Ming Pao Daily News'* employers and the Chinese government ... (we) did not want to see the issue being politicised in the tense atmosphere of the Sino-British row.'[330] At this stage, *SCMP* tended to speak about the scale of damage through foreign voices. For example, the paper printed large photographs depicting a 'protest hunger strike', with a strong statement from the International Federation of Journalists.

However, *SCMP*'s immediate response to the sentence was not entirely pessimistic. For instance, they pinned hope on the appeal mechanism, and the willingness of a mainland Chinese lawyer to act as defence counsel,[331] despite the fact that many Chinese lawyers tried to stay away from politically sensitive cases such as this one.[332] At the same time, this injustice came under strong criticism from a *SCMP* analyst. In his piece, he compared the fate of Xi to that of the most famous Chinese dissident, Wei Jinsheng. 'The system provides the administration with a handy weapon to penalize foreign and Hong Kong journalists ... the Xi case is a deliberate attempt by the Chinese Communist Party to gag the Hong Kong press, deplete the people's right to know.'[333] In this article, the writer argued that Xi's case arose mainly because China was not content with self-censorship. It wanted total control over Hong Kong reporters, which would extend to their western and Asian colleagues. During this transition period, the 1997 factor also played a role, in the sense that China was engaged in psychological warfare with Britain. The analyst expressed the view that, after 1997, much of the Hong Kong media would be dominated by the Chinese media. His prophecy came true a few years later, not only in relation to *SCMP*, but also to himself.[334]

SCMP adopted a human interest angle in respect of Xi's ordeal by revealing the emotions of his father, which in turn further illustrated how unreasonable the Chinese handling of the case was. The paper reported that, having learnt about his son's heavy sentence, Xi Yang's father had a heart attack and was hospitalised. Xi's father said, 'My son was only doing the job of a reporter. Why should he deserve such a severe sentence?' Furthermore, he said he had not received any formal notice of his jailing and had only met him for 30 minutes the year before. Xi's trial had driven his whole family to despair and they were living in deep depression.[335]

SCMP not only carried the Chinese version of the story, it also covered a warning from China's allies. For instance, it argued the merits of supporting the appeal privately: 'emotional public reaction may harm Xi's appeal...', and 'appealed to legislative councillors and reporters not to resort to the British government for help, saying this would complicate the issue.'[336] By the same token, *SCMP* also printed an alternative public opinion of 'people appalled by [the] journalists' immature action' in taking to the streets to protest against a Chinese law that Hong Kong people were not familiar with.[337] The opinion was that Hong Kong journalists had to abide by Chinese law when they worked in China.

While journalists and other supporters were organising a signature campaign to lobby for Xi's appeal, the outcome of the appeal was handed down by the Beijing Municipal Supreme People's Court swiftly: it upheld the conviction. At this point, the coverage of *SCMP* seemed to shift to highlight the head-on confrontation between Chinese ideology and that of Hong Kong, in a last ditch attempt to preserve the Hong Kong media system over the Chinese one. The journalists' outcry was demonstrated in the news front page of *SCMP*, with prominent pictures of angry protestors, together with a strongly worded editorial.[338] *MPDN* expressed its anger by leaving its editorial blank except for 20 Chinese characters, which can be translated as: 'Salute to our reporter Xi Yang; in the wake of Chinese oppression we might as well throw our pens away to protest against the Chinese judicial system.' *SCMP* supported *MPDN*'s angle by reporting and translating its 20 Chinese character editorial.

Again, *SCMP* was up-front in depicting the journalistic protest, as more and more journalists took to the streets to express their anger. They burned gauze masks to symbolise the fact that they would no longer keep silent and vowed to voice their opposition. 'If we don't fight for the release of Xi, *Ming Pao Daily News* will certainly leave a bad name in the history of Hong Kong journalism.' It was important 'to tell the Beijing authorities that they couldn't do whatever they liked to journalists from Hong Kong ... they have to respect the freedom of the press.'[339]

SCMP's editorial strongly criticised the Chinese for giving such a heavy sentence, saying it was not only damaging for media confidence and freedom, but also for the confidence of Hong Kong and international business. The editorial said it would hurt its own reputation in the long run. It sent a 'clear danger signal to Hong Kong reporters [that they might in future be] subject to arbitrary and heavy-handed punishment ... [T]he fundamental issue is not how the case was handled, but whether Xi's action constituted a criminal act at all ... what China can do to its own citizen before 1997, it will feel at liberty to do to Hong Kong people after 1997, putting at risk the issue of press freedom included in the Basic Law and Joint Declaration.'[340] *SCMP*'s editorial highlighted the risk of restraints on press freedom and the presumed doom of Hong Kong following the handover.

On the one hand, *SCMP* reported on the criticism and condemnation by liberal political groups in Hong Kong. For instance, the United Democrats were reported as saying the outcome was not acceptable. Another grass-roots political group, the Alliance for Democracy and People's Livelihood, was reported as stating the verdict shook public confidence and 'showed [that] Beijing disregards the Hong Kong people's will to set Xi free'.[341]

On the other hand, *SCMP* also showed the Chinese perspective, albeit not as convincingly as the opposition's. For instance, a vice-director of *Xinhua News Agency*, Zhang Junsheng, reiterated that the case was an individual one and had nothing to do with press freedom in Hong Kong. 'It is not a question of the free press, it is a question of the breaking of law on the media when one is carrying out the job of reporting.'[342] Furthermore, *SCMP* also put forth the counter-arguments orchestrated by China's allies. For instance, a Hong Kong Affairs Adviser to China said the appeal reflected 'different standards between Hong Kong and China'.[343] This was echoed by another adviser to China, who said that it showed a 'clear gap between the ways China and Hong Kong handled such incidents'.[344] Another pro-China politician, also a delegate to the Chinese People's Political Consultative Conference, explained that the upholding of the original verdict might be due to the fact that the court was put under pressure.[345]

To further represent the appeal trial as an unjust show, *SCMP* published the findings of a public poll which indicated in the aftermath of the Xi case that Hong Kong people thought Beijing had used the Xi case as a warning to the Hong Kong media. *SCMP* also printed an opinion-editorial piece written by a journalist-turned-legislator showing how the press was being squeezed by China. 'It is a signal to Hong Kong and foreign journalists that free and independent news reporting will not be tolerated.' The writer concluded her piece by asking 'what can and should the British do for the six million Hong Kong people ... should they lose their freedom after 1997?'[346]

In the coverage of *SCMP*, the feeling of helplessness seemed to be dominant, just as a reader's letter remarked, 'don't abandon Xi'.[347] Indeed having taken to the streets, and held a hunger strike and signatory campaign, the journalists' campaign seemed to go nowhere; the protest became passive and symbolic as no improvement was expected in the foreseeable future. The lobbying for Xi's release became low key.

Xi Yang got released on parole in early 1997, after disappearing from the public eye for three and a half years. *SCMP* remarked sarcastically that the uncompromising campaign for his early release had paid off.[348] The revealing part of the story, however, was the response *SCMP* demonstrated in its coverage.

The front-page story underlined Xi's gratitude to the Chinese authorities, but also indicated the real political reason behind the move: 'Harmonious atmosphere in the lead-up to the handover ... it's a good thing for my company (*Ming Pao Daily News*) and a blessing to Hong Kong people ... our whole family is grateful for the lenient policy of the Chinese government, this is a very sincere act indeed.'[349]

However, the coverage of *SCMP* remained subtly political in the way it juxtaposed pictures to indicate the ordeal's effect on Xi. In a story entitled 'Handover "key freedom factor"', there was an accompanying picture of a young-looking Xi Yang before his imprisonment. Another story entitled 'Yellow ribbon campaign pays off' was illustrated by a picture of a grey-haired Xi Yang showing the strain of his three-year imprisonment. There were further stories indicating doubts about the happy ending to the incident. For instance, there was a report stating that the whereabouts of a jailed source, Tian Ye, remained unknown.[350] Nothing had so far been reported on the status and whereabouts of Tian Ye, a former official with the Bank of China, who was alleged to have helped Xi Yang with spying and theft of state secrets. The opaqueness of the incident further enhanced the media's doubts about the Chinese judicial system. On the day following Xi's release, *SCMP* reported an activists' warning that Hong Kong reporters faced the same risk as the mainland arrest procedure was still in place. The story was published together with a picture of Xi Yang, the caption of which expresses a sense of relief for Xi's early release but 'fears continue over press freedom'.[351] There was another story reporting that a 'group considers taking up battle against censor'. The aftermath of the Xi case was far from an end to the battle for press freedom.

While the reportage remained largely factual, the overall tone of the coverage was conciliatory and accepting of the realities of the situation, especially in the editorial. The editorial on the day of Xi's release, which was entitled 'Growing appreciation', said 'Beijing should appreciate Hong Kong has a different set of measures for press and other freedoms.... [T]he unexpected release ... illustrated Beijing's leniency and appreciation of Hong Kong press concern [and] underscores China's growing confidence in dealing with Hong Kong.' It concluded by saying that the release demonstrated 'the mainland government could be reasoned with' though this required 'patience and persistence'. However, the crucial thing the editorial did not say explicitly was left to its news report, in which a senior U.S. official in Washington received the release, with a note of cautious welcome; but he added: 'it doesn't change our view that how he was arrested in the first place was unjustified ... it is difficult to know what this means in the larger scheme of things [in China].'[352]

Conclusion

The theme underlining the coverage of the English-language newspaper, *SCMP*, of the Xi Yang case was that the Chinese government had been heavy-handed and unfair in their treatment of a reporter who covered financial news in China. The Chinese authorities were depicted as taking heed of neither the wishes nor the feelings of the Hong Kong people.

It is tempting to conclude that the paper's coverage of the Xi case was relatively independent. However, my analysis of the paper's coverage suggests that even a relatively liberal and independent paper, with a long critical tradition, had shifted its editorial stance in anticipation of 1997.

Coverage of the case was the first major head-on confrontation between the Hong Kong press and the mainland Chinese authorities over the suppression of a journalist. In the past, reporters on the China beat reportedly experienced various forms of harassment during their work on the mainland. The reporting of *SCMP* showed how this relatively independent and critical paper first presented the fears of the parties concerned. The paper could not find out the truth for its readers, but its analysis rightly pointed to a worrying trend. The fear of the Hong Kong press was real, and Hong Kong journalists' battle against Chinese suppression was defeated. Although there was praise because the 'uncompromising effort of *Ming Pao Daily News* reporters, the journalist operation and many others paid off', there was also a warning that the 'growing signs of China's readiness to limit its tolerance to dissent have showed there is a real threat to broader freedom of expression after July 1'.[353]

There occurred a shift in the paper's position over time, from a critical to a more compromising stance, which is evident when the coverage is seen as a whole. The paper appears to have disengaged itself from the controversy while Xi was in prison. This will be written about further in the part with the interviews with the journalists themselves in Chapter 6.

Ming Pao Daily News

The obvious question in relation to the Xi case was why it happened and why, in particular, this happened to the well respected Chinese-language daily, *Ming Pao Daily News* (*MPDN*). It is perhaps useful to outline the background in respect of the paper's tradition and its place in the wider context of society at the time.

The Xi incident was not an accident. Many reporters on the China beat had previously experienced detention, interrogation, harassment and even arrest during their work in mainland China.[354] Although it appeared to be unfortunate for *MPDN* that its reporter got caught up in a politicised incident, there were also implicit social and professional reasons for this. First, *MPDN*, which used to be a critical and independent paper, specialised in reporting on China's current affairs. The political stance of its founder and former journalist-turned-proprietor, Louis Cha, had been an asset for this paper. The paper was particularly acclaimed in the 1970s and 1980s for acting as a 'critical friend' of China.[355] In the late 1980s, Louis Cha was successfully enlisted to do Chinese united front work, and was appointed a delegate to the Chinese People's Political Consultative Conference. Contrary to his previous political leanings towards democracy, his political stance had since become conservative and thus controversial, in particular, with regards to the promulgation of the Basic Law consequent to the Sino-British Declarations (1984), the mini-constitution that laid down the ground rules for Hong Kong's future as a Special Administrative Region (SAR) of the PRC come 1997. At the high point of his political career, he sold most of his shares in *MPDN* to a young Hong Kong Chinese businessman, Yu Pun-hoi, whose main goal was to create his own media empire by using *MPDN* as a stepping stone to the mainland market.[356] At the same time, *MPDN* continued to play an important role in monitoring and reporting on the latest developments in China, in particular, its economic and reform policies.[357]

On the political front, *MPDN*'s once vigorous support for mainland grassroot reform, such as the 1989 Beijing student movement, had become muted following a crackdown all over the country. The phasing out of dissident news was to be replaced by a unique feature of the transition period,[358] that is, the expansion of news about China, with special attention to the on-the-spot reportage that attracted both local young professionals as well as their mainland counterparts coming to Hong Kong. The growth in first-hand reporting on China was in demand both domestically and internationally. Undoubtedly, as Hong Kong moved towards the handover year of 1997, this demand became all the more urgent. Another pragmatic reason was the growing western interest in doing business with, or investing in, China. This was given impetus when China embraced an open market economy after the late senior Chinese leader, Deng Xiaoping, reconfirmed the 'Southern Progress' policy[359] by touring the Special Economic Zone of Shenzhen in south China in 1992.[360]

For practical reasons, local newspaper organisations started to employ mainlanders. They had the edge over local journalists because of their apparent good connections and understanding of the political landscape there. Nevertheless, in the case of Xi, this "native-informer" perspective proved insufficient, even problematic as the Chinese authorities both expected and insisted that reporters on the China beat, whether mainlander or otherwise, to abide by its standard for journalistic practices.[361]

On this occasion, China punished one of its own nationals who chose to reside in Hong Kong and work for a Hong Kong press.[362] It is unlikely that the Chinese authorities expected the outcry the case triggered in all walks of life in the colony. The confrontation happened because Hong Kong was about to revert to China. In these specific circumstances, a seemingly one-off journalistic incident turned into an unprecedented head-on confrontation between Hong Kong and China.

Nature of news coverage: a story in three phases

MPDN 's coverage of Xi Yang's case tended towards selective factual reporting at times. This could be seen in its headlines. At the start of Xi Yang's detention, the daily tended to use Chinese authorities as their main source of information. For instance, on the day the news broke, its headline was 'Beijing said *Ming Pao Daily News* reporter broke the national security law so he was arrested'[363] and the news source was *Xinhua (New China) News Agency.* It also named pro-China politicians, and a top Chinese official in Hong Kong, in headlines, who either showed their sympathy or promised to find out more details about the arrest and the charge for the paper.[364]

In another instance, the headline showed the restrictive nature of the Chinese authorities in respect of press freedom: '*Xinhua (New China News Agency) News* official said, "It is unrealistic to withdraw the rules and regulations imposed on Hong Kong coverage of mainland news".' Even under such restrictions, the paper held high hopes that the incident would be resolved quickly. There was a conciliatory tone, for example, one headline praised security officials, saying 'Officials of state security bureau are polite and friendly.[365] Although *MPDN*'s management had made contact with the Chinese authorities, it was hard for its readers to share the artificially induced optimism encapsulated in the Chinese promise that 'the matter will be resolved soon'.

MPDN also juxtaposed non-related, and sometimes contradictory messages, in the headlines apparently to bring out the pros and cons of the argument, for instance, 'Allen Lee [a Hong Kong legislator] intends to understand more about the incident; state security bureau refuses to accept signatory letter by *Ming Pao Daily News*' editorial department'.[366] On another occasion, the juxtaposition of two messages in a headline helped to set up an impending confrontation which: 'Beijing arrests Xi Yang according to the state security law; *Ming Pao Daily News* presses for open and fair trial'.[367] Sometimes the contrast between two different official lines in the same headline revealed a thorn in Sino-British relations, for instance, 'Hong Kong government urges clarification of Xi Yang incident; Beijing Foreign Ministry says there is no need'.[368] *MPDN* and other groups had pressed hard for details of the secret trial, the Chinese authorities disclosed through a semi-official news outlet, *China News Services.* However, sometimes the Chinese position was counter-balanced in the same headline by *MPDN*'s own position: 'Chinese official line: Xi Yang submits secrets to be published in *Ming Pao Daily News*; however, the paper believes that Xi only fulfils his reporting duty'.[369]

Apart from its headlines, the paper used special graphics showing a count for chalking up the number of days Xi has been arrested, for instance, the happenings of the second day, the third day, the fourth day and so on, thus highlighting the unlawful detention by the Chinese authorities.[370] In spite of this adoption of graphics, the news coverage of the paper on the detention and before the formal arrest was relatively inconspicuous, though the story usually appeared on the first page of news.[371]

The special graphics were also used to give the gist of the news showing the paper's perspective, especially after a higher court upheld the previous verdict. For instance, in the first two weeks of Xi's detention, as described above, *MPDN* used the special graphics to highlight the number of days Xi had been held in detention. The graphics were later used usually to show the different sides of the story, namely, the official Chinese line, and those of the British and Hong Kong governments, local politicians and Xi's supporters. Sometimes the paper put more emphasis on events.

Besides, the news layout changed and shifted strategically as events unfolded. There was a sudden twist on the third day of Xi's arrest. The day before, the paper had published an editorial entitled: 'To help Xi Yang to get a fair and reasonable trial.' But the next day, the proprietor openly offered an apology to China. In an effort not to undermine its credibility, the paper managed to hide its self-contradictory position by billing an inconsistent message in its headline: 'If Xi Yang committed a crime because of work, *Ming Pao Daily News* will apologize on his behalf. However, the group's chairman reiterates that the paper will not change its stand on covering the news event'.[372]

In an apparent effort to compensate for its embarrassing apology, the paper displayed related news quite prominently. It started by allocating half a page on the first news page to related news, together with the paper's statement, and responses from the Taiwan press, the Hong Kong Journalists Association and political parties. On the fourth day, the paper again allocated half the first news page to its editorial and news reporting, and showed a big picture of the three senior editorial managers of the paper briefing reporters on the progress of the case.

The newspaper's sudden admission on Xi's behalf that he had committed unlawful deeds provoked internal controversy and external dispute. The paper's excuse that it was adopting a bargaining position to facilitate Xi's early release was received negatively. On the same day, the daily used local and overseas responses to point out that the Xi case was adversely affecting press freedom. For instance, the page was filled with comments from Taiwanese culture and media representatives saying that the Xi case was 'a threat to press freedom'. Pro-democratic legislators were interviewed and their comments on the Xi case appeared in the paper, including quotes such as, 'a very important signal to Hong Kong' and 'have to clarify the reasonableness of the incident'.[373] However, there was no further justification for why the paper had dumped its earlier argument that its reporter was only doing his job in China and had not engaged in any criminal activities.

Unsurprisingly, the paper changed its stance again when its apology strategy did not pay off, this time focusing on the protest against Chinese suppression consequent to the court announcement of Xi's sentence. It sometimes gave the news a full-page treatment; at other times, the news was scattered throughout the inside pages.

MPDN actively orchestrated a protest campaign after the appeal court upheld the previous verdict. It vigorously protested, not only by allocating the whole front page to news and pictures related to the public protests, but also by publishing a full page of messages from readers, and the paper's call for further letters, cartoons, drawings or any other kind of messages to be sent to the paper in the self-addressed envelope printed on the paper.

As well as using headlines and layout to relay the paper's main message, the paper also made full use of the effect of news pictures to support its aim of 'propagating' the truth, and thus further mobilising public opinion. When the paper changed its stance to offer an apology, it printed prominent pictures of its proprietor being interviewed by reporters. He used the occasion to announce that the paper would apologise, despite the fact that he and the management insisted that their reporter had always covered news professionally.

After Xi was given a heavy sentence, news pictures appeared showing the general sentiment of *MPDN* and the profession in general. Prominent pictures showed a series of campaigning actions, for example, journalists and members of the public taking to the streets, and *MPDN* 's staff holding a sit-in protest together with a 72-hour hunger strike. The pictures tellingly showed the proprietor lending his support to his staff by visiting their sit-in demonstration and appearing as the leading figure in his staff-initiated street demonstration. This helped to cover up explicit differences between the interests of the proprietor (who was more concerned with the paper's good relationship with China and its business prospects) and those of perhaps the senior management and certainly rank-and-file journalists (who were more concerned with the well-being of the jailed journalist). Pictures thus helped to demonstrate the apparent solidarity between newspaper employer and employees, sympathisers included.

In the beginning, *MPDN* tended to relay and play up Chinese official sources. It also played down British sources, and even openly rejected their concerns and offer of assistance. This apparently was as a result of pressure from the Chinese authorities. The paper, however, used the excuses of not wanting to 'politicise' a purely journalistic incident, and of further aggravating the far from amicable relations between the Chinese and British governments.[374] Another reason might also have been that the paper believed it could negotiate with the Chinese authorities using its own power as a media organisation.

Indeed, *MPDN* had been known to use go-betweens to resolve the 'dispute'.[375] The paper published the latest news on Xi Yang creating an optimistic atmosphere by using Chinese allies or officials as sources. This reliance on one particular channel of sources contributed to a biased assessment of the whole situation that did not have the endorsement of the paper's own staff. Thus when Xi was sentenced, the paper published a remark made by one of its staff that 'the low profile contributed to Xi's heavy sentence'.[376] This manipulation of information was also pointed out by Martin Lee, the chairman of the opposition United Democrats, who criticised conservative/ pro-China legislators for saying that they were waiting for the result of the appeal as an excuse for refusing to sign the signatory campaign to the Chinese leadership.[377] These criticisms were not, however, reflected in the paper's editorial position.

Apart from using one-sided sources, *MPDN* appeared to adhere to professional reporting standards, but at times it exploited the chance to make news. For instance, during the paper's shift in position, the paper printed a full transcript of the interview with its own proprietor to explain his concerns and thinking. This kind of 'scoop' story could be found later (for example, after Xi was released, his only interview appeared in *MPDN*), but more often consisted of pictures showing either the proprietor lending support to his staff or senior management sharing the anger of its staff.

After Xi Yang's sentence was handed down by the Beijing court, the paper explicitly made use of its layout and allocation of pages to highlight the confrontation. It also printed a selection of editorials from ten mainstream newspapers protesting against the heavy sentence.[378]

When the paper chose to engage in vigorous protesting and lobbying for domestic and foreign help, it used grass-roots organisations and ordinary people as its sources. It even made use of anonymous or pseudonymous letters, cartoons, drawings or one-sentence messages posted to the paper, which demonstrated the general sentiment of the community at large. The nature of sources employed could be seen as both homogenous and highly selective, as the information was largely used to support the paper's main campaign goal.

Furthermore the paper also gave space to personal human interest columns and articles written by Xi's father, his colleagues and unrelated contributors. All these articles had a common purpose, that is, to create an image of Xi Yang as a kind-hearted and obedient son: he had saved people after the Tongshan (not far from Beijing) earthquake in the late 1970s; he had been respectful and obedient to his sick mother; he was not afraid of difficulties, and had published a book. From the perspective of his colleague on the China news desk, Xi was a conscientious, hard-working journalist. Xi's colleague also wrote an analysis attempting to counter the Chinese authorities' argument that Xi's reports had caused the country serious economic loss. His column analysed the fluctuations in interest rates so as to prove that the Chinese government should have increased its revenue and showed that Xi's reports constituted a way of testing public opinion. It also cited other sources such as in the Beijing-funded daily, *Wen Wei Po*.

This is not to say that *MPDN* should or should not have invited Xi's relatives and co-workers to contribute this information; only that it was unusual for the Hong Kong press, and in particular for an independent paper, to set aside such prominent space for what was not strictly a news feature item. For instance, before Xi's case, another mainland journalist, Gao Yu, was given a heavy sentence in China for the alleged crime of leaking state secrets. In contrast, she had not received such prominent and insistent reportage on her background, together with related news stories.

At the peak of the protest against Xi's sentence, a full page, or even two pages, of readers' letters, supporting notes and other text messages filled the news section, alongside prominent pictures of Xi Yang. To get the paper's point across, opinion and editorial sections printed consecutive high-sounding editorials, together with sympathetic contributors' articles. Related news stories were played up, and inside the news page an envelope was printed encouraging readers or letter writers to reveal their contact address and write to protest directly.

A comparison of *MPDN* 's coverage of the release of Xi Yang with its reports of three years before undoubtedly gave readers a feeling that Hong Kong had entered a new era – one of decolonisation and sinicisation (change to a mainland Chinese style of conduct).

In late January 1997, the news headline read 'Xi Yang comes back!' Other related news filled up the whole first news page. The editorial, entitled, 'A unification ending', denoted a complete appeasement of the Chinese authorities, without any mention of the injustices involved in putting a journalist behind bars for three and a half years. Instead, it hailed Xi's parole release as marking a 'lenient spirit' on the part of the Chinese Judicial Ministry. According to *MPDN*, the release was a 'thoughtful consideration' of Xi Yang's special circumstances by the Chinese Government; it coincided with the Chinese Lunar New Year and so was presented as a 'new year present' to Xi's family, and also an occasion for reunion for *MPDN*'s big family.

> The *kindness* of the Chinese government has realised the long-standing wish of all *Ming Pao Daily News* staff. Beijing's early release of Xi has created a *harmonious* atmosphere prior to the handover. . . . It has allayed Hong Kong people's worries. *Chinese leniency* towards Xi Yang and his early release demonstrate Beijing's wish to maintain stability and ensure a better outlook for Hong Kong's future. This *kind-heartedness* will be appreciated by all the Hong Kong people. . . . Xi Yang's case has closed with his return in time for reunification. Therefore, we would like to thank the Chinese government and all other officials.[379] (emphasis added)

In the 1,000-word editorial, the writer used the words 'leniency', 'kind-hearted' and 'kindness' more than once to describe the action of the Chinese authorities, including the Judicial Ministry, and used words and phrases such as 'grateful', 'happy ending' and 'harmonious and moving atmosphere' to express the paper's gratitude for Xi's release.

In addition, there was a separate statement by the new owner, Tiong Hiew-king, a Malaysian Chinese businessman, printed under the name of the paper, giving a personal welcome to, and expression of gratitude for, this Chinese leniency. The statement also asked reporters and the like not to disturb Xi's ailing father in Beijing.

In the news item describing Xi's comeback and his father's gratitude for Chinese leniency, Xi Yang in fact did not express gratitude. Rather he thanked all those who had been concerned for his well-being. Xi reportedly said,

> I am happy and moved because I am on parole release and could come back to Hong Kong and come back to *Ming Pao Daily News* where I previously

worked. My parole is a surprise for me and for my family. I suppose it is also good news for my company. To all Hong Kong people, the news is also a blessing. I believe and hope this harmonious atmosphere and confidence will prevail as the theme of the year 1997. I believe all Hong Kong people share my wishes. I wish to thank all my colleagues and all the others. I'll pray for Hong Kong and all the people.[380]

With his imprisonment following an unfair trial, it did not make sense for Xi Yang to thank the Chinese authorities. He could not, however, speak his mind freely because of the restrictions in the terms of his parole. *MPDN*'s layout of its news was highly selective, and only reported on what the paper wanted the reader to know or recall. Apart from the headline news, the editorial and *MPDN*'s statement, there was a press release by *Xinhua News Agency* officially announcing that Xi's repentance provided the rationale for his release on parole; a statement 'wishing everyone good luck in 1997' by Xi's father, Xi Linsheng; a brief report on parole regulation according to Chinese criminal law; a brief response from the Hong Kong governor proclaiming 'good news before Chinese Lunar New Year'; and a short piece written by a reporter who witnessed Xi Yang's arrival at Hong Kong airport and his emotional welcome by colleagues in his newsroom.

The news coverage of the release did not make any reference to the campaign and protest launched three years before. Even more problematically, there was no acknowledgement of the unfairness of the trial nor of the jailed reporter's own insistence on his innocence throughout the ordeal. The only voice countering all the 'good news' was that of the Hong Kong Journalists Association, which stated that 'Xi's release before the handover signifies positive news. But the union always believed Xi only performed his duty as a reporter and he is innocent.' The union expressed the hope that the 'Chinese authorities would respect Hong Kong journalists' rights and freedom to cover news in mainland China'. It seems that this discordant reaction was not appreciated by the daily, as it was buried at the end of the Hong Kong Governor's welcoming reaction, without even a subtitle. The paper also printed several prominent emotionally loaded pictures showing a grinning Xi Yang beside a huge cake at a welcome party; Xi's emotional reunion with his elderly father; Xi sitting at his desk in the office with his colleagues; and close-ups of Xi opening a bottle of champagne and slicing the cake. All these features contributed to the construction of the so-called 'harmonious' scene through which the paper compromised its independent and critical stance.

On the day following Xi's release, the conciliatory tone was further elaborated in a special feature report. This sentimental piece, which was entitled 'Reunion of Xi and his father, silence is golden' and written by a reporter with a by-line, cited Xi Yang talking about his life in prison. He had 'privileges', for example, he was allowed time to learn Buddhism and practice *qigong* (a meditation exercise that can help to improve one's health). Every morning and evening, he would practice Zen meditation to relax and avoid negative thinking. 'Now I can even help heal others by massage, though I am not yet very good at it.' He continued:

I am privileged in that I didn't have to do labourous work. Apart from the three daily meals, I have read a lot of books and have drawn a lot of paintings ... the prison permits inmates to subscribe to journals and periodicals; the newspaper is the official *Beijing Daily*. Every night I could watch television news ... sometimes I played chess, sometimes I read books: novels, prose, biographies, history, philosophy, political theories ... all kinds of topics are accessible.[381]

According to this special report, Xi's three-year term of unjust imprisonment seemed to be a sojourn of rest and nourishment.

However, the independent daily could not afford not to print remarks by one of the major campaigners for Xi's release. At the end of the special report on Xi Yang, there was a short news report of less than 300 words, entitled '"Operation to Save Xi Yang" welcomes the release of Xi Yang'. However, the content did not exactly match the headline. The report opened by saying, '"Operation to Save Xi Yang" issued a statement yesterday to welcome Xi's release back to Hong Kong but the group pointed out that the release of Xi Yang could not reduce Hong Kong people's worry about future press freedom.' The story was interrupted, however, by a brief description of how Xi Yang passed his first day in Hong Kong. It was followed by another paragraph from the statement by the group, 'Operation to Save Xi Yang', saying,

> Xi Yang should have been released three years ago. His current release was the result of the concerted effort of various Hong Kong parties. The group is concerned that Tian Ye, the mainlander who provided news information for Xi Yang, is still in jail.[382]

On the following day, there was no news about Xi Yang apart from a 150-word clarification from a senior Chinese official in Hong Kong. In the brief report entitled 'Xi Yang's parole is in accordance with Chinese law', a vice-director of *Xinhua News Agency*, Zhang Junsheng, was quoted as saying that 'The parole of Xi Yang was done in accordance with Chinese law. The Chinese authorities did not release Xi in order to create a good political atmosphere during Hong Kong's period of transition. However, he added, "I think all are happy, though, to have such an outcome".'[383]

Analysis

In spite of the fact that there is strong evidence of manipulation in terms of form and content with regards to the reportage on the Xi case, *MPDN* largely maintained its outlook as an independent paper, initially seeking to negotiate with the Chinese authorities, and later mounting a fierce defence against Chinese coercion. Undoubtedly, the paper's editorial line highlighted the ideological nature of this confrontation between two different systems.

When Xi was convicted, the paper questioned 'what kind of crime has Xi

Yang committed knowingly?'[384] On the following day, under the headline 'Reporter's duty is to find out the truth', the paper attacked the Chinese authorities' allegation that Xi Yang persuaded an 'insider' (Tian Ye, a mainland finance officer) to spy and steal finance information for an 'outsider' (*MPDN*), saying that it was normal practice for independent reporters in Hong Kong and the western world to find out the truth for their readers. In its third consecutive editorial, the writer echoed the Hong Kong Journalists Association's argument[385] by saying that Xi did not have an open trial in accordance with the law, so the trial was in fact unlawful. It went on to say that although the Chinese authorities alleged that Xi's crime was spying and stealing information for *MPDN* to publish, the Chinese official version of the events proved that Xi was not engaged in any spying activities.[386] The fourth editorial, under the title 'We are in the same boat through stormy weather; fairness stays within our hearts', signified a shift in *MPDN*'s position of addressing the Hong Kong public at large by referring to an independent survey commissioned by the paper. The poll's findings showed that a majority of respondents largely supported the paper's argument that there was not sufficient evidence to justify Xi's guilt and that the sentence was too heavy.

When the appeal court upheld Xi's sentence, *MPDN* could not express its anger and frustration, but, as stated above, left its editorial blank save for 20 Chinese characters saying: 'Salute to our reporter Xi Yang; in the wake of Chinese oppression we might as well throw our pens away to protest against the Chinese judicial system.'[387] In this rare move of leaving its editorial blank, the daily not only questioned Chinese press freedom, but it also pointed to a miscarriage of justice. However, the editorial stopped short of pointing out the heart of the matter, which was in fact a structural problem: that there are no checks and balances in an authoritarian system, and that China needed a representative and democratic political system. On the following day, the paper printed another editorial stating that a 'journalist is not a government's mouthpiece, he/she should be the people's eyes and ears'. However, these eloquent editorials elicited no response from the Chinese government, nor any improvement in Xi's position. Apparently, *MPDN* had totally failed in its negotiations with the Chinese regime, which insisted on imposing its control over the Hong Kong press.

Conclusion

In hindsight, we can see that *MPDN* was pursuing its own agenda in favour of press freedom, and how the paper actually succeeded in producing a social movement in that direction. On the other hand, the daily was so involved in the case that it was manipulated by the Chinese authorities and their allies.[388] In some instances, it appeared not to know where it stood – whether it supported the principle of press freedom or its journalist's freedom to report about China or its good relations with Chinese authorities – or why it fought the battle. Therefore its strategies of dealing with this crisis swung from one end of the pendulum to the other, fluctuating according to the whims of the proprietor/top management as they listened to various channels of so-called Chinese advice.

Apart from external pressures, there was also peer pressure from internal forces to do something for their jailed reporter. The staff was seen as taking the lead in initiating demonstrations and protests against Chinese coercion.

The proprietors' influence was clear, for example, in 1993–1994 Yu Pun-hoi openly apologised to the Chinese authorities, and in 1997, Tiong Hiew-king made a personal statement welcoming Xi's release on parole. The lobbying and campaigning for Xi's release was initially represented as a battle for press freedom, but later as political circumstances changed the paper followed a policy of conciliation under Chinese pressure. The paper's editorial position in its post-release coverage revealed a daunting political influence. However, this political influence took a different form in the popular daily, *Oriental Daily News*.

Oriental Daily News

Oriental Daily News (*ODN*) is generally regarded as being a relatively independent and popular paper.[389] It can be characterised as a mass circulation, grass-roots paper concentrating largely on Hong Kong, whose aim is to speak out for the less fortunate.[390] This Chinese-language daily was historically connected to Taiwan, but had adjusted its position since the 1980s apparently in anticipation of the change of sovereignty in 1997. In the coverage of the Xi Yang case, the news was usually succinct and factual. At times the news reports could be so telling that they became subtly analytical. The daily generally made use of sources of information, including official ones, to clarify its position.

Nature of news coverage: a study in distancing

ODN sometimes used its headlines to bring out the tensions underlying the subject matter. For instance, when the Chinese authorities announced the official arrest of Xi Yang after detaining him for a fortnight, the headline read, 'Beijing alleges a Hong Kong reporter admitting to stealing secrets, and officially arrests him according to national security law. *Ming Pao Daily News* hopes there will be a fair trial and a clarification of the boundaries for news coverage.'[391] The headline itself suggests that the Chinese authorities had the upper hand. Indeed, the report began by quoting *Xinhua News Agency* who set out the Chinese position, according to which the incident was not related to press reporting. However, the argument was countered by the quotation of *MPDN*'s reaction that the paper believed Xi Yang innocent. This counter-argument was further supported by a remark from the News Executives Association in Hong Kong, according to which *MPDN* had not published important financial secrets. The report ended by stating the concerns of the two largest political parties in Hong Kong, the Liberal Party and the main opposition party, the United Democrats.[392]

Also, its headlines helped to reveal the issues at stake and bring out the twists in the story. For instance, on the day following Xi's official arrest, there was a news report entitled 'The way *Ming Pao Daily News* reported on the Xi Yang incident apparently invited Beijing criticism; *Ming Pao Daily News* has been tipped off that if it takes a low profile, Xi Yang will be released'. According to a senior source at *MPDN*, the *ODN* report said, *MPDN* had made contact with Chinese sources. *ODN* disclosed that Chinese sources had told *MPDN* that printing the news of the Xi case on its first news page constituted a 'confrontation'. Such high profile reporting apparently upset the Chinese authorities, so that the case was formally sent to the court; this hindered the process of a private settlement. The *ODN* report added that *MPDN* insisted that Xi had conducted his reporting in a normal professional manner, and had reiterated its position that, prior to an open and fair trial, Xi should be considered innocent.[393]

In such a highly sensitive and political case, *ODN* protected the anonymity of its sources so as to avoid exposing those concerned to possible Chinese reprisals. At times, however, by quoting Chinese officials or Chinese allies as the main protagonists, and putting their names in the headlines, *ODN* subtly identified those who were pulling the strings, real or imaginary, behind the scenes. For instance, the daily quoted senior Chinese officials in the headlines, including the vice-director of *New China News Agency*, Zhang Junsheng;[394] the Chinese Justice Minister, Xiao Yang;[395] the Chinese delegate to the Chinese People's Political Consultative Conference, Tsui Si-min;[396] the vice-director of the Hong Kong and Macau Affairs Office, State Ministry, Wang Qiren;[397] and the deputy to the National People's Congress, Cheng Yiu-tong.[398] On the other hand, in the headlines *ODN* also named professional bodies and political groups that acted as opposition forces, so readers could easily tell which sources were more authoritative and which arguments might be more accurate. The opposition forces included the Hong Kong Journalists Association,[399] the Committee to Protect Journalists,[400] British journalists[401] and the Hong Kong Legislative Council.[402]

Apart from identifying the main players or involved parties in the headlines, the choice of adjectives used helped to signify the level of community involvement, and the strength of emotion in the public at large. For instance, after the appeal court upheld the original sentence, *ODN* used strong words such as 'angry' in the news story entitled 'Hong Kong Journalists are angry with the appeal as it is not done in accordance with law, they urge the release of trial details and stress that people from all walks of life wish the whole verdict be disclosed.'[403] However, the story itself only included reactions from pro-PRC politicians urging an explanation and transparency in the trial, apart from the main opposition reaction, rather than presenting the views of the so-called 'all walks of life'. It seems to be the case that the daily assumed that the urge for transparency could be viewed as generally representative since it came from across the political spectrum.

The choice of language also reveals the political perspective of *ODN*, for instance, expressions like 'a show',[404] 'trial not fair',[405] 'heavy-handed sentence',[406] were used to describe the appeal.[407] After the appeal, *ODN* reported that more than '100 groups'[408] had joined forces to save Xi Yang, and on the following day, the United Democrats had got 8,500 signatures[409] posted outside the Hong Kong headquarters of *Xinhua News Agency* to support Xi Yang. These numbers represented a collective protest against the Chinese decision, and made the headlines appear more impressive.

The general stance of *ODN* towards the Xi Yang case is apparent, since it printed stories with pictures on its first Hong Kong news page[410] to chart developments in the case, such as the change in the political position of *MPDN*, the protest march, demonstration and hunger strike organised by *MPDN*'s staff, and so on. Also its coverage could be critical at times, for example, it revealed Chinese manipulation of the news media, including *MPDN*, through coercion and advice from China's allies.[411]

It is evident that the strategy of *ODN* reporting was not to take sides, but it was not neutral either. In another example of its critical approach, it quoted a disillusioned senior Chinese official in charge of Hong Kong propaganda, Lo Fu, so as to highlight the miscarriage of justice of Xi's appeal trial. Lo Fu, a former Hong Kong editor of a China-funded evening newspaper, *New Evening Post*, who had endured house arrest in Beijing for ten years for the alleged crime of leaking state secrets, was quoted as describing Xi's appeal trial as 'a show put out by the Chinese authorities'. Lo Fu pointed out that Xi Yang and his co-defendant, Tian Ye, appeared in the news footage of *China Central Television (CCTV)* covering the appeal trial. However, since Tian Ye had not appealed, there was no reason why he showed up in court. Thus, Lo Fu reportedly concluded that this demonstrated that the Chinese authorities were not acting in accordance with the law.[412] There was further evidence for this in *CCTV* broadcasting footage, which showed that more than 100 Beijing inhabitants were seen to be witnesses in that secret trial, but neither Xi Yang's family members nor Xi Yang's company were informed that the trial was to be held on that day.

Although the paper occasionally used critical sources, it usually used authoritative official sources, namely the Chinese and the British or Hong Kong governments, since one of the main factors affecting the negotiations in Xi Yang's case was the Sino-British tension. For instance, *ODN* published a senior Chinese official's 'no meddling' warning to the Hong Kong governor and the British government.[413] Two days later, the paper published a follow-up story stating that the 'British Embassy and Hong Kong government continue to be concerned about the Xi Yang incident, they urge an early clarification of the alleged criminal offence and ask for an open and fair trial.'[414]

The daily also printed stories from non-official sources, from professional and political outlets. However, the non-official sources were usually used to counter Chinese arguments, or criticise the Chinese authoritarian measures taken against this lone Hong Kong reporter.

On other occasions, the daily effectively made use of anonymous sources to indicate the underlying causes behind the twists and turns in the case. These news reports pointed to manipulation by the Chinese authorities. For instance, a story attributed to an anonymous source at *MPDN* disclosed how Chinese sources denounced *MPDN*'s reports, and the paper was thus depicted as being harassed by the Chinese authorities for its independent handling of news reports related to Xi's ordeal.[415]

ODN printed another news story tracing and uncovering the reason behind *MPDN*'s sudden change of position when it offered both an open apology and admission of the alleged crime on behalf of its reporter. The news report of *ODN* cited anonymous sources pointing to the implicit conflict of interest between *MPDN*'s proprietor and his staff, indicating that *MPDN*'s proprietor, Yu Pun-hoi, was advised by Chinese sources to accept three conditions openly, so as to secure Xi Yang's early release. The three conditions, according to *ODN*, were that *MPDN* must openly admit: its reporter had committed a criminal offence; apologise to the Chinese authorities; and reject any help or assistance from the British and Hong Kong governments.[416] By attributing the story to anonymous sources, *ODN* could reveal the complications in the Xi case. The paper also demonstrated its independence without taking the risk of offending the Chinese authorities.

ODN did not directly comment on the Xi case except at three key moments, that is, when Xi's first trial verdict became known, when he lost his appeal and when he was released on parole. *ODN* consistently maintained its independence and critical stance throughout the case. In its first editorial, entitled 'Chinese implementation of justice is in doubt', the headline itself demonstrated its critical position. In the editorial, there was a strong argument throughout, saying that China had engaged in a 'black-box operation' from the start of the investigation to the first trial, so it was hard to convince people that Xi Yang had a fair, just and reasonable trial. It also criticised the matters that Xi's family members and his employer were not formally informed of the verdict, which was only conveyed through the Federation of All China Journalists, a semi-official professional organisation. The editorial concluded that it was obvious that the heavy sentence had a political function, that is, to intimidate the Hong Kong press so as to prevent similar journalistic behaviour. Although senior Chinese officials stated that the case would not affect Hong Kong reporters covering mainland Chinese news, the editorial said, this was not credible.

In its second editorial on the case, *ODN* suggested that the outcome of Xi's appeal had damaged Hong Kong people's confidence in the future. The editorial added that the Xi case was a vivid example of the discrepancy between the two systems, the Hong Kong and the Chinese, as regards press freedom.[417]

After Xi Yang's release, *ODN*'s editorial pointed to the heart of the matter, that is 'Xi Yang regains his freedom and it is an end to a thorn in the Sino-Hong Kong relationship'. Unlike *MPDN*'s editorial, *ODN* explicitly looked back over the past three years and examined why the case had attracted such strong protests locally. It concluded that the Chinese authorities needed to understand and tolerate Hong Kong's value systems, and to engage in a two-way communication so as to help the 'one country, two systems' scheme live up to its name.[418]

The post-release coverage of *ODN* was comprehensive, and remained subtly critical of the Chinese handling of the Xi case. On the one hand, it reported the gratitude of Xi's whole family and the welcome Xi Yang got back in Hong

Kong. On the other hand, the news report explained why Xi Yang could not answer reporters' questions, mainly because he was restricted from speaking freely because of his parole conditions. However, though Xi Yang remained silent about his own case, neither did he indicate his gratitude for Chinese 'leniency'. He only said his release was a piece of good news for his family and company. It was also a blessing for the Hong Kong people, and he hoped such a harmonious atmosphere would prevail for the year 1997. The report also reminded readers that the Xi case had aroused grave concerns for all walks of life in Hong Kong. Unlike *MPDN*'s editorial, that of *ODN* was revealing, and served as a footnote to the so-called 'happy ending'.

Its post-release coverage also followed up on and investigated the real reasons behind the lenient release. On the second day of Xi's release, *ODN* printed a head-line story clarifying some conciliatory remarks made by *MPDN*. In its story enti-tled 'Beijing attempts to create a political atmosphere as the provisional legislative council elects its chairperson, so China releases Xi', it argued that the timing of Xi Yang's release was chosen by Beijing to coincide with the election of the chairper-son of the provisional legislative council, which was set up by the Chinese authori-ties to replace the incumbent legislative council on the day of the handover. Both the nature, and election procedure, of the provisional legislative council had attracted criticism and concerns locally and internationally.[419] Also, *ODN*'s news reports covered the reaction of 'Operation to Save Xi Yang', a group which cam-paigned for his release. The group criticised China for not admitting Xi's inno-cence, and stressed that Xi Yang had only been carrying out his duty as a reporter. The group also rejected the position advocated by *MPDN* that Xi's release hap-pened out of Chinese leniency. Instead, the group pointed out that Xi obtained an early release owing to a concerted effort by people from all walks of life in Hong Kong. It said it had nothing to do with China's mercy.

ODN supported the above argument by drawing parallels with a precedence: the case of Gao Yu,[420] a mainland journalist who similarly endured imprison-ment for leaking 'state secrets'. Gao's son believed Xi Yang's release had to do with the handover which was due in six months' time. Gao's verdict also seemed to be a warning to Hong Kong journalists.[421]

On the third day, *ODN* printed the reaction of the Hong Kong Governor, Chris Patten, who raised the issue of a possible backlash against the Hong Kong press. In that brief news report entitled 'Fears for self-censorship by the Hong Kong press', Patten was quoted as saying he did not worry that the Hong Kong press would be suppressed after the handover. Instead, he worried that there would be self-censorship in the press. He believed Xi Yang had not violated Chinese law, but had only fulfilled his duty as a reporter, which was to find out the truth and report it.[422]

Conclusion

ODN, as the best-selling daily, covered the Xi case in a restrained and cautious way. At first this was because the news section of the paper was highly competitive. Thus, in the beginning of Xi's ordeal, the paper only allocated brief space to its reports. Only when Xi's heavy sentence was passed, did the paper start to allocate half a page or a full page to reports on the development of the case, accompanied by critical editorials. It appears that *ODN* was well aware of the potential conflict of interests, as it seems to have kept its distance from the whole incident. This strategy may also be explained as a way of not attracting Chinese criticism. Also, it seems quite clear that its staff's position was a lot easier due to the owner's apparent non-interference.[423]

Concluding remarks

One of the questions posed in the first section of this chapter was 'How independent was the press during the transition?' It was assumed that, because the press vigorously protested against the Chinese treatment of Xi Yang, it had been fiercely defending its freedom. After investigating the news coverage from the beginning to the end of the case in three mainstream papers, the analysis reveals a complicated picture.

Still, it might be concluded at this stage that all three newspapers underwent various degrees of changes in editorial stance in order to accommodate pressure from the Chinese authorities. It appears that the English-language *SCMP* was least affected, and *MPDN* most seriously affected, whereas *ODN* managed to keep its relatively independent position and not bow to the pressure completely.

Yet, it seemed that the media played an active part in their own decline. The problem is apparent in all three newspapers. *MPDN*, in a sense, was 'broken' by Xi's case. It made a dramatic turnaround in its coverage in Xi's case after just a few days, though the major influence behind the change in editorial strategy remains unclear. For instance, did it end its high-profile campaign on Xi's behalf due to external pressures, or purely out of consideration for Xi's well-being? Was it motivated by a genuine belief that a low-profile campaign was the best way to free Xi? Or did it reflect the natural self-censorship instincts of its proprietor and his subsequent instruction of, and influence on, its editorial staff?

In respect of *SCMP*, a comparison of its coverage at the time of Xi's arrest and its coverage at the time of his release shows how the paper's attitude shifted during this period. The shift was not the result of the controversies surrounding Xi's case, unlike that of *MPDN*. However, the change of tone between 1994 and 1997 is apparent: it had moved from a clear position within the western liberal framework of newspapers to being something akin to China's 'friend', who though disappointed by China's action, was willing to sympathise with China's position and the difficult decisions faced by Chinese leaders. Within this more friendly framework, the paper refrained from commenting on ethical issues, concentrating instead on the methods adopted by the various interested parties.

As for *ODN*, it is rather difficult to fit it into the established framework. It used distancing techniques at all stages of its coverage. While reporting fully, it seldom displayed its own stance on the issue, despite the fact that this was an historic turning point in the Hong Kong media's relationship with Beijing. In a sense, this newspaper's coverage is something of a yardstick. It comes from a very different intellectual direction than that of *SCMP*. Although touched by the western liberal newspaper tradition, it is a very different paper to most newspapers in the west. Perhaps among western-style papers it is closest in spirit to a small-town paper with a fiercely independent publisher and owner. The owner of *ODN* had no aspirations to do business, media or non-media, in mainland China.[424] Generally, the paper's main tactic in dealing with sensitive issues was to maintain its distance, reporting without compromise, but adhering carefully to rules of attribution and sourcing. *ODN* is not really part of the western liberal newspaper tradition, otherwise it would have got rid of its pornography and some controversial columns,[425] and started giving reporters credit to their reports. Thus the distancing appears to be done for political, not professional, reasons.

To sum up, the editorial presentation of the media in respect of this particular case reflects the beginning of a major decline in news professionalism. The changes were not implemented voluntarily, but were the result of external pressure, and were probably also variously countered and encouraged by peer pressure and internal forces. The crucial questions behind all these editorial changes will require an investigation of the journalists' own perceptions.[426] Before I do that, however, I shall next undertake another textual analysis to study the media response in the post-handover period.

4 Reporting on the Taiwanese presidential election

A textual analysis of news coverage in the post-handover period

Introduction

After 1989, many former communist countries collapsed. The end of communist political rule brought about economic change.[427] In the case of China, however, the sequence of events was reversed. Economic change took place in China before any relaxation in political control and redistribution of political power. In other words, the Chinese government allowed capitalism to go hand in hand with communist rule. The capitalist economy developed within a closed political system.[428]

Hong Kong reverted to Chinese rule in 1997, and holds a unique place within Chinese politics. It is unique not only because it is an example of a capitalist system that has come under Chinese Communist rule, but also because the Chinese have promised it a measure of flexibility.[429] This promise to Hong Kong was unprecedented since, following the Chinese Communist Party's take-over of China in 1949, none of the capitalist cities managed to survive in a command economy.[430]

During the late 1970s and early 1980s, the Chinese leader, Deng Xiaoping, invented the 'one country, two systems' scheme in order to accommodate the Hong Kong people who live in a system vastly different to that of their mainland Chinese counterparts. Since 1997, the Hong Kong Special Administrative Region (HKSAR) has been allowed to continue its capitalist economy and will enjoy a high degree of autonomy until 2047. Despite the promise of economic and political freedom, however, there have been restrictions imposed on political freedom in Hong Kong.[431] This has caused concern as regards the way the media have described social changes ever since.

The role of the Hong Kong media in the post-colonial period offers some insight into the scope of political and civil freedom in Hong Kong under Chinese rule. The press has influenced public opinion, as far as agenda-setting and ideological consensus are concerned, as can be seen from many scholarly research findings during Hong Kong's transition period.[432] The press has also tended to describe and represent social and political changes since 1997. On the one hand, the press has helped to report on, and shape, post-colonial ideology; on the other hand, it has also formed part of the post-colonial setting. Therefore, it is intriguing to investigate the complicated interaction between the press and its environment, and the political influences on the press and its subsequent organisation of news.

Contrary to general concern in the run-up to 1997, there has been no apparent direct repression of the press from the central government since the handover.[433] However, it could be argued that the integration of state pressure and ideological thinking through proprietary control and corporate management appeared to have been so effective that the Chinese government did not need to resort to repressive measures. Press freedom was effectively curtailed for business reasons.[434]

An integrated and chronological exploration of key media policy and media developments can illustrate the tensions within Hong Kong. This chapter attempts to demonstrate how state pressure and ideological thinking provoked many of the political shifts that came to define the period. While on the surface the Hong Kong media seemed to collaborate with, and even capitulate to, Chinese rule, there were pockets of resistance. As the media operated within a market economy with numerous competing interests, the response to Chinese control was diverse and complex. In other words, the Hong Kong media's position was ambiguous and contradictory, resistant to a blanket theory of Chinese control. The first section of this chapter discusses how the scope of political freedom has been affected, and examines the shift in political culture and media development in the post-colonial period. This is followed by an analysis of the interaction between political influence and the media, with a close textual analysis of the Taiwanese presidential election in 2000.

Background to Hong Kong

The notion that Hong Kong is part of China can be traced back to ancient times.[435] As mentioned in earlier chapters, in the late 1970s, China's insistence that Hong Kong should be reverted to its control arose from a nationalist concern. While the rhetoric in official publications reaffirmed this position, the senior Chinese leader, Deng Xiaoping, only laid down the policy for bringing Hong Kong under central government in the early 1980s.[436] Since the beginning of that decade, the British government had sought to persuade the Chinese government to extend the period of British administration of Hong Kong.[437] However, China rejected this suggestion immediately. It argued that if China did not reclaim Hong Kong before the end of the twentieth century, the Chinese leadership would be no better than Li Hongjen (who was synonymous with a traitor) who had ceded Chinese territory to a foreign imperial power during the Qing Dynasty in the nineteenth century.

Hong Kong and its colonial context

This concern with sovereignty was not only about reclaiming the remaining territories that fell under British control under the 'unequal treaties'[438] more than a century ago, it was also about demonstrating that China had become 'prosperous and strong' at last.[439] In fact, one of the long-standing goals set by Deng Xiaoping to demonstrate how powerful China had become in the late 1970s and early 1980s was to reunify Hong Kong, Taiwan and Macau (a Portuguese colony). Of China's three primary goals – economic growth, modernisation and unification – the latter was particularly important for strengthening the Chinese Communist Party's (CCP's) legitimacy to rule. To this end, the senior Chinese leadership promoted itself as an architect of economic growth and a guardian of national pride.[440] In order to pursue this goal, it was decided that while China would adhere to socialism, the Central Government would introduce a different system for Hong Kong and, more importantly, for Taiwan, promising that both places would be allowed to maintain their capitalist economies, and have a high degree of autonomy with regard to local administration. This was the scheme of 'one country, two systems' that especially catered to the six million ethnic Chinese in Hong Kong, and 22 million in Taiwan, who had largely lived their lives outside mainland China and outside Communist rule. Indeed, many in both countries had fled the Chinese regime.[441] Since the CCP took over mainland China and formed the People's Republic of China (the PRC) in 1949, the nationalist Kuomintang (KMT) fled to Taiwan and established its state, the Republic of China on the island.

Reunification, the Chinese Government believed, would put an end to a century old 'shame and humiliation'[442] that China had suffered as a result of imperialism and foreign invasion, signs of Chinese weakness. Deng Xiaoping insisted that the return of Hong Kong fulfilled the wishes of the whole nation and people; it was his personal ambition to come to Hong Kong in the year of handover. He passed away, however, in early 1997. Although he never realised his dream of coming to Hong Kong, he successfully laid down the blueprint of 'Hong Kong rule by Hong Kong People' with a nationalistic overtone.[443]

China's development and historical role in Hong Kong

Chinese nationalism first arose during the 1949 Chinese Communist revolution, although there were nineteenth-century antecedents. The reclamation of Chinese territory was a long-standing aspiration, though the notion of nationalism was a recent concept in modern China. It can be traced back to the call for the people's resistance to Japanese invasion during the second quarter of the twentieth century. The nationalist call aimed at creating a strong sense of nation statehood, China having undergone decades of suffering from foreign invasion and civil war. The aim was to reclaim a national identity by unifying different ethnicities and territorial groups. During the early twentieth century, the Chinese people were called upon to resist their enemies, and fight. During the Chinese civil war between the KMT and the CCP, the CCP won the war because it played upon nationalist sentiment.[444] In 1949, the government of the PRC was officially set up.[445] After that, the new sacred emblems of nationhood served also as symbols for the party-state: Chairman Mao Tze-tung (Mao Zidong), who was portrayed as the founder and father-figure of nation and party, the Tiananmen Square in

Beijing, the CCP, the red flag and the National Day, all emerged in school education as symbols of a unified Chinese identity.

This concept of nationalism, during and after the communist revolution, was debatably imported from the west but redefined as patriotism-nationalism. The Chinese communist triumph of 1949 brought with it a narrow, increasingly exclusive, view of nationalism.[446] In contrast to the nationalist KMT's preservation of traditional Chinese culture in Taiwan, the nationalist ideologies of the PRC were shaped and driven by the state and its needs.[447]

Under Mao, nationalism was one of the core sources of loyalty to the state. It was also largely a mixture of political nationalism, and ethnic Han (the majority Chinese originated from Han ethnicity) identity in which the state made an effort to transform and monopolise the meaning of nation, and achieve a politically driven shift in Chinese national thought.[448]

The changing economics in the post-Mao era opened up new economic zones. The reform policy was intended to create space and flexibility for trade with the outside world in the hope that the experience and investment would benefit the whole country.[449] This economic drive was behind the Chinese revitalisation of the idea of nationalism. Concurrently, there were new demands on government to accommodate difference. In the post-Mao era, nationalism was still defined as 'love of the state' but with a new dimension. In 1989, the Chinese dissident scientist, Fang Li-zhi, said, 'love of country has been indistinct from love of the state'.[450] However, in modern China, this idea of patriotism-nationalism was linked to new Chinese economic policies that were used to unify South China, Taiwan and Hong Kong, whilst recognising their individuality. As with other terms associated with the west, such as capitalism, the Chinese government adopted the term, but attached to it Chinese terms of reference. For instance, in order to adapt capitalism to the environment of socialist China, and distinguish Chinese socialism from Soviet Union style socialism, capitalism was renamed 'socialist market economy' or 'socialism with Chinese characteristics'. Indeed, Deng Xiaoping said foreign capitalist investment would enhance and supplement the socialist system. To open certain coastal cities to the capitalist system might encourage foreign investment that benefits the whole country.[451] In this way, the political legitimacy of the CCP would not be affected adversely, but paradoxically strengthened, especially at a time when both Maoism and Marxism-Leninism were in decline; yet much of Latin and South America is telling a different story.

The strange union between 'socialism', 'nationalism' and 'capitalism' has created an alternative Chinese identity. The special economic zones that emerged and flourished along China's coast in the post-Mao era eventually formed the so-called 'southern narrative' of Chinese identity.[452] The special zones and economic practices were initially portrayed as exceptions to Chineseness, as a form of 'otherness'. But over time, and through strategic leadership, the Special Economic Zones (SEZ) came to represent national aspirations and a shift in the paradigm of China's national identity. This redefinition of Chinese identity to include a 'southern narrative' has enabled people from the southern province of Guangdong, the city of Shanghai, the coastal province of Fujian and other cities of the coastal south to repudiate the historical myth of a single and unified image, that of the northern Chinese. In contrast to an inward-looking national image built upon the northern interior, the southern narrative posited a new national identity, one that was business-oriented, open, internationally inter-active, decentralised and that allowed for the emergence of southern cultural tra-ditions.[453] The modernising Chinese culture of the coastal treaty ports provided a potential alternative to the ideas of national identity of the two main Chinese rival parties across the Taiwan Strait, the KMT and the CCP.[454]

However, state-defined nationalism is very different from popular national-ism. Official nationalism was almost a synonym for 'patriotism', which requires the people to support the socialist state unconditionally, and to love their mother country, regardless of whether they believe in the system or not. Also, the people are supposed to help the mother country to establish political stability and economic development.[455] To serve this larger cause, official nationalism tweaked to accommodate popular nationalism. In this way, the notion of one country, two systems was designed to reclaim a territory separated from the mainland such as Hong Kong. The return of this territory was so significant to China that it was willing to give concessions to ease this political transaction, and also to woo Taiwan into unification with China.[456]

Official 'nationalism' tried to accommodate a wider group of people, allow-ing flexibility for a more diverse kind of nationalism. This opened up the 'south-ern narratives'. The specific result of the 'patriotism-nationalism' policy in South China, Taiwan and Hong Kong was the unique concept of 'one country, two systems' in Hong Kong. Deng Xiaoping said the ruling elite of Hong Kong should be patriots, by which he meant the senior officials there had to support the Central Government's policy.[457] Hong Kong, with its history of geopolitical limitation and constraint, seemed to be satisfied with Chinese nationalism as long as it accommodated its economic and cultural differences. Unlike Taiwan or Tibet, Hong Kong has never had a chance to pursue territorial independence from the mainland.[458]

Hong Kong in its post-colonial period

Despite the rhetoric of patriotism, Deng Xiaoping allowed public criticism in the HKSAR. He also accommodated national differences under the umbrella of Chinese nationalism. Amid the political and cultural contests regarding Chinese nationalism, the Central Government promulgated its Sino-Hong Kong policy. It set the boundaries and scope of political freedom. Deng emphasised that criti-cism of the CCP was acceptable after the handover of Hong Kong sover-eignty.[459] Right-wing institutions such as pro-Taiwanese organisations and official representatives of Taiwan could stay behind and operate, while the administrative set up of the SAR government could comprise members of differ-ent political persuasion. He suggested that 'a small percentage of leftists and rightists could play a part in the SAR administration, but the majority should be made up of apolitical administrators.'[460]

While Deng appeared to be liberal in promoting the concept of the SAR formation, the Central Government was firmly against any pro-sovereignty movements in Hong Kong. From the outset, the advocacy of 'two Chinas' (mainland China and Taiwan) was not allowed.[461] At the same time, senior Central Government officials made it clear there would be restrictions on the media. Though the slogan promised 'one country, two systems', the Hong Kong press would not enjoy 'one country, two systems' protection if it dared to touch on politically sensitive issues, such as national sovereignty and central authority. Prior to the change of political regime, Lu Ping, a senior Chinese official in charge of Hong Kong and Macau affairs, gave advance warning about the guidelines that would apply after 1997:

I don't want to create any illusions for you.... After 1997, it will not be possible for you to advocate two Chinas, or one China and one Taiwan, or Hong Kong independence, or Taiwan independence.... The press will not be allowed to do so. It is a different issue from press freedom.[462]

The sovereignty movement became one of the most contentious issues, as the Hong Kong press continued to fulfil its duty as an independent distributor of information to the public at large. This political inflexibility was complex in its operation. In April 2000, a Central Government official in Hong Kong criticised a Hong Kong reporter for interviewing the elected deputy Taiwanese president. The reporter argued that this was a normal and regular follow-up of news events.[463] In early June 2000, a senior official of the Taiwan Affairs Department of the Central Government's Liaison Office warned business people at the Chinese Chamber of Commerce not to do business with Taiwan firms that supported Taiwan independence.[464] Many observers were likewise deeply concerned by the interference.[465]

These new political prohibitions were not only restrictive for the press, but also applied to politicians and other officials. In contrast to what Deng Xiaoping had promised, Cheng An-kuo, the senior Taiwanese representative, was in effect thrown out of Hong Kong when his visa was not renewed in November 1999.[466] His main political mistake was to describe the Taiwanese President Lee Teng-hui's position on the Sino-Taiwanese relationship openly as a 'special state-to-state' one. This subsequently precipitated a domestic Hong Kong government reshuffle. Cheung Man-yee, the Director of Broadcasting, was apparently removed from her position and transferred to an overseas appointment: she allegedly acted against the patriotic policy by giving approval to the airing of the Taiwanese representative's opinion.[467] Her removal from Hong Kong was regarded as a penalty, a warning for those who deviated from the Central Government's policy.[468]

China's hard-line approach on the sovereignty issue, first applied in the media, extended to the political and cultural realm. Another major political controversy that occurred in the post-colonial era was also related to political challenges within China. The Falun Gong Movement began in China and caused concern to the CCP.[469] The Falun Gong started as a meditation and breathing exercise and body-mind training group that attracted hundreds of thousands of followers in mainland China.[470]

The Hong Kong branch of Falun Gong was legally registered, and had conducted its activities in a peaceful and lawful manner.[471] As the official Chinese attack on Falun Gong intensified, the legitimacy of Falun Gong supporters in Hong Kong was called into question. The central issue in the Falun Gong episode was whether Hong Kong could really claim to be a privileged free city within the orbit of socialist China. The promise of 'one country, two systems' was put to the test as many pro-Chinese politicians and central officials put pressure on the SAR administration to outlaw the Falun Gong. The position of SAR officials shifted as the pressure from the North escalated and the 'loyalty' of individual officials was tested. Finally, the Chief Executive of the SAR, Tung Chee-hwa, relented and agreed that the Falun Gong was a 'kind of cult' and 'more or less an evil cult'.[472] He also stated that the Hong Kong government would not tolerate any activities intended to upset the stability of Hong Kong and China.

Factionalism within SAR

Despite the rhetoric of senior Hong Kong government figures, legislation has still not been promulgated outlawing the local branch of Falun Gong as of 2004. It was also reportedly said that the reason behind the Central Government's pulling its punches was that it wished to avoid creating the appearance of meddling with Hong Kong's autonomy. So Beijing left it to the Chief Executive to handle the Falun Gong issue in Hong Kong.[473]

In such a political atmosphere in the post-colonial era, it was very difficult to reconcile Chinese nationalism and HKSAR autonomy, especially since China feared that Hong Kong could be used as a base for subversion. Despite increasing political pressure, a local organiser of Falun Gong rented the Hong Kong City Hall to host its annual conference. The Beijing-funded press criticised the Hong Kong administration for allowing such a subversive group to hold events in Hong Kong. Beijing-backed Hong Kong *Wen Wei Po* doubted the wisdom of allowing this kind of function to be held on Hong Kong soil, even worse on government-controlled soil, and asked: 'Is Hong Kong being used as a "subversive base" against the motherland?'[474]

This criticism of the SAR administration implied that factionalism existed within the Hong Kong government. The fact that Hong Kong could exercise its political freedom reflected that there was no lack of support in the administration for maintaining the status quo. However, this split within the administration was not without consequences. The early resignation of Anson Chan, the Chief Secretary and deputy to the Chief Executive, exposed the acute differences between these two top officials.[475] Also, Anson Chan was reportedly strongly criticised by the Central Government official for not helping the Chief Executive to administer the SAR effectively.[476] The allegation pointed to her unpatriotic deeds, including her personal approval of Falun Gong's 'defiant' meeting on Chinese soil.[477] As with the Director of Broadcasting, Anson Chan was marginalised, but chose to leave of her own accord.[478]

Apart from eliminating factionalism within the SAR administration, the Central Government tried to iron out the ideological differences between China and Hong Kong by issuing political guidelines, for example, the news media were forbidden to criticise the Chinese leadership. Even before 1997, some newspapers accepted the limits imposed on them. For example, *Sing Tao Daily News* set out guidelines in black and white on how sensitive issues should be reported:

> According to Chinese official rules, all incidents mentioned in non-governmental media, incidents like leaders' speeches, leaders' whereabouts, government policy, fire, explosion or air crash, are classified as 'state secrets'. Therefore, if aforementioned incidents are used in any news reports, the report will become a 'sensitive news story'. There is a danger of stealing 'state secrets' too.[479]

According to the guidelines, the aim was 'not to antagonize the Chinese side or attract denials from them' when handling 'sensitive news stories'.[480] What was remarkable, however, was the reasoning behind the rules. It explicitly sought to appease Chinese officials by ceding to the Central Government's imperatives for reporting on the Chinese scene.

This issue of self-censorship remained a serious structural problem. This was particularly the case among media organisations owned by those with wide-ranging economic interests in China. One notable example was the manner in which *Television Broadcast (TVB)*, the leading television station, played down an incident in which one of its news reporters was berated by a senior Chinese diplomat for asking 'inappropriate' questions of Chinese Premier, Zhu Rongji. If other journalists had not reported the case, and brought pressure to bear, *TVB* might well not have reported the incident on its own news, nor would *TVB* have made any official protest to the Central Government.[481]

This case also demonstrates the clash between the news ideologies of Hong Kong and China. The 'inappropriate' question related to a protest during Zhu's official visit to France. The rationale of the Chinese official was that Hong Kong reporters formed part of the Chinese press, and should therefore follow the rules and be respectful to the Chinese Premier.[482]

Similarly, in October 2000, the Chinese President, Jiang Zemin, accused the Hong Kong media of naiveté and low journalistic standards after a series of questions from journalists about whether he supported another term for Chief Executive, Tung Chee-hwa. President Jiang also warned journalists that they would be held accountable if their reports were not accurate enough. On 20 December, the President warned the residents of Macau and Hong Kong against using their freedom to oppose the state. He also said that both Hong Kong's and Macau's news media should value news freedom but also consider their 'social responsibility when fielding questions or filing reports'.[483] Not ashamed of repeating the Central Government's position, the Hong Kong Chief Executive, Tung Chee-hwa, called upon the Hong Kong media to have 'social responsibility', by which he meant that the press should have respect for the Chinese leadership. It should not question, challenge, or cast doubts upon the leadership's motives with respect to Hong Kong. This position was in contrast to the western liberal journalistic tradition of the Hong Kong press.

However, one year later, in December 2001, the Chinese President voluntarily came out to meet Hong Kong reporters and invite them to ask him questions after a meeting with Tung Chee-hwa in Beijing.[484] This was an example of the Central Government's effort to pull its punches so as not to damage Hong Kong's reputation as a free city.

The role of the media in Hong Kong

The mini-constitution of the Basic Law provides for freedom of the press, and the HKSAR Government appeared to respect this freedom following the handover. During the first year after the handover, even media analysts observed that there was no overt rollback of press freedom.[485] Yet, some journalists and news media continued to practise a degree of self-censorship, particularly in respect of reporting about mainland China.[486] Direct repression from the Central Government was not a necessary measure.[487]

In the past few years, some Hong Kong daily newspapers have either had new owners or major new shareholders.[488] This often resulted in rapid structural change to the management as well as the editorial direction of particular press. The pressure on journalists to self-censor was subtle and indirect. There was also a widely shared perception of the need to take special care on topics of particular sensitivity to China or when covering the Central Government's relations with Hong Kong's powerful business people. Related matter however, continued to appear in the press.[489]

The way journalists worked revealed tensions between Chinese policy makers and Hong Kong media operators.[490] The ideological tension between China and Hong Kong described in the last section has been reflected in media organisations, where these tensions have infiltrated institutional policy and affected editorial management. The Chinese strategy was to control mainstream newspapers using pro-China business people. As the Hong Kong business community was keen to develop its share of the mainland market, many in the business sector were keen to be China-friendly. Newspaper proprietors thus practiced self-censorship through internal management control.

The Chinese policy of media control can be traced back to the transition period. Before the handover, Kam Yiu-yu, the former chief editor of Beijing-controlled daily newspaper, *Wen Wei Po*, revealed China's long-term policy towards the Hong Kong press.[491] Kam, who had been in Hong Kong performing propaganda work for the CCP for over 40 years, confirmed that Beijing's strategy was to 'control the economic bases' by ensuring the media were held by pro-China proprietors. There was thus no need for any overt interference.

This policy had been in operation since the transition period. According to Xu Jiatun, the self-exiled director of *New China News Agency* (the de facto Chinese embassy in Hong Kong under British rule), the Chinese government considered buying *South China Morning Post* (*SCMP*) with the cooperation of a local businessman in the 1980s, but missed the opportunity owing to its unfamiliarity with the procedures of Hong Kong's stock market. Subsequently a Malaysian Chinese businessman, Robert Kuok, was apparently approached by Xu Jiatun with the aim of persuading him to relocate his base of operations to Hong Kong and also with the view of using this press for promoting investment opportunities in China and the official viewpoint on Chinese matter.[492] In 1993, Kuok successfully acquired the controlling shares in the leading English-language daily from Rupert Murdoch, when the Australian media mogul decided that *SCMP*, a traditional pro-British daily, could not help, and could even hinder, his entry into the mainland market.

Colonial period

On the media front, apart from the three Beijing-funded and controlled newspapers, *Wen Wei Po*, *Ta Kung Pao* and *Hong Kong Commercial Daily*, and the one individual-owned newspaper, *Hong Kong Economic Journal*, all other mainstream newspapers are owned by either public or private companies. During the colonial period, for example, the 1980s, newspapers were usually owned by journalist-turned-proprietors. However, the media scene has changed rapidly since the early 1990s, with ownership and financial restructuring. Newspapers have fallen into the hands of either business people or conglomerates, more often than not those with links to Chinese affiliated companies.

THE REWARD FOR BEFRIENDING CHINA

Since the 1989 Tiananmen massacre, Beijing has been criticised by, and isolated from, the rest of the world. The act of befriending China in the early 1990s when most of the business community was hesitant appears particularly impressive. When Sally Aw, proprietor of the English-language daily, *Hong Kong Standard*, was allegedly involved in a fraud case concerning the distribution figures of her newspaper, she was not prosecuted. The excuse given by the Secretary for Justice, Elsie Leung, was that it was not 'in the public interest to do that'. However, this aroused public speculation about Aw's personal political connections with China, and it seemed that her adjustment of the editorial position of her papers was seen as a service to the Chinese. Also, the SAR Chief Executive, Tung Chee-hwa, was a board director of *Sing Tao* Group (and *Hong Kong Standard*) before he ran for office.[493]

DIMINISHING TAIWANESE INFLUENCE

One of the major changes in the Hong Kong media scene was the diminishing influence of Taiwan. In view of the Central Government's hostility towards Taiwan's sovereignty movement, all Taiwan-funded newspapers were either shut down or returned to Taiwan before the political handover of Hong Kong.[494] In addition, political correctness became the order of the day. Newspapers historically closely connected to Taiwan started to downplay such links.[495]

Under such circumstances, Taiwanese influence largely diminished. For instance, major changes happened to a leading pro-nationalist KMT quality newspaper. Though historically tied to Taiwan, *Sing Tao Daily News* had kept a safe distance from the KMT since 1992. When its proprietor, Sally Aw, paid her first visit to Beijing, President Jiang Zemin received her personally. This was an achievement that the Chinese United Front Department had worked towards for a long time. That Department was supposed to be one of the democratic mechanisms whereby the CCP could at best consult minority groups, and at worst, be aware of any dissident opinions among such groups. It aimed to convert the political opposition. To this end, a series of unprecedented media joint ventures were lined up between *Sing Tao* Group and Chinese-owned conglomerates in certain major cities, namely Beijing, Guangzhou and the Shen Zhen Special Economic Zones, over the next few years. In the end, all of them failed to exist in the market.[496]

THE DECLINING BRITISH FACTOR

Another distinctive shift emerging from the transition period was the declining influence of the British Government. Its traditional unofficial 'flagship', *SCMP*,[497] was sold to Australian media mogul, Rupert Murdoch, who in turn sold it to Robert Kuok. Kuok's Kerry Group had a lot of business in the mainland. Kuok was initially persuaded by Chinese officials to transfer his base to Hong Kong. He was then rewarded with the chance of serving Beijing as an adviser.[498] When he bought the controlling shares of *SCMP*, the Bank of China backed him with a loan. On the management front, nothing drastic seemed to be done by the new proprietor. However, a Chinese consultant, Feng Xiliang, a founder editor of the Chinese official English-language newspaper, *China Daily*, was appointed to the newspaper without prior notice to the editor. This move had triggered journalistic concern[499]

Post-colonial period

In the case of *SCMP*, after Robert Kuok acquired the newspaper, the news content and management appeared to remain much the same for the first few years.[500] The whole picture changed when one of the paper's high-ranking journalists was forced to leave.[501] The abrupt departure of one of the most prominent China-watchers in the English-language media, Willy Wo-lap Lam, was a sign that even the most senior and well-known journalists could be removed if they incurred the wrath of Beijing and its allies. In what many observers saw as an example of media self-censorship, *SCMP* demoted Willy Lam from the position of a senior editor of the daily's China coverage section to that of an associate editor on mainland politics. Lam subsequently resigned in protest, claiming that the newspaper's management had begun to 'tone down' his column on China to avoid antagonising the Central Government. The editor-in-chief denied the charges, and attributed the change to a structural reorganisation.[502] However, the incident followed a published letter to the editor from the newspaper's owner, who denied a claim in Lam's column that a group of Hong Kong businesspeople, including the newspaper owner himself, had been offered commercial advantages by Chinese leaders in return for supporting Chief Executive, Tung Chee-hwa, for a second term.[503] He described the column as an 'absolute exaggeration and fabrication' that was full of 'distortions and speculation'.[504]

A former editor of *SCMP* also described earlier pressure from the owner and management to sack Lam and others before the handover of Hong Kong.[505] The incident illustrates the increasing attempts by the Chinese to depoliticise newspaper coverage, as well to tighten up political control over news reporting. Lam resigned because he felt he had been sidelined and stripped of his editorial powers. After working on the newspaper for more than 12 years, he was concerned about 'increasing attempts [at *SCMP*] to depoliticise China coverage to avoid sensitive political matters'.[506] He believed Beijing had a hand in pressuring the newspaper's management to censor his coverage of China, and that this had become a common phenomenon in Hong Kong. According to Lam, Beijing was extremely sensitive towards the Hong Kong media, so it was possible they had put pressure on other news media to rein in journalists whose work they did not like.

However, this showdown can be looked at from another perspective. It shows that journalism's norms can play a countervailing role. Murdoch once said that the paper was the only one of his businesses he could not fully control.[507] Despite the fact that Lam had become a marked man in the eyes of the proprietor and his senior management staff for some years, he was only forced to go when the newsroom was reorganised. Moreover, Lam's concern about the Central Government's possible meddling in the Hong Kong press was shared by more than 100 in-house journalists, who published a letter in *SCMP* stating their worries for the organisation they served.[508] Their concern was based on the fact that Lam was sidelined only months after his proprietor published the scathing letter in *SCMP* described above.

Another distinct feature of the post-colonial period was the lack of a critical voice concerning Chinese policy. For example, *Ming Pao Daily News* (*MPDN*), a leading critical Chinese-language daily newspaper in Hong Kong, had previously been branded one of the most outspoken press on the CCP's policies, especially back in the 1960s and 1970s.[509] At that time, its journalist-turned-proprietor, Louis Cha, was in charge of editorials. Its editorial position changed after it came under the ownership of Oei Hong Nien, Yu Pun-hoi at first, and then Tiong Hiew-king. Oei and Tiong were both overseas Chinese businessmen from Indonesia and Malaysia, respectively, whereas Yu was a local Hong Kong Chinese businessman. Initially, the purchase of *MPDN* was apparently a means of appeasing China by taming this otherwise outspoken paper. Furthermore all its new proprietors aspired to enter the important mainland market. After Tiong Hiew-king took control, *MPDN* became part of a company with business interests ranging from travel, timber and even forestry in both Hong Kong and China, with a newspaper business on the side.[510] Tiong Hiew-king's vision was to make *MPDN* a 'Chinese people's newspaper'.[511] It seems, however, that Tiong was equating 'Chinese people' with the 'Chinese government in Beijing'.

Yet, there was an implicit conflict between a pro-China position on the one hand, and a pro-Hong Kong one on the other, with the interests of Hong Kong coming second to the interests of the Central Government. Tiong's vision of a 'Chinese people's paper' backfired in Hong Kong. The paper later adjusted its editorial position again, though it remained mild in terms of printing dissenting views on China.[512]

PUNISHMENT FOR UNPOPULARITY

The case of the Next Media group and its proprietor provides an example of how far the integration of economic and political factors had the effect of controlling the press and thus curtailing press freedom. A self-made entrepreneur, Jimmy Lai, was hailed as a 'freedom fighter' for Hong Kong because he launched a popular newspaper, *Apple Daily*, in 1995. The story began when he wrote an article entitled 'Li Peng, a tortoise egg with zero IQ' in *Next Magazine*. In it he criticised the Chinese Premier Li Peng for ordering the killing of students and civilians in Tiananmen in 1989. Despite the fact that the article was a serious insult to the Chinese leader, and perhaps constituted a crime in China, Lai was untouchable in Hong Kong because of the right to free speech. His boldness won him applause from Hong Kong readers. After that, the Central Government regarded Lai as its enemy. Coincidentally, he not only suffered from personal harassment when his house was bombed, but his garment outlets in China also had licensing problems. Although it was unclear who caused his bad fortunes, his newspaper has been totally banned from China from the beginning. *Apple Daily*'s journalists were under a blanket ban from entering mainland China to cover any news, even the most routine and jingoistic stories.

Subsequently, Lai resigned and severed all links with Giordano, his garment group. But the group's ten outlets in China continued to suffer problems with licensing. Furthermore, Next Media Group, which owned *Apple Daily* and *Next Magazine*, met many obstacles to getting listed in the Hong Kong Stock Exchange. The listing sponsor, Sun Hung Kai Investment Company, withdrew at the last minute, apparently out of concern that the transaction would be economically risky because of political factors. The Next Media Group was later listed in Hong Kong, with the help of an investment banker, Tony Fung. However, Fung, who had represented the anti-establishment media baron Jimmy Lai in a corporate take-over, was blocked from being reappointed to the governing council of the Chinese University (the second leading university) by the Chief Executive, Tung Chee-hwa.[513] This political intervention attracted international press attention, though the SAR administration denied any political involvement in this academic appointment.

The newspaper also suffered from a reduction in advertising revenue. At least two large Hong Kong property companies were asked to steer advertising business away from *Apple Daily* newspaper owned by Jimmy Lai, who was a vocal critic of Beijing and the Tung Chee-hwa administration.[514]

It is true that the early success of *Apple Daily* and its sister publications had to do with its outspoken position on Chinese politics, especially after the Tiananmen massacre of 4 June 1989. The fact that the paper rose to be the second best-selling daily newspaper shortly after its launch in 1995 was largely due to its proprietor's management philosophy and his treatment of the paper as a 'commodity'. On the one hand, Lai injected a dose of tabloid style and content into the broadsheet. On the other hand, he also served the new middle class with a combination of critical views and reports on China and the SAR. As Ip Yat-Kin, the editor of *Apple Daily* once said: 'As long as democracy sells, we will print.'[515] The financial success of *Apple Daily* indicated a substantial demand for pro-democracy, anti-China publications; this in turn put pressure on other publications to moderate their pro-China stance to try and capture some of this market.

Ip Yat-Kin's remark highlights the extent to which market forces can help journalists counter proprietary and management pressure, and how the reader's need to be informed can serve as a legitimate reason for journalists to uphold their professional principles. But how far could market pressure help? This will be discussed in the case study on the Taiwan election in the next section.

Despite hostility from the Central Government, *Apple Daily* survived. This again demonstrates the power of the free market. Still, in 2001, given that the Hong Kong public sphere was contracting, and the political situation in Taiwan became more dynamic, Jimmy Lai denounced the suppression by the Hong Kong and Central Governments by moving his headquarters to Taipei, the capital of Taiwan. He started a new publication, *Taiwan Next Weekly*, in Taipei, leaving his staff to manage *Apple Daily* and Hong Kong *Next Magazine*.

Concluding remarks

Yet the most severe short-term challenge following the handover of Hong Kong was not political but economic.[516] The Hong Kong economy deteriorated following the Asian financial crisis of 1997. The upshot of this was that some proprietors withdrew their resources from the mainland and concentrated on the local market.

Chinese-language journalists reported in accordance with a tacit understanding of their editors' and publishers' requirements. There was also pressure because some publishers and editors believed that advertising revenue or their business interests in China would suffer if their papers were seen to be antagonistic to China. However, because of keen competition, the press continued to report and comment on sensitive issues such as Taiwan and the Falun Gong.[517]

Case study: Hong Kong's media at a historical crossroads – covering elections in Taiwan

Background to Taiwan and its relationships with Hong Kong and China

In 2000, the Chinese mainland Government was very concerned about the outcome of the Taiwanese Presidential election.[518] That the Taiwanese had progessively moved away from authoritarian rule since the late 1980s in the direction of democracy was indeed impressive. This had at least two significant implications for all Chinese in PRC, HK and Taiwan and elsewhere. First, Taiwan transformed from an authoritarian one-party rule to a multi-party political system. The fact that the Taiwanese people were allowed to vote for their president through universal franchise was unimaginable to the rival Chinese Communist Party (CCP). Second, the success of the Taiwanese political system illustrated that there could be an alternative system to that of socialist China, not just a feasible one, but also, perhaps, a better one.

The Hong Kong news media treated the Taiwanese election as one of the most significant Chinese political events at the turn of the century.[520] Domestically, the influence of this Taiwanese election was huge, and its effect on Chinese democracy was wide-ranging and significant. Not only the Hong Kong press, but media from all over the world, sent reporters to cover this unprecedented election. The development of events, especially in respect of Chinese reaction, was reported and followed closely by the news media worldwide.

The Hong Kong media reports not only revealed the post-colonial situation, but also formed part of the post-colonial context. Journalists were constantly under internal and external environmental constraints, both knowingly and unknowingly.[521] The press played the role of observer, but the pressure they were under was reflected in their article. For example, mainland Chinese leaders repeatedly demanded a unification of ideology;[522] and some news organisations internalised this way of thinking and adopted a policy of not advocating Taiwanese independence.[523] There was a constant struggle between the post-colonial and nationalistic discourse, on the one hand, and journalistic discourse on the other. So did the press succumb to, or resist, the pressure to conform? How did it strike a balance between fulfilling its role as an independent distributor of information and toeing the CCP's line of 'social responsibility' based on patriotism?

Unique significance of Taiwan's elections in 2000

Three years after Hong Kong reverted to China, and one year after Macau was reunited with China, the mainland government was desperate to achieve the next goal – reunification with Taiwan – seeing this as one of the main goals for the twenty-first century.[524] Chinese officials attempted to intervene and prevent the candidate for pro-Taiwanese independence being elected. Although the Hong Kong press had already been warned several times in the past that it should not advocate Taiwanese independence, as discussed earlier, it continued the work by adopting various tactics and strategies.[525] It was hard, however, to distinguish between reporting on Taiwanese independence, and advocating it.

Contrary to Chinese wishes, and despite a month-long bombardment of verbal threats against pro-independence tendencies, the Taiwanese exercised their democratic rights and elected the pro-independence Democratic Progressive Party (DPP) candidate, Chen Shui-bian, as president. This was the first genuine presidential election in Taiwan.

This expression of popular pro-independence sentiment on the part of the Taiwanese people, in defiance of the Chinese desire for unification of Taiwan with China, was not only significant to Taiwan, but also to the Hong Kong press. The press coverage of the Taiwanese election has thus been chosen as the case study here.[526]

How the campaigns unfolded

There was a steady escalation in Chinese rhetoric in the run-up to Taiwan's election. First, one month before the poll, the Chinese Government published a White Paper stipulating its policy on Taiwan. It stressed that if Taiwan continued to delay negotiations for its reunification with China, then China would not hesitate to take the island by force. The Chinese Government had already said that if Taiwan made a declaration of independence, and if there were direct foreign intervention in Taiwan's politics, the Chinese would recover Taiwan by military means. This was seen by the Taiwanese as an attempt to intervene in Taiwan's domestic affairs.

Second, the month-long election campaign coincided with the annual session of the Chinese National People's Congress (NPC) and the Chinese People's Political Consultative Conference (CPPCC). More than 3,000 deputies and delegates from all over China attended the two-week long political convention. This was exactly the kind of occasion that allowed the Chinese leadership to reiterate its position, and set the stage for the people's representatives, in particular the military, both to put pressure on Taiwan and, more often, to reiterate the Central Government line with regard to Taiwan as a Chinese territory.

Thus the Taiwanese election in 2000 was held under enormous domestic pressure. It was a local election involving the long-standing rival to the CCP, the KMT, which fled to Taiwan after its bitter defeat in mainland China in 1949. The presidential election was a three-way contest between KMT candidate Lien Chan, Chen Shui-bian, the pro-independence DPP, and independent James Soong, an ex-KMT member, also a long-serving ally of the incumbent Taiwanese President, Lee Teng-hui. All three aspired to political and territorial independence to a varying degree and had explicitly expressed their willingness to work on improving Sino-Taiwan relations.

The lesson of the 1996 election is revealing. At that time, to exert influence on the incumbent President, Lee Teng-hui, the Chinese Government staged a military exercise aimed at intimidating Taiwanese people near Taiwan waters. Lee Teng-hui, however, was elected with a large number of votes, even though the Taiwanese were under imminent threat of war, with missiles landing in the Taiwan Strait. The Chinese release of the White Paper in 2000 was therefore regarded by the Hong Kong press as a tactical moderation. This time, the mainland strategy appeared to move from the threat of military might to the power of verbal might – a 'paper missile' that is.[527]

Foreign politics added a new dimension to Chinese politics, which complicated this supposedly domestic dispute. For instance, the United States sent a warship to the Taiwan Strait to discourage further harassment by China. After the publication of the White Paper in 2000, the United States warned China of dire consequences if it waged a war.[528] Thus, different interests were at work, and several different negotiation processes were in place, simultaneously during the month-long election campaign, that is, the Sino-Taiwanese, the U.S.-Taiwanese and the Sino-U.S. This complex domestic/foreign interrelationship dominated the Taiwanese election campaign. For instance, the three main candidates were seen to modify their pro-independence stance so as not to provoke China further, and claimed that they were all willing to resume talks with China upon victory.

The newspapers selected for the case study: Context and reasons for choice

The three papers chosen for this case study – *Oriental Daily News* (*ODN*), *South China Morning Post* (*SCMP*) and *Ming Pao Daily News* (*MPDN*) – represent positions ranging from relatively independent to relatively patriotic, and include both Chinese- and English-language newspapers. They were selected partly for the reasons stated in Chapter 3, but also because they were the three main papers that allocated resources and prominent space to cover the election. For instance, all three papers sent correspondents or made use of stringers there, and the news dispatches from Taiwan were usually given prominent coverage. The case study covers the period from late February to late March 2000, to include the actual election campaign and its immediate aftermath.

Oriental Daily News

Sources used

It was extremely difficult, if not impossible, to get news on the rapidly changing political situation in mainland China, especially as the Chinese government retained tight control over the flow of information so as to keep people in the dark. Apart from sending its team of reporters to Taiwan to report on the latest developments there, *Oriental Daily News* (*ODN*) relied heavily on information printed in foreign countries. For instance, *ODN* relayed stories printed in the local Taiwanese media, including *Liberty Times*, *United Evening News* and *China Evening Times*, and those covered by Taiwan's official agency, the Central News Service. For the latest Chinese moves and the reactions of the different power factions in PRC, the paper quoted from sources such as *Liberation Army Daily* for military matters and the leading *People's Daily* for the mainland official position on Taiwan affairs. However, *ODN* also used foreign media such as United States' *Associated Press*, *CNN*, *Science and Technology Journal*, *The New York Times*, *The Washington Post* and Japanese *NHK* (Japanese Broadcasting Corporation, Japan's sole public broadcaster), *Asahi Shimbun* and *Yumiuri Shimbun* which had interviews with high-ranking Chinese officials. Sometimes *ODN* would quote anonymous sources in China; so it did to prevent the sources from getting into trouble for speaking to journalists outside China proper.

Nature of coverage, headline, use of pictures etc.

ODN in general adhered to its journalistic norms by printing up-to-date news concerning Chinese actions and Taiwanese response. Thus, for example, it covered the fact that the Chinese backed Lian Chan, the nationalist KMT candidate. On the other hand, it also covered the latest developments concerning Taiwan's ability to strike back militarily, the United States' firm support for Taiwan as regards to defence, and the moderation of Chinese rhetoric, particularly that of the non-military leaders, following U.S. intervention. The paper also described candidates' efforts to downplay their pro-independence stance, and to rally local political heavyweights to support their cause.[529]

The paper appeared to uphold professional journalism. Thus, their assessment of this Sino-Taiwanese confrontation tended to be descriptive and factual. For instance, regarding the military capability of Taiwan vis-à-vis that of the mainland, the paper on the one hand showed very vaguely, also the headlines, etc that follow shows Taiwan's 'dependence' on the U.S. as an ally. The story of 12 March 2000 was headed 'U.S. missile carrier will sail to Taiwan next month' and attributed the source to *The New York Times*, and Taiwanese military publications. The subheading of the story was 'the ability to wage war has increased and that makes mainland uncomfortable'. However, there was a side photo story originating from the U.S. *Associated Press* showing how a Beijing newspaper had printed the photograph of a United States carrier about to head for the Taiwan Strait. This photo story seems to highlight the Chinese position that the United States were 'obstructing' the peaceful re-unification of Taiwan with China. However, the paper tactically avoided saying this explicitly, but rather left it to readers to form their own opinion.

Similarly, in respect of the military build-up across the Taiwan Strait, the paper carried a report by a Taiwanese official in a Taiwanese military magazine entitled 'The anti-submarine capacity of China-made carrier is low'.[530] On Taiwan's defence against possible invasion from the mainland, the paper quoted a story from Taiwan's *Liberty Times* entitled 'Lee Teng-hui instructed to fend off China's intervention'.[531] Here, doubt was cast on the military strength of China while Taiwan was portrayed as defence ready.

While interpretations appear open, the justification of the cross-Strait tension was surely in doubt. *ODN* indicated the essence of the disagreement using Taiwanese officials' reactions. For instance, *ODN* quoted a Taiwanese defence ministry spokesman in a story entitled 'Taiwan points out that Beijing has deepened the tension across Taiwan Strait', with subtitles 'China's attempt to deny the reality of Taiwan's sovereignty amounts to disregarding the facts; [they should] recognize separate rule and give up threats'. However, at the end of the story it added a paragraph with the subtitle 'Beijing reiterates "one China" policy'.[532] This juxtaposition was one of the measures most often used, as a means of making the paper appear objective and expressing the point of view of both sides.

The United States' support for Taiwan was duly reported and the coverage shed light on the imbalance between the two powers across the Taiwan Strait on the one hand, and the potential meddling of a foreign power on the other. For instance, on the same day the Taiwanese defence ministry spokesman made the above remarks, there was another story about the United States carrier, which served as an anti-Chinese missile system, arriving on schedule despite Chinese threats: 'The U.S. missile pad arrives in Taiwan as scheduled'.[533] The fact that the island had tightened up its security according to *Associated Press* was used in another article entitled 'Taiwan tightens up measures to prevent mainland Chinese intervening in the election – "the loyalists" can resist missiles, no fear of disturbance of the vote counting'.[534] However, the subheading indicated the fear prevailing in the island: '[the island] worries that mainland China will assassinate candidates, a critical moment so they [the Taiwanese] will not mention any increase in defence measures'.

The ODN's attempt at 'balance' and how this was achieved

The news coverage of *Oriental Daily News* appears to show efforts at striking a balance between journalistic and nationalistic discourses, with the former attempting to paint an objective picture of events by printing nine separate public opinion polls[535] on the Taiwanese presidential election. These covered subjects ranging from Taiwanese candidates' popularity to the preferences of the Hong Kong public and its youngsters. The sponsors of the polls ranged from the Taiwanese local media such as *United Daily News*,[536] to *ODN*'s own poll,[537] and those conducted by Hong Kong institutes.[538] On the other hand, because of its mass circulation, the paper also helped to shape public opinion.

With regards to the balance of power across the Taiwan Strait and the possibility of a war, *ODN* occasionally revealed local Taiwanese people's sentiments. For instance, it carried a reporter's own analysis summing up Taiwanese people's confidence: 'Taiwanese people believe even though [Chen Shui-] Bian gets elected, there will not be a war'.[539]

The juxtaposition of conflicting views continued, especially at the peak of the crisis. For instance, at the side of a story entitled 'U.S. summons Lee Zhaoxing and urges China to exercise restraint', there was a picture by *Associated Press* illustrating a gathering of 300 students in Nanjing, the captial of KMT China, holding a banner with the slogan 'Hoping for an early reunification of China'.[540] The message here, on the eve of polling day, was intriguingly ambiguous, but it gives the impression that the paper was providing a balanced story.

Indeed, the juxtaposition of seemingly factual news reports covering both sides across the Taiwan Strait, without any explicit analysis, creates an impression of ambiguity throughout the coverage. While some reports indicated Taiwanese strength, *ODN* also covered Chinese movements, in particular those of the People's Liberation Army. For instance, the paper quoted *Liberation Army Daily* and *Science and Technology Daily* saying 'Jinan air force parades'.[541] On the following day, *ODN* carried news of the White Paper published by *People's Daily* overseas edition: 'Infinite deferral of peace talks will become an excuse for invading Taiwan – Beijing publishes the White Paper condemning Taiwanese independence and opposing any universal suffrage to change Taiwan's status as part of China'.[542] However, when the Chinese position changed, *ODN* reflected this: 'Beijing: the White Paper is not an ultimatum, China strongly resents the United States' intervention in its domestic affairs'.[543]

When *ODN* printed a story on the independent position of the incumbent president, Lee Teng-hui, it made sure to include the Chinese position, which opposed the pro-independence candidate, Chen Shui-bian. Again, *ODN* combined a story about Taiwan's official reaction to China with an interview by a Japanese *NHK* TV reporter with a mainland official in charge of Taiwanese affairs. Thus, the story became a precarious mix entitled 'Lee [Teng-hui]: make sure the election will resist mainland's intervention – [Taiwanese] mainland affairs committee reiterates "one China" [policy] with its own definition of statehood and urges resumption of talks'. The content of the story on the one hand highlights Lee Teng-hui's belief that 'the two countries' position was realistic; on the other hand, this was balanced by Beijing's rhetoric saying that the relationship across the Taiwan Strait would deteriorate if Chen Shui-bian won the election.[544] Again it was left to the reader to interpret the situation.

However, *ODN* sometimes appeared to be upfront when reporting Chinese interference. For instance, it quoted Lee Teng-hui: 'Lee: mainland resembles hooligan beating people if the latter rejects talk – Asian wisdom is in Taiwan, the mainland should learn from Taiwan'.[545] This occasional upfront interpretation of news developments might have something to do with the daily's mass appeal to the public. Newspapers in general sold better in a non-local crisis such as this. Here, market forces apparently helped to counter state pressure.

The coverage of the three main candidates' tactics and strategies in their campaign also helps to illustrate this point. During the election campaign, the three candidates all felt the heat from China. Amid coverage of the emotional participation of the Taiwanese people in this large-scale election campaign, *ODN* reported on the moderation of the candidates' response to the mainland's imminent threat. Reports followed the mood of the rapidly changing atmosphere, for example, 'Taiwanese election special – the three candidates play the stability card, Bian guarantees that he will not change national symbols/ emblems'. In another Taiwan election special: 'Nearly a million people campaign, 3 candidates confront each other' with subtitles saying, 'In Taipei 150,000 people took to the streets to support Lian Chan. Lian and Ah Bian each have 300,000 supporters'.[546] Taiwanese people's emotions and aspirations had never before run so high, as these reports show.

Similarly, mass circulation *ODN* printed sensational stories with graphic pictures concerning the preparations for war on both sides of the Taiwan Strait. For instance, on polling day, 18 March, there was a story about military movements entitled 'The two sides across Taiwan Strait actively prepare for war' with a subheading 'It is rumoured that mainland China chooses this time to wage war; Fuzhou [the capital of Fukien province which faces Taiwan] restricts military personnel from leaving camp ... Taiwanese military has proclaimed highest alert in war preparation'.

Editorial line: mixed

As a means of providing balanced reporting, *ODN* also reported the Chinese official line in general, and that of the military in particular. For instance, it relayed a report printed in *Liberation Army Daily*: '*Liberation Army Daily* warns Taiwanese people: do not elect Ah Bian [Chen Shui-bian, the pro-independence candidate] – millions of soldiers stand by to combat Taiwan independence activists'.[547] This was highly informative, but also helped to reinforce the message of the Chinese propaganda machine.

The three Taiwanese terrestrial TV stations, which were under the ruling KMT's control, openly lobbied in support of the KMT's candidate. *ODN* also relayed stories from Taiwan's *United Evening News* entitled 'Terrestrial TV stations openly lobby in support of Lian Chan', with a subheading 'Only permitted to approve; not allowed to criticise current affairs'.[548]

As social, political and cultural changes took place in post-colonial Hong Kong, the press could not help being affected. This post-colonial or nationalistic discourse can be detected in both the way reporting was conducted and the editorial position. First, the framing of reports apparently adopted a Chinese perspective. For instance, a week before polling day, there was a report seemingly toeing the Chinese line: 'If the new president elected has no tendency towards Taiwanese independence, political talks can be anticipated – Beijing's new condition influences the Taiwanese election campaign'. However, the content of the story was very different to what the title said. The lead paragraph was about the announcement of a famous Chinese Nobel laureate scientist, Lee Yuan-tseh, that he was openly lending support to Chen Shui-bian. Lee Yuan-tseh was highly respected worldwide and could mobilise local support for Chen. His popularity was said to be next to that of the incumbent Taiwanese president, Lee Teng-hui. However, there was a tail to the main story – the reaction from the Chinese Foreign Minister, Tang Shu-bei, saying that 'If Taiwan's new leader has no pro-Taiwan independence colour, Beijing will consider re-opening talks across the Taiwan Strait.'[549] By the side, there was a report by a staff reporter entitled 'Beijing's soft intervention is more effective' with a sub-heading 'Taiwanese society is finally dominated by reason.'[550] Here, the Chinese position was again repeated, but they were encouraged to adopt a 'softer', and therefore more 'effective', stance.

Relating the election to Hong Kong readers

Very few Hong Kong residents had a vote in the Taiwanese election. Those who did were either permanent residents in Taiwan, or originated from there. Thus the majority of people in Hong Kong had no say in what happened to Taiwan, and could only express their opinion. One story said '50% of Hong Kong people think [James] Soong's victory will benefit Hong Kong', with a subheading stating 'Ah Bian's [Chen Shui-bian's] victory is not beneficial to Hong Kong's stability'.[551] This article indicated the sentiments of the Hong Kong people who were, to a large extent, influenced by both the Chinese rhetoric and the mass media.

ODN picked a human interest story from a Taiwanese newspaper to provide a Hong Kong connection. In a story entitled 'Tung Chee-hwa "campaigns" for the election', it reported that Chen Shui-bian's election team placed a one-page advertisement in mainstream Taiwan newspapers to remind Taiwan voters: 'We are here to elect a president, we are not here to appoint a Chief Executive of the Hong Kong SAR [Special Administrative Region]'.[552] In the middle of the full-page advertisement, there was a two and a half inch photograph of Tung Chee-hwa, with the caption 'Chinese Hong Kong Chief Executive, Tung Chee-hwa'. By publicising Chen Shui-bian's position towards the Hong Kong administration led by Beijing-appointed Tung Chee-hwa, the advertisement criticised Hong Kong's 'one country, two systems' position that deprived Hong Kong citizens from enjoying election rights. It also served as a protest against Beijing's intervention in the Taiwanese election.

Apart from this kind of reportage which had political connotations, Chen Shui-bian's success was largely presented from a human interest angle. For instance, upon Chen's victory, *ODN* printed several pages of reports with headlines such as 'Peasant's son, once jailed for political struggle, elected president'[553] and 'Bian wears bullet-proof vest to celebration rally'.[554] These human interest stories were aimed at the general reader who might be more interested in details about the president-elect's personality than the never-ending arguments and threats across the Taiwan Strait.

Contradictions and confusion within coverage

If there was ambiguity in the news reports' representation of the nationalistic discourse, the position of the editorial was even more confused and inconsistent.

For instance, on the eve of election day, *ODN* printed an editorial entitled 'Civilian officials rule above Tiananmen [square], only in the crystal coffin do Chinese heroes lie – an analysis of the level of safety in the Taiwan Strait'.[555] Here, the editorial compares the bravery of Mao Tse-tung, in his crystal coffin inside Mao's museum in Beijing's Tiananmen Square, to that of the current Chinese leadership, implying that they dared not start a war because of the role played by the United States in Taiwan's affairs. This was an implicit criticism of the Chinese leadership, and implied that the danger of a war across the Taiwan Strait was minimal.

However, on polling day, the paper printed another editorial apparently endorsing the Chinese goal of reunification entitled 'To choose for Chinese betterment in the years to come', in which it stated that 'today is the day the Taiwanese people choose their president, but it is also a historical day when all Chinese people choose between war and peace...'[556] This implies that the vote of the Taiwanese people would have an impact on war and peace, though it is unclear to whom 'all Chinese people' refers. It could literally mean Chinese people from mainland China, or others living outside China including those in Hong Kong, Macau and overseas. However the Chinese outside China and Taiwan neither had a vote nor the power to make a choice between war and peace. Perhaps the editorial intentionally blurred the issue.

At the same time, *ODN* carried a report about a rare advertisement in the Chinese official propaganda organ, *People's Daily*. A full-page advertisement appeared on the front page of its Huadong (eastern) edition saying 'If Taiwan is to split from China – will Chinese people agree? Never ever!'[557] Thus the official Chinese position was emphasised again, and was reported in a Hong Kong mass circulation daily.

Post-election coverage

Nevertheless, the editorial position of *ODN* became clearer in its condemnation of the KMT's pro-independence position following that party's defeat by Chen Shui-bian, the candidate of the Democratic Progressive Party (DPP): 'The KMT was divided so it was defeated. Chen Shui-bian steps up, the future is worrisome'.[558] Although the editorial seemingly criticised the KMT and adopted the Chinese thinking that if Chen was elected, the future of the Sino-Taiwan relationship would be worrisome, in its last paragraph; the editorial used the incident to criticise the CCP's role in Chen's victory. It even concluded that the DPP came to power largely as a result of Beijing's repressive measures in the past two decades. In this case, the editorial line was more than ambiguous, it was actually contradictory. On the one hand, it toed the Chinese line by linking the KMT's downfall to corruption; on the other hand, it made use of the occasion to criticise China's wrongful policy by stating that Taiwan's independent DPP was victorious largely due to the mainland's unrelenting threats or war. Here, the editorial took heed of both the Chinese official nationalistic call and the popular Taiwanese nationalistic sentiment at the same time, though in a clumsy way.

Though *ODN* did not allocate an opinion/editorial section to contributors and staff analysts, they did have a small column in their China section. Before the election, the column traced the Taiwanese independence movement's history; more importantly it also wrote about the 'Taiwan independence movement having the support of the United States' and 'carrying out terrorist attacks in support of independence.' As the column was supposed to be expressing an individual's opinion, there was no mechanism for news checking or balanced reporting. The column did not, however, occupy a prominent position.

Analysis and summary

In sum, the mass circulation *Oriental Daily News* put more emphasis on journalistic discourse than other papers, in terms of the selection, emphasis and presentation of stories. However, the paper also operated under contextual constraints, in the sense that it could not disagree with the larger goal of national unification. There was a widespread impression among both journalists and the public that it was prudent for the press to engage in a degree of self-censorship. The pressures on journalists to self-censor are usually subtle and indirect.[559]

Although numerous articles on these subjects continued to appear in print, the reports of Chinese-language journalists seem to show a pervasive, if tacit, understanding that editors expected those reporting on China to be particularly certain of their facts and careful in their wording.

Another source of pressure came from the belief held by some publishers and editors that advertising revenues or their business interests in China would suffer if they were seen to be too antagonistic to China or powerful local interests. There are no reports of direct orders to refrain from covering a certain issue, but there was a widely shared perception of a need for special care on topics of particular sensitivity to China or Hong Kong's powerful business interests, such as the matter of Taiwanese independence, or the relations of powerful businessmen and women with the Central Government.

It appears that they adopted a series of measures such as juxtaposition of facts, and ambiguity in tone to create space for readers to form their own opinions. It might be partly due to the fact that the Taiwanese election was such a media event that the mass circulation paper could not afford to ignore those news items with mass appeal. Market forces, with their economic implications, hence played a role in countering state pressure. Also, popular nationalistic sentiment was so overwhelming that it occasionally overshadowed the official Chinese nationalistic call. Furthermore, the factionalism within the SAR discussed earlier shows that members of the Hong Kong elite were not necessarily in agreement on sensitive Chinese political issues such as this Sino-Taiwanese confrontation.

Ming Pao Daily News

Sources used

The coverage of the Chinese-language quality newspaper, *Ming Pao Daily News* (*MPDN*), gave more support to the nationalistic discourse. It dominated over the journalistic discourse in the following ways. First, the predominance of official and related Chinese sources in news coverage, in terms of both number and importance, is the crux of the problem. For instance, there were numerous interviews with Deputies to the NPC and Delegates of the CPPCC. While the NPC was generally regarded as the Chinese Parliament, whose main job was to pass the Central Government's annual budget, bills and motions, the CPPCC acted as the major consultative instrument for the Central Government to gauge support from other representatives. These were the two main approved political bodies in China, though neither the Deputies nor the Delegates were democratically elected.

The Chinese leadership used the occasion of a meeting of the NPC to pronounce their dislike of Taiwan's outgoing President, Lee Teng-hui. This was covered in a report in *MPDN* entitled 'Lee Teng-hui was the representative of pro-Taiwan independence – the Government Work Report criticised Lee for the first time'.[560] This was the first time China openly criticised Lee in the Annual Report of the Chinese Government. The paper also quoted General Zhang Wannian as saying if Taiwan went independent, that would mean war.[561] The fact that Chinese Premier, Zhu Rongji, 'received most applause' when he read his report to the NPC Deputies and the CPPCC Delegates, became a major news story.[562]

The fact that the Chinese Premier criticised the Taiwanese leader was naturally big news. There was, however, hardly any explanation for such a high profile accusation. The reason China promoted this anti-Lee Teng-hui sentiment was only explained in a regular column under a pen name.[563] The open condemnation was said to be risk-free because Lee was an outgoing political figure. The column said: 'In the opening session of the CPPCC, the Deputy Chairman Yep Xuan-ping strongly criticized Lee Teng-hui as the representative of Taiwanese separatism ... in the eyes of the Chinese leadership, Lee is a former political heavyweight, he cannot represent anyone, so Beijing dares to criticize him openly.'[564]

With the above coverage, *MPDN* is exercising a kind of unthinking acceptance of the importance (in terms of both news sense and politics) of what NPC and CPPCC had told the nation and the world about Taiwan. Likewise it is an unthinking assumption by *MPDN* of the mouthpiece role of propagating what both organisations said, without giving alternative interpretations of what they said, to say the least. The daily thus helped to construct a 'reality' by giving out this 'risk-free' but casual analysis.

Nature of coverage, headlines, use of pictures etc.

There is further evidence indicating that *MPDN* tended to adopt a nationalistic discourse. First, its reporters tended to have a preconceived position as regards the reunification controversy. For instance, interviews with Taiwanese candidates were usually conducted in accordance with the mainland's unification framework. For example, one of the questions put to all three main candidates was loaded:

> The Beijing authorities have indicated that they, the people from across the Taiwan Strait, do not want to see a pro-Taiwan independence candidate elected. Also, Hong Kong and overseas Chinese are worried that Chen Shui-bian, the candidate of the Democratic Progressive Party (DPP) will be elected, as they think that would make the Sino-Taiwanese relationship even more tense. But if Chen does get elected, what do you think the effect will be on the development of relations across the Strait and the development of Taiwan politics?[565]

Here the reporter seemed to represent Chinese not only in Hong Kong but also all over the world. How does the journalist get the impression that Chen Shui-bian's victory would adversely affect Sino-Taiwanese relations? The legitimacy of the question is seriously doubtful – there was no explanation whatsoever as to how the reporter came up with such a leading question. One possibility is that the daily adopted, and indeed endorsed, the nationalistic framework of analysis.

Similarly, the allocation of space to news coverage tended to favour a 'pro-China'[566] position. For instance, a lot of prominent coverage was given to Chinese leaders explaining Chinese policy. Although there appeared to be differences in the positions of the various power factions as events unfolded, the coverage closely followed the Chinese line. Very often, the paper simply reported the rhetoric of the Chinese leaders, namely Chinese President, Jiang Zemin, Chinese Premier, Zhu Rongji and Vice Premier, Qian Qichen, without critical interpretations and analyses.

For instance, after the publication of the White Paper in late February 2000, the United States strongly reacted to the mainland's threat of war against Taiwan. Chinese Vice Premier, Qian Qichen, dismissed the threat allegation as resulting from the 'Taiwanese guilty conscience'. A report quoted Qian in its title 'Qian: it will be best if reunification takes place as soon as possible – he rejected the allegation that China uses military force to intimidate Taiwan, and he pointed out that the Taiwanese felt guilty and so perceived [China as] a threat to themselves'.[567] During a session with a group of Hong Kong Deputies, who were selected from certain constituencies in Hong Kong by the Central Government, Qian explained: 'When we published the White Paper, they [the Taiwanese] said it was a threat, when the People's Liberation Army said something, again they said it was a threat. In reality there was no threat, they felt that way because they were timid and had a guilty conscience. So they were afraid of this and that.'[568] The report took for granted that Qian said this, and neither analysed the truthfulness of the content, nor attempted to get any reaction from the other side.

Likewise, on the following day, the Chinese President, Jiang Zemin, stated that 'there would be no war in March', making an effort to alleviate fears of an imminent war before the Taiwanese election.[569] The story quoted Jiang and used ancient Chinese poems to imply the Taiwanese worry was an imaginary one. Again, the daily did not attempt to explain why the Chinese leader's position had softened. This, in fact, was apparently in response to the strong reaction of the U.S. following the publication of the White Paper mentioned above.

This method of reporting without explanation meant the paper could avoid taking a stand on the rights and wrongs of political events. At one time, *MPDN* reported that Beijing has softened and therefore not prepared to go to war. But at another time it propagated what the Chinese leadership wanted to warn Taipei. Without giving any explanation on the two-prong strategy of Beijing's leadership, *MPDN*'s coverage in itself looks incoherent. The Chinese position towards Taiwan did not soften; in fact, it was tactically adjusted, but stayed as vigilant as ever. Three days before polling day, the Chinese Premier, Zhu Rongji, emerged with the toughest warning yet. *MPDN* used the Chinese Premier's strong words as headings and subheadings.[570]

The headline was indeed daunting: 'Zhu: those who are pro-Taiwan independence will not have a good ending – strong warning, we will not spare blood to defend re-unification'. Subtitles read: 'We will support whoever endorses one China' / 'The Taiwanese people face an urgent historical moment' / 'Will there be a military demonstration? Zhu: "wait and see"'. At the side, there was another strong warning entitled 'Deputy Commissioner of Nanjing military zone: If Taiwanese people opt for Chen Shui-bian this implies they opt for war'.[571] It is worth going into details about this news report because it demonstrates how the layout and presentation all helped to promote an escalation in tension. Apart from the fact that the Chinese leader's reiteration of his position came on the eve of Taiwan's polling day, there appeared not to be much actual news in the incident. The real news, of course, was the fierce emotion expressed by the Chinese Premier, Zhu Rongji. *MPDN* illustrated the escalation in Sino-Taiwanese tension by printing several large pictures of Zhu's fierce facial expressions and the story covered half a broadsheet to make the point. The timing of this very tough warning perhaps had to do with the final recognition by the mainland government that the pro-independence candidate, Chen Shui-bian, was gaining momentum. It also indicates the Chinese leadership's urgent desire both to swing voters and pressure the candidates into giving up their pro-independence stances. However, there was no explanation of this in the news reporting, merely shots from the Chinese side.

The reaction from Chen Shui-bian was given a far from proportional space, and was instead buried on an inside page. He stressed that Taiwan would not accept the notion of 'one country, two systems' and it would neither be a 'second Hong Kong' nor a 'second Macau'. Chen had made a valid point and it appears to be a newsworthy story. The fact his response was not prominently displayed can be explained by the fact that it was contrary to the story-telling of a unification discourse.

The layout and presentation of news reports also sometimes enhanced the Chinese propaganda, and gave readers the impression that war was imminent. For instance, a graphic of a type common in mass-circulation papers was put in front of the election news, apparently indicating the two main issues relating to the Taiwanese presidential election: the election campaign war in Taiwan itself; and more importantly, the implied threat of imminent war on the part of the Central Government. A senior Chinese official in charge of the cross-Strait negotiations, Tang Shu-bei, issued a warning should the Taiwanese election deliver a pro-independence victory:

> Sino-Taiwanese trade will be terminated if Taiwan stops being part of China, and if across the Taiwan Strait there are two Chinese countries. We cannot imagine that Taiwan will be able to get 15 billion U.S. dollars trade surplus, nor can we imagine that the people [of the mainland and Taiwan] will be able to marry, study and travel freely across the Strait.'[572]

This was another attempt to sway Taiwanese voters and candidates by threatening them with material loss and other restrictions.

Ming Pao*'s embrace of China's official position*

Stories about the United States' intervention were seemingly framed from a Chinese perspective. For example, when the U.S. government summoned Li Zhaoxing, the Chinese ambassador in Washington D.C., the story, entitled 'The U.S. is concerned about the consequences of the "White Paper"',[573] scaled down the serious tone of the U.S. reaction. However, the tone was more forceful and upbeat when covering the Chinese response to the U.S. statement: 'China condemns America's Taiwanese policy as an interference with Chinese sovereignty'.[574]

MPDN reporters also toned down the language used, and sometimes omitted words, because of the repressive nature of Chinese strictures against reporting on the Chinese scene. For example, Lee Teng-hui, the Taiwanese President, branded Beijing as a 'hooligan' for threatening to invade unless the island reunited with the mainland. In a report entitled 'Lee Teng-hui: mainland should not rely on their forces; the White Paper is a threatening tactic',[575] terms such as 'hooligan' and 'hegemony' used by Lee were either omitted altogether or buried in the story. Instead, the daily played up another story ridiculing Lee Teng-hui by quoting his ex-ally: 'James Soong laughs at Lee Teng-hui's threatening tactics, saying they are similar to those of the Chinese Communist Party.'[576]

EDITORIAL LINE: PATRIOTIC

In such a nationalistic reporting framework, the editorial line developed its own patriotic theme in favour of the 'one China' policy. The editorial content ranged from elaboration on the need for 'reunification' with Taiwan to avoid the threat of war, to tactics for handling pro-Taiwanese independence representatives, namely Lee Teng-hui and Chen Shui-bian. Anti-Lee Teng-hui and anti-Chen Shui-bian sub-themes also developed.

The nationalistic tendency was most obvious in editorials such as 'Reunification must proceed with patience'[577] and 'Beijing is increasing pressure on Taipei'.[578] The latter dismissed the 'threat and harassment' to the island saying that it was just another 'offensive by the pen and intimidation by the sword' trick designed to influence the presidential election in Taiwan. However, it added that 'the tactic has moved from an ordinary declaration of policy towards a nationwide mobilisation ... it also aims to put pressure on the president-elect and compel Taipei to come to the conference table.'

According to the editorial, Beijing was worried that under a new administration, Taiwan might resort to 'overt procrastination and covert independence'. It was because of this worry that the CPPCC launched a high-profile attack on Lee Teng-hui's 'state-to-state special relationship' theory and warned that 'to opt for *taidu* [Taiwan independence] would be to opt for war'.

The analysis went further to show evidence that Chinese tactics were effective:

> Chen Shui-bian ... has indicated he will neither have the 'state-to-state special relationship' theory included in the constitution nor propose a referendum on *taidu* [Taiwan independence] ... What they have done shows Beijing's offensive has roused a response from the Taiwan people.... Beijing has completed its preparations for mobilising the party, the government, the armed services and non-government groups.

The editorial concluded by endorsing the position of Beijing that:

> Taipei must come to the conference table rather than resort to delaying tactics when the election is over and that, unless it does so, Taipei will feel increasing political and military pressure from the mainland. That point merits the attention of those to whom the Taiwan question is of concern.[579]

Two days before polling day, things seemed to be going Chen Shui-bian's way, and *MPDN* came up with some advice for China on how to tackle the potential new president. In an editorial entitled 'Beijing "attack Bian"; but must have strategy',[580] it began questioning how Beijing could possibly tackle issues if Chen really got elected given that the Chinese leadership had repeatedly condemned him. It said 'Even though Chinese Premier Zhu Rongji sent out a severe warning, in fact, he has since had some reservations. In comparison, the position of the military generals seems to be more rigid. Thus it will be difficult to maintain face.' The editorial sensibly concluded by saying that 'in fact, Beijing should keep a cool head and give a period of grace to observe developments in Taiwan.' The ambivalent and conciliatory tone of the editorial can be explained by the rivalry between popular nationalism and Chinese official nationalism discussed in the contextual analysis. Because *MPDN* claimed to be the 'Chinese people's paper', it largely adopted the official Chinese viewpoint. However, as a leading Hong Kong Chinese-language daily, it also needed to take heed of local popular nationalistic sentiment, which was on the whole aspiring to, and impressed by, Taiwan's democratic movement and the success of Taiwan's peaceful transfer of power.

Relating the elections to Hong Kong readers

In order to establish the relevance of Chinese politics to Hong Kong, *MPDN* traditionally allocated space to regular commentators and occasional contributors to comment on current affairs. The opinions represented a wide political spectrum ranging from pro-China to relatively liberal commentators, from the viewpoints of academics to those of politicians. However, without substantial independent news reports and in-depth news analysis, this handful of views tended to be irrelevant and could not provide a vibrant forum. The views expressed appeared more and more incoherent following the 1997 handover. These commentaries had another function: to demonstrate that the paper remained a public space for various interests. Examining the distribution of authors, and the concerns raised, during the Taiwanese election campaign period may give an idea of how even an opinion-editorial page was affected by contextual constraints. For instance, in the paper's forum section, Timothy Wong Ka-ying, a research coordinator from Lingnan University (a Hong Kong university operating under the western liberal tradition), wrote, 'Beijing cannot tolerate permanent separation of the two places.'[581] Here, the message explicitly elaborated on the Chinese line, but, in any case, the Chinese position could not have been any clearer, the contribution simply served as an endorsement by the elite – an academic in this instance.

Contributions by politicians from both conservative and liberal camps were included as well. For example, Ng Hong-man, a Hong Kong Deputy to the NPC (a Chinese parliament without any democratically elected element), twice aired his views.[582] The Chairman of the pro-China political party, the Democratic Alliances for the Betterment of Hong Kong (DAB), wrote a commentary after the election;[583] so did the Chairman of the Hong Kong Democratic Party, the largest pro-democratic party in Hong Kong.[584] Other commentaries appeared to be making practical suggestions such as 'giving more time to Taiwan'[585] since the goal of 'making the most distasteful candidate unelectable'[586] had been defeated, and the Taiwanese had 'chosen one among the three bad apples'.[587]

Post-election coverage

The post-election coverage of *MPDN* was misconceived, especially its explanation for the downfall of the KMT and the victory of Taiwan's pro-independence movement. After the victory of Chen Shui-bian, the daily continued to advocate a cooling down period in its editorials, for instance, the one entitled 'A cooling down period and time for reflection is required across the Taiwan Strait'. In the post-election coverage, editorials never described the newly elected Chen Shui-bian as 'Taiwanese President'. Instead, they referred to him as the 'new Taiwanese leader'.[588] Of course, this was in line with the Chinese position, which regarded Taiwan as a renegade province of China. When the paper came to examine the aftermath of the defeat of the KMT, it printed two consecutive editorials to criticise both the KMT and the former president, Lee Teng-hui. In an editorial entitled 'The Kuomintang lost because it is not in touch with the people's will', it addressed the issue, and attributed the main reason for the defeat to Lee Teng-hui's pro-independence policy. It illustrated the point by saying, 'this is not the first time the KMT has lost power: last time it lost to the CCP because of its own corruption. This time it lost power in Taiwan for the same reason.'[589]

The KMT might well have lost power because of corruption. However, what the editorial did not explain was why the pro-independence standard-bearer, Chen Shui-bian, won the election. In another editorial entitled 'Lee Teng-hui promotes Taiwan independence and was taught a lesson',[590] the daily concluded that Lee Teng-hui was the 'black hand' behind the Taiwanese pro-independence movement, and that now his real face was exposed, more and more KMT members asked him to step down. 'More importantly, he will be responsible for any potential damage and loss of life in a future war across the Taiwan Strait.' It was indisputable that KMT party members had protested against Lee Teng-hui and demanded his resignation from the party's chairmanship. However, the editorial seemed to be far-fetched in predicting, first, that there would be a war and, second, that he would be responsible for 'damage and loss of life' in a war that had not yet happened.

The problem lies with political blindness. It blinded itself by blindly following the Beijing perspective in interpreting the outcome of Taiwan election. The political space for imagination is thus curtailed and the coverage is bounded to be misjudged and misleading.

Analysis

In sum, the Chinese Government perspective appeared to be predominant in this quality Chinese-language paper whose proprietor wished to turn it into a 'Chinese people's paper'. Here, the factor of popular nationalism was playing its role in countering official Chinese nationalism. The split within the Hong Kong elite may also have played a part in the paper's decision to allocate equal space to commentaries by both liberal and conservative politicians and academics.

Similarly, journalistic discourse could still be found in both news reports and commentary, though it was not given as much weight as nationalistic discourse. This perhaps could be explained by the economic implications for a newspaper operating in a market economy.

South China Morning Post

Sources used

South China Morning Post (*SCMP*) represents in its purest form the western liberal newspaper tradition. It is an English-language paper with a western editor, and many of the writers and editors are Europeans. While *MPDN* and *ODN* are in Chinese, and have mainly employed reporters and contributors from Hong Kong and mainland China in recent years, *SCMP* has a couple of Hong Kong Chinese and mainland Chinese reporters to cover both local Hong Kong news and news about China. The story-telling of *SCMP* was more or less in the tradition of the British liberal press with a fact-finding approach. In other words, it printed analysis, traced the background and attempted to explain the issues. For instance, it described the background to the clash across the Taiwan Strait and also the close economic relationship between Taiwan and the mainland. In an interview with the Vice-Director of the Institute of Taiwan Studies at the Chinese Academy of Social Sciences in Beijing, *SCMP* reported that Taiwanese investors had invested about US$40 million (Hong Kong $312 million) in the mainland by directing it through third parties, principally those in Hong Kong.[591]

Nature of coverage, headlines, use of pictures, etc.

Concerning the difference between the mainland 'one China' policy and the Taiwanese 'special-state-to-state' relationship advocated by the Taiwanese president, Lee Teng-hui, it reported what had been agreed in 1992. The report revealed that representatives from Taipei and Beijing had agreed that 'while there is one China, both sides can give their own definition [of statehood]'.[592]

Key elements of the Sino-Taiwanese controversy, namely the Chinese military exercise in 1996, Lee Teng-hui's pronouncement of a 'special-state-to-state' relationship with China, and China's current anxiety concerning the Taiwanese independence movement in 2000, were described in related news reports. The coverage was largely issue-oriented, and the analysis favoured the Taiwanese perspective and concerns about human rights.

The turning point was the publication of the White Paper, documenting the mainland's policy on Taiwan concerning the issue of reunification.[593] The news reports used loaded terms such as 'big stick' and 'carrot' to describe the Chinese policy. For instance, in an agency story entitled 'Sabre-rattling replaced with direct-trade lure', *SCMP* said: 'after threatening Taiwan with the stick of war, Beijing held out the carrot of direct trade.'[594] However, in another report entitled 'U.S. "inflating Taiwan arrogance" – Washington bears unshakable responsibility for tensions in Taiwan Strait, says Beijing', the English-language daily explained the origin of China's Taiwan policy. This policy was laid down by Deng Xiaoping, a senior Chinese leader who advocated economic reform in the late 1970s and early 1980s.[595] Moreover, the White Paper was dismissed by Taiwan's political commentator who said: 'Last time [4 years before] they fired a real missile and it drew voters to President Lee Teng-hui. This time they fired a paper missile instead.'[596]

SCMP generally also only used one large picture per page, like most modern English-language papers, so the choice of picture was key in determining subliminal messages.

SCMP coverage of U.S./western involvement

The English-language daily not only covered the subject matter of the Sino-Taiwanese confrontation, it also pointed out the involvement of western countries. As events unfolded, the paper covered issues that were concerned with the two governments across the Taiwan Strait as well as those involving foreign powers, particularly the U.S. For instance, in a report entitled 'U.S. warns Beijing over Taiwan threat', it was reported from Washington D.C. that 'the U.S. intensified its concern over mainland threats to use force to reunify with Taiwan, with a senior Pentagon official warning of "incalculable consequences".'[597] The role of the U.S. was given substantially more weight in *SCMP*'s coverage than the Chinese-language papers. Apart from the updated report on the United States' influence on the Sino-Taiwanese confrontation, the positions of other foreign governments such as Australia were reported as well. In a news report from Sydney entitled 'Australia warns over Taipei threat', *SCMP* said: 'a tumultuous week in Sino-Australian relations has culminated in the Chinese Ambassador being officially warned of Canberra's opposition to Beijing's recent threat to Taiwan.' These reports helped to shed light on Chinese repression and added an international dimension to what was seemingly a Chinese dispute.

SCMP provided analytical reporting on the latest developments in the situation. Regarding the Chinese publication of the White Paper, *SCMP* printed a report entitled 'Beijing issues new war threat'[598] that went to the heart of the matter. With regards to Taiwan's response, a report stated explicitly in the headline that Taiwan felt intimidated: 'Taipei stays defiant on sovereignty – stop intimidation, Beijing told'.[599] The report also gave space in the lead paragraph to a Taiwanese official who said: 'Taiwan yesterday issued a defiant riposte to Beijing's threat to use force to achieve reunification, insisting the island is an independent, sovereign state.'[600]

In dealing with the complexity of the subject matter, *SCMP* adopted straightforward journalistic tactics, relaying information that was newsworthy. On the one hand, an *SCMP* report relayed an editorial from the Chinese official newspaper, *People's Daily*, indicating that the Central Government could be flexible:

Beijing wanted reunification as soon as possible, but was willing to offer concessions, including pushing forward personnel exchanges in the economic and cultural fields and establishing direct links in trade, transport and postal services.[601]

On the other hand, and more importantly, the *SCMP* report pointed out Chinese lies and also the White Paper's unreasonable demands concerning reunification by quoting a Taiwanese official:

'Despite going through various internal and external environmental changes since 1912, the Republic of China [Taiwan] has not only not ceased [to exist], rather it has stood firm and continued to grow strong', Mr. Lin said ... In its White Paper, Beijing said that in 1949, 'the Republic of China's historic position was terminated' and the People's Republic [of China] was the sole government exercising sovereignty over all of China, including Taiwan. 'These positions completely deny reality', Mr. Lin said.[602]

Furthermore, it also indicated that there was not yet a unanimous position regarding the schedule for reunification with Taiwan by quoting the semi-official *China News Services*. In a report entitled 'Reunification in 20 years, says scholar – Beijing 'remains committed to peaceful solution', a researcher at the Institute of Taiwan Studies at the Chinese Academy of Social Sciences in Beijing told *China News Services* that the White Paper did not include a reunification timetable, so that there would be 'greater flexibility' for Beijing to seize the initiative on the Taiwan issue.[603]

Editorial line: lacking in conviction

Although the coverage of *SCMP* appeared to adhere to journalistic discourse that revealed the repressive nature of the Central Government, the paper's editorial position tended to lack conviction as regards to expressing it explicitly. During the Sino-Taiwanese conflict, Hong Kong was placed in a sensitive position. Paradoxically, although Hong Kong had benefited from the animosity between the two powers, it was now part of China.[604] In these circumstances, although *SCMP* carried upfront reports on Sino-Taiwanese tensions, it nevertheless appeared unable to criticise China's reunification policy on Taiwan openly. For example, it refrained from discussing the justification for Beijing's threat to Taiwan. In its editorial entitled 'Helpful ambiguity', it attempted to explain the reason behind Beijing's policy on Taiwan:

In response to the 'three ifs' in Beijing's recently published White Paper on Taiwan are three 'whys' ... Beijing's policy of alternating between tough and soft words on Taiwan could be connected with the need to placate the hard-line old guard which yearns to see the island back in the fold, like Hong Kong and Macau.[605]

While the editorial acknowledges that Taiwan was different from Hong Kong and Macau in the sense that unlike the latter two it was not a colony but 'a thriving democracy whose people do not react well to threats', it did not give an upfront critique of Chinese intimidation. Instead it advocated the need for 'delicate behind-the-scenes diplomacy to calm matters'. Finally it concluded that this could best be done by 'restoring the ambiguity that existed previously in cross-Strait relations'.[606]

Post-election coverage relating to Hong Kong readers

In the aftermath of the Taiwanese election, the relevance of the election for Hong Kong was seen in both news reports and the commentary section, which seemingly represented Hong Kong's aspiration to have a similar democratic system. In one *SCMP* news report, Hong Kong residents were said to praise the Taiwanese electorate for casting 'courageous' votes, saying 'Hong Kong people say they should be allowed to choose their own political leader'.[607]

In another analysis entitled 'Taiwan vote "good for Hong Kong" ',[608] the staff writer aspired to Taiwan's peaceful transfer of political power via general election. Moreover, there were contributors and columnists who favourably reported on Taiwan's success in conducting the presidential election smoothly, despite mainland China's threats.[610]

However, *SCMP* also printed articles casting doubt on Chen Shui-bian's stature and experience, for example, 'Chen's political skills face a daunting test'[611] and the editorial entitled 'Party Hangover'.[612]

The contrast between Hong Kong's undemocratic post-colonial situation and Taiwan's newly acquired democracy has become an issue since the Taiwanese election. The relevance of Hong Kong was best illustrated by president-elect, Chen Shui-bian, when he was quoted in *SCMP* as saying: 'we don't want "one country, two systems" and Taiwanese voters don't want Taiwan to become like Hong Kong and Macau'.[613] After Chen crushed the KMT in the election, he offered an olive branch to Beijing but warned, 'Taiwan must never become a second Hong Kong'.[614] The undemocratic nature of Hong Kong's political system, which was much inferior to the democracy of Taiwan, was rightly pointed out. The Hong Kong system was held up as an unviable model; this helped explain why Taiwan did not want to accept the Chinese offer of 'one country, two systems'.[615]

Similarly, Martin Lee, Chairman of the Hong Kong Democratic Party and the most outspoken of China's critics, was quoted in a report as saying that he 'lauded Taiwan democracy'. Yet, although he praised Taiwan's system of government, he also said 'promoting democratic reform had become harder in Hong Kong since the 1997 handover ... I hope Taiwan and Hong Kong can continue [to] influence progress in the mainland towards [the] democratic rule of law.'[616]

SCMP's coverage in the context of western liberal media values

As discussed earlier in the contextual analysis, there was a constant struggle between the official Chinese nationalistic/patriotic call and the popular nationalistic appeal. The English-language daily was keen to report on the response of the general populace to the Taiwanese election, and to contrast the Taiwanese with the people on China's side of the Taiwan Strait, who were denied democracy based on popular election.

The gap between China and Taiwan was shown to be huge when it was reported that the 1.2 billion mainland Chinese were kept in the dark over the island's politics. Covering an Agence France-Presse (AFP) story entitled 'Mainland in dark on island politics', *SCMP* said, 'Most mainland Chinese have only a vague idea about the 13 years of democratic reforms in Taiwan and are in the dark about this week's election which has been banished from the pages of the state press.'[617] The press blackout on the mainland and the consequent ignorance of the mainland Chinese were reflected in the question asked by a Beijing souvenir vendor: 'Will Lee Teng-hui be re-elected?' The mainland Chinese were unaware that Taiwan's President was not standing for re-election. The information circulating in mainland China was at best partial and at worst biased. For instance, Lee Teng-hui was regularly vilified in the mainland press as a 'trouble-maker' and 'splitter' working to ensure Taiwan's separation from China.

Analysis

Although *SCMP* apparently chose to stick to the journalistic discourse in reporting the cross-Strait tensions, it also appeared not to dispute the 'one-China' policy. In the sensitive post-colonial circumstances, it appeared difficult to deny the integrity of Chinese territory and national sovereignty; so it was natural for the mainland to claim back Taiwan. The logic followed that if Taiwan indefinitely delayed negotiations on reunification, the mainland had cause to speed up the process by any means, including the use of military force. As the Chinese Foreign Ministry spokesman, Zhu Bangzao, was quoted in *SCMP* as saying: 'after the return of Hong Kong and Macau's return to the embrace of the motherland, it is natural that we have this urgency in solving the problem of Taiwan, the question of Taiwan cannot be dragged on indefinitely.'[618] Bearing in mind the change in ownership of *SCMP*, and the Chinese leadership's repeated nationalistic call and warnings, the paper was under enormous pressure to conform. It is not surprising that it included analyses from the pro-China camp, such as a commentary by Shiu Sin-por, a researcher from the China camp, entitled 'Taiwan mocks the election process'.[619] It was not, in fact, entirely new for the paper to include opinions from the pro-China camp. More telling perhaps was the editorial position of the paper on the eve of polling day. In its editorial entitled 'Turning up the heat', *SCMP* said:

> Mindful of the fact that most Taiwanese are not prepared to go to war with the mainland now that they have already achieved de facto independence

> ... the risk is that belligerent statements by Mr. Zhu Rongji [the Chinese
> Premier] may so offend the Taiwanese electorate that they will ignore his
> warnings and vote for the candidate Beijing considers most undesirable.[620]

Although mild, this was a key statement. It was one of the few times the Hong
Kong press stated the true and obvious fact that Taiwan was functioning as a
nation in all but name. But neither *ODN* nor *MPDN* ever made this obvious
point in their editorials.

Differences and similarities between coverage

To sum up, in covering such a major media event, all three newspapers deployed
their resources to ensure they received dispatches from Washington D.C.,
Taipei, Keelung (a coastal city in Taiwan), Kaohsiung (a southern city in
Taiwan), Beijing and Shanghai. They also relied on anonymous sources and
non-staff contributors for up-to-date news reports and commentaries.

ODN tended to be ambiguous in terms of its editorials, but it covered stories
ranging from the political to the human interest. This mass circulation Chinese-
language daily often turned political news into sensational stories in order to
appeal to the widest readership. It adopted tactics such as juxtaposing a news
story and a photo story, when the tone of the latter might not necessarily be consistent with that of the former. In this way, readers were not led to a definite conclusion but were rather given space to form their own opinion.

MPDN was more definite in its editorial position in terms of selection and
display of news reports. This intellectual daily, which appealed to the Chinese
elite in Hong Kong, represented the dominant discourse in the post-colonial
period, which was largely a patriotic-nationalist one. However, even *MPDN*,
which attempted to live up to its claim to be the 'Chinese people's paper', could
not totally disregard western liberal journalistic norms. In other words, it could
not afford to omit significant news, though it might cast it in a particular light in
the way it framed the story, and by the adoption of official terminology.

The English-language daily, *SCMP*, was relatively liberal and seemingly created
a public space in which readers could interpret news events and formulate their own
opinions. However, even in respect of such a relatively liberal paper, which enjoyed
a journalistic tradition lasting over a century, evidence still showed that it also operated under the constraints of the internal and external environment.

Analysis

Common ground between papers: a shared discourse

The three daily newspapers all shared a common discourse, i.e. the post-
colonial/nationalistic discourse. In other words, during the Taiwanese election,
they all chose not to dispute the Chinese line of national sovereignty and territorial integrity. Even though we can see that *ODN* and *SCMP* sometimes deviated

from this line by employing 'factual reporting' or measures (such as using anonymous or foreign sources occasionally), the political guideline of taking 'social responsibility' was faithfully followed.

Regarding newspapers attempting to make the issue more relevant to Hong Kong readers: there were reports that Hong Kong could be involved in any military action, and reports that the Hong Kong garrison of the People's Liberation Army (PLA) was on 'high alert' etc.[621] To some reporters, the 'high alert' story was 'released by China explicitly to try and raise tensions in Hong Kong and make Hong Kong people turn against Taiwan and its democratic system, making democracy appear disruptive and troublesome'.[622] According to one reporter, at least one of the photographs released by *Xinhua News Agency*, the Chinese official news propaganda machine, and used by Hong Kong papers was 'faked to make pictures of China's military might appear more impressive'.[623] The three papers in this study seem not to have handled this news. They neither questioned nor analysed it.

Key differences

IMPACT OF PRESENTATION

The key differences among the three dailies, however, resulted from differences in presentation, and the degree to which their proprietor interfered with editorial content. While *MPDN* very often adopted the official Chinese terminology, *ODN* chose to adopt evasive tactics, such as juxtaposition and ambiguity, and the use of misleading emphasis in headlines. The English-language *SCMP* chose to adhere to the British liberal press tradition, and appeared to be the most upfront, factual and balanced of the three in its reportage and commentary.

IMPACT OF OWNER

The impact of the owners on the three dailies can only be seen by implication at this stage. The mass circulation *ODN* may have been concerned about its appeal to the general reader. The strong emphasis on economic profits might have meant that journalists were able to counter the apparent state and ideological pressures in the changing political environment. The reason for this is that most Hong Kong people after just three years of Chinese rule did not subscribe to mainland political thinking, and papers that explicitly adopted China's line on all matters sold fewer copies. Therefore, profit-chasing caused the paper to reject the mainland political framework. While the proprietor's influence on *ODN* in this specific case study may not be absolutely clear, the impact of the Malaysian Chinese businessman/proprietor on *MPDN* can be demonstrated more confidently. The evidence of the paper's selection of news topics, news angle and even choice of questions to election candidates all point the same way, that is, the paper has completely adopted China's viewpoint on the Taiwan issue. This complete acceptance of China's position might have something to do with the owner's desire to turn the paper into the 'Chinese people's paper'.

Contrary to the nationalistic position of *MPDN*, *SCMP*, though also owned by a Malaysian Chinese businessman, perhaps found a way to absorb the owner's impact and continue to uphold its journalistic professionalism in a distinct way.

IMPACT OF JOURNALISTIC CULTURE

The generally balanced and factual analytical reporting of *SCMP* demonstrates the impact of journalistic culture on the complex interaction between the political economy of the media and the journalistic profession. Even in the cases of nationalistic *MPDN* and mass circulation *ODN*, we can find evidence of the impact of journalistic culture here and there.

Concluding remarks

The three arguments discussed in the section on contextual analysis, namely official nationalism versus popular nationalism, factionalism within Hong Kong and the political economy factor in the media, all played a role in either restricting or enhancing the journalistic practices of the Hong Kong press.

From a media coverage viewpoint, this Taiwanese election was unprecedented in Chinese society: a popular election involving millions of people rallying and campaigning that also inspired the 7 million inhabitants of Hong Kong.

Similarly, the highly sensitive nature of the confrontation between the mainland and Taiwan had an impact on the Hong Kong economy and disrupted the balance of stability in Asia. On the surface, newspapers like *ODN*, *MPDN* and even *SCMP*, on the whole adopted the Chinese perspective on the ideological battle between Taiwan and the mainland. The Chinese call for reunification with Taiwan appeared to be natural and legitimate within the national goal of accomplishing and maintaining national sovereignty and territorial integrity. According to this way of thinking, it was not right to argue otherwise. Therefore, news reports of a Chinese nationalistic nature were prominently displayed and presented as authoritative. However, because market forces and the western liberal journalistic culture exerted a pull in the opposite direction, the reporting and editorial line could appear confused, and sometimes contradictory.

5   Regime change and media control

Introduction

The Chinese regime's media policy aimed to place restrictions on, and stream-line, its media to serve its purpose. However, the Hong Kong media were far from cooperative, though some have compromised even if they have not entirely complied with the new rules. The introduction to the annual report on freedom of expression in Hong Kong, compiled by the Hong Kong Journalists Association and Article 19, described the five years since the political regime change as 'hav[ing] proved worrisome ones for freedom of expression – not worrisome in the sense that there has been a definitive and unambiguous erosion of this important right, but worrisome nonetheless. The coming five years may yet prove more challenging.'[624] The report then went on to describe how 'the environment for vibrant and healthy free expression, and a free press, in Hong Kong has become hazy, and more ambiguous, since 1997.' What caused the press freedom watchdogs to condemn the erosion of freedom of expression was a growing awareness that the media were being manipulated in a number of ways including political control, economic corruption and suppression.

My argument in this chapter is that a control mechanism was at work during the five years since 1997. Though this mechanism was not unique, and had been operating since the transition period, it had nevertheless become more sophistic-ated. However, the effect of this control mechanism was uncertain, judging from the resistance of practitioners to it and the ongoing negotiations revealed by interviewees who included management and senior editorial staff.

Two trends in media development can be noted in 2002: a rising political caution, and a strong inclination to 'dumb down' the media five years after the political handover of Hong Kong. Political intervention was regarded not as overt but a result of market forces producing corruption and suppression, as it became increasingly evident that political caution and sensationalism/ trivialisation have become two sides of the same coin. The political caution included, for instance, limited coverage of Taiwanese politics and actions related to the independence of Taiwan; the activities of the spiritual meditation group, Falun Gong; Tibet and Xinjiang; and criticism of the Chinese leadership.

This chapter does not attempt to investigate the degree to which press freedom in Hong Kong has been eroded. Rather, it traces the causes of the contraction of press freedom by analysing the control exerted, primarily, by the owner; and the effect of the decolonisation process and its subsequent impact on the political economy, and cultural and social aspects. I shall specifically investigate the structural change in Hong Kong society, and the structural change that took place in news organisations and institutes, to find an explanation for the materialisation of this apparently 'hazy, and more ambiguous' environment, and its link to the instalment of a new political regime.

This chapter and Chapter 6 are based primarily on the findings of face-to-face in-depth interviews with 56 journalists and senior news executives at major print media and some broadcasting media in Hong Kong. They were selected primarily according to two guiding principles.[625] First, they had personal knowledge of the issues and events covered in the case studies analysed in Chapters 2 to 4. Second, almost two-thirds of them were high-ranking editorial or managerial news practitioners who were either policy and decision-makers, or enjoyed access to the daily deliberative process. Journalists at all levels were approached using the press list of the Hong Kong Journalists Association, but the focus is more on senior people as they are rarely interviewed, and were more involved in decision-making and policy-making.[626] Fifty-seven individuals were contacted, with only one refusal. The purpose of the interviews was to understand better the influence of politics and economics on the functioning of news organisations in general, and the influence of political change in particular. The following people were interviewed: six senior reporters, columnists or editorial writers; ten news editors and five academic contributors; 35 senior news executives, including 15 deputy or chief editors, two chief executive officers and a manager; 11 executive producers or broadcasters; and six publishers or proprietors. Interviewees were drawn from different levels of the hierarchy as well as from different mainstream media organisations, so that there was both vertical and horizontal representation.

The investigation is intended to be representative of the political spectrum as well as of opinion within a particular news organisation. Representing the left were journalists from Beijing-backed *Wen Wei Po*, *Ta Kung Pao* and *Xinhua News Agency*. The more liberal news organisations included *SCMP*, *Hong Kong Economic Journal* and *MPDN*. The mass circulation newspapers, *ODN* and *Apple Daily*, represent the middle ground. A full list highlighting representation across news organisations can be found in Tables 4.1 to 4.3 of the appendix. Some of the interviewees were interviewed and written to more than once. The average time spent on each interview was between 60 and 90 minutes. The total time devoted to interviews amounted to around 4,000 minutes. The interviewees have mostly remained anonymous in order to protect their confidentiality. However, there are exceptions, in which case the prior consent of the person in question was secured. In addition to these interviews, the two chapters also draw upon a large amount of information published in newspapers, journals and research publications.

Flak

From the transition period to the post-colonial era, there were concerns regarding state policy towards the Hong Kong media. First, the tightening of policy was exemplified by a series of tirades by senior Chinese officials in the 1990s, especially after the Tiananmen crackdown. For example, Chinese Vice Premier, Qian Qichen, issued seven guidelines to be observed by the Hong Kong, Macau, Taiwanese and foreign media when covering news about China.[627] The attack on the Hong Kong press included condemnation of the so-called promotion and advocacy of 'subversive and separatist' views relating to the Chinese dissident states, Taiwan, Xinjiang and Tibet, with Taiwan as the most sensitive issue in the five years following the handover.[628] However, China did not forbid the commemoration of the 1989 Beijing Student Movement.[629] One explanation for China's accommodation of the 1989 and 4 June vigil held in Hong Kong was that Beijing believed that those in self-exile did not pose an immediate threat to the rule of the Chinese Communist Party (CCP). However, this does not mean that the CCP relaxed its grip on the Hong Kong media.

As 1997 drew closer, China aimed strong rhetoric at certain Hong Kong media organisations and their journalists who continued to be outspoken about China. It is known that the CCP traditionally regarded the news media as one of the four best weapons for control and rule; the others being the military, the party and propaganda. Thus the news media were regarded as being as important as the military.[630] The flak directed at the Hong Kong media created psychological pressure on journalists and management alike. This psychological pressure caused writers to limit the legitimate scope of their reporting voluntarily and to set political boundaries. The effect of this was apparent in respect of issues such as Taiwan and its relations with China, as shown in Chapter 4. Attacks on the media took a variety of forms. Before 1997, Lu Ping, the director of the Hong Kong and Macau Affairs Office, State Council, issued a warning against advocating the independence of Taiwan, Tibet and Xinjiang province.[631] As described above, Qian Qichen, Chinese Vice Premier, laid down clear ground rules for post-1997 reportage, for example, no criticism of the Chinese leadership was allowed.[632] The Central Government's representative in Hong Kong, Wang Fengchao, the deputy director of the China Liaison Office in Hong Kong,[633] together with other pro-China allies, took the lead in condemning a *Cable TV* reporter's interview with the newly elected Taiwanese deputy president, Annette Lu.[634]

Flak from all sides continued after 1997 and became even more explicit and direct. Posing questions to Chinese leaders was interpreted as challenging the authorities, so it was condemned. A Hong Kong reporter was criticised for asking the Chinese Premier, Zhu Rongji, for his reaction to the protest by Reporters Sans Frontières (Reporters Without Borders).[635] The spokesman lectured the reporter saying that she should have been grateful to be part of the Chinese press delegation allowed to cover the Premier's foreign trip.[636]

In a separate incident, Jiang Zemin, General Secretary of the CCP, attacked the professionalism of Hong Kong journalists, calling them 'simpl[istic] and sometimes naïve'. He reacted incredibly strongly when asked whether it was an 'imperial order' from Beijing for Tung Chee-hwa, the Chief Executive of the Hong Kong Special Administrative Region (HKSAR), to serve a second term of office from the year 2002.[637] The Chinese leader regarded the question as embarrassing, and complained that the Hong Kong press was not sufficiently patriotic to show political sensitivity. Although the Hong Kong Chief Executive was elected by a group of several hundred representatives, it was nothing close to a democratic election.[638]

Central and provincial influence

Not only top Chinese leaders, but provincial officials also pointed the finger at the Hong Kong press when the latter continued to practise critical and independent journalism on mainland China's territory. This also reveals a sharp rivalry between the HKSAR and other provinces in terms of promoting local interests.[639] For instance, in early 2003, a mayor of Guangzhou city (the capital of Guangdong province, the southern Chinese province neighbouring Hong Kong) openly criticised a Hong Kong reporter for bringing a Hong Kong journalistic way of doing things to Guangdong province.[640] The Chinese official found it irritating to face unexpected questions, so he rebuked the reporter for pointing out the government's accountability on certain issues.

This indicates that two levels of control mechanism were at work: first, the Central Government versus the HKSAR, and second, the HKSAR administration versus provincial ones. Local people, such as the Hong Kong representative and pro-China allies, helped to keep the control mechanism operating, but sometimes they overdid things in their efforts to make the press conform. For example, a journalist who unsuccessfully attempted to interview the deputy Taiwanese President, Annette Lu, was accused of contravening the Chinese media regulations.[641]

From China's perspective, the importance of Hong Kong declined following Hong Kong's return to China. China had progressed enormously both economically and socially over time. The economic boom of China's southern and coastal provinces, for example, following reform and the open door policy put in place two decades before, meant China need not rely so heavily on Hong Kong for investment, information and a window to the west. Both overseas and domestic business opportunities could be enjoyed without the mediation of Hong Kong. In fact, both the Hong Kong business community and professionals turned to the mainland Chinese market for investment opportunities and jobs.

Marginalisation

The Chinese authorities could in turn make use of the new interest in China to make journalists as well as publishers fall into line with the official Chinese position. Coercion has taken different forms, such as interrogation of journalists, and blacklisting them and their newspapers from covering official events in mainland China. In some of the worst cases journalists were detained for periods lasting from several hours to days, and only released after signing letters of repentance. Journalists have been put behind bars for years or been deported from the country, having had their travel documents confiscated and being permanently banned from re-entering the country.[642]

Physical restrictions have been a serious blow to news reporters on the China beat, as well as foreign correspondents. This has not been carried out randomly; unwanted visitors/journalists have been targeted to serve as a deterrent to others. Their only 'crime' has been either that their reportage/writing has been categorised as 'unfavourable' to China,[643] or simply because of the reporter's association with a 'hostile' or 'unfriendly' news organisation.[644]

Economic suppression

The Chinese specifically targeted those who owned media organisations or who had influence within them. They used verbal threats and economic sanctions against their enemies, but actively solicited the support of those they considered to be their friends. Amongst the former was Jimmy Lai, an entrepreneur born in China who had fled to Hong Kong for a better life, and later became a media tycoon. Lai wept when he talked about the imminent reunification with China, apparently because he feared that the incoming government would take away all the freedom he had hoped to enjoy.[645] Lai had started as an entrepreneur specialising in the garment business. In contrast to previous newspaper proprietors, whose newspapers were their only business, his newspaper businesses, including *Apple Daily*, were a secondary interest for him. After he started *Next Magazine* in Hong Kong in the early 1990s, his garment business in mainland China was subjected to violence and regulatory restrictions, apparently because of the critical and popular stance of *Next Magazine* and *Apple Daily*. After his garment business was sabotaged by the Chinese authorities he sold all his shares and severed links with the company completely. His media business then became his only business. The prohibition on *Next Magazine* and *Apple Daily* from covering news in China continued, however.[646]

Carrot tactics

The Chinese authorities, on the other hand, were skilled at wooing specific businessmen and women whom they regarded as potential friends. The rewards they offered to those who contributed to Chinese reunification were not at all dissimilar to those the British had in the past given to members of the Chinese elite for help in ruling their colony. The rewards offered by the Chinese after 1997 ranged from Bauhinia Award[647] and appointments as advisers on Hong Kong affairs, to recommendations to Beijing that their favoured should become people's representatives, such as deputies of the National People's Congress (NPC) and delegates to the Chinese People's Political Consultative Conference (CPPCC).

The distinctive feature here is that the central authorities as well as the HKSAR government appeared to be keen to give prestige status or a nationalistic identity to newspaper proprietors, such as Sally Aw (the former proprietor of Chinese-language *Sing Tao Daily News*), Charles Ho (the current proprietor of *Sing Tao Daily News*) and Robert Kuok (the proprietor of the English-language daily, *South China Morning Post (SCMP)*). These tactics helped to influence media organisations to write about the administration in a favourable light. As well as wooing newspaper proprietors, special efforts were made to facilitate and respond to journalistic demands. For instance, an exclusive interview was granted to Thomas Abraham, the editor of *SCMP*, by Chinese vice premier, Qian Qichen, on the eve of the fifth anniversary of the establishment of the HKSAR.[648] Unsurprisingly, the interview proved mutually beneficial. In that article, *SCMP* helped to convey the Chinese message that 'there would not be any major change in the election concerning Hong Kong Legislative Council and the Chief Executive in 2007 as promised by the mini-constitution of the Hong Kong Basic Law.'[649]

Other tactics included giving special briefings to certain inner circle daily newspapers. Some senior journalists received personal phone calls from the Chief Executive, Tung Chee-hwa, requesting them to tone down negative news, for example, that he had secretly abolished a controversial project to build 85,000 public housing units a year. However, the papers he contacted largely maintained their 'independence'.[650] Apart from one quality paper that did what the Chief Executive asked, other papers, informed by an anonymous official source, maintained their 'independent' judgement and covered the story in various ways.[651] Special trips were also arranged for journalists at the provincial level so as to familiarise them with the country so they could help paint a rosy picture of China. Even the 'unfriendly' *Apple Daily* was wooed to the same end. It was invited to apply for these field trips, though it was turned down at the last minute. This indicates the rigidity of the central policy whereas there might be some leeway at provincial level.[652]

The British legacy

The Chinese authorities consciously and actively made the media fall into line with a central policy that emphasised 'social responsibility' and 'patriotism'. Some journalists were reminded of the British way of handling the media. During the last decade of British rule, the Hong Kong government shifted on the whole from a suppressive and heavy-handed policy[653] to a more persuasive approach aimed at building up mutual trust and bonds with the press. One journalist who has worked in both London and Hong Kong for many years commented on the British style of media manipulation: 'Sometimes they [the British] only carried out a certain policy with no discussion; sometimes they made lots of noise but in fact made no concrete moves.'[654] In this way, the British could manipulate the media behind the scenes without being perceived as disturbing public life too much. Unlike its predecessor, the HKSAR government rushed to announce policies such as the plan to construct 85,000 public housing units a year without taking heed of the impact on the property market and in turn on the economy. Once that plan was announced, the property market collapsed, which adversely affected the public at large and damaged the economy. Yet some journalists appreciated the new regime, as they regarded it as being more 'open and fair'. Following the handover, the government, as the major source of information, consciously cultivated different newspapers as their leak channels.[655]

Rivalry among the elite

The attitude of the HKSAR government towards the media did, however, differ from that of its predecessor in the sense that, on the whole, it adopted the Chinese perception of what the media's role should be. That is, the media should take up the role of 'social responsibility' and be patriotic to the country. This attitude was most apparent during a crisis. During the initial spread of the Severe Acute Respiratory Symptom (SARS) epidemic, the Hong Kong media in general gave it prominent and extensive coverage. However, Long Yong-tu, a senior Chinese official, said that the media had 'exaggerated and over-reacted' which might cause unnecessary public panic.[656] A member of the old elite, Donald Tsang, then Chief Secretary, defended the Hong Kong media saying that they had done a good job, and a favour to Hong Kong and China.[657] In contrast to the 'residual liberty' enjoyed by the Hong Kong press, two *Xinhua News Agency* editors were sacked when they released confidential documents relating to SARS.[658] This discrepancy in attitude towards the news media shows the inherent problems with the 'one country, two systems' policy[659] and the incompatibility between the official Chinese mentality and that of its Hong Kong counterpart.

Even within Hong Kong, the rivalry among the elite was acute. During the implementation of HKSAR policy (including media policy), discrepancies in attitude appeared between the old and the new elite. This gave the media space to manoeuvre. On a deeper level, Chinese attacks on the media jeopardised Hong Kong's enjoyment of a high degree of autonomy, and revealed the rivalry between the centrally appointed new elite and the British-groomed old elite. For example, as regards the approach to the Falun Gong, Chinese officials and pro-China allies were seen as interfering with Hong Kong's autonomy when they openly condemned the Falun Gong in Hong Kong, whereas some Hong Kong officials, including Anson Chan, the Chief Secretary and deputy to the Chief Executive, allowed them to hold functions in Hong Kong government owned venues. The Beijing-backed *Wen Wei Po* said that 'to allow a subversive group to hold functions on Chinese land' was unacceptable, and indicative of the 'uncooperative' attitude of the old elite who were suspected of retaining allegiance to the former regime.[660]

It is doubtful whether the theory that Anson Chan continued to owe allegiance to the British holds water, despite the fact she wrote an article in *Financial Times* after she retired from her job, criticising the way the HKSAR handled clashes with provincial interests, and expressing concerns about the enactment of anti-subversion laws in Hong Kong.[661] However, it is quite obvious that British-groomed senior officials might have very different concerns regarding the definition of Hong Kong jurisdiction, and indeed the concept of the rule of law. Apparently, the government was playing a game on this – they threatened to ban the Falun Gong, as a way to ease pressure from Beijing. It appeared that Anson Chan was more concerned about the future direction of political reform and the setting up of the accountability system, which weakened the power of Chan's beloved civil service.

During the first five years following the handover, the clash between the old and new regimes was exemplified by the different mentalities of, and approaches adopted by, the Chief Executive and the Chief Secretary. Although both of the two top officials openly denied that they had any differences, when Anson Chan, the Chief Secretary, offered her resignation for personal reasons, the Chief Executive, Tung Chee-hwa, accepted it right away without trying to persuade her to stay. The main differences were apparent in the implementation of policy, and in sensitive matters such as whether Hong Kong should ban the Falun Gong. The Chief Executive openly said it was an 'evil cult', but the Chief Secretary approved the rental of public venues to the Falun Gong to hold its functions.[662] Anson Chan also emphasised the importance of civil service neutrality and immunity from party politics, but this was not echoed by the Chief Executive, Tung Chee-hwa.[663]

During the Chief Executive's second term of service, the split was not just between the old and new elite, there was also acute competition among the new elite themselves. Rivals within the cabinet of the Chief Executive leaked to the press highly confidential minutes of the Executive Council, which showed the malpractice of the Finance Secretary, Anthony Leung, who had benefited from insider information.[664] It appears that no consensus was reached and the colonial legacy was still at work.

Restructuring and reorientation of the media

In anticipation of a new political culture triggered by a new political regime, there appeared to be a major restructuring of media ownership, and indeed a reorientation of the media during the political transition as well as in the post-colonial period.[665] Broadly speaking, the changes were a fading out of Taiwanese influence and British domination, and a new pro-China atmosphere with a pro-unification ideology. For instance, long-standing Taiwan-funded newspapers closed down, in one case because it was financially unviable,[666] in the case of two others because of the political consideration that it might not be safe for Taiwan-funded papers to remain beyond 1997.[667] The handover 'deadline' also witnessed the closure of a China-funded daily, *New Evening Post*, with the excuse given that its historical role was completed.[668] The more likely cause, in fact, was that there was no longer such a desperate need for so many China-funded dailies[669] to exist beyond 1997 as other 'independent' dailies started to come into line with the official position.

The majority of newspapers with historical connections to Taiwan severed their links, and instead adopted a pro-Hong Kong stance. These included the best-selling *Oriental Daily News*, the quality *Sing Tao Daily News* (*STDN*) and mass circulation *Sing Pao Daily News*. This perhaps can be explained as a reaction to the guidelines laid down by the Chinese authorities that prohibited criticism of the Chinese leadership, and advocacy of the sovereignty of Taiwan, Xinjiang and Tibet. Some daily newspapers, such as English-language *SCMP*, Chinese-language *Ming Pao Daily News* (*MPDN*) and *STDN*, were sold to pro-China proprietors. It can only be assumed that the pro-China business community was interested in buying up newspapers that previously might have had a clear anti-China or pro-establishment position in order to help the new political masters.[670] As a result of the restructuring of ownership, there emerged a pattern that the business interests of the corporation became paramount. Thus the independence of the press might not be the priority of the whole company. The management might wish to reorganise the editorial emphasis and resources actively, and this in turn affected both journalists and readers.

Subsequently, the political spectrum of the news media narrowed. First, the pro-Taiwan and anti-CCP news media virtually faded out; although some retained their old title and format, they stopped using the kind of language or tone that might be interpreted as hostile or critical to the Chinese regime. Second, the ownership shifted from 'journalist/proprietor' to corporate/business, for example, *MPDN* and *STDN*.[671] Third, along with the restructuring of ownership, there was a reorientation of the editorial positions of newspapers to cater for the new political and economic environment.

Effect on the organisation of news

As a result of the above-mentioned control mechanism, there was a change in the attitude towards professional journalists. The respect for journalism's norms and routines appeared to be diminishing, and management no longer regarded journalists as an asset as much as before, but rather regarded them as a liability.[672] In the conflict between management and staff, the editor was seemingly 'sandwiched' between the publisher and the journalists – sometimes acting as an unsuccessful negotiating agent. The difficulty was that often even the editor could not convince himself/herself that it was right for the management to intervene in journalistic routines, by, for example, sacking an outstanding journalist.

South China Morning Post

Under these circumstances, the case of *SCMP*, a westernised and relatively independent English-language newspaper, is a telling example. It has been described as slowly 'heading to its death'[673] – editorial independence was slowly eroded, and management interests became so rampant and overriding that, in the end, the publisher had the last word in the editorial department. Over time, the newspaper changed from being a long-standing pro-British daily to a newspaper supporting the rule of the Chinese regime.

However, although this editorial change was pushed over time, it met with resistance. During the triangular struggle between journalists, management and proprietor, the latter at first appeared to act discreetly. This may have been partly due to resistance coming from the long tradition of western journalism, and also concern over the paper's reputation. *SCMP* was founded in 1903 and has long been Hong Kong's dominant English-language newspaper. As such, it was an important source for political news about mainland China for both Hong Kong's English speaking community, and for China watchers elsewhere in the world. *SCMP* was the largest English-language newspaper in the territory. In the latter half of 2001, it had a circulation of 100,000 and a readership of around 300,000.[674] The restraint exercised by the proprietor was partly due to external criticism and partly to the countervailing force of public opinion and market forces.

The fact that *SCMP* was one of the best selling and profitable papers might also have helped to sustain its reputation and image during this critical period. Not long after Robert Kuok acquired the paper, he created the position of 'China adviser' and invited Feng Xiling, a founding editor of the English-language mouthpiece, *China Daily*, to take up the post.[675] At the time, this move invited criticism, and speculation on a possible shift in the paper's editorial position in favour of China. Apparently, there was no clear move initiated by the proprietor for some time, though it was revealed later that pressure continued to be exerted on the editor.[676]

The cumulative interference with editorial freedom meant that, within a few years, a handful of well-respected and outspoken journalists, critical cartoonists, satirical columnists and, above all, three chief editors were removed from their posts.[677] According to a former staff member at *SCMP*, this removal of heavy-weight journalists helped to disperse obstacles to institutional changes.[678] This all took place in the five years following the political handover, though changes could be traced back to the time before the handover, when the current proprietor, Robert Kuok, took over this British flagship from Rupert Murdoch in 1993.[679] Murdoch reportedly said that *SCMP* could not help him to enter the China market. That explains why he wanted to sell it to pro-China allies. Robert Kuok was the first of a batch of overseas Chinese businessmen and women to return to China to invest after the 1989 crackdown. Evidence shows that he was rewarded with contracts and business sites and opportunities to expand his hotel and other businesses in China.[680] For instance, Robert Kuok's Kerry Group owned and operated the Shangri-la chain of hotels in China and Asia.

In connection with this, a senior Chinese official revealed the complicated relationship between the state and business. According to Xu Jiatun, the former director of *Xinhua News Agency* (the de facto Chinese embassy in Hong Kong under colonial rule), the CCP attempted unsuccessfully to take control of *SCMP* through a third party.[681] However, it succeeded in its aim with the intervention by Robert Kuok. With the help of the Bank of China, Robert Kuok successfully got a controlling share of the paper.[682] The Chinese input was not revealed until later. After Robert Kuok stepped down as chairman, his son helped to get rid of journalists seen to be obstacles to editorial change. Jonathan Fenby, the former editor (who was also the former editor of the *Observer* in London), has suggested that the management acted on its boss's wishes to sack columnists and journalists seen to be critical of China. At that time, Fenby carried out some of these demands, but not all of them.[683] Unsurprisingly, the work of China editor, Willy Lam (one of the paper's long-standing assets), was not appreciated by the proprietor. He was regarded as not fitting in in the new political atmosphere, and seen as an obstacle to institutional change.

Lam had written a column entitled 'Marshalling the [Hong Kong] SAR's Tycoons', in which he claimed that a group of tycoons (including Kuok) had gone to Beijing to meet with Chinese leaders, and had been urged to lend their support to Tung Chee-hwa, the Chief Executive of the HKSAR, in his bid to return to office for a second time. The story went on to analyse how Hong Kong tycoons were ready to follow central instruction because they were promised business opportunities and other advantages. This article apparently infuriated the proprietor. Robert Kuok himself wrote to the editor to register his unhappiness with Willy Lam, condemning Lam's article as an 'absolute exaggeration and fabrication'.[684] He was later supported by letters from other tycoons as well.[685]

Two analyses at the time are worth noting.[686] One observer initially hailed Kuok's decision to register his unhappiness through publication as 'liberal'. By sending a letter to the editor of his own paper, Robert Kuok earned a reputation for seeking to be treated just as one of the many 'ordinary' readers of the paper. Some even went further to conclude that Lam must be the most secure journalist in the group – 'the untouchable' – as no one would dare to sack him after this episode. However, others including Lam himself did not feel the same way. In fact, the boss was so furious that he sent an ultimatum to the head of the editorial department, saying action needed to be taken. Not long afterwards, Lam resigned.

One editor on the paper had a theory that problems between the proprietor and journalist were exaggerated because there was no Chief Executive Officer (CEO) to act as a buffer.[687] Owen Jonathan, a long serving in-house lawyer in the Kerry Group, and a personal friend of Robert Kuok's, had acted as an effective buffer and minimised the head on collision between management and editorial. When he stepped down as CEO, his role was taken over by the new chairman, Ean Kuok, Robert Kuok's son, so the CEO's role as buffer was removed.

From the perspective of the journalism profession, it is worth noting how senior journalists attempted to contain and control the undesirable clash between the proprietor and their reputable colleague. Kuok's letter was an unprecedented move. It can be seen as the beginning of the end of editorial freedom, a sign of intolerance and disapproval from on high. When Kuok's letter was faxed through, an alarmed opinion page editor went to consult the Editor. The editor in charge of the opinion page, after discussion with the Editor, decided that they would follow the normal procedure and printed the letter as it was, but describing the correspondent as the 'former chairman of *South China Morning Post* group'. After the letter was printed, Robert Kuok was apparently annoyed because he did not want to have his old job title printed as well. The Editor, however, thought the paper should tell its readers openly that the letter came from the group's former chairman. Having read the letter, Lam continued to stand by his column.

The deadlock continued for a while, so the management resolved the situation by other means. The Editor wrote to ask one assistant editor to sub-edit Lam's copy, the assistant editor subsequently refused. The move was interpreted as an attempt to censor Lam's article before it went to press. Lam was warned about this unusual state of affairs. Soon after, the Editor talked to Lam about problems with his style of writing and expressed his wish to read Lam's copy prior to its going to press. The last column Lam wrote was about the sensitive issue of the Xinjiang minority and Chinese policy. It was vetted by the Editor before going to press.[688]

Apparently, the Editor was being squeezed between his staff and his boss. Despite all the pressure from above, the Editor did not agree with the management that Lam should be removed because that would amount to censorship, however, the pressure to remove Lam did not relax. Even the Editor, who came from a western journalistic tradition, could not defend press freedom, but had to carry out the proprietor's instructions. It was learnt that the then chief editor, Robert Keatley (former editor, *Wall Street Journal*), told Ean Kuok, the chairman, that the news of Willy Lam's sacking would surely become the front page lead story of *The New York Times* the following day. Ean Kuok replied that if that was the case, he was willing to pay the price. After an apparently vigorous exchange, a deal was reached that Lam was to be removed from his China editor position, but retain his associate editor job.[689] This incident reflects the dilemma of the top editor who was attempting to negotiate some space in the face of management control. One editor summed up the situation:

> Ultimately, probably only the editor at the time, Robert Keatley, knows what happened and he is unlikely to tell the truth. He may simply have deceived himself into believing Willy [Lam] would not object to being moved from his job as China editor to columnist [although his title of associate editor would be retained], which was the original offer made to him.[690]

From a journalist's perspective, the choice was very limited. Lam chose to quit in protest at his unfair treatment. He did not, in general, like the idea of being sidelined, and, in particular, being removed from his position as head of the China desk without consultation after he had worked for more than a decade at *SCMP*. He turned down the offer of a columnist's job and planned his protest. He told his friends at other newspapers that he was prepared to resign in protest at *SCMP*'s compromise on reporting about China.[691]

The situation, even for such a well-known journalist, was bleak. In an interview, Lam said he did not like to play office politics with the management. He believed that even if he stayed on now, he would have to leave later.[692] In hindsight, he was right. Another 22 journalists were made redundant in the name of budget cuts, including Danny Gittings, the op-ed page editor, and one of the key figures on the signature letter to rally support for Willy Lam. A group of 115 reporters and editors of *SCMP* backed Lam with a signature campaign, registering their concern over the management's handling of the incident.[693]

However, some people held a very different view regarding the journalists' concerted efforts to register their resentment towards the management and sympathy for their colleague. One senior journalist, who was made redundant afterwards, remarked that he did not believe that the paper could sack all the journalists who put their names on the letter in support of Lam. He urged those who remained there to stay and work, because he believed journalists could be more 'effective' inside *SCMP* than outside.[694]

The impact on the paper's quality, credibility and reputation for morality is impossible to imagine. One senior editor remarked, 'I never thought that they would let Willy [Lam] go ... so I won't be surprised if things happen to me too.'[695] Another editor resigned because of Willy Lam's dismissal.[696]

Feelings ran high both inside and outside the newsroom. It was observed that Robert Keatley, the editor, was a bit shaken by the peer pressure: there was not only the signature letter mentioned above, but also a fax from the former CEO, Owen Jonathan.[697] However, Keatley was unable to change the chairman's decision. Neither did peer pressure help. Lam had to leave the organisation he had served for more than a decade. The erosion of the quality of the paper continued, though there was a setback, and the Willy Lam incident had a bearing on the later incident. Danny Gittings (the son of John Gittings, a long standing China correspondent for the *Guardian* in London), the op-ed page editor, pressed for the serialisation of *The Tiananmen Papers*, a book compiled by Zhang Liang, a Chinese dissident, and edited by Andrew Nathan and Perry Link. The content of the book, which claimed to have documented the decision-making process of the Chinese leadership during the 4 June crackdown, was denied by Beijing. The decision to print the book excerpt was not unopposed, even though the paper had specifically bought the copyright to print the book excerpt. This time the intervention came from the acting chief editor, Thomas Abraham, an Indian journalist who used to be based in London and was a family friend of the former chairman, Robert Kuok.[698] Objecting to the serialisation of *The Tiananmen Papers*, Abraham quoted Rupert Murdoch's saying that 'those who sign the cheque decide what goes in the paper'. Abraham relayed to his staff that Ean Kuok, the chairman, objected to the serialisation of the book, even though they had bought the right to do so. Later, Abraham resigned as well of his own accord.

The decision was overturned by Robert Keatley when he came back from holiday. He instructed that the excerpt of *The Tiananmen Papers* be printed. Journalists inside *SCMP* suspected that Keatley felt 'guilty' at not being able to retain Lam.[699] So this time, he pressed for the printing of the excerpts, even though this would attract criticism from Beijing.[700] More journalists, including senior editors who were involved with the signature letter, were sacked. In less than 12 months, another batch of journalists was made redundant; among them was Danny Gittings who was seen as being involved in organising the staff action. The pressure on journalists to comply continued. This time the casualty happened in the Chinese capital. After the handover, the Chinese authorities changed the rules; reporters sent by the bureau of Hong Kong media organisations to be based in mainland China were required to be Chinese nationals. Chinese nationals were believed to be likely to be more cooperative in abiding by 'Chinese rules and regulations' than foreigners. For historical reasons, *SCMP* was regarded as being a British and foreign paper because it was printed in English and was under foreign ownership. Following the handover, the Beijing bureau of *SCMP* was placed under the administration of the Hong Kong and Macau Affairs Office of the State Council.

It was reportedly said that the Chinese authorities had required *SCMP* to deploy local Chinese to replace foreign correspondents in China so that Chinese officials could have better control over their reports. Against this background, Jasper Becker, chief of *SCMP*'s Beijing Bureau, was sacked.[701] Abraham Thomas, the then editor said Becker was sacked because of alleged insubordination towards the new China editor, Wang Xiangwei.[702] The sacking of Jasper Becker did not attract as much outcry and attention as Willy Lam's case, partly because *SCMP* had since made a couple more senior journalists redundant, but also because Hong Kong was suffering from an economic downturn, and most of the public seemed to be getting used to these kinds of political incidents. Another explanation was that this was not entirely a case of conflict between editor and journalist, but was the result of a reorientation of news arising from the new political circumstances, so that new expertise was required. Still, it is worth noting the background of the clash between the correspondent and the China editor. Jasper Becker is a veteran China correspondent who has written several books on China, such as *Hungry Ghosts: Mao's Secret Famine*. Wang Xiangwei was a former reporter on the Beijing mouthpiece, *China Daily*, before he moved to Hong Kong. Wang first joined *Oriental Daily News* Group's English-language newspaper, the defunct *Eastern Express*, in Hong Kong, and later moved on to join *SCMP* as business reporter. He did not enjoy the same internal respect and external reputation as his predecessor, Willy Lam.

However, one credible journalist observed that *SCMP* could not tolerate Lam any more, because it wanted to have a different emphasis on China news, that is, more social and economic news, and less highly political news. 'Wang, with his background, had at least got one "strong point" over Lam, that is, Wang's connections in China and his willingness to extend his duties to help with business exploration in Shanghai, on top of his duties as China editor', the journalist added. It was suggested that the management might have required different expertise at this juncture.[703] Thus the sacking of Willy Lam was not simply an example of management suppression, a row between the editor and his staff, nor was that of Jasper Becker. It was rather that the journalist was redundant in the new editorial positioning that resulted from the new political environment.

SCMP's China coverage has changed over a decade, though it still reports on China's politics, it tends to carry wire stories rather than reporting by its own reporters.[704]

Apart from the new emphasis on China news, *SCMP* dismantled its political desk and cancelled the position of Political Editor, leaving the original political editor 'at large'.[705] This move further indicated the changes taking place in the larger environment. At the turn of the century, *SCMP* had departed from its conventional position. 'It is indeed unusual not to have a political desk for an English broadsheet that claims to be the leading regional paper...' noted a senior editor at *SCMP*. *SCMP* was not alone, however. Mass market papers similarly got rid of their political desks and redeployed their political beat reporters.[706]

Commercialism

This kind of political caution was in fact an expression of commercialism. There may also be a political element to the decision. People are getting fed up with politics. So the argument would go. Thus, give them human interest stories. In fact, political caution and commercialism were, in effect, two sides of the same coin. Coincidentally, the popular *Apple Daily* also scrapped its political desk about the same time, using the excuse that in the post-colonial era, there was less interesting political news, so it would make more sense in terms of deployment of human resources to make political reporters join the general news desk.[707] Thus, it appears that political caution was hampering the efforts of journalists to produce quality political news. Both up-market and mass market papers shared similar views on the need to trivialise the news rather than cover political news in depth. In general, *SCMP* did not reduce its political coverage and, in fact, appeared to increase it by using wired stories.[708] This posed a challenge to the journalists themselves, however. 'It became harder to investigate and do in-depth political stories because you no longer had political beat reporters, leaving general reporters having to squeeze time to follow stories through,' one senior journalist said.[709]

Perhaps Hong Kong is at the moment heading towards having a strong corporate media. According to a veteran journalist, the trend of having business considerations override other concerns was not surprising given that the government has also gone corporate, starting right at the top with the Chief Executive who brought in outsiders on the pretext of increasing accountability.[710] Since July 2002, a stream of policies and proposals has shown the way Hong Kong is heading, including charging for accident and emergency services, pay cuts, taxes on overseas domestic helpers, etc. Therefore, one journalist concluded that big business would thrive, while people on the street were likely to suffer, and added:

> I believe that Hong Kong is well on its way to having a very strong corporate media such as exists in the United States. Newspapers and TV, etc. have to make profits to survive. But the profit motive takes on a different aspect

in the United States. . . . I feel that the Hong Kong media is following the U.S. trend. Business stories feature more frequently and prominently than social and political issues.[711]

The state government, as one of the biggest advertising sources, can exert more and more control over media organisations. Indeed, after 1989, there was a blacklist of newspaper organisations. China-funded and pro-China companies stopped placing advertisements with them, so as to penalise those who were regarded as 'subversive' or critical of Beijing's crackdown on the student movement.[712]

Furthermore, companies who enjoyed a good relationship with the government were likely to adopt a similar attitude towards media organisations. 'Corporations like Li Ka-shing's group did not place advertisements in our paper because *Apple Daily* was critical of Tung Chee-hwa,' according to a senior staff member at *Apple Daily*.[713] Li Ka-shing was reportedly supportive of Tung's running for the position of first Chief Executive of the HKSAR. It was later discovered that Li's company was in fact the second largest shareholder in Tung's family company.[714] Furthermore, there was a lot of criticism from the business community and the public alike that Tung's government had been favouring Li's company and his son's company in their bids for government projects.[715]

Complication of self-censorship

However, in the commercial world, the fittest survive. It would be hard to ban a popular medium altogether. Advertisements found their way into papers that enjoyed mass appeal. For instance, Pacific Century Cyberworks (PCCW), which was owned by Richard Li, Li Ka-shing's son, did place an advertisement in *Apple Daily* because the paper catered to affluent middle class readers, and was the second leading mass circulation paper. It was an effective vehicle to reach not only the mass market, but also the middle classes. Nevertheless, economic suppression could affect every section of the leading quality papers. To maintain a critical and independent stance and restrict the influence of businessmen required alertness and skill. The following anecdote illustrates how journalists worked around censorship.

As stated above, the lack of a CEO to act as a 'buffer' led to a head-on clash between the proprietor and the editorial staff of *SCMP*. It was traditional at *SCMP* for a nightly news list to be faxed to the CEO. Following the departure of Owen Jonathan, the former CEO, the new chairman, Ean Kuok, took over the CEO's role. On one occasion an item, written by an *SCMP* staff writer, appeared on the news list with the title 'Li Ka-shing should shut up and show a little humility'.[716] The chairman called a duty editor in an attempt to censor the story. It was a serious situation. After several telephone exchanges, and some persuasion, the article was toned down by removing the offending line, and finally went to press. In the aftermath, the deputy and assistant editors learned the lesson that only 'very boring terms' should be used on the nightly news list.

They adopted this technique, which was not entirely unknown to their mainland Chinese counterparts.

Eventually, the publisher's interference became so widespread that he had the last word on editorial policy. He became, in effect, the virtual head of the editorial department.[717] There also appeared to be more management intervention than before. For instance, in an open message from the publisher, printed in the paper, he said the paper would now aim to serve the national interests of China.[718] As well as taking care of the needs of readers, the publisher said, he would also take care of the interests of shareholders and advertisers. The shift in the positioning of *SCMP* could not be more clearly revealed than by this publisher's message.

Other unusual things happened at *SCMP* that showed that editorial freedom was being further undermined. There was no immediate appointment of a new editor following the departure of Thomas Abraham, the previous editor. Instead, three senior editors were appointed to an editorial team that took up the responsibility for making daily editorial decisions.[719] It was later announced that a former editor during Rupert Murdoch's reign would return from Australia to lead the team after eight months during which the top post was vacant.[720] One journalist at *SCMP* remarked:

> The significant trend nowadays is that the intervention of the management has become clear and strong. You can tell from the editorial meeting – in recent years, the editor has lost his authority, not to mention his replacement by the 'team of four' [including the publisher, Thaddeus Beczak (a former banker), who became responsible for the paper] ... the editorial management appears to be confused and indecisive ... it would never have happened in the past.[721]

In the case of *SCMP*, the erosion of press freedom took a while, at least during the first few years following Robert Kuok's take-over. This may be explained by the fact that there was resistance from journalists, and negotiation between management and editorial. However, in the case of *Metro Broadcast*, owned by Li Ka-shing, the business interests of the group, and the tendency of the proprietor to support the HKSAR government, were clearly spelt out right from the start. The management implemented company policy swiftly and directly.

Proprietorial influence

If the case of *SCMP* is the worst example of a newsroom where newspaper proprietors and management exercised control over editorials, the case of *Metro Broadcast* is another telling example of how journalists became casualties in conflicts between journalistic norms and corporate interests when there were no intermediaries in between. One journalist said: 'The news controller and senior editor should act as a buffer, but they are unwilling to shoulder this responsibility. If senior people have the guts to do it, we could have more space to do our job.'[722]

Proprietorial influence was invisible but omnipresent. Li Ka-shing, Hong Kong's leading tycoon, once said he did not want to get involved in the newspaper business because, first, he did not work in business sectors with which he was unfamiliar and, second, he was worried that operating news media might create enemies and problems for himself. He was certainly no friend to journalists. He complained that the Hong Kong news media practitioners were too critical of him and his group. He even repeatedly threatened that he would cease to invest in Hong Kong if criticism did not stop.[723] However, the scenario changed at least in respect of the radio broadcasting station he owned. Once the businessman acquired the controlling share in *Metro Broadcast*, there appeared to begin a programme of self-censorship, especially in areas concerning news about Li Ka-shing's business interests, and Tung Chee-hwa's HKSAR government, to which Li openly lent his support and loyalty. As stated above, it was later revealed that Li Ka-shing held 6 per cent of the shares and was the second largest shareholder in the Tung family's company. In August 2002, Paul Cheung Chung-wah, the chief news editor at *Metro Broadcast*, was sacked in the name of budget cuts. However, observers noted that the excuse was not particularly convincing, as Cheung was the only one to be made redundant at the time.[724]

It has since been revealed that Paul Cheung accused the management of censorship; for example, there were several instances of management bans concerning: coverage of negative news about the group; reports on Falun Gong activities; and protests against Tung Chee-hwa's policy in the last couple of months before his dismissal.[725] According to Cheung, he put up with pressure from senior editors for more than a year, but would have resigned if the job market had been more promising. He had hoped that he could retain enough space to do his job, and that his immediate boss would help to allay some of the pressure and mediate on his behalf. After several fierce exchanges and meetings, he naively believed that the management would leave him alone to make editorial decisions provided he followed the mutually agreed principles of objectivity, accuracy and factual reporting. He also agreed to abide by the rule that if there were any negative news about the group, he would clear it first with the company before release. Moreover, he also agreed that his news team would not actively run 'dumb-Tung [Chee-hwa]' news.

Unfortunately, the conflict between management and editorial staff was not resolved, and the atmosphere became one of acute mistrust. Although mutual agreement was reached on how 'sensitive' news should be reported, there continued to be clashes between the management and Cheung's news team. After less than 12 months', without further notice, he was sacked.[726] Cheung was devastated by the sudden termination of his employment. Subsequently, he took his case to the Hong Kong Journalists Association for justice.[727] In an interview, he said he did not hope to get his job back, but he still wanted justice. He thought the company sacked him because he acted as an obstacle to self-censorship.

Journalistic resistance

In 1995, even before the political handover, six senior editors at *Asia Television Limited* (*ATV*), the second leading terrestrial TV station in Hong Kong, collectively resigned as a protest against censorship.[728] The journalists had wished to screen a Spanish documentary about the 4 June Tiananmen massacre,[729] and even though the documentary said that no one died, the management was so sensitive about the issue that they wanted to censor it. According to one of the journalists who resigned, the censorship of the documentary was 'unnecessary' and 'stupid' as the film was not an attempt to oppose the Chinese position. However, the incident exemplifies the extreme sensitivity of the media management and its tendency to over-react on the brink of the political handover. It also at times acted before it was instructed to do so, showing that the mechanism of censorship has become more and more ingrained in the hierarchy. The case also reflects the lengths to which journalists would go when the situation was bleak.

One senior journalist remarked that, in hindsight, although they were defending their right to do their job professionally, and defending the audience's right to know, the incident largely resulted from a lack of communication and a lack of negotiation. The journalist added that another minor, but not unimportant, factor was that the economy at that time was much better, so they did not have to worry about finding another job. That indirectly encouraged them to move on, and indeed, not long after all of them had found another journalistic job.[730]

The position of these six editors is in contrast to that of Paul Cheung's at *Metro Broadcast*, described above. Because the economic conditions were poor, he did not dare to resign, even though he found the working environment hostile and not conducive to his work. He was later humiliated and sacked.

Market liberation versus market distortion

Market forces could be a liberating as well as restrictive. *Apple Daily* was an exceptional paper that made good use of the political space left by other papers. It held itself out as an outspoken paper that represented Hong Kong's interests and maintained the image that it was prepared to criticise the Chinese authorities.[731] However, even Lai, *Apple Daily*'s proprietor, who was usually hailed as a 'democracy fighter' by some western media,[732] laid down parameters on the scope of reporting about China. He once issued the guideline to his editorial staff that there was to be 'no breaking news on China',[733] after certain mistakes were found in his daily's China section that attracted condemnation from Chinese mouthpieces such as *Xinhua News Agency*.

The general impression was that, as the political parameters had changed after 1997, so had the critical stance of outspoken papers.[734] Under the Chinese regime, the news media were required to be 'patriotic' to China and to adopt a 'nationalistic responsibility' in Hong Kong.[735] This had an impact on news operations in the sense that, while journalists continued to maintain their own criteria for 'newsworthiness', publishers were eager to comply with China's requirements, and this caused a clash between media owners and their staff. Under these circumstances, it is significant to note that the mass circulation paper, *Apple Daily*, printed a full-page apology,[736] at the instigation of its proprietor, Lai, after rejecting an advertisement from a group that was seen as an outcast by the Chinese authorities.[737] *Apple Daily*, out of political concerns, rejected a full-page advertisement from the Hong Kong branch of Falun Gong, a meditation exercise group outlawed by mainland China. The advertisement was protesting against the Hong Kong government's purge of its mainland counterparts.

This story reflects the narrowing of the public sphere as well as sensitivity concerning the activities of some dissident groups in the post-colonial era. When the chief editor of *Apple Daily* received the advertisement, he was unsure of the implications of printing it, since the day of publication would be the day of the verdict of a case taken by the Hong Kong government against Falun Gong. There were concerns as to whether publishing the advertisement would amount to a contempt of court. The paper's legal adviser gave her view that there would be a slim risk, leaving the decision to the editorial department.[738] Since the group did not want to change the wording that might constitute a contempt of court, they decided to reject the advertisement altogether. The advertisement was subsequently placed in the quality daily, *Hong Kong Economic Journal*, on the day of the verdict.[739]

This decision was later repudiated and put right by the publisher. When Lai heard about it in Taiwan, where he was preparing for the inauguration of *Taiwan Apple Daily*, he immediately returned to Hong Kong. 'He was grumbling over the phone, asking who made the decision. And the chief editor thought he would be sacked this time,' one senior journalist at *Apple Daily* recalled.[740] When Lai came back, he met with his senior staff. One senior journalist recalled:

> He was hysterical and furious ... he swore and scolded us vigorously ... and he was in tears. He asked us how could we have done this thing to the paper ... how could we possibly turn down the advertisement – now the Falun Gong had no freedom to express itself, even though they were prepared to pay for it? At the end, he demanded an open apology from the editorial department. That was passed without dispute.[741]

Apparently, the editorial staff dared not argue with the proprietor. Thus, a full-page apology was printed but attracted little notice from either the public or the press. 'We were very worried that rival papers might take this chance to attack us. Luckily, they don't give a damn – perhaps that is because it is related to the Falun Gong, a group which is outlawed by the central authorities.'[742]

This incident shows the timidity of the press in general, regarding highly sensitive groups and news related to them. Lai's response, however, was unusual. When the chief executive officer of a quality newspaper was asked whether he would have run the advertisement, his response was completely different. Their decision would have been based on a completely different set of values, and the ultimate interests of the paper and hence the group would have guided their policy. The chief executive said, 'we would never ever accept that kind of advertisement. It is not a matter of press freedom. We, as a newspaper should have the right to choose what advertisements we want to place. We guard freedom of expression as well as our "own freedom of publication" – we should have the freedom of not placing an advertisement, if that could potentially incur loss on our part.'[743] He meant that, if they printed a political advertisement that would definitely upset the official position, this would lose them advertising revenue from organisations at the other end of the political spectrum. Thus political correctness would always prevail in such circumstances. He pointed out that the problem was greater among the Chinese diasporas.[744] In other words, the paper in Hong Kong and its foreign editions in North America, Britain, Europe and Australia always took advertisements, and indeed covered political news, that supported the pro-China line instead of dissident positions such as pro-Taiwan or pro-democracy ones, so as to guarantee that the paper stayed within the Chinese mainstream.

'Toadying culture'

This attitude of 'political correctness' stemmed from an awareness of the new political environment and culture under the new regime. The political parameters had apparently shifted, and the media did not challenge the very root of power but instead abided by the 'one country, two systems' policy. As a result, the systems and guidelines of China were apparently adopted without proper scrutiny of the impact of sinicisation (the Chinese way of doing things), such as an increase in authoritarianism and a lack of transparency concerning formulation of government policy. The suppression of negative information in order to save the national image became a priority. As pointed out earlier, the most recent example was the spread of the SARS epidemic in 2003, which highlighted the inability of the mainland Chinese press to expose, and report in a timely manner on the issue.[745] The Hong Kong news media were struggling to fulfil their duty as a watchdog as well as being a Chinese institution.

As the 1997 handover drew nearer, political correctness prevailed and greater control was exercised over the press by both owners and the state. This had a direct impact on news coverage of relatively sensitive political issues, for example, anything to do with the legitimacy of the Chinese authorities, and there were many instances of censorship. For example, political terms such as 'massacre', which indicated the suppressive nature of the central regime, became highly sensitive. The Chinese authorities exerted pressure on individual newspapers to make them clean up their act. One editor at *SCMP* recalled:

> I was told in June 1996 by the then deputy editor, Victor Fung, that the newspaper should not refer to the events of 4 June 1989 [in Beijing] as a 'massacre', though we had of course always done so previously. He said he had been told this by the chief executive, Lyndley Holloway. Later, the editor, Jonathan Fenby, said the word 'massacre' enraged the [Chinese]

authorities and could not therefore be used. I said I would comply if he put up a public memo to that effect. He declined. The outcome was that the backbench [the night editor and the sub-editors] would not alter the word if it was already in reporters' copy, but would [also] not change other terms (such as crackdown) to 'massacre'.[746]

After 1997, there were not only changes of terminology but also a shift in attitudes towards Chinese sovereignty. There were several key incidents of censorship relating to mainland China news at *SCMP*, which shows the level of self-censorship taking place in an English-language daily with a long tradition of liberalism and professionalism. For example:

In November 1996, Fenby instructed an assistant editor, Keith Wales, to alter the intro[duction] to a Jasper Becker [then the Beijing bureau chief] story about flooding in Hunan [a province in China]. Becker's story said something along the lines of 'Chinese authorities covered up the deaths of thousands of people in flooding . . . the *Post* can reveal'. Fenby changed it to 'thousands of people died in flooding . . . the *Post* can reveal'.[747]

By deleting several words, the implication that China had acted wrongly was removed. That was how self-censorship operated – through routine editorial decisions. Journalists cited many more cases. 'In June 1996, Fenby instructed another assistant editor, Colin Kerr, to tone down a splash headline about Lu Ping [the Chinese senior official in charge of Hong Kong and Macau affairs] and press freedom.'[748] This kind of news was consciously censored because it implied that the Chinese authorities were attacking Hong Kong's freedom of the press, and the paper's management wanted to make every effort to avoid irritating the incoming regime.

There was a general 'toadying culture' in the post-colonial era,[749] which was closely linked to Confucianism and decolonisation.[750] This was not a coincidence. Once Hong Kong became part of China, many people automatically made adjustments, even before receiving instructions to do so, so as to win the heart and soul of the new masters. Despite the fact that both the external and internal working environment had deteriorated, there was a general acceptance of this new 'reality', and journalists attempted to work around it.

Framing of news

One of the obvious changes in 'political correctness' related to the framing of news, for example, the coverage of Taiwan-related news such as the Taiwanese presidential election in 2000, as mentioned in the textual analysis in Chapter 4. The Taiwanese President Chen Shui-bian, the first popularly elected opposition leader, was described as 'leader of Taiwan' rather than 'president' by the two terrestrial television stations at the time of his inauguration as president. A senior broadcast journalist remarked on the change in description:

The official rationale was that Jiang Zemin was the president of China, and Taiwan was only part of the country. As far as I know no one in *ATV* [*Asia Television*] was convinced by the argument, but staff had no choice but to follow orders. . . . I do not know if *ATV*'s news bosses were instructed by anyone outside to stop referring to Chen as president of Taiwan. . . . There was no need to wait for instructions. If someone feels that by taking a certain step he will win praise from a powerful party, he will certainly go ahead.[751]

However, the long-standing journalistic culture of Hong Kong journalists was still there. The controls imposed on the news editorial were met with resistance. The same senior journalist recalled that he had tried to argue against the change to Chen's title:

I maintained that Taiwan and Beijing are separate governments (of course not separate countries) and we should stick to the titles each side has for its leaders. For instance both sides have premiers and *ATV* News still referred to the Taiwanese premier as such . . . [however] I considered my argument wasted because I was told that Chen was only 'a' leader (presumably not 'the' leader even if his jurisdiction is only Taiwan) and so it would be inappropriate to refer to him as president (even though prior to this Chen was described as President of Taiwan).[752]

Furthermore, under the new regime, there were mounting concerns about national security. Falun Gong, an outlawed meditation group in China, was perceived as a legally tolerated organisation in Hong Kong. The fact that the Hong Kong government could not eradicate a group unless it was proved to be illegal reflects the merits of their system in contrast to that of the mainland Chinese. However, the Hong Kong news media appeared to exercise extra caution in covering news about the group as it was deemed to be banned in one way or another by the state/central regime. According to a senior journalist, the Falun Gong protests were covered whenever the assignment desk sent crews to the protests. Whenever there was a news story, the English channel would use it. The reason why the English and Chinese channels adopted different policies was historical: the English channel traditionally catered for non-Chinese speaking expatriates, and operated in a more liberal and flexible style. Still, there were a lot of ways to screen stories from public sight. The management could censor sensitive stories by saying that resources were better allocated elsewhere:

But sometimes Falun Gong protests were not covered. The assignment desk claimed in those instances that there were no crews or that the team got there too late. It's hard to say whether there was a deliberate move by the assignment desk not to cover controversial issues. The same happens sometimes with stories, such as protests against genetically modified food or news conferences given by pro-democracy figures. ATV's absence is noted but whether the reason is censorship is hard to prove. The assignment editors can also say they have their own priorities or they have a lack of resources.[753]

Having said that, the journalist indicated that the English side still enjoyed more flexibility and freedom than its Chinese counterpart. Sometimes, the English side was given a freer rein, for instance:

> As for stories on China my former Chinese colleagues were very alert. In fact the English side would get information from them. But how the information is used, apparently in some cases, is different (and if so, the directions must come I suppose from the higher-ups).[754]

A similar situation can be seen with the mainland's news media, for example, the English-language *China Daily* was supposed to have enjoyed more freedom and flexibility than its Chinese counterpart, *People's Daily*.

Yet in the case of 'negative' news, such as natural disasters, the news media were more and more adapted to the Chinese style of 'responsible' reporting. One example cited by columnist and commentator, Andy Ho, is how *ATV* Home (the Chinese Channel) reported on the floods on the mainland.[755] In Ho's article, he said that natural disasters had become a major component of the Hong Kong daily news diet since Hong Kong had reverted to China. The local media spent considerable airtime covering such incidents on the mainland. However, these news reports increasingly resembled propaganda from the Chinese authorities rather than accounts by an independent news organisation. He noted that the case of *ATV* Home was particularly conspicuous. The way the channel described the official response sounded exactly like a government press release. Ho said:

> It is understandable that local news organisations often have to rely on their mainland counterparts as the primary source of info[rmation] on spot news across the country, especially immediately after a tragic accident. [However, t]he local media [are] under no obligation to duplicate on air what has been fed to them from across the border. Yet the station's editors appear to have given up their job to edit news stories. They do not see the need to cut out typical Chinese official lines designed to project a caring and efficient image for party cadres.[756]

Apparently, this practice of toeing the official Chinese line has emerged as a recurring pattern at the TV station. It appears that there was a completely different set of standards in force for disasters that might involve official neglect or oversight on the mainland. This may have been partly due to the fact that the Hong Kong TV station's broadcasting spilled on to its neighbouring southern province in China, and the station was targeting that affluent advertising market.[757]

Epilogue: broadcasting

The control mechanism on the press also had an enormous effect on broadcasting. First, there was a tendency to reframe terminology to reflect the 'one China' concept in support of Chinese sovereignty, despite the fact that Taiwan had existed as a political entity for decades.

Broadcasting, especially television broadcasting, was generally regarded as having a far-reaching influence on audiences. This was particularly true in a country without press freedom such as China. In many ways, the Chinese authorities were very concerned about broadcasting from Hong Kong, and imposed restrictions on it. Part of the reason for this was the fact that residents of southern provinces could easily receive the signal from neighbouring Hong Kong. In these circumstances, enormous pressure was put on TV journalists to fall into line with the official position. As a result of the collaboration between the HKSAR, the Chinese Liaison Office in Hong Kong[758] and pro-China allies, there was a general de facto ban on reporting on Taiwan. For instance, in a *Radio Television Hong Kong (RTHK)* programme – 'Hong Kong Letter' – a Chinese-language radio programme, Cheng An-kuo, the Taiwanese representative in Hong Kong, clarified Taiwan's official position on the former Taiwanese president Lee Teng-hui's 'state-to-state' rhetoric. Pro-China allies criticised not only Cheng but also *RTHK* for failing to live up to its position as a government broadcaster.

Cheung Man-yee, the Director of Broadcasting and head of *RTHK*, was 'promoted' and removed from her position, apparently as a 'penalty' for this broadcast. However, a source commented that, in fact, her transfer was announced long before the incident happened so it could not be regarded as a 'punishment'.[759] 'Nobody will remember that, and, of course, more important is the fact that *RTHK* is under criticism from the leftist press and pro-China figures,' a senior *RTHK* journalist said.[760] Referring to the mounting pressure experienced by those responsible for the programme, the senior journalist said:

> There are always comments afterwards on whether it could have been done better. There is no clear dividing line between editorial judgment and censorship. On the whole, no one has come up to me to tell me to do this, not to do that. *RTHK* is always under outside pressure from the left wing.[761]

As regards to the reason why *RTHK* had decided to air the thorny issue of Chinese sovereignty, the journalist added:

> We solely decided on the basis of news value. The 'Two-state theory'[762] had been strongly attacked by the Mainland, and it is time to air Cheng's [the Taiwan official's] view. We found that the views of the Taiwanese government apparently departed from those of Lee Teng-hui, therefore we went ahead and arranged our program.[763]

To the journalist's surprise, public criticism was strong, though society as a whole was supportive to *RTHK*. 'This was crucial for a public broadcaster.

My rationale is: it is always legitimate for Chinese people to talk about China's future, at any time, in any place. Cheng's views had news value, why couldn't they be aired?' he added. However, he also admitted that the programme format of 'Hong Kong Letter' might have invited criticism because only one view was presented, without the opposing one. More importantly, someone might 'feel safe to interpret the "One Country" principle narrowly'. The journalist defended the format of allowing a monologue broadcast, however, by holding that the diversity of speakers in other programmes would balance the programme in the long run. The ultimate question was whether the Taiwanese official's sound bite could be broadcast on the publicly funded *RTHK*. Remarkably, the producer in question later produced many programmes about the Taiwanese election following the controversy of Cheng An-kuo. One of these included a live relay of the inauguration ceremony of the newly elected Taiwanese President, Chen Shui-bian. His whole speech was broadcast, and a panel discussion followed. At first the producer was worried about inviting criticism again. He said:

> I expected there might be criticism from the left wing, but nothing came up. The broadcast was justified on the ground that Chen's speech had great news value. Everyone at that time worried that Chen might announce a radical stance and this might trigger war in the Taiwan Strait. [But in fact, he did not.][764]

In order to make it easier to change the institutional structure, and, in turn, the culture of Hong Kong broadcasting, the Chinese tactics used were not entirely dissimilar to the removal of heavy-weight journalists from newspapers.[765] Although some might argue that the announcement of the transfer of Cheung Man-yee, Director of Broadcasting, to another position was not related to these events, the fact remains that she was removed from her long-standing influence on the public broadcaster. This was particularly felt when *RTHK* was later under attack again. The public broadcaster was left without an upfront and vigorous defender.

In a separate incident, a news story about Taiwanese politics broke in 2000. A *Cable TV* reporter interviewed Annette Lu, the first female and popularly elected deputy president of Taiwan. After a week or so, there was an organised effort to criticise and discredit the story.[766] There was even more pressure on the leading terrestrial station, *Television Broadcast* (*TVB*), when it broadcast an interview with the Taiwanese President, Chen Shui-bian. It was broken into parts and interrupted by comments from the political commentator, Timothy Wong Ka-ying, an expert in Taiwan politics and an independent scholarly commentator. 'They were successful in making the point that if you attempted to interview certain politicians or office-bearers who were outside the legitimate boundary, you would be categorized as "naïve and stupid" because you were unaware of the new political order; and you had very likely burdened your news organisation with unnecessary consequences,' a senior broadcasting journalist said.[767]

One senior journalist who undertook to conduct these highly sensitive interviews did indeed suffer. A message was relayed to the journalist, saying that in the opinion of the management, the reporter was pro-Bian (i.e. pro Chen Shuibian, which was equivalent to being pro-Taiwanese independence). This was a serious allegation, which would not only damage the credibility of the staff, but would also constitute a criminal offence when the enactment of the proposed anti-subversion law of Basic Law article 23 is completed. 'The thing is, if after 12 months or so I'm sacked or forced to go, no one will know that this is as a result of a single news story in year 2000 ... our sacrifice won't even have a heroic face because no one will believe our words,' the reporter said.[768]

Flak came from all sides and affected both the private and public broadcasting sector. In 2002, Annette Lu was again approached by *RTHK*. Candy Chea, a senior presenter of entertainment programmes, disclosed casually to a reporter that she intended to interview Annette Lu for her response to the early release of a Hong Kong singer, William So Wing-hong who was convicted of possession of drugs in Taiwan. This was meant to be a soft news story on the social-entertainment side, nothing to do with hard politics. However, the interview was subsequently cancelled, apparently because of strong pressure from the left-wing press and pro-China allies. Xu Simin, a delegate to the Chinese People's Political Consultative Conference (CPPCC) said, 'Other news organisations can interview Annette Lu as many as ten times and I would not care. But I would not tolerate *RTHK* doing it even once because it is a government-funded broadcaster.'[769] However, one senior producer held different views regarding the disagreement:

> If Candy Chea had conducted her interview, she would have challenged [Annette] Lu on whether she had used her personal capacity to release So Wing-hong, a Hong Kong singer. But of course, no one talked about it.... Lu might have been discredited. In a sense, Chea was on the 'same side' as the left wing people.[770]

Yet the content of the interview was still considered to be sensitive. The significant issue was that Chea was discouraged from carrying out her duties according to her professional judgement. Ironically, the incident blew up to such an absurd degree that an anonymous Hong Kong official reportedly suggested that government departmental staff (including *RTHK*) should follow the seven guidelines laid down by Chinese Vice-premier, Qian Qichen in the event of making contact with Taiwanese officials. 'It is a laugh because *RTHK*, as a news organisation, has to handle news from all over the world, including Taiwan on a daily basis. How can we follow the guidelines and seek prior approval? It is simply not viable,' a *RTHK* spokesman said.[771] In the aftermath, on the one hand, journalists working at *RTHK* said that there was no interference with their work; on the other hand, there were more occasions in which it was incumbent upon them to discuss and clarify certain politically sensitive topics before they went ahead with publication.[772]

This was not just rhetoric; it was a battle for control of the publicly funded broadcaster, *RTHK*. Both Chinese officials and pro-China allies attempted to make it revert to the role of 'mouthpiece' that it had held in the old colonial days. One of *RTHK*'s most popular television programmes of the past decade has been the 'Headliners', which satirised current affairs on a weekly basis. However, when the inefficient and badly performing HKSAR government was satirised as the 'Taliban', the Chief Executive, Tung Chee-hwa, criticised the broadcaster for having 'bad taste'.[773] Tung's comment triggered another major debate on whether the public broadcaster should use government money to satirise its own administration. Commenting on the difficult situation *RTHK* encountered, one senior producer said that ultimately support must come from the public at large.

> We always have to fight for our own space. If society and the public stop supporting us, then that is the end ... there is no use for just one person or one station to act as the hero. Ultimately ... it hinges on whether society and the people appreciate this kind of program ... whether *RTHK* serves the public good.[774]

The dilemma for *RTHK* was in fact due to its dual role. On the one hand, it is a government department subsidised by government revenue, but on the other hand, it is also a news medium enlisting editorial independence in its institutional code of practice.[775]

Concluding remarks

The control mechanism affecting the Hong Kong press has various aspects. First, there are the implications of the application of the Chinese family business philosophy to the press business, by which media owners, rather than professional journalists, exerted increasing control over the editorial position. Second, because of the influence of the notion of Confucianism and loyalty, many journalists had to come to terms with the core issues of survival and the pursuit of collective interests. This in turn led to the decline of the intellectual press.[776] Third, during the process of decolonisation, there was a restructuring of news media ownership along with a re-alignment of economic and political players, including media tycoons or tycoons who became media proprietors. Consequently, Chinese entrepreneurs have largely taken on the leading role in various fields including the media, and as a result, the political spectrum of media organisations has become narrower instead of broadening.

The restructuring of press ownership and re-orientation of the news media has had a major impact on the organisation of news, as is evident from the previous discussion. It shows that self-censorship is already in place. For most reporters, politics is not the issue; this is left to those higher up the hierarchy. As pointed out by one senior journalist, reporters learn what their bosses want and write accordingly. The bosses (the sub-editors and editors) then fine-tune pieces, because they in turn know what the media owners require of them, so self-censorship is subtle and comes with the job, so to speak. One journalist remarked: 'Self-censorship is not confined to Hong Kong alone. The much publicized fears of self-censorship in Hong Kong after the handover overlook the very same process taking place in the west (where the consequences are more severe).'[777] The trend appears to be that the Hong Kong news media are well on the way to having a very strong corporate identity, as is the case in the United States. Yet, there were quite a number of junior reporters who did their day-to-day work with courage as one editor argued:

> It should be remembered that, apart from the censorship outlined above, the *Post* [*SCMP*] did a reasonable (and sometimes excellent) job at reporting sensitive issues prominently in a fair manner, and that this often required a good deal of courage from relatively junior staff on the political, China and news desks. During the handover period, there was a lot of criticism of the *Post* from foreign correspondents based in Hong Kong, much of which was simply wrong.[778]

On the other hand, it is evident that there was no organised up-front resistance, though there was resistance from the rank and file, and even the management, in the case of *SCMP*. Undoubtedly, it could be risky for those who lent their support and indeed some paid the price by, for example, losing their jobs.

Thus, media owners controlled the organisation, and had control over editorial positioning, and in turn pursued their own or their group's interests rather than those of the media organisation. That is to say, media owners may not have made the reputation and credibility of the medium their first priority. There were no concessions, even though in certain cases the staff registered their concern. This illustrates the acute difference between journalists and news media proprietors. Yet neither the owners nor the management used the pretext of editorial differences, or objections to a journalist's independence or critical position, to sack them. Perhaps this shows that there is still concern about the professional image and reputation of individual media organisations. On the other hand, there was no effort to retain those who were forced to give up their jobs.

It is clear that there was an enormous influence coming from the owner who was very likely to be influenced by the regime change. This is evident in the re-alignment of political as well as economic players during the decolonisation process, starting during the transition period and for the five years following the handover. This allegiance to the new political regime resulted in the political repositioning of certain news organisations. The relationship between media and state (both central and local) can only be inferred here, because very few proprietors are available for interview.[779] However, the strong journalistic tradition and no less vigilant institutional forces were both at work. In the next chapter I shall examine and analyse the traditions and values of the Hong Kong press and its institutional alliances, which help to counter both internal and external intervention, and to sustain a degree of press freedom following the handover.

6 Journalistic norms and people power

Introduction

In the last chapter, I argued that the Hong Kong news media, including broadcasting (though my major concern is with the press), were under state control, primarily because the owners and their managerial staff exercised control via the institutional structure, and professional routines and practices. Although the majority of the press accommodated the new regime, the response from publishers and journalists appears to have been varied. Some showed signs of resistance and even rebellious activities. Even more importantly, the public broadcaster seems to have been resilient and Hong Kong public opinion was not compliant.

While political control over the media was not complete following the political handover seven years ago, the latest political developments are intriguing. On 1 July 2003, more than half a million Hong Kong people peacefully took to the streets to demonstrate their resentment of, and grievances against, the administration led by Tung Chee-hwa, and to protest at the enactment of a new national security bill in particular. This unprecedented move by the Hong Kong people to mark the sixth anniversary of the inauguration of the Hong Kong Special Administrative Region (HKSAR) alarmed even the most stubborn pro-China politician.[780] As a result, the Chinese authorities made major concessions: the enactment of the bill in question was postponed indefinitely, and the two most unpopular local cabinet ministers were sacked.[781] Although Tung, the chief executive, kept his position, the Chinese authorities took steps to rectify the situation in order to resolve the most serious political crisis since the take-over. It was believed that had it not been for these prompt measures, the crisis would have worsened and would likely have affected mainland China as well.[782] Analysts perceived the struggle for Hong Kong press freedom to be the beginning of a fight for Chinese press freedom. But why would the central authorities have allowed Hong Kong people power to have its way?

Unsurprisingly the two phenomena were closely related. The radical press and political institutional forces (such as the Catholic church) were pointed out as the main instigators of the latest general dissent, which successfully mobilised the public in general and the middle class in particular to mass demonstration.[783] The large turnout at the July march in Hong Kong was arguably due to the activities of the radical press, namely *Apple Daily* and *Commercial Radio* broadcaster, according to both the Chinese official media as well as to independent Hong Kong scholarly assessment.[784] Furthermore, senior Chinese officials also made the accusation that a 'foreign force/element' had played a role in instigating the incident.[785]

Under such sophisticated control and enormous pressure from the regime, how could the press (and broadcasters) resist so effectively? Were the media alone in the struggle? Were they supported by political and social institutional forces, both local and foreign? Why did the Chinese authorities concede to the power of the Hong Kong people? I shall address these questions in this chapter. I shall also attempt to trace the roots of resistance, namely the long-standing journalistic tradition and norms, and the infrastructure of the news industry that helped to generate and shape an alliance of resistance. As seen in Chapter 5, the regime change increased hierarchical controls to curtail civil liberty in general, and press freedom in particular. Paradoxically, this worsening of the situation helped to raise awareness and stirred up a general resentment in which institutional pressure groups, professionals and the middle class were mobilised and given a voice in certain of the critical media.[786]

Further to the criteria mentioned in Chapter 5, the selection of the 56 journalists with whom I conducted face-to-face interviews was based primarily on two guiding principles. First, they had personal knowledge of the details of the case studies analysed in the previous chapter. Second, they were usually high-ranking editorial or managerial news practitioners who were either policy and decision-makers, or enjoyed access to the daily deliberative process. Interviewees were drawn from different levels of the hierarchy as well as from different mainstream media organisations, so that there was both vertical and horizontal representation. For instance, the following were interviewed: the publishers of the two leading dailies, *Apple Daily* and *The Sun*, and the quality paper, *Hong Kong Economic Journal*; the chief executive of quality papers such as *Sing Tao Daily News* and the news controller of the leading television broadcaster, *TVB*; the former chief editor of the leftist *Hong Kong Wen Wei Po* and *New Evening Post*; the current chief editors of *Sing Tao Daily News*; senior editors at *Ming Pao Daily News*, *South China Morning Post*, *Hong Kong Economic Times* and *Hong Kong Economic Journal*; and senior producers at *Wharf Cable*, *Metro Broadcast*, *Commercial Radio*, *TVB*, and the public broadcaster, *Radio Television Hong Kong (RTHK)*.[787] Some of them were interviewed and written to more than once.

Proposed new national security bill

As already mentioned, in mid-2003, more than half a million people took to the streets peacefully to air their resentment towards the Chief Executive, appointed by the Chinese regime that had taken over Hong Kong seven years previously, and the proposed national security legislation. Apart from curtailing other civil liberties, the law is believed to enable the resumption of colonial restrictions on

Hong Kong press freedom. The idea of compiling a draconian law in the name of national security can be traced back to the year 1989. After the crackdown on the Beijing student movement, the Chinese authorities felt a pressing need to prevent Hong Kong from becoming a subversive base that could be used against China. So the Chinese authorities strengthened article 23 of the Hong Kong Basic Law considerably in direct reaction to Hong Kong's support for the pro-democracy movement.[788] Under that clause, Hong Kong would have to enact legislation to prohibit Hong Kong people in general, and the press in particular, from committing acts of subversion, secession, sedition and theft of state secrets.

The new Hong Kong Special Administrative Region (HKSAR) government did not try to enact the law until recently. Seven years after the change of political regime, in fact, many leading lawyers argue that there is no imminent threat that the law will be enacted. However, from the perspective of the Chinese authorities, the law is intended to safeguard national security in general and to 'implement the reunification of Hong Kong with China'.[789] The HKSAR government's popularity in implementing its policy reached a record low when it tried to push this unpopular law through by force. The reason I mention this incident is because, first, it was seen to be a revival of draconian colonial measures, which would certainly have an impact on the press; and, second, the high turnout in protest against this enactment was arguably a result of the mobilisation of certain parts of the radical press and a broadcaster.[790] The resistance of certain media proprietors and journalists to the new political regime, and indeed their reluctance to toe the official line, reveals that the journalistic tradition and norms remained strong in the media culture, despite the change of political regime. But what are these journalistic traditions and norms, and how do they evolve and influence media practices?

First of all, I shall look at one of the leading media watchdogs, the Hong Kong Journalists Association (HKJA), whose embedded journalistic norms are mostly recognised by Hong Kong people in general and journalists in particular. This professionally oriented union brought the imminent threat of the incoming regime in general and the threat of the new national security law in particular to the attention of the Hong Kong people more than a decade ago. As mentioned earlier, Article 23 of the mini-constitution, the Basic Law, was strengthened considerably following the crackdown of 4 June 1989, with the intention of preventing any threat to the central government. After half-a-million people demonstrated against the proposed national security law and the maladministration of the HKSAR government, the Chinese authorities alleged that the HKJA was one of the organisations that instigated foreign media/journalistic groups to campaign against the new national security bill.[791]

Emerging union embraces western journalistic norms

Paradoxically, the HKJA was originally set up to fight for journalistic rights under colonial rule, but after more than three decades' work, it turned out to be more of a professionally oriented union, and indeed a 'watchdog' for press freedom under Chinese rule. The HKJA, the first journalistic trade union in Hong Kong, was set up in 1968, a year after major political disturbances against British rule. It was intended to help colleagues get the working conditions they deserved and also to achieve an increase in their wages. 'It was undignified, I remember, that local firefighters should turn their hoses on reporters and photographers, as they once did,' said Jack Spackman, the founder chairman.[792] Indeed, two years after it had been officially established, on 1 April 1968, the Association was still complaining to the Director of Fire Services about one of these hosings, as well as protesting to the police about reporters being threatened and pushed around.

> We were given better typhoon gear at the *SCMP* [*South China Morning Post*] and *China Mail* after pushing for it. We also, after considerable argument, obtained blankets and pillows to go with the camp stretchers provided for reporters and editors trapped in the office during typhoons. Small issues in the context of today's headlong rush towards a new political and social order, but big issues back then for our men and women in the trenches.[793]

The Association, from the outset, worked to make the government, business leaders and media owners aware of new ideas about the proper treatment of journalists. The union, which was established by some 30–50 journalists, survived and continued to grow throughout its lifespan and worked hard on education too. They ran 'forums and lectures, and ploughed out newsletters, essential marketing techniques for a union seeking to build a membership in the face both of apathy among colleagues and antagonism from certain media barons.'[794] Thus the HKJA was initially set up to negotiate rights for journalists. The original founders were mainly expatriate journalists, but they were later joined by local journalists, as more and more were educated in local journalism schools.[795]

Journalism training in Hong Kong was primarily based on the U.S. model. It was based on the premise that freedom of the press was a right to freedom of expression and information. The role of the press was two-fold. First, it must be objective, fair and impartial so as to make available to the public the diverse views on a news event or any issue of public concern, so that members of the public could form their own views and make their own judgements. Second, the press was also a watchdog against the government to ensure that the government functioned properly and acted within its proper scope, i.e. according to the model of liberal democracy. These two roles, however, may be seen as conflicting.[796]

> For instance, some may criticize journalists for joining the 'campaign for Xi Yang's early release' and the latest anti-article 23 rally as it may jeopardize their impartiality or the image of it. But one may argue the contrary is the case. If we do nothing or do not exhaust all means of stopping the government from committing basic wrongs, we fail to perform the second role properly. In times of peace or operating under a full-fledged democracy, the press may not face intense pressure from both sides. But in Hong Kong where the political

system is basically undemocratic and the government somehow threatens basic human rights, journalists always ponder whether they should go beyond objective reporting and campaign for a better society.[797]

Raising awareness in anticipation of political handover

Indeed, when the announcement of Hong Kong's handover back to China came two decades ago, this conflicting role became obvious. As a union, the HKJA foresaw that Hong Kong journalists would face major challenges. Its role began to shift. To start with, raising political awareness and defending journalists' political rights in the face of the incoming Chinese communist regime became an urgent matter. This was a very significant time in Hong Kong's history, with the announcement of the Sino-British Joint Declaration (an agreement resolving Hong Kong's future) in September 1984, and the subsequent politicisation of Hong Kong as it faced an uncertain march towards 1997. Like many other organisations in Hong Kong at the time, the HKJA became more active politically, in many respects acting more like a pressure group than a traditional trade union. The HKJA began focusing its attention on press freedom issues, and the need for the reform of outdated colonial laws affecting freedom of expression. The union was also to become more actively involved with international media organisations, joining both the International Federation of Journalists and the Commonwealth Journalists Association. Mobilising international support and raising political awareness became the new focus, and this new focus was, on the whole, supported by its members. Membership reached a peak of more than 800 (which was said to represent at least one third of professional journalists in Hong Kong) by 1997, during which year there was a contested election for the position of chairperson.[798]

In a bid to consolidate the local rank-and-file so that a concerted effort could be made to meet the challenges ahead, the HKJA established its own identity in the mid-1980s by changing its organisational structural and increasing localisation, so that it was no longer dominated by expatriate correspondents. A Chinese executive committee member proposed that the HKJA should make a clear-cut move to establish its own image and set out its long-term goals. So it was decided that the union should rent its own offices and hire a full-time organiser to carry out its executive duties.[799] At that time, the Foreign Correspondents' Club (FCC) premises were rented out by the Hong Kong government at a minimal fee, and were supposed to be shared between the FCC and the HKJA. However, the latter was eventually forced to squeeze into a single room in 1986. The union was facing a financial crisis.[800]

We did not (and still do not) have many members; we have always been constrained by the comparatively small number of journalists in the workforce. Membership dues were barely covering the union's daily expenses, and to top it off we were fighting an isolated battle for press freedom in Hong Kong.[801]

Financial independence was crucial, especially if the union was to become truly independent and free from either public influence or private ones. A major source of income for them in those days was an appropriation of several tens of thousands of dollars from the profits of the Press Ball, the annual fund-raising event organised jointly with the Hong Kong Press Club, a body composed mainly of non-journalists and non-locals. At the Annual General Meeting of that year the important decision not to be reliant in the future on joint fund-raising efforts with the Press Club was made. Instead the union would organise its very own fund-raising ball.[802]

Agenda-setting: lobbying the colonial administration to redress the draconian law

The HKJA's major role as a pressure group for press freedom began to take shape at this time. The campaign for law reform bore fruit with the repeal of the outdated press control laws, and the scrapping of government powers to review and prohibit TV programmes. The starting point for the HKJA's media law reform campaign, in many ways, was the publication of the draft Joint Declaration in September 1984.[803]

Ironically, many of the draconian laws were meant to target the two Chinese regimes facing each other across the Taiwan Strait. Historically, many of the outdated and draconian colonial laws came into existence at the time of the formation of the People's Republic of China (PRC), and were at the time considered necessary to prevent the China/Taiwan rivalry from affecting the smooth running of the colony. They gave the government sweeping, undefined powers to control the media. By the mid-1980s, these laws were considered obsolete, as China no longer constituted a potential threat to the security of Hong Kong. There was also a growing feeling that the statute book should be cleaned up, and that this was an essential part of the process of removing the 'taints of colonialism', as the 1984 report of the assessment office put it. The first target for the HKJA in its law reform programme was the Control of Publications Consolidation Ordinance, which was enacted in 1951. This was repealed in early 1987, though it was replaced by a new offence of maliciously publishing false news.[804]

As one of the leading lobbyists against repressive media laws, the HKJA fought the entrenched reluctance of the colonial authorities to give up their many instruments of control over the media. This was to become more evident in a later battle for reform of broadcasting laws. The HKJA, in seeking changes to media-related laws, was becoming more aware of the need to carry out political lobbying work, both in Britain and Hong Kong.[805] However, the ice seemed to thaw following a change in British policy on Hong Kong in the last few years of British rule after John Major took over as British Prime Minister. Things seemed to move rapidly upon the arrival of the last Governor, Chris Patten, who, for various reasons (including the preparation for the handover of Hong Kong back to China), took greater interest in press freedom issues. He also attended the HKJA's fund-raising ball in 1993 as guest of honour. Although this was not the first time that a British governor attended an HKJA function, Patten nevertheless demonstrated his willingness to listen and indeed take heed of journalistic concerns about the need for legal reform.[806]

In light of these subtle changes in the larger environment, the HKJA saw the need to push through demands for a more open and accountable government in anticipation of a possible roll-back after the Chinese take-over in 1997. Indeed, there was an urgent need for the HKJA as a trade union to participate in, and press for, open and transparent government as Hong Kong constitutional reform had slowed down as a result of the Sino-British arrangement. Prior to the signing of the Joint Declaration in 1984, and the introduction of an elected element to the Legislative Council, few people were interested in challenging the government's virtual monopoly on information.[807] It was extremely difficult for the public to obtain information from the government, unless its release was to the administration's advantage. The greater political awareness created in the mid-1980s, plus more aggressive politicians and pressure groups, led Hong Kong residents to think about whether the colonial government should become more open and transparent in its dealings with society. Unfortunately, the China factor became a major obstacle in the course of media liberalisation. For instance, in 1991, the HKJA formed a core group to press the government for access legislation.[808] In 1994, the campaign bore fruit, but the government move was condemned by the Chinese authorities who said it constituted a major change to the government system, with post-1997 implications.[809]

Standard-setting body

During the transition period, the defence of the integrity and credibility of the news profession became an important role for the HKJA. The political rift between the British and Chinese became so great that the news media found it hard not to get involved in one way or another. The imminent threat of the incoming new regime was real, and journalists were warned that the price of freedom was 'eternal vigilance' as noted by Emily Lau:

> Although the Hong Kong people will be delivered to Chinese Communist rule in 4 years' time, there is a feeling that 1997 has already arrived. Seemingly every day the Chinese government throws its attacks, insults and intimidations towards Governor Chris Patten, among others, for having the temerity to demand a quicker pace of democracy. Beijing's objective, simply, is to undermine the governor and the colonial administration.[810]

Emily Lau, the journalist-turned-legislator, said one of the casualties of the Sino-British row was the local news media, which in many instances had failed to offer the troubled community high quality, critical and analytical reporting.

> The Hong Kong people are fed a daily overdose of anti-Patten propaganda and invectives generated by Beijing, by local pro-communist factions and

by short-sighted, selfish business people. If one were to rely entirely on the news media for information, one would surely reach the conclusion that the overwhelming majority of the community is against the governor and his political reform proposals. Alas, public opinion polls have for months consistently told a different story – that those who support the governor's package outnumber those who oppose it by 2 to 1.[811]

Because of the incoming Chinese regime, the colony was arguably in need of fearless, independent and vibrant news media to present the many sides of these tortuous arguments. Unsurprisingly, the Chinese authorities exerted pressure on certain news media, seeking an explanation for why the HKJA's core activists were concentrated in a particular newspaper, *Ming Pao Daily News*.[812]

According to Emily Lau, what Hong Kong did not need was a media too frightened to report and speak the truth. Yet Hong Kong journalists were under constant and increasing pressure. She believed that the HKJA had a role in fending off this disturbing force. Indeed the HKJA was at first the only organisation to press for the Johannesburg principles to be used as a guideline in the promulgation of the new national security law, though the idea was later picked up by other NGOs as well.[813]

> I have repeatedly warned that Hong Kong could lose its press freedom before 1997 in the face of China's increasingly relentless pressure on local journalists, some of whom are too spineless or too inexperienced to fight back. Thus the task of defending the integrity and credibility of the news profession has fallen on the Hong Kong Journalists Association, which has a number of tireless and determined fighters.[814]

The Chinese imposed tight restrictions on the Hong Kong press, mainly because Hong Kong newspapers had extensively reported and commented on the student movement and the aftermath of the Tiananmen massacre in Beijing in 1989. It was at this point that the Chinese authorities started to label Hong Kong reporters in general, and the HKJA in particular, 'subversive' elements, and imposed the seven guidelines on them.[815] Indeed, the HKJA has been instrumental in resisting pressure from Beijing, and consistently campaigned for the early release of Xi Yang and other mainland journalists.[816] Specifically, it has been active in criticising the Beijing authorities for malpractices and ill treatment of Hong Kong journalists, namely interrogation, detainment, confiscation of return-home-permits and bans on entering the country. The union has publicised all the major shortcomings of both the central and local government and other adversaries, as well as incidents of oppression of journalists.[817]

To facilitate its role as one of the leading lobbying groups, the union has annually documented, and campaigned against, any political and economic interference. In anticipation of the 1997 handover, one crucial step taken by the HKJA was the publication of an Annual Report on freedom of expression, starting in 1993. The emphasis has been on monitoring and documenting the escalating Chinese interference with Hong Kong journalists covering news in China. The document has since become the only annual booklet documenting self-censorship and restrictions affecting the freedom of the press, and serves as the only primary systematic documentation for further research and lobbying for freedom of speech, both locally and abroad.[818]

Yet defining its role and direction in the post-1997 reality became problematic even for the HKJA: partly because the restrictions on civil liberties in general were not as clear-cut as previously envisaged, particularly there was no direct interference with the press on the part of the central authorities, but rather a more subtle and more effective mechanism, such as 'carrot and stick' tactics, and economic censorship exercised by, for example, owners, managements and advertisers. Above all, the political culture was also shifting. This resulted in the emergence of a pro-China organisation, the Hong Kong Federation of Journalists (HKFJ). In an apparent bid to counter the lobbying influence of the HKJA, the Federation, founded by journalists primarily from China-funded newspapers such as *Wen Wei Po, Ta Kung Pao, New Evening Post* and *Hong Kong Commercial Daily*, was set up on the eve of the handover. The Federation was reportedly said to have received subsidies and support from central authorities in the form of educational and professional exchanges in China.[819] Apart from that, News Executives Association (NEA) and Newspaper Society (NS) became more actively involved, and played a more important role after 1997.[820]

Despite the fact that the HKJA no longer enjoyed the reputation of being the only trade union, it remained the most recognised one in the profession. A senior journalist noted:

> It has only been in the past 10 years or so that there have been noticeable and comparable changes within local journalism. And yet in many ways the profession has still not been given the respect and recognition it deserves: this is amply demonstrated by the low wages many journalists continue to be paid ... yet despite this, the HKJA, with the support of its members, has contributed a great deal to improving the lot of fellow journalists and to protecting freedom of the press. As a consequence, step by step, the union has gained broad recognition and respect among the public.[821]

Despite this, the union could not develop into a fully fledged force, partly due to the apparent discouragement by media publishers and bosses of the formation of in-house unions. Only the public broadcaster *Radio Television Hong Kong* and *Reuters News Agency* managed to set one up. Almost all other news organisations were denied permission to form a union. Neither was the HKJA effective as a professional body in setting an ethical standard for members to abide by, because even though most news practitioners firmly believed in journalistic principles, once they sent their copy to the editorial desk, they lost control of it. Sometimes they had to follow the editorial position of their own news organisations receiving instruction from their seniors, or they were not in a position to decide the content of the news product, as shown in Chapter 5. This lack of trade unions in individual news organisations has largely created a 'firewall' that has reduced the ability of the rank and file to engage in political activities. Yet journalistic values and norms, upheld by the HKJA for more than three decades, are still shared by most professional journalists and embedded in their working principles, although many have had to compromise in the face of economic pressure.[822] A strong journalistic culture remained firmly in place, however, and in the case of conflict between journalists and management, even the latter apparently respected the norms and could not intervene explicitly as described in Chapter 5. More often than not, management had to resort to making excuses to cover up their real motives.

Despite the fact that the HKJA is regarded as being a 'tiger without teeth', it is fair to say that it has played an important role in setting ethical standards for journalists to follow. The HKJA has the power to fine a member and even to expel a member, who has the right to appeal to the HKJA's appeal committee. In reality, predictably, these powers have not been used. Also, because only a few news organisations have in-house unions, as described above, the union remains weak in negotiating journalists' rights. Despite that, the HKJA remains the only territory-wide trade union representing journalists.[823] Being the only representative of journalists, it has relentlessly monitored the erosion of press freedom, giving expression to journalistic aspirations and upholding professionalism. Above all, it has provided an independent and critical voice against both the British colonial and Chinese regimes in the face of their interference with press freedom. During the transition and post-colonial periods, in particular, its roles of raising awareness, supporting repressed journalists, and monitoring, documenting and campaigning against Chinese interference in press freedom, became significant. However, in order to make this happen, the HKJA has had to rely on the profession in general and individual journalists in particular for their fearless resistance and struggle against meddling.[824]

Rebel journalists

The Hong Kong Journalists Association set out professional guidelines for journalists, but these could only be implemented by the journalists themselves. In cases such as those of Xi Yang, Willy Lam, Jasper Becker, Danny Gittings and Paul Cheung, journalists in one way or another demonstrated their relentless independent professional judgment, and their will to resist the meddling of political or economic interests, by either exposing the oppressors or complaining of unfair treatment. Although in the end, most of these dissident and non-conformist journalists were sacked or resigned voluntarily, they confronted their publishers or editors and stood up for their professional principles. Inevitably, the development of Hong Kong's journalistic norms was influenced by the larger political and social environment. As indicated in Chapters 2 and 3, historically, Hong Kong has always been a haven for political activists to launch journals and newspapers to promote their cause. Such causes have opposed, at different times, the imperial Qing Dynasty, the warlords, the Japanese invasion, and lately the two contemporary main Chinese rival parties – the Chinese Communist Party (CCP) and the nationalist Taiwanese Kuomintang (KMT) party.[825]

Because of Hong Kong's special status as a colony, a major Chinese diaspora city and a window to the west, its press was tolerated by the coloniser, as long as the media did not contravene the legal framework and pose a threat to British rule.[826] Subsequently, a diversified media helped to maintain the status quo and keep a balance between the CCP and the KMT. This balance in Chinese politics arguably helped the British to maintain their rule.

After the CCP took over China in 1949, Hong Kong initially benefited from the capital and enterprise introduced by émigré newspapermen and women from Shanghai.[827] Pro-KMT and anti-CCP journalists fled to Hong Kong to start a new agency. Yet those who supported or had sympathy with the CCP also came to Hong Kong to carry on with their united-front work for Taiwan, mediated through Hong Kong publications. In the late 1970s and early 1980s, on the whole, the leftist press was a minority while the mainstream Hong Kong press was regarded as being anti-CCP or KMT-friendly or pro-British.

In Hong Kong, journalistic norms were affected and indeed shaped by this political division. That is to say, journalists on the whole largely held one of two editorial positions – they either identified with, or shared the ideology of, the leftist or the rightist position. In private, however, journalists socialised with each other in their leisure time through sports activities (as evidenced by the HKJA's annual football league) and games of majong. However, it was only after the early 1980s when Hong Kong's future had been resolved through Sino-British talks that the Hong Kong press began to shift structurally and editorially in preparation for political change and in anticipation of new norms under the new regime. This was true for the quality press, such as *Wah Kiu Yat Po* (*Overseas Chinese Daily News*) and *Sing Tao Daily News*, and even for the mass circulation/tabloid press, such as *Oriental Daily News, Sing Pao Daily News* and *The Express*, all of which largely kept their historical link with Taiwan. One indication of these links was that they all followed the way the Republic of China (ROC) printed dates. Another was that they mostly labelled the Chinese Communist Party (CCP) 'communist thief', and referred to China proper as the 'thief's land'. These indications were erased during the late 1980s and early 1990s.[828] *Ming Pao Daily News* was initially set up as a commercial paper, but later shifted to the style of the quality press after establishing itself as a critical/anti-CCP newspaper following the 1967 disturbances. Thus, it is fair to say that, prior to the late 1970s/early 1980s, the mainstream Hong Kong press had a strong tradition of being anti-CCP and KMT-friendly or pro-establishment.

The shift in the larger environment also affected journalistic norms. First, the quality/elite press, for example, *Ming Pao Daily News* and *Sing Tao Daily News*, shifted from an anti-CCP position to a pro-CCP/CCP-friendly one, and severed links with Taiwan officially. Second, similar structural changes occurred in mass circulation papers, such as *Oriental Daily News*. Third, the elite press, such as *South China Morning Post*, shifted from a pro-British establishment position to a China-friendly one. Journalistic attitudes were also subtly affected in the following ways. First, there was a new interpretation of the political terms 'left' and 'right'. Second, in private and implicitly, 'leftist' or ex-leftist journalists were stereotyped and described as radicals, lunatics and extremists because they once served the pro-CCP media. Third, and most importantly, although journalists in general claimed that they respected journalistic norms such as 'objectivity, impartiality and fairness' regarding the production of news, their position also shifted, though the basic notion of journalistic rights remained. Although there was a shift to a general acceptance of mainland China as the incoming regime, there was scepticism regarding China's promise to allow Hong Kong to maintain its status quo, and even a general fear in the profession about the prospects for press freedom in Hong Kong.

As seen in Chapter 3 (the textual analysis of selective news coverage in the pre-handover period), the journalistic response to the treatment of Xi Yang was fearless, furious and above all rebellious, especially in the beginning and during the campaign for his release. Here, we can identify quite a strong tradition of independent professionalism arguing vigorously for Hong Kong journalistic rights against mainland China's loosely defined law. Their response can also be explained by the anxieties they felt concerning the future of the Hong Kong press and their apparent fear that they might share Xi's fate following the handover in 1997. Whatever the underlying motivation, it is indisputable that Hong Kong journalists organised a strong protest and signature campaign to lobby for Xi's early release. This could not have been accomplished without the desire to fight for the preservation of press freedom.

Commercial radio

Under the circumstances of a new political reality, it is not surprising that phone-in/talk-back public affairs programmes would be increasingly well received. The independent watchdog spirit was best demonstrated by Albert Cheng King-hon, a *Commercial Radio* broadcaster who fearlessly and vigorously confronted the powerful and the rich, through his leading popular phone-in/talk-back programme, 'Teacup in a Storm' (*sic*). The news agenda he pushed was recycled as news content in the following day's newspapers, and was sometimes even heard or seen promptly in the news bulletins of other broadcasting media. The speedy turnover of news content explains why Cheng was regarded as one of the most powerful and influential individuals in Hong Kong.[829] The competitive nature of the media and its advanced technology explains why issues of public concern could blow up within hours rather than days or months. One case in point was when the Hong Kong chief executive, Tung Chee-hwa, had to retreat from his original intention of hosting a birthday party for a heavyweight politician, Sir Sze-Yuen Chung, at the colonial Government House because of public opposition.[830] Cheng's programme was the first to mobilise public opinion to speak out against the proposal, and both the mass circulation and quality daily newspapers covered the story the following day. So within 24 hours, amid official complacency and slow spin, Tung had no choice but to withdraw his original proposal. Subsequently, the Hong Kong administration appeared to be less tolerant, and wanted to exert tighter control over this critical broadcasting programme. Despite the popularity of the radio station, *Commercial Radio* was under threat of not having its licence renewed after its expiry, partly because of the performance of its top-rating phone-in programme, 'Teacup in a Storm', which aired public criticism of the head of the administration and senior officials on a daily basis. This is another example of state suppression using rules and regulations.[831]

Significantly, amid concerns over the freedom of expression in the five years following the handover, the radio phone-in programme emerged as one of the most popular media for gauging and expressing public opinion. Among them, Albert Cheng's 'Teacup in a Storm' was notable, as many Hong Kongers, particularly the working class, tuned into his programme first thing in the morning to listen to his coarse voice, and be reassured that it was 'business as usual'. Albert Cheng, popularly known as 'Tai-pan',[832] has created a successful model of speaking up for ordinary people. He invented himself as an 'independent watchdog' and set the news agenda for the day. 'Government officials have had to come and respond to us in the past two to three years because we are the radio station with the highest ratings and our programme is the most popular one among programmes of a similar nature at a prime time slot,' Albert Cheng said.[833] His fearlessness is best demonstrated by his resilience after a serious assault in August 1998, when he almost died. Sceptics believed he was attacked for his outspokenness, and the whole society was shocked.[834] Although he was afraid, he continued to speak up on issues of public concern. Having experienced this life threatening attack, he underwent a mental struggle, but decided that he should continue his programme because he did not want to give his supporters the idea that violence would prevail.

> Before the assault, I almost decided to quit since I have been hosting the 'teacup in a storm' [*sic*] for so many years ... I had already suffered before that, for instance, in 1983, I sat next to the director of the party's United Front Department, but in 1984 I was not allowed to enter the country because of my work as a TV public affairs talk show host [critical of Chinese politics].[835]

> I used to be a businessman [and a publisher], since I took up the job of hosting current affairs and later a phone-in program, I have lost many old friends ... and peer pressure has been brought to bear on me, but fortunately I am not a sociable person. I quite enjoy my solitude ... I accept perhaps that is the price I have to pay for being outspoken.[836]

What with the risks to his personal security, several libel cases and state suppression, his feelings of loneliness steadily grew after 1997, partly due to the changes in the political environment, which surely had a bearing on his work. Like Lam Hang-chi, the proprietor of *Hong Kong Economic Journal* (whose situation will be discussed below), Cheng sensed that there was an obvious change in the political culture of the news media. For instance, he found news organisations politically cautious, and uninterested in following up on sensitive issues and policies. It was vastly different from the past when, if he covered an issue, other news organisations would follow it up.[837]

Furthermore, even a famous radio broadcaster like him was not totally immune from internal and external pressures. The difference was that he was supported by his proprietor, mainly because of the commercial value of his top-rating programme that apparently helped to draw in advertising. Cheng complained about one heavyweight political figure, Selina Chow, a veteran legislator of the pro-business Liberal Party and chairperson of the Hong Kong Tourist Association. She wrote to Cheng's boss, George Ho, the chairman and owner of *Commercial Radio*, complaining that Cheng did not provide adequate time for her to respond. Ho refused to get personally involved.[838] Apart from exerting pressure through one's boss, Cheng reflected:

> The two most powerful weapons to silence journalistic practitioners are to use violence and legal means to sue. They could make you and your family live in anxiety all the time. An ordinary person could not easily deal with personal security as well as a financial burden at the same time.[839]

A returnee from Canada, having lived there from 1968 to the early 1980s, he was initially fearful of the CCP, but he shifted to a position of reconciliation and wished to make a contribution to Hong Kong's future. The popularity of his programme showed that he successfully made use of the political space left by the elite, and above all the mainstream, press who on the whole exercised political caution and self-censorship under the new political regime.[840] Yet Cheng came under pressure to self-censor because *Commercial Radio*'s broadcasting license was due to expire in August 2003, and the station's performance was under close scrutiny and there were fears it might be given a probation period.[841] Observers noted that the latest warning issued by the Broadcasting Authority about Cheng's style of broadcasting was 'unfair' as he had been doing the same thing for the past few years.[842] Cheng abruptly took early summer leave, threatening not to return, as a protest against the Broadcasting Authority's warning. He said:

> I have been threatened by the triad, sued in a libel case, and badly assaulted. Never have I experienced such intimidation. The worst thing is I don't even know where I can see justice done.[843]

His protest proved to be fruitful: he earned enormous sympathy – tens of thousands of supporters wrote to the Broadcasting Authority in support of him.[844] As a result, the HKSAR administration extended the licence of the *Commercial Radio* station for another 12 years, with an interim review in six years' time.

To sum up, because of its historical, political and cultural context, Hong Kong was not allowed to develop into a democracy, but the Hong Kong people have eventually developed a sense of democracy and become freedom lovers.[845] This was first because the last generation of refugees risked their lives to come to Hong Kong and, second, because the second generation became more and more westernised and generally educated to liberal thinking and freedom. In the case of journalists, they were usually trained in a school of journalism that was largely modelled on similar schools in western liberal democracies, such as the U.S. The nature of the phone-in/talk-back programme gave the people a voice. Given Cheng's outspoken style, he successfully negotiated with various departments, got results and speedy responses and, above all, helped ordinary and powerless people to air their grievances and dissent. He once told undergraduate students that in fact he did much more than a normal journalist/broadcaster. He referred many cases to government departments, legal firms, social services and NGOs on a daily basis.[846]

At the same time, he was also empowered by his audience, and public support encouraged him to continue. Indeed, the popularity he enjoyed apparently helped to fend off interference as it meant he received support from his proprietor. The fact that there was a broadcaster who could act as a watchdog and set the agenda for members of the public helped to reassure people that Hong Kong continued to be free. As with the HKJA's role in the case of journalists – even though on the surface, more often than not, there was no immediate substantive social change – Cheng's gestures made a difference because justice appeared to have been done, even if it was only on air.

Rebel publishers

Hong Kong Economic Journal

> Strictly speaking, there was no legal restriction on press freedom before 1997; however, after 1997, the HKSAR came up with a proposal to enact article 23 of the Basic Law, which would change the situation in respect of Hong Kong's press freedom.[847]

It was not just journalists who were rebels; there were also maverick publishers and proprietors. *Hong Kong Economic Journal* (*HKEJ*) has been named as one of the two papers that remained independent and relatively free of self-censorship.[848] In the general atmosphere of rampant self-censorship, Lam Hang-chi, the proprietor of the *HKEJ*, announced on the thirtieth anniversary of the paper that he might need to sell the paper in light of the HKSAR's intention of rushing through the new national security bill. By this action, he highlighted the imminent threat posed by the bill in question.[849] He thought that it would pose an unprecedented threat to press freedom, and did not want to risk his staff going to jail for working for the press.[850]

A critical elite press tradition

Lam's ideology, and the principles by which he managed an elite paper, largely echoed the long tradition of the critical Chinese press. As mentioned earlier, historically, there was a long-standing tradition of the Chinese press rebelling against a totalitarian monarchy and authoritarian governments. Back in the early twentieth century, mainland Chinese revolutionaries came to Hong Kong to set up newspapers to rebel against the Manchurian government, later the Kuomintang (KMT) military and then the Chinese Communist Party (CCP). Intellectuals and elites, fired by this spirit of Confucianism and conviction,[851] criticised and opposed administrations, and sought to reform them. Their mantle was inherited by media proprietors who fled to Hong Kong after the Communist take-over of China, and who helped to maintain a flourishing Hong Kong press in the 1970s and 1980s.[852] As stated above, the anti-CCP position became the mainstream ideology for both mass circulation and quality papers at that time.

In a written communication with the author, Lam Hang-chi, proprietor and publisher of *Hong Kong Economic Journal*, summarised his experience of owning and publishing an outspoken paper under the rule of the British as well as the Chinese. He said that, in the decade prior to the handover, there was a market for reporting and commentary on Hong Kong economics and politics because of the changing position of Hong Kong and its struggle to move from being a British colony to a Chinese Special Administrative Region. However, following the peaceful regime change, interest in Hong Kong politics shifted from big events to local issues. Despite the shift towards Chinese politics in the larger political environment, Lam's viewpoint remained largely the same.

> As I am not an entrepreneur, my paper is a creation of a newspaperman/ intellectual. I undergo a quest for spirituality and put stress on knowledge and rationality.... As for political commentary, I always consider issues as they really are, and hope to preserve (not advocate) freedom and democracy and ... hope to make stable progress [i.e. not abrupt and 'revolutionary' progress – author's note].
>
> My inclination is the same after the handover as it was before, because it is a matter of principle and not a strategy for managing a newspaper.[853]

New journalistic norms in a new political climate

Understandably, other newspapers might have to put on a 'new face' to pursue political interests, Lam said. He added that if there was any newspaper that needed to change its principles in order to adapt to the change-over, it must have a private reason for doing so that an outsider might not fully appreciate. In the past, newspapers subsidised by the nationalist Kuomintang (KMT) government in China changed their editorial position overnight following the take-over of the Chinese Communist Party. He added that this had not happened in the changeover from British Hong Kong to Chinese Hong Kong. Nevertheless he admitted that there was a change in mentality of Hong Kong people in many ways because of the change of political regime:

> After the handover of Hong Kong, the public sphere has not been narrowed, but the perspective of Hong Kong people has. Among the many reasons are: firstly, along with the retreat of the British, Hong Kong lost a group of experts who used to maintain constant contact and connection with western politics and culture. That constitutes a loss of active intermediaries who could act as inspiring agents of thoughts.[854]

The risks involved in running a paper in the post-colonial era also include changing economic factors, resulting from decolonisation and sinicisation. Market forces became restrictive to the Hong Kong press because market increasingly meant the Chinese market. According to Lam Hang-chi, the second major blow was that Hong Kong could not establish its own identity following the handover, so it had to find a way of identifying with China. Based on the rationale of cultivating a better relationship with China, contact with the international community had become less intense and more indirect. More and more businessmen and women put their efforts into exploring the mainland market. They tended to appreciate and follow the Chinese way of doing things, which largely eroded the existing system, such as respect for the rule of law and the level playing field for business. This further distanced Hong Kong from Europe and America in terms of culture and institutions. In fact, even before the handover, the *Hong Kong Economic Journal* was under enormous pressure, particularly on the economic front.

> During Sino-British negotiations, China-funded organizations boycotted *Hong Kong Economic Journal* and did not place advertisements in the paper, saying that the paper's editorial board was 'pro-British'. However, in the post-handover era, perhaps the British factor was no longer important, their biased view of us has become less obvious.[855]

The economic sanction of an advertising ban by China-funded companies had a serious impact on the newspaper. However, the tactics have changed slightly following the handover. The administration distanced itself from influencing the paper (for example, the chief executive of the HKSAR constantly refused to give interviews to the paper), but dared not isolate this paper altogether because of the paper's influence on senior Chinese officials. The tactics they employed were subtle.[856]

> The leading officials of the HKSAR administration have never boycotted *Hong Kong Economic Journal*. All they did was to treat an individual medium as 'more friendly'. The 'more friendly' media may find it more convenient to get certain news, but they have to pay a price for that, that is, they can't be reserved, distant and objective in commenting on the government.[857]

As pointed out in Chapter 5, some management staff of certain papers adopted a completely different perspective regarding the 'price' of acting as the official channel of the administration. Yet, with the imminent enactment of the proposed anti-subversion law, Lam was pessimistic about the prospects for the press.

> If the attitude of the HKSAR officials does not change, and the enactment of the proposed anti-subversion law [Basic Law article 23] is not abandoned, that would be detrimental to the Hong Kong press. If operating a paper means easily committing a criminal offence, then we would have to think whether it is worthwhile to continue.[858]

Notwithstanding these warnings, he notably refrained from commenting on self-censorship by saying that it was difficult to tell whether there was self-censorship. 'I can only tell from my experience of writing and managing a newspaper. I do not feel there is a need to self-censor myself. In terms of commentary, Hong Kong continues to be very free. But it is hard to say what will happen after the enactment of the anti-subversion law.'[859] In other words, self-censorship would be necessary after the anti-subversion law was formally in place.

Undoubtedly, Lam, an outspoken writer and widely respected newspaperman, enjoyed both respect and popularity, but he was constantly being wooed by the Chinese to engage in united-front work, apparently because of his influence in the community. His books were first published by a Taiwanese publisher, who referred to him as the number one writer in Hong Kong. Mainland China followed suit in printing his book. The potential readership in the mainland was much bigger than in Taiwan given the huge Chinese population there. Observers noted that the Chinese authorities were trying to involve Lam in united-front work in a more subtle way. For instance, Lam's commentary and past editorial writings were reprinted in mainland China, though the controversial and critical political essays on China were removed. Furthermore, an interview with Lam conducted by *Shanghai Wen Hui Bao*, a leading municipal daily in Shanghai, was subsequently printed nationally.[860]

To sum up, Lam, educated in the west, namely in Britain, admired western liberalism and civilisation. He learnt to be a journalist by working at *Ming Pao Daily News* first as a translator. Though *Hong Kong Economic Journal* specialises in finance and business, it is also strong on political reporting and commentary. The running of the quality paper, *Ming Pao Daily News*, may have had an impact on him. Seeing himself as an intellectual and a member of the elite, he differed from other proprietors in the way he managed and operated his papers. He has his own philosophy for running a specialised paper, for example, he did not rush to get listed, as many other proprietors did, to get capital for reinvestment. Nevertheless, in face of imminent political suppression, his response was realistic and involved commercial calculation. As he reportedly said, once the national security law was passed, it is doubtful whether he would continue to be so outspoken as that would likely incur business loss, as well as jeopardising both his own and his staff's personal security.

Apple Daily

Although certain proprietors regarded media prospects as gloomy, others adopted a different perspective. As mentioned earlier, political caution became a trend in the political transition period. However, Jimmy Lai saw this as a precious opportunity for him to employ capitalist methods to make use of the space left by the shift in the position of other newspapers.[861] Given the fact that many mainstream/broadsheet newspapers were falling into the hands of pro-China businessmen and women in the 1990s, who then, on the whole, exercised political caution and exerted full control over their news medium, certain mass newspapers seized the opportunity and operated in a way that helped to sustain their readership as well as to build up their reputation.[862] However, this is not to suggest that every newspaper that adopted a critical position necessarily succeeded in the market. For instance, *Mad-dog Daily*[863] only existed for a brief time prior to the handover. The quality press, such as *Hong Kong Economic Journal*, suffered hardship. In the highly sophisticated and competitive market economy of Hong Kong, in order to survive and flourish, a paper not only needed enormous investment, but also had to employ highly sophisticated marketing, new technologies, advertising and publicity, as in the case of *Apple Daily*. It was unusual in that it combined 'sensationalism' with a critical voice.

After 30 years in the garment business, Lai saw an opportunity to change his career path – from garment entrepreneur to media mogul. He asked around about the feasibility of launching a new Chinese daily newspaper. In the months following the Tiananmen crackdown, Lai went to Albert Cheng King-hon, then publisher of *Forbes* magazine in Hong Kong, for advice about publishing. In an interview, Cheng said 'I am his mentor. He was in the fashion business, then he was my apprentice for three months. At one time, we were almost like brothers. I'm the monster creator. I told him about newspapers, I told him to follow *USA Today*.'[864] Cheng, also a broadcaster (as described above), later broke up with Lai. He is reported as saying 'Jimmy is a monster'. According to Cheng, the way Jimmy did business was ruthless. Cheng thought Lai was in fact contaminating the environment and every other newspaper that followed him.[865]

In the mid-1990s, it was rumoured that most of the news media proprietors had been co-opted by the Chinese authorities. For example, the owners of the two terrestrial TV stations and the only cable TV station were all invited to be advisers on Hong Kong affairs to Beijing.[866] Lai was keen to launch a daily after his success with his popular weekly magazine – *Next Magazine*. A founding editor of *Apple Daily* reckoned that there should be room in the market for an outspoken mass circulation daily, so Lai invited him to line up staff and set up the paper.[867] Lai set aside an enormous amount of cash – 0.7 billion Hong Kong dollars (approximately equivalent to £50 million) – to sustain the anticipated losses of the first three years. 'Apple' was presumably a tribute to his growing interest in the Bible. Lai converted to Catholicism a week after Hong Kong was handed back to China. He said to a reporter that there had been news ever since Eve had bitten the apple in the Garden of Eden.[868] Without evil, there was no news. But the evil he referred to also included the impending arrival of China, which *Apple Daily* intended to monitor as a pro-democracy newspaper.

The success of the mass circulation paper had much to do with Lai's management skills and above all his reinvention of himself as the icon of an uncertain city. At first Lai portrayed himself through the foreign media as a freedom-fighter.[869] He constructed an impressive image of himself and of *Apple Daily* as a daring paper. However, the downside was the acute competition *Apple Daily* created. Since its launch in 1995, *Apple Daily* has changed the press culture drastically.[870] It has influenced not only other tabloids but also quality papers, which have followed its style of succinct and graphic layout and reporting, and the playing up of trivial and sensational stories. His accomplishment, according to one founding staff member of *Apple Daily*, was to 'rebel against the complacency of the Chinese press and he applied a whole lot of western technology and ideas in making the mass appeal paper work'.[871]

Lai's entrepreneurial style, as described in Chapter 5, was tough and clear-cut. He would fire anybody he wanted to silence, though he paid them compensation. He also gave financial rewards to motivate his staff, and encouraged journalists to stay by giving them shares.[872] He also broke the newspaper retail price cartel that had been controlled by the Hong Kong Newspaper Society for years.[873] This turned the Hong Kong newspaper industry upside down and introduced unprecedented and cut-throat competition; subsequently some papers ceased publication. This had a tremendous impact on the newspaper environment as many, including the quality papers, followed *Apple Daily*'s successful model, not only in content and outlook, but also in language and the tone of trivialisation and commercialism, and above all in diminishing moral and professional standards. However, Lai had his own philosophy:

> 'Otherwise, we can't survive. It is . . . a lesser evil. To sustain press freedom is a greater good . . . But if we don't have it [pornography], we probably sell 30 percent less and I can't sustain the newspaper. If I had a choice, I wouldn't do it. It's the heat of the kitchen. I've got to stay in it,' Jimmy Lai said.[874]

The fact remains that Lai's worldview shaped the paper over which he had absolute control. The proprietor, who despised journalists, had an enormous impact on the tone of the paper. On the one hand, Lai did not censor the daily news before it went to print. On the other hand, it was an open secret how his worldview shaped the paper's content and style. He often chaired meetings with senior staff and did not refrain from disclosing his strong views on news in general, and on politics in particular. Most of the senior editors would know his views on, for example, Falun Gong or the proposed enactment of the anti-subversion law.[875]

However, some working journalists welcomed the establishment of such a paper. One senior editor, who has also worked for a quality paper for many years, remarked that not many papers in Hong Kong could provide such space for journalists to work in.[876] This may be true, but on the other hand, not every one could tolerate Lai's hot temper and the way he treated his staff. Those journalists who had worked under him complained that he did not respect people but just pushed for the boosting of circulation by all means. 'He is the kind of person who is willing to cooperate with his partners in an uphill struggle, but perhaps that's not equally true when he is prosperous,' one founding editor, who chose to resign after helping to steer the paper for the first few years, remarked.[877]

New media culture

Even a popular paper like *Apple Daily* had to face the cruel realities of survival under state as well as corporate bans. Lai was determined to turn *Apple Daily* into one of the leading tabloid dailies, but one with a critical tone. His success in getting both working class as well as middle class readers is explained by the fact that other so-called quality papers were in fact less bold in pointing out the malpractices of the new regime. One senior editor noted:

> Other quality papers are hypocritical when they complain that the *Apple* culture has destroyed the next generation – with its sex, violence and opinion mixed with facts, very often unfair to politicians, officials as well as to ordinary people.[878]

A veteran editor who has worked on a quality paper for some time reflected that it was, in a sense, a waste of time working for those papers that claimed to abide by professional standards, when in fact they did not.[879] Another feature of Lai's success as a media publisher was his keenness in taking things to the limit: he checked the circulation weekly, if there was any drop, he would press for the reason. 'What lead story goes on the front page make a big difference – one can tell immediately whether the story will sell papers,' one senior member of staff said.[880] Though tycoons, such as Li Ka-shing, banned advertising in *Apple Daily*, the paper, with its large middle-class readership, attracted other up-market advertising, including real estate and expensive consumer goods such as watches, jewellery and cars.

So was *Apple Daily* a freedom fighter or a market exploiter? There have been debates about the media phenomenon *Apple Daily* helped to create, and whether the paper truly represented the Hong Kong people's voice. Remarkably, a senior manager noted that if the 'market' changed, so would the editorial position of the paper. 'If Hong Kong people no longer support democracy and civil liberty, then we would change our position because we follow the market mechanism.'[881] In other words, 'democracy sells, so papers sell'. However, the ideology Lai claimed to uphold and the commercialism he championed were two sides of the same coin. Lai proclaimed, for instance, his anti-Chinese Communist position that may or may not have been fully represented in his paper.[882] Despite this, both the mass circulation daily and its proprietor reaped fame and profits.

On the other hand, according to one of his senior executives, after the paper's coverage of the 1 July march protesting against the new national security bill, the paper received a lot of messages saying 'well done'.[883] Although this good-will did not immediately translate into advertising revenue, hopefully it would later.

> It's more symbolic. Advertising hasn't increased because of our support for the protest. It's more like a brand building exercise with more people linking our name to a popular cause.[884]

Indeed, before and on the eve of the mass protest, the daily and the weekly owned by Lai were actively involved in mobilising their readers. For instance, on the eve of the 1 July pro-democracy protest, the cover of *Next Magazine*, the city's muckraking weekly, featured a photographic mock-up of the Hong Kong Chief Executive, Tung Chee-hwa, taking a pie right in the face. The caption urged readers to 'take to the streets'. During the days leading up to the demon-stration against the proposed new national security bill, *Next*'s sister publication, *Apple Daily*, distributed cartoon stickers calling for Tung to be ousted, and dis-tributed posters on the day of the march.[885] Regarding the question whether the publisher ordered this anti-government move, an executive said:

> It's not an order from Jimmy [Lai]. The editorial team just decided to do it. We on the business side just went along with the decision editorial made. I'm sure when editorial made the decision they didn't have advertising in mind at all.
>   That [the good response] doesn't help us directly. No one is going to come to us and say we would like to advertise in your paper because it's anti-government. What we're hoping instead is to give the impression that *Apple Daily* is *the* paper people are buying and reading these days. By doing so, we hope more advertisers will come as a result of the paper getting more popular and talked about, rather than as a result of our political stand.[886]

However, he admitted that what they did was controversial, and he did worry, from a business perspective, about the consequences of overstepping the mark as a newspaper.

> Yes, I do worry about an ad [advertisement] boycott. But there's nothing I can do as a business manager here. Editorial is in charge and I'm not in a position to tell them what to do. . . . What we did was of course controver-sial. My answer would be: let the market/reader decide. If we stepped beyond what a paper should be doing, we would be punished commercially. If not, if readers like it, then we would go ahead. The market is our only yardstick here.[887]

The market factor

Undoubtedly, marketing was the name of the game. Another special feature of *Apple Daily* was that through its proprietor's personal efforts, the paper had formed an informal alliance with civil institutions and celebrities. This informal networking had built up quite a strong resistance to some of the government's policy, including the campaign for the enactment of the proposed anti-subversion law. Among these allies, liberal politicians and a religious leader, opinions concerning the paper were vague, sometimes ambivalent and sometimes endorsing. Martin Lee, the founding chairman of the opposition Democratic Party, said:

> I'm not saying everything he [Lai] does is right. Some pages are extremely good, some are extremely bad. Some of those photographs are ghastly, and I certainly do not approve. But if you want a large circulation you may have to compromise. If you run a paper that is respectable and gentlemanly, like *Hong Kong Economic Journal*, the influence is low. I have a lot of respect for Mr Lam [Lam Hang-chi, the Journal's founder and publisher] but how far can he reach? That's the problem.[888]

A barrister and legislator also agreed with Lee. '*Apple Daily* is a mixed blessing. It's often unbearable, but when you hear a symphony of voices of people putting on kid gloves about some government proposal, it is often the only paper that doesn't mince words.'[889] For the outspoken and respected Roman Catholic Bishop, Joseph Zen, Lai was a good friend and a very special businessman who did not have much interest in making money. 'He has high ideals and a keen sense of cultivating his own personality with his love for reading. . . . I think he himself leaves much freedom to his editorial staff,' Bishop Zen reportedly said.[890]

However, although he allowed his editorial staff considerable freedom, that did not mean he had no political influence. With regards to the biggest controversy in post-colonial Hong Kong, Lai's stance as proprietor had a bearing on the paper's position. Given his strong opposition to the proposed enactment of the anti-subversion law, on the one hand, his staff had to follow his position, on the other hand, they also needed to consider the market and circulation figures, and strike a balance.[891] He was the first newspaper proprietor to take to the streets, and marched with 60,000-plus other Hong Kongers to protest against the proposed enactment of Basic Law article 23.[892] Lai reportedly said that the law was like 'an invisible, tightening collar'.[893] The informal human network he formed included: the Roman Catholic Bishop, Joseph Zen, who is the leader of over 200,000 Christians in Hong Kong; Yeung Sum, a directly elected legislator, former chairman of the Democratic Party (DP) and Lai's brother-in-law; Martin Lee, another directly elected legislator and founding chairman of the DP, a good friend of Lai's and a Catholic; Albert Cheng, the broadcaster and a good friend of Martin Lee's; and Lam Hang-chi, founder and publisher of the *HKEJ* and a long standing friend of Martin Lee's.

To sum up, Lam and Lai represented two different kinds of rebel publisher – the former regarded himself as an intellectual who had undergone an education in western liberal thinking and put forward his ideas mainly through his own column.[894] Whereas the latter proclaimed himself a refugee, a street child from China, and a self-trained entrepreneur and self-invented media mogul who challenged the state by vigorously mobilising readers to stage a massive protest against the malpractice of the state. Both took to the streets to demonstrate their firm belief in press freedom and placed themselves in the firing line by challenging the suppressive measures the state was about to impose. This demonstration of personal belief and professional spirit was an example, if not exactly a model, for their staff, their colleagues and above all, the public. It showed that their papers (including their news content) were uniquely independent from political and economic influences, and also acted as a watchdog, setting the agenda of the day. It also served to create a unique brand.

Their vision coincided in being very critical of the maladministration of the state, for instance, state interference in the market, sinicisation and disregard for the rule of law following the handover. They both, however, avoided provoking the central government (although Lai once called the former Chinese leader a 'tortoise egg with a zero IQ'),[895] and perhaps that gave them some leeway to negotiate with the central regime. Still, Lai suffered more, because there was a ban on advertising in his publications, and his journalists were not allowed to enter mainland China to cover stories. Obstacles were also placed in the way of his company getting listed. The Chinese was more keen to involve Lam in united-front work, however. The existence of these two papers – one mass circulation and one quality – exerted pressure on other, more conformist, papers, which, in order to compete, could not afford to ignore public sentiment completely. For instance, in respect of the proposed national security bill, it was evident that the press, other than *Apple Daily* and *Hong Kong Economic Journal*, shifted their position in reaction to social sentiment, particularly after the big march on 1 July 2003.[896]

Resilient public broadcaster

While *Apple Daily* demonstrated a strongly opinionated position and strived to set the agenda for Hong Kong, Hong Kong's public broadcaster struggled to retain its impartiality and independence. Just as the Hong Kong Journalists Association evolved from being an expatriate body to a localised one, *Radio Television Hong Kong* (*RTHK*) also evolved from a colonial mouthpiece to a relatively independent media organisation with its own editorial code of practice. The paradox was that, on the brink of Hong Kong's return to China, the pressure on *RTHK* to revert to its old 'colonial' role was enormous. According to a veteran journalist, the news section of *RTHK* was established in the aftermath of the 1967 disturbances.[897] At that point, *RTHK* started to have its own editorial responsibility and identity.

> Between 1967 and 1970, the attitude of the Hong Kong government in relation to her people changed subtly. This had a bearing on *RTHK* too. For

instance, those officials who used to write news bulletins were transferred back to the Government Information Services (GIS) and editorial respons- ibility was handed back to *RTHK*.[898]

According to the retired veteran journalist, this was part of the Hong Kong government's policy of relaxing its grip on the media. *RTHK* was also indirectly forced to have its own news section in order to compete with other news media that enjoyed press freedom. For instance, at around the same time, *Hong Kong Commercial Radio* also set up its own news team to replace its previous practice of getting news bulletins from the GIS and broadcast them accordingly. *RTHK* was set up in 1928, but its news team was only officially set up in 1973. During the political transition period, in the face of repeated calls from the pro-China camp demanding that *RTHK* resume its role of government mouthpiece, Wong Chi-keung, a retired founding editor of *RTHK*, commented openly that the rela- tive freedom of the Hong Kong news media was the result of a 'long bloody struggle'.

> Nowadays, people take it for granted and fail to notice that in fact it was hard to get!... In fact editorial independence is not a gift, but a great responsibility. Staff of *RTHK* was brave to bear this responsibility ... but it wasn't appreciated by the Chinese officials who usually had tight control and wished to force the media to serve party and state.[899]

Role of a public broadcaster

The Broadcasting Review Board recommended in 1985 that RTHK be made independent of the government, but this proposal was blocked by the Chinese side of the Joint Liaison Group in 1992. In the post-handover era, the govern- ment's broadcasting arm continued to be targeted by pro-Beijing politicians. There was strong pressure for the broadcaster to revert to its colonial role. This was an important issue, because *RTHK* offers an alternative viewpoint to that of the two commercial radio broadcasters, *Hong Kong Commercial Radio* and *Metro Broadcast*, and the two terrestrial television stations, *Asia Television* (*ATV*) and *Television Broadcasts* (*TVB*).[900] *RTHK* came under political pressure on the issue of Chinese sovereignty. According to an experienced journalist, *RTHK* has an irreplaceable role in providing a platform for alternative views, for example, covering Taiwanese issues and providing criticism of the incumbent administration.[901]

In May 2001, the pro-Beijing daily, *Wen Wei Po*, lashed out at the station over comments by a *RTHK* presenter to the effect that Tibet was a country. The presenter was discussing the fiftieth anniversary of an agreement whereby China took over the region in the wake of the Communist take-over. In a subsequent statement, *RTHK* said that there was no doubt that Tibet was a part of China. It also said that the presenter was quoting other people's views. It added that the segment was 'lacking in impartiality', and a more complete explanation of the

Tibet question was given on the day after the initial broadcast, including the stance of the Central Government.[902] Further pressure was put on *RTHK* following a decision by *TVB* and *ATV* to call Taiwan's president, Chen Shui-bian, the island's 'leader', instead of 'president'. The terminology was closer to that of the mainland Chinese media.[903] The public broadcaster was expected to follow suit. The National People's Congress delegate, Ma Lik, called on the government to issue guidelines to *RTHK* concerning Mr. Chen's title. The government broadcaster insisted that it would not change its current practice of using the term 'president', and the government said, 'it is not our practice to issue guidelines to *RTHK* regarding its news reporting.'[904] The issue was whether or not *RTHK* should play the role of a government supporter.[905]

Struggle for independence

RTHK continued to use public support to stand up for its norms and to fend off intervention. In its own defence, the broadcaster sought to stress its editorial independence.[906] Operationally, *RTHK* was modelled on the British Broadcasting Corporation (BBC) and a few Directors of Broadcasting were seconded from the BBC in the 1970s to mid-1980s.[907] However, structurally it was, and still is, under the full control of the government in terms of financial subsidies and the appointment of the broadcasting director who also acts as the editor-in-chief of *RTHK*. *RTHK* claims that it upholds independent journalistic values such as impartiality, balanced views and diversity of culture and viewpoint in its producers' guidelines.

> We are a public broadcasting body which aims at serving the public and operates in the interest of the public ... when there are important government policies to be implemented, we will give sufficient airtime for government officials to explain the policies and to exchange views with the public in our program.[908]

Yet, there had been growing pressure since the handover, which prompted observers to question whether *RTHK* itself had become involved in self-censorship. The station's satirical television series, 'Headliners' (which had often been criticised by the pro-Beijing media), was briefly suspended to make way for a series of profiles on top government and business leaders. It returned to the air in January 2001. However, internally opinion was divided concerning *RTHK*'s performance.

> The Headliners has become 'outdated' and boring at times, it indeed needs to adopt a drastic change ... you can't just keep on criticizing the HKSAR and the CE as your only gimmicks.[909]

The framework agreement

Overall, *RTHK* retained its editorial independence, even if at times it was overly cautious to ensure that it presented news in a factual and impartial manner. However, this did not alter the fact that the position of *RTHK* was precarious. It operated under a 'framework agreement' with the government's Secretary for Information Technology and Broadcasting,[910] which guarantees the station's editorial independence. As an administration document, the agreement was open to administrative change. To secure adequate safeguards for *RTHK*'s editorial independence, the government should have formalised the framework agreement through legislation. Unlike the BBC, *RTHK* has neither the solid guarantee of constitutional protection, nor the 12 members of the board of governors appointed by the Queen on the advice of ministers.

To sum up, the independence of *RTHK* was attained through both the relaxation of the colonial grip and the long-term struggle of journalists inside and outside the public broadcaster. However, without public support, it could not have stood so firmly or for so long. It was not just the press and the public broadcaster who were under pressure, however. Following the change in regime, control over institutions, exerted through structural and hierarchical means, was evident as well.

Role of the press in the struggle for academic freedom

In the new political reality, if the public broadcaster was struggling hard to sustain its independence, so were 'civilized institutions'.[911]

The informal collaboration between a columnist and a broadsheet paper helped to expose state control over institutional freedom in 2000. In addition to support from a specialist paper and a mass circulation paper, public opinion was also on the side of academic freedom in the face of state interference. In July 2000, a social scientist at the University of Hong Kong, Dr. Robert Chung, alleged in *South China Morning Post (SCMP)* that the Chief Executive, Tung Chee-hwa, had tried, through a 'special channel', to suppress opinion polls on his popularity conducted by Chung.[912]

Public opinion prevails

Remarkably, the case aroused an unprecedented public outcry. Public pressure to determine the veracity of the allegations was such that the university council found itself taking the unusual step, albeit reluctantly, of setting up a three-member inquiry panel. The panel, headed by a former Court of Appeal judge, found that two professors Cheng and Wong had indeed tried to put a stop to Chung's polls, and that the pair had twice conveyed messages to Chung that were 'calculated to inhibit his right to academic freedom'. The two professors resigned shortly afterwards. More importantly, the inquiry panel also found that the Hong Kong Chief Executive's special assistant, Andrew Lo, who had denied asking Professor Cheng to put pressure on Dr. Chung, was a 'poor and untruth-ful witness'.[913] There were calls for a wider investigation of the case.[914] The special assistant to Tung was later removed from the governmental payroll, but only transferred to Tung's family company, Oriental Overseas (International). The incident also shows how media practitioners helped to raise the issue and blew the whistle. The case also reveals how the news media and public opinion could come together to form a countervailing force to government pressure. The story unfolded like this. A journalist on *SCMP* spotted a column in the paper, and helped to turn it into a front-page story.

> The allegation about Tung interfering with opinion polls was in a column written by Robert Chung, which I saw on a proof of the comment page passed to the backbench [night editors] that evening. I said to the deputy editor, that, if we had time, we should write a news story based on the column and lead on paper with it. Otherwise we should remove the column (so other papers would not see it the next day) and do the story the next day. The deputy editor said it could not be removed because there was no replacement and perhaps a few pars [paragraphs] on page 1 would do. I told the political editor, about it and suggested him [sic] try to get hold of Chung. One of his staff did so and, after some persuasion, the deputy editor agreed to lead with it. He asked not to use the word 'gag' in the headline.[915]

The story was followed up by both local and foreign media. The next day, the Chief Executive, Tung Chee-hwa, was giving a speech to a Chamber of Commerce and was asked by a foreign businessman whether he had interfered with opinion polls. He denied it categorically and the following day every paper splashed the story. The story gave *SCMP* something in excess of 20 splashes over the next few months. That was one of the few times when *SCMP* actually set the agenda and led the story. Yet there was pressure from the Chinese camp, accusing the paper and the journalist alike of 'dumping on CH Tung and the HKSAR administration'.[916] Specifically, there were accusations by the pro-China press and pro-Beijing figures (usually made to political desk reporters and sometimes publicly on radio phone-in programmes) that *SCMP* was involved in some kind of post-colonial conspiracy. However, nothing was ever said to senior journalists by the *SCMP* management, and there was no attempt to interfere.[917] The story simply kept gathering momen-tum. There were a lot of new angles, for example, the inquiry itself and the resigna-tion of the vice-chancellor of Hong Kong University.[918]

However, the pressure on academics remained apparent. It was not until two years after the incident that Robert Chung emerged again with a clear and deter-mined voice to stand by his profession. He had seemingly kept a low profile since the incident apparently triggered the resignation of the former vice-chancellor of the University of Hong Kong and the transfer of Andrew Lo, special aide to Tung Chee-hwa. In early 2003, Chung said that he would con-tinue to conduct and publicise his polling results and speak out against any infringement of academic freedom.[919]

It would not have been possible for Robert Chung to have triggered such an outcry had the news industry infrastructure not been so well in place. It was because of the long-standing liberal tradition and the well-embedded journalistic values and routines, that the journalists and editors were so effective in turning a column into major news. With the help of other news media, a tiny piece of news could be developed into a series of issues confronting the new government and the powerful closed circle of the Chief Executive. Thus the media are seen to have fulfilled their independent 'fourth estate/watchdog' role in the best possible way. However, it should be noted that the proprietor himself was unhappy with the Chief Executive, Tung Chee-hwa. For instance, there was an editorial that called on Tung to 'step up and sit back'.[920] But would journalists have enjoyed such freedom if the proprietor had had a cordial relationship with Tung?[921] This question perhaps can only be answered in the light of the cultural infrastructure of Hong Kong society, which is described in the next section.

In retrospect

According to the evidence, the Hong Kong press used to hold a strong anti-Chinese Communist position. Only in recent decades, mainly because of the imminent political handover, did the mainstream press begin to restructure itself in anticipation of the change in social environment that would accompany regime change. The anti-Chinese Communist standpoint became a minority position. Yet fear and scepticism continued.

In the post-colonial era, apparently only one mass circulation paper, *Apple Daily*, one specialist paper, *Hong Kong Economic Journal*, and one commercial broadcaster, *Commercial Radio*, maintained a critical stance towards the HKSAR and expressed concerns about the Chinese meddling in Hong Kong affairs.

Although it appears that these media organisations remained on the periphery, the fact that they could mobilise such enormous support indicates that they enjoyed substantial institutional support, both in the form of moral support and also sources of information.[922] To explain this, we have to look at the cultural constitution of Hong Kong society. First, it has almost become a common goal for the Hong Kong people to defend their civil liberties, namely the rule of law, a level playing field for business and freedom of expression, given the long process of civil and political education that started in the early 1980s. To begin with, there were the talks on Hong Kong's future, although the people of Hong Kong were excluded from the negotiations. Hong Kong people started to recognise the importance of free media as Hong Kongers relied heavily on the Hong Kong media for information.[923] Furthermore, the Hong Kong media's active role in reporting on the 4 June Beijing student movement and its aftermath made an impression on the public, and they could see what a difference Hong Kong could make as an information haven.[924]

The development of the concept of the rule of law led many to respect the legal profession. The outspokenness and involvement of leading lawyers had a major impact. For example, successive chairpersons of the Hong Kong Bar Association worked to attract the moral support of their foreign counterparts, such as the British and New York Bar Associations.[925] Community leaders made great efforts over a long period of time to support the 'refugee' society, for instance, the Roman Catholic Church in Hong Kong helped to provide free, quality education during the 1960s, 1970s and even the early 1980s. The respect the church enjoyed and the influence it could command extended far beyond its more than 200,000 Catholic followers. Above all, the Catholic Bishop, Joseph Zen, who was hailed by both local and foreign media as the 'conscience of Hong Kong', spoke out fearlessly for the weak and minorities, especially when Hong Kong was very much in need of leadership.[926]

Unsurprisingly, at a time when the economy was in a slump, and the administration was in a state of confusion following the handover,[927] this kind of formal and informal institutional support coincided with the aspirations of both the professionals and the middle class.[928] Thus the roots of resistance can be traced back to the general fear that the Chinese Communist Party would not live up to its word and allow Hong Kong to maintain its capitalist and free economy system. Other social factors apparently facilitated the defence of press freedom, for instance, the business community (including British, American and Hong Kong representatives) and leading bankers (such as David Li Kwok-po), all denounced the HKSAR's handling of the enactment of the proposed new national security bill, in one way or another. In the wake of the peaceful mass demonstration, public sentiment has shifted, the leader of the pro-China political party and some business celebrities even went so far as to say that it might not be a bad idea to allow Hong Kong to have more democracy.[929] One more external factor was at work, Taiwan would have a very good excuse to reject the proposed 'one country, two systems' arrangement if the reunification with China did not work well in Hong Kong. Thus anxiety about Chinese communist rule united all walks of life, and above all gave the media space to manoeuvre, even though they remained on the periphery.

Faced with a wayward mass media, an alienated Legislative Council and a dispirited society, the government has encountered grave problems trying to get the community to support its policies, as a local political scientist, has reportedly said.[930] The mass media were regarded as having become the 'single, most important intermediary'. However, the lack of intermediaries between the government and the people had severely undermined the government's legitimacy and capacity to govern. It would arguably be 'wrong to think that a partnership between the government and selected mass media can ensure good governance'. Thus, it is evident that Hong Kong journalists were not alone in seeking to defend Hong Kong's press freedom and above all freedom of expression. Apart from local practitioners, the regional and foreign press provided rather comprehensive coverage and commentary on the proposed new national security bill and Hong Kong's organised efforts to protest against it.[931] Foreign consulates, trade representatives and banking communities in Hong Kong also registered their concerns about the potential impact of the proposed legislation on free speech and the free flow of information in the former colony.[932] More-over, the Catholic Church, the richest and most popular religious institution in Hong Kong, has shown a similar determination in resisting intervention from Beijing.[933] The Hong Kong Bar Association too has played an important part in attempting to defend judicial autonomy and issuing a stern warning about a possible backlash if the proposed anti-subversion law is enacted and its implications for freedom of the press and freedom of speech. Thus key institutions of civil society played important roles as allies of the press.[934]

7 Conclusion

This study has explored the significance of media professionalism and media organisation, the role of the media in political change, and the relationship between the media and a society's power base, taking as an example the case of Hong Kong. It has adopted a historical political economy approach in its exploration of the Hong Kong press in three significant periods, namely: at the time of colonial rule in the late 1960s; during the political transition in the 1990s; and in the post-handover period in the early 2000s.

The late 1960s

The case study of the late 1960s provides a useful corrective to the uncritical acceptance of the liberal argument. It reveals the repressive role of a liberal democracy that adopts a series of oppressive measures against opposition voices. As the case study of the public records of the British government shows, part of the radical press was suppressed by the colonial government in the late 1960s. Although the British government repeatedly proclaimed the importance of a free press in Hong Kong, in practice its approach was largely and consistently repressive. Britain's main concern was to maintain public order, and nip any threat to the colonial regime in the bud. While within the society at large there was a commitment to resisting infringements of press freedom, the government gave higher priority to maintaining its own authority than to issues of freedom of the press. It is worth noting remarkably, that the British colonial way of political suppression was usually not that explicit. One strategy was to follow a policy of divide-and-rule, so, for example, they allowed the pro-Nationalist Taiwanese groups to survive. The other strategy was to leave some room for anti-colonial political forces. So, at least until the riot of 1967, the communist group were left relatively free to do what they wanted so as to provide a balance to the pro-Nationalist Kuomintang (KMT) group.[935]

As mentioned in Chapter 2, the radical press's provocative, condemnatory, and even rebellious, attitude towards the colonial government was largely due to its perception of the British as running an exploitative regime. There was neither democratic representation nor any attempt to reduce social injustice and inequality in the late 1960s. Hence, the press backed by the People's Republic of China

(PRC) was arguably the main radical force at the time, playing the role of 'watchdog' and campaigning for more democracy, although, regrettably, they adopted an extremist strategy later on.

As evidenced in Chapter 2, part of the local English press were sympathetic towards the communist press. It was observed that the widespread disturbance in 1967 was largely due to a general grievance among the working class and to the prevalence of social injustice in society. On occasions, some of the local English press criticised the heavy-handed measures adopted by the Hong Kong administration. Also, some legal professionals relentlessly attacked the absolute power the British Hong Kong government sought to retain even after the disturbance. The English press dared to criticise the colonial government on how the riot was handled. It speaks to the fact that the English press enjoyed relative autonomy; certainly it belonged to the ruling class then. But how could it possible play out its professional role? In fact it reflected the higher echelon of power which was then divided over how to handle the riot, thereby allowing for dissenting opinion expressed in the English newspaper. That could be of relevance to the developing relative autonomy of the press in Hong Kong now and in the future.

However, there were factors that prevented the radical press from continuing to play their provocative role. Although the PRC-backed press helped to stir up and mobilise the working class, and to turn the labour dispute into a social movement, it did not command support from media across the political spectrum. In particular, the radical press was criticised and condemned by its rivals and the self-proclaimed centrist press. This was partly due to there being a clear political cleavage between left and right, with the pro-colonial/establishment press in between. Moreover, the political cleavage between the communist and anti-communist gangs has swept under the carpet the ideological difference between the left (progressive taking sides with the underprivileged) and the right (conservative defending the status quo) properly understood.

In addition, when the movement against colonial rule turned to anarchy, widespread public support declined – a fact that also contributed to the failure of the radical press. This lack of cultural support was due more to a 'communist-fearing' or 'anti-communist' sentiment (which was shared by many Hong Kong inhabitants during the Chinese Communist take-over in the late 1940s), rather than to an approval of colonial rule.[936]

Moreover, despite the existence of a long tradition of a Chinese press acting as a critical and progressive voice of Chinese society as mentioned in Chapter 1, professional journalism was not widely practised. In the 1960s, the Hong Kong press was mainly ideologically oriented, with a clear division between the leftist (pro-CCP) and the rightist (pro-Nationalist Taiwanese KMT) press. Journalism education was not widely available until the 1980s following the founding of a number of journalism schools in the 1960s.[937] Overall the contemporary society could be characterised in the words of a political scientist as a 'minimally socially and politically integrated' society with an embedded refugee mentality, and a not yet fully developed sense of belonging to Hong Kong.[938] This was because the majority of Hong Kong residents moved there during the late

1940s and early 1950s when mainland China was taken over by the Chinese Communists.

Paradoxically, the failure of the radical press occurred not only as a result of colonial coercion and legal repression, but also as a consequence of a decrease in the influence of the Chinese authorities. Although most of the leftist press was at the time registered locally, and claimed to be privately funded, in fact, it was heavily subsidised by the Chinese authorities. In other words, the ultimate owner of the leftist press was the Chinese regime. While the radical press relentlessly maintained its resistance to, and indeed rebellion against, the authoritarian colonial regime, it was restrained by its owners, and indeed by its role as an ideological apparatus of the Chinese regime.

The case study in Chapter 2 reveals an intriguing power struggle. Despite the fact that the British were considering withdrawing from Hong Kong in the wake of the strong local rebellion, it was the Chinese calling upon the leftist press to discontinue resistance to colonial rule. The Chinese ordered the PRC-backed press to call off the struggle against the British because it did not serve Chinese ends. At that time, the CCP's policy was to retain Hong Kong as its window to the west during the Cold War. As the Beijing authorities resumed control over the situation in mainland China, they introduced their own policy, according to which the best way in which Hong Kong served China's interests was as a colony. Furthermore, the fact that Peking called off the struggle against the British Hong Kong government in the late 1960s is also a standing determinant of Hong Kong's press freedom, since local left-wing newspapers are state-owned enterprises serving the dictates of the ruling regime in Beijing. Whilst such state behaviour in the late 1960s has been documented, it can be taken as a working premise in understanding the logic and behaviour of these Beijing-owned papers in Hong Kong before and after 1997.

Despite the failure of the radical press in the 1960s to overthrow the colonial regime, it helped to prompt a thorough review of British local policy that resulted in a more soft-handed approach, which in turn led to a series of social changes in the following decades.[939] These included the British Hong Kong administration establishing channels for communication with the Chinese press. For instance, the Hong Kong government compiled a daily précis of all the Chinese press for senior government officials to read first thing in the morning.[940]

Another remarkable finding is that the case of the prosecution of the three PRC-backed newspapers (*Tin Fung Daily News, Afternoon News,* and *Hong Kong Evening News*) was not included in any available law reports in Hong Kong. One explanation is that the judgment may have been buried in the High Court during these turbulent years.[941] However, in view of the careful and lengthy exchange among senior officers in London and Hong Kong concerning this selective prosecution of senior newspapermen and women and the ban of newspapers by legal instrument, all of which was highly sensitive, it seems very strange that the law report would have been omitted. Although it is tempting to conclude that it was done for political reasons, such a conclusion requires more evidence and further research to shed light on this legal dimension, which is not the task of this study.

In sum, political influence was significant in shaping the press in the late 1960s. Yet the political power structure was not monolithic, and tension within and between various British offices acted as a countervailing force, as seen in the case study of the late 1960s. However, in the aftermath of this British suppression, the Hong Kong press apparently exercised restraint during the following decades until a critical press began to emerge as a result of the weakening of the colonial government authorities.

The 1990s

During the transition period of the late 1980s and 1990s, new political journals and daily newspapers flourished,[942] and, remarkably, an independent critical press emerged. This was due to the diminishing political influence of the colonial government, but also partly to a last major effort by the British to relax their legal grip on the Hong Kong news media before their departure. Whilst the emergence of a critical press is largely a result of the process of de-colonisation, it is also the outcome of the growth of maturity of the local political community/civil society. In contrast to the 1960s (when the press lacked the support of a fully fledged civil society due to insufficient popular education and a lack of civil rights awareness amongst the middle class), during the 1990s a counter-force emerged from the developing civil society that provided new sources of information, journalistic professionalism and support from other civic institutions.

Against strong opposition from the Chinese side, liberalising steps were also taken towards constitutional reform, which provided greater opportunity for various interest groups, political parties and minority groups to participate in public debates, and even established partially democratic elections to the Hong Kong legislature. At the time when British rule was fading and the Chinese had not yet formally established legitimate authority in the colony, there was an ongoing tension and disagreement between the British and the Chinese regarding what Hong Kong policy should be following the handover. This situation resulted in a kind of 'political power vacuum' in which media organisations manoeuvred.[943] Their critical approach, however, was not aimed solely at the new masters but also at the colonial regime. In anticipation of the political changeover, the public tended to support a resilient and free press, as evidenced by the public backing of the press across the political spectrum who campaigned for the open trial and early release of reporter, Xi Yang.

Yet, it was not only political developments, but also social ones that contributed to the evolution of a critical press. In Hong Kong society as a whole, scepticism towards the new masters could be detected, and in particular an anxiety concerning a potential negative impact on civil liberties and press freedom. Under these circumstances, the threat of possible press censorship appeared real to the already anxious public. Thus an event that was perceived as an interference with the freedom of the press, such as the jailing of a Hong Kong journalist who was just 'doing his job', became a 'case' to fight for, as shown in the case study in Chapter 3. This vehement reaction was not just a response to a perceived threat to the press as an industry, but was also due to the fact that the Chinese government was, as a result of such interference, perceived as a common enemy. Scepticism and anxiety indeed became so widespread that the media across the political spectrum (including a fraction of the Beijing-funded leftist press) pushed for clarification regarding this case, and assurances in respect of press freedom following the handover in 1997.[944]

In addition, Hong Kong's civil society can be seen as one of the key entities supporting the press who made extensive use of civic institutions as a source of information for the mass media. From the early 1990s to 1997, however, the mass media tended to shift to a conforming mode (as seen in the analysis of news coverage in Chapter 3), and that despite vigorous rank-and-file resistance to internal and external intervention. The civil society played an even more apparent role in the early 2000s.[945]

Professional awareness and knowledge have been on the increase due to the growing popularity of journalism studies since the 1980s. The generation of journalists who gained their education at such institutions was educated and trained according to western journalistic ideals, values and norms. The increasing opportunities for journalists to enter China to cover news also played a role. Many could compare the freedoms and rights Hong Kong people enjoyed with those of their mainland counterparts. Thus, a dilemma arose, on the one hand, proprietors intended to appease China but, on the other, were forced to 'confront' and exercise pressure for the cause of press freedom, as in the case of Xi Yang. Indeed, the case study shows how senior editors and management, such as publishers and editors-in-chief, joined the coalition force to campaign for the early release of the jailed reporter, but this usually occurred at the initiative of the concerted efforts of the rank-and-file.[946]

At the same time, the Hong Kong market also flourished thanks to China's open-door policy. With its close proximity to China, the Hong Kong economy prospered. On the media front, information about development in China was especially sought after locally and internationally, which in many ways helped to enable further development of the Hong Kong press.

However, in anticipation of the handover, the Chinese also stepped up their pressure on the Hong Kong press. This period was marked by Chinese attacks on, and unrelenting hostility towards, Hong Kong journalists. A notable example was the imprisonment of Xi Yang. With this severe penalty, the Chinese laid down the new ground rules for reporting and journalistic work in the post-handover era. Another distinctive feature of the period was that newspaper owners acted as 'proxies' for the new regime. Newspaper proprietors, apparently acting on behalf of the new regime, began to have an effect on media organisations with a subsequent influence on news content.

Indeed, the restructuring of media organisations began before the political handover. In anticipation of 1997, Hong Kong society was changing rapidly. The roots of systematic control originated from a wide-ranging restructuring at the institutional and organisational levels which resulted in a major shift in political orientation, and consequently in editorial content and position, as shown in the analysis of media control in Chapter 5. Businessmen and women, through buying up majority shares in newspapers, fully controlled both operational and allocational power. A new proprietor would revamp the paper by, for example, systematically removing contributors and columnists, and replacing them with new staff; abolishing the political news desk; re-distributing staff; and changing the editorial orientation. Although some journalists fearlessly resisted this intervention, the proprietor usually succeeded in the restructuring process.

As a result, as evident from the textual analysis in Chapters 3 and 4, an inclination towards political caution was taking shape, involving a drift away from politically sensitive topics such as criticism of the central leadership, and an increasing prevalence of consumerism and commercialism in news content. It pointed out that political caution is exercised when the press handled sensitive issues. Combined with consumerism and commercialism, this political caution serves to silence the press itself over sensitive issues and shrugs off press responsibility in reflecting views of importance on issues such as Taiwan independence. This is what is commonly called 'self-censorship'. But this account gives substance to what is behind the self-censorship. Commonly conceived, it is taken as an act on the part of the media itself to self-restrain itself. But it is a kind of self-negating act, that is, not to tell the public what you believe is true or not to honour what you believe you should do. But such thinking may wrongly focus on individual decisions or integrity. It is also extremely hard to find evidence to prove any allegation. The way we conceive it in this study, however, means we could identify a self-censoring act by referring to the larger political picture where we can identify causes for self-censorship, without looking for evidence that is hard to obtain.

In general, the news media organisations shifted their diverse political allegiances towards the dominant ideological power and the future masters. This led to the complete disappearance of references to the historical connection with Taiwan and the severed links with it, and the decreasing influence of the British on the press.[947]

In this connection, infotainment frequently replaced dry politics. As a result, trivialised news helped to neutralise hard politics and served as a tactic towards sensitive political news. Even though most of the titles and key staff remained intact, this structural shift nevertheless marked a defining moment for the press. Political influence was clearly evident in the trajectory of the shift of most of the mainstream newspapers.

Furthermore, there was an acknowledgement of imminent political change – from a British colony to a Chinese Special Administrative Region (SAR) and an acceptance, albeit reluctantly, of a new master. In the highly politicised society at large, a gradual paradigmatic shift in perspective occurred, which involved a growing acceptance and understanding of the incoming political regime.[948] In the case of the news media, the shift was manifested by the fact that many proprietors, and indeed journalists themselves, moved from a previously hostile attitude, to a friendly and even subservient one.[949]

On the media front, resistance was sporadic, one example being the campaign for the early release of Xi Yang, in mainland China. Unsurprisingly, resistance from individual journalists and even the journalistic profession produced clashes with media owners because of an acute conflict of interest between proprietors and employees. For instance, some proprietors had business interests in mainland China or attempted to explore the mainland market. Even in the case of those who did not have clear political allegiances and investment in China, the goal of maximising profits played a key role. This is particularly important as the Chinese authorities represent the biggest state institutions, and thus at the same time act as the most significant potential advertisers domestically and internationally. Hence, there is a tension between owners and employees when faced with external intervention, although professional journalists have attempted to use their day-to-day autonomy to mediate pressures within the organisation.

Under such circumstances – although there occurred a shift in political orientation and editorial policy towards an apolitical stance – the restructuring of the news media was not completed, and was affected and complicated by the on-going Sino-British disagreement on major Hong Kong policy.[950] The restructuring happened through changes of ownership and the buying up of shares in the quality press. In the face of these changes, professional resistance remained strong, but mainly at the individual and professional levels, rather than at the organisational level. Although in the civil society there remained strong support for the media as a source of information, and for journalistic norms, around 1997 a conciliatory tone prevailed in media organisations themselves, especially at the institutional level, and most clearly at the editorial level.[951]

It was under such circumstances that the Hong Kong press manifested ambiguity and ambivalence in terms of its content and strategy in response to the many influences, pressures and constraints experienced in this period. However, with the escalation of pressure, the countervailing forces appear to be equally complex and strong. Simultaneously, a 'space' for the critical press re-emerged and was seized by some entrepreneurs in the following years.

In sum, Hong Kong during the transition was under contradictory pressures – on the one hand, the civil society provided new sources of information, and journalistic norms benefited from a relaxed political environment. On the other hand, there was increasing pressure from the Chinese who exerted more and more influence at various levels of the organisational hierarchy. Newspaper proprietors, acting as a 'proxy' for the new political power, helped to induce an institutional and structural shift in news organisation. Media control was manifested in the form of self-censorship. These were the key features that defined this period of press history. However, the political implications were only fully manifested in the post-handover period when more independently critical journalists were removed in the guise of a re-organisation of newsrooms.

The 2000s

Political influence played a significant role in shaping the press in the 2000s. During the transition, the press came under contradictory pressures, whereas in the post-handover years, part of the Hong Kong press at least demonstrated a resilient resistance to media control.

Although control exercised by owners and the state tightened, it was uneven and complex. While personnel changes within media organisations appeared to be complete, some media remained resilient in their support of civil liberties by turning to diverse, and sometimes even critical, sources of information. For example, a pollster-scholar was able to use the quality press to expose the government's suppression of free speech.[952] Market competition encouraged further coverage and exposure of the incident as a major case of state intervention. As the interview findings indicate, the staff and the editor had the power to turn a lone scholar's article into a breaking news story despite the fact that the paper was undergoing restructuring. Moreover, consumers and readers helped to empower journalists, and indeed provided sources of information to support continuing media coverage and exposure of the event.

This shows that although direct influences, pressures and constraints exerted by owners, and indirect coercion and legal repression imposed by the government, could be enormously strong, other factors, such as market influence, consumer power, journalistic norms and the civil society as a source of information, all help to resist and countervail them. Here, the countervailing factors such as professional routine, civil society as a source of information, public aspiration and market logic are related to each other and help to expose the attempt to suppress academic freedom in 2000. These countervailing factors help to fend off pressure from political power and economic censorship. And it illuminates the picture of how and why the media work at a specific historical juncture.

In a highly sophisticated capitalist society, these countervailing factors all act to influence the media to report and follow up an important news story because they cannot afford to ignore it once it becomes breaking news. This is especially true as strong competition stems not only from one type of medium but also from across various media such as radio, TV broadcasting and public broadcasting.

As mentioned earlier, as well as one fearless columnist exposing intervention by the Chief Executive of the Hong Kong government, defiant veteran journalists refused to submit to the new political order. Journalists on the government broadcaster, *Radio Television Hong Kong*, also refused to work within the new political boundaries.[953] These defiant examples helped to raise public awareness and indeed triggered an alarm concerning the imminent curb on press freedom. Nevertheless, during these past few years, many experienced journalists were forced to leave their positions or were sacked for refusing to abide by new guidelines. Yet, a few were able to become even more defiant by joining the critical press or foreign media organisations.[954]

Significantly, parts of the press stepped outside the limits imposed by politics, and flourished. This phenomenon marks one of the key characteristics of the

Hong Kong press, that is, its use of market forces to achieve its ends. The proprietor of the mass circulation paper, *Apple Daily*, revealed that he spotted the market gap vacated by the quality press that used to be critical of both the colonial government and the Chinese regime, and moved to fill it.[955] The paper also expanded its content according to the mass circulation/tabloid formula based on 'consumerism' and 'commercialism'. These moves combined ensured the success of the *Apple Daily*. However, this is not to say that *Apple Daily* is critical of every instance of malpractice committed by the Chinese government. Instead, its highly contentious stance is calculated to match the majority sentiment of a Hong Kong civil society anxious about threats to civil liberties and press freedom.

Yet the very purpose of privately owned media in a market-driven economy is to make profits. Thus, the influence of advertisers and shareholders is of key importance for the success of the commercial press. The case of *Apple Daily* is illustrative. Although it is generally seen as a critical paper, its ideology is largely conservative. It helps to promote consumerism and a capitalist, commercialised way of living as a norm. Although it reports on minority/marginalised groups, such news is usually framed in a sensational way and fails to investigate the larger social background.[956] The infotainment style tends to water down the political element of highly sensitive political news.

Whilst maintaining its critical role, the paper's campaign against the proposed new national security bill largely echoed mainstream Hong Kong middle class interests.[957] It also coincided with interests across the political spectrum (e.g. from NGOs such as Amnesty International and the Hong Kong Journalists Association, to the banking, business and overseas investment communities), although for very different reasons. The business sector, for example, was anxious that economic/business information would be suppressed if the proposed new national security bill were passed.

Unsurprisingly, in the post-handover era, the political pressure from the Chinese regime was enormous and this tended to shape the Hong Kong press in an unprecedented manner. Change occurred within a capitalist context, however. The restructuring of media ownership in Hong Kong seemed to be settled, with the mainstream press largely in support of the status quo. One of the marked features continued from the transition was that newspaper proprietors appeared to be acting on behalf of the new regime, and curbed press freedom in a quiet manner. With new editorial policies installed along with structural change, sensitive news stories or documentaries were either spiked or put on the back burner.

This kind of self-censorship was effective in the sense that some outspoken Chinese critics and editors were marginalised or removed from the local scene as a result of newsroom and news desk reorganisation carried out in the guise of a new market strategy. A news desk or news section could be removed, and columns cancelled, all in the name of a redeployment of resources to cater for a new market environment as shown in Chapter 6.[958]

The case study presented in Chapter 4 reveals that Taiwan remained one of the most contentious news items (as it has not yet agreed to submit to the 'reunification scheme'), as demonstrated in the analysis of the Taiwanese presidential election in 2000. The Hong Kong press, in terms of its news freedom, was constrained largely by control exercised by its owners and the government. Self-censorship was rampant under these internal and external constraints. Yet findings show that the press was not entirely intimidated. They still retained a little independence, and appeared to have adopted tactics to report on this sensitive news item.

The news content of the case study in 2000 demonstrates a general shift in the political orientation of the press. For instance, reporting on Taiwan has become a sensitive issue, if not entirely a political no-go area. It is illustrative that the Taiwanese President is generally described as the 'Taiwan leader', and the 'June Four massacre' was largely replaced by the 'Tiananmen incident'.

Legal instruments such as Article 23 of the mini-constitution of the Basic Law were also on the agenda. Its enactment was suspended after half a million people took to the streets to protest against it. This illustrates that even an authoritarian regime like China cannot entirely disregard a mass popular protest.

Retrospect

As mentioned in Chapter 1, radical political economists tend to view capitalist society as being class dominated. The media are seen as part of an ideological arena in which various class ideas are contested. Although dominated by certain classes, ultimate control is increasingly exercised by the monopoly of capital. Analysts of this tradition are concerned that the increasing concentration of power coincides with dominant political and economic power interests. The media operate within the framework of the dominant power structures and are dependent upon the dominant ideology, which in turn reflects and reinforces the status quo.

In contrast, according to the liberal tradition, the media respond to, and reflect, the views and values of the public, thus ensuring consumer control. The liberal theorists' view differs significantly from that of the radicals. While the radical approach emphasises media censorship, the liberal approach emphasises the market that enables consumers to exercise control over the media. The central liberal idea is that the general shape and nature of the press is ultimately determined by its readers because of the hidden hand of the free market. Thus liberal theorists tend to see the media as neutral, independent and owing allegiance to the public interest rather than to the organised political interests of society.

However, historical analysis reveals more complex situations than these two positions propose. The findings of this study have a number of theoretical implications. First, one strand of the western radical political economy argument emphasises market censorship. It sees control as being exercised primarily through economic processes. What this study reveals, however, is that political power was a key influence in shaping the Hong Kong press. In the late 1960s, the colonial government repressed the Chinese Communist press; in the 2000s, a new government curbed the independence of the press in a variety of ways; and between these periods, there was a transitional phase during which the press were able to become increasingly independent and critical as a result of the weakening of government authorities.

In the latest developments in spring 2004, there is evidence that increasing political pressure is being put on critical commentators to deter them from speaking out for the common people.[959] Raymond Wong, the broadcaster and outspoken critic of the Chinese authorities, temporarily left his job claiming that there were attempts to silence him using coercion and offers of bribes. He is reported to have said that if there were a threat to his or his family's personal security he would stop broadcasting. Another leading broadcaster, Albert Cheng, said that the political pressure was suffocating and that he had received death threats. 'I am not afraid of people in power, but I shudder at the threat of violence. It is only human and natural for me to be deeply disturbed by death threats,' he wrote.[960] Mr Cheng was seriously injured in a knife attack in 1998 and in a letter to *South China Morning Post* he said he simply could not risk another attack.[961] The trend is worrying as these are not isolated cases.[962] A political scientist reportedly said ' "orchestrated action" is being taken against some media.'[963]

These latest developments largely arise from Hong Kong's unique political position. As has been mentioned before, China has promised to allow Hong Kong to continue its capitalist system under its 'one country, two systems' policy, partly in order to tempt Taiwan to come to the reunification table. Under this peculiar political arrangement, China has laid down the rule that 'river water should not mix with well water', meaning that Hong Kong's capitalist system should not interfere with the mainland Chinese socialist system. The original goal was to allow China to benefit from the Hong Kong capitalist system. During the last decade of colonial rule, Britain relaxed its grip on the Hong Kong media (for whatever reason), whereas the Chinese wanted to tighten their grip on the Hong Kong press following the handover. They were worried about the risk of Hong Kong's well water interfering with mainland China's river water, with good reason, as in certain instances the influence of the Hong Kong media was great. For example, its coverage of the SARS epidemic (in 2003) had a significant impact on mainland Chinese people, particularly those living in the vicinity of the Pearl River Delta and the southern province of China who had ready access to Hong Kong TV and radio broadcasters (see Chapter 5).

Second, with notable exceptions,[964] this strand of the political economy approach tends to underestimate the inter-connection between political and economic factors. For instance, as this study shows, newspaper owners may act on behalf of the government to curb press freedom. Furthermore, the proposed new national security bill and the latest attacks on radio broadcasters mentioned above, all point to a tendency on the part of the Central Government and the HKSAR government to control the media using legal and non-legal means. Response from the media is varied and sporadic. Increasingly, newspaper proprietors choose to be proxies acting on behalf of the new regime. They may even risk loss in circulation figures, a reduction in staff morale, media credibility and indeed readers' support in order to reap long term material rewards for their personal and business interests. There are exceptions, however. Certain newspaper proprietors and journalists continue to make themselves heard. Some jeopardise their personal security and perhaps even their business viability, though, in the case of Jimmy Lai and *Apple Daily* there are also opportunities to exploit a market gap, as described in Chapter 6.

Third, the radical political economy tradition tends to overstate the monolithic nature of the power structure, and tends to underestimate other countervailing forces such as journalistic norms, civil society as a source of information, and influences exerted by competitors, all of which enable some papers to maintain different levels of independence.

Fourth, the media are subjected to, and shaped by, different combinations of influence at different times and in different places, so an understanding of the historical context is required. This theme of variability of influence is increasingly apparent in the case studies of the 1990s and the 2000s. These show that the Hong Kong media were exposed to contradictory influences and had an ambivalent relationship with the dominant power structures. Factors in the wider environment are significant. For example, before 1997, some journalists could resist pressure and even protest by resigning because there was a secure economic environment.[965] However, this kind of active protest became rare after 1997 due to the economic downturn.[966]

In addition, the pressure put on the media results in an ambivalent relationship with the dominant power structures. In the case of the Hong Kong press, the press is neither fully part of the power structure (for example, *South China Morning Post* and *Oriental Daily News* have undergone shifting positions in editorial orientation) nor is it fully independent of the power structure/dominant ideology (for example, *Apple Daily* and *Hong Kong Economic Journal* can be selective in maintaining their critical position). Both the above-mentioned dailies respond to pressures and adjust accordingly. For example, the proprietor of *Apple Daily* laid down guidelines saying there was to be no breaking news about China, and *Hong Kong Economic Journal* rarely sent journalists to cover Chinese political news in order to avoid a direct clash with the Chinese authorities, despite the fact that both newspapers represent a leading critical voice in Hong Kong. Although in the case of Hong Kong it is not possible to talk about a liberal democracy, it has nevertheless developed most of the features of a highly sophisticated capitalist city embedded with market values and civil society culture with a strong appreciation of a free flow of information. There are ways in which popular forces can influence the media in liberal democracies. Although some of these are considered contentious within the radical tradition, they do, nonetheless, play the role of powerful countervailing forces as shown in the above-mentioned study.

Drawing on what I learnt from the Hong Kong experience, I would like to reconstruct the paradigm of radical political economy in order to make allowance for elements of the liberal democracy models (such as the role of professional norms and standards, public expectation and aspiration, and the power of civil society) which counteract the infrastructural/economic factors and superstructural/political reasons that cut press freedom down. The experience of Hong Kong, where the first HKSAR chief executive had not been able to carry out his mandate fully and where elite opinion was split over government major policies (such as on the enactment of the proposed new national security bill), the power of agents and actors (such as from the pan-democratic alliance) may override the dominant power of economic commands and political censorship. The overwhelming importance of political and economic reality in shaping media content can subsequently be undermined. However, we can also rework the liberal democracy model to take seriously into account the overwhelming importance of political and economic reality in shaping media content. In my reconstructed account of the liberal democracy model, during the colonial suppression in the 1960s, given the media system as a relatively open and competitive process in which various actors are competing for influence, political power (British colonial administration) and economic ownership produce media content that is biased/class-biased against the underdogs/underprivileged and in favour of the ruling political and economic elites.

In short, the larger environment of Hong Kong is changing rapidly. So is public sentiment. However, the political culture, journalistic norms and institutional support remain strong. It is evident that the British colonial government was highly oppressive at one point, but it also changed enormously over time. Although the Chinese regime is an authoritarian regime in nature, it has been adjusting its strategy, if not entirely its policy, towards Hong Kong.

As has already been pointed out, media organisations are subject to influences that can make them conform to the establishment's ideology. The media in liberal democracies are often subjected to influences from above and below. How these pressures and constraints are manifested, and whether countervailing forces are present in a vigorous form, however, depends upon the specific context in which the media operate. In the case of a hybrid authoritarian/bureaucratic/capitalist/city state such as Hong Kong, which is a transitional society and largely deviates from the static model of a western liberal democracy, the interaction is even more complex.

Appendix

Table 1 Newspaper readership in 1966, 1976, 1986 and 1996[1]

Rank	Newspaper	Readership[2]
Newspaper readership in 1966		
1	*Sing Tao Wen Pao*	21%
2	*Sing Pao Daily News*	18%
3	*Kung Sheung Daily News*	10%
4	*Ming Pao Daily News*	8%
4	*Hong Kong Commercial Daily*	8%
6	*Sing Tao Jih Pao*	7%
6	*Wah Kiu Yat Pao*	7%
8	*Ching Pao*	6%
8	*Express Daily News*	6%
10	*Tin Tin Daily News*	5%
11	*South China Morning Post*	4%
12	*Wah Kiu Man Pao*	3%
12	*Star*	3%
14	*Hong Kong Standard*	2%
15	*China Mail*	1%
(N)		(3,036,000)
Newspaper readership in 1976		
1	*Sing Pao Daily News*	649,000 (19%)
2	*Sing Tao Wen Pao*	519,000 (15%)
3	*Oriental Daily News*	470,000 (14%)
4	*Sing Tao Jih Pao*	354,000 (10%)
5	*Ming Pao Daily News*	298,000 (9%)
6	*Express Daily News*	235,000 (7%)
7	*Wah Kiu Yat Pao*	226,000 (7%)
8	*Hong Kong Daily News*	190,000 (5%)
9	*Kung Sheung Daily News*	130,000 (4%)
10	*Hong Kong Commercial Daily*	127,000 (4%)
11	*South China Morning Post*	125,000 (4%)
12	*Ching Pao*	104,000 (3%)
13	*Chinese Star*	69,000 (2%)
14	*Ming Pao Evening News*	45,000 (1%)
15	*Star*	32,000 (1%)
16	*Hong Kong Standard*	31,000 (1%)
(N)		(3,460,000) *contd.*

Table 1 Continued

Rank	Newspaper	Readership[2]
Newspaper readership in 1986		
1	Oriental Daily News	1,767,000 (38%)
2	Sing Pao Daily News	850,000(19%)
3	Ming Pao Daily News	423,000 (9%)
4	South China Morning Post	278,000 (6%)
5	Tin Tin Daily News	258,000 (6%)
5	Hong Kong Daily News	258,000 (6%)
7	Sing Tao Jih Pao	199,000 (4%)
8	Express Daily News	108,000 (2%)
9	Wah Kiu Yat Pao	100,000 (2%)
10	Sing Tao Wen Pao	88,000 (2%)
11	Hong Kong Economic Journal	66,000 (1%)
12	Hong Kong Commercial Daily	58,000 (1%)
13	Wen Wei Po	55,000 (1%)
14	Hong Kong Standard	37,000 (1%)
15	Ching Pao	32,000 (1%)
(N)		(4,718,000)
Newspaper readership in 1996		
1	Oriental Daily News	1,601,000 (29%)
2	Apple Daily	1,338,000 (24%)
3	Sing Pao Daily News	630,000 (11%)
4	Tin Tin Daily News	465,000 (8%)
5	Ming Pao Daily News	345,000 (6%)
6	Hong Kong Daily News	323,000 (6%)
7	South China Morning Post	253,000 (5%)
8	Sing Tao Daily	221,000 (4%)
9	Hong Kong Economic Times	95,000 (2%)
10	Hong Kong Economic Journal	61,000 (1%)
(N)		(5,481,000)

Sources: Hong Kong Media Survey 1996, SRH Media Index 1976, SRH Media Index 1986, AC Nielsen. [*sic*] SRG Hong Kong Media Index 1996.

Notes
1 Adopted from So, Clement Y. K. and Joseph M. Chan, eds., *Press and Politics in Hong Kong – Case Studies from 1967 to 1997* (Hong Kong: Hong Kong Institute of Asia-Pacific Studies, Chinese UP, 1999) 9–10.
2 Ibid. The population figures (N) for the respective years are based on age 9+ projects. [*sic*]

Table 2 Selected chronology of the 1967 disturbances[1]

Phase 1	Demonstrations and riots
6 May	Police arrest 21 men at Hong Kong Artificial Flower Works in San Po Kong owned by Hong Kong businessman, Li Ka-shing.
11 May	Pickets threaten to break into the factory and clash with police. Riots break out.
11–13 May	Rioting in Kowloon. Buses set alight; government offices looted.
14 May	Order restored.
15 May	Statement from Ministry of Foreign Affairs in Beijing demanding an end to violence allegedly started by the police and British colonial authorities.
22 May	Attempts to demonstrate outside Hong Kong Government House thwarted by police. Clashes between police and demonstrators in Garden Road, Central.
1 June	Emergency regulations introduced forbidding the display of wall posters.

Phase 2	Work stoppages, economic disruption and further violence
June	Transport services disrupted. Intermittent strikes. Police break into government electrical and mechanical workshops and the Kowloon depot of the Hong Kong and China Gas Company. Five hundred people arrested.
23 June	Police break into Hong Kong Rubber and Plastic Workers Union. Fifty-three arrested, three die.
24 June	Call for a general strike.
24 June	Attack on the police station at Sha Tau Kok.
July	Drought. No response to request for additional water supplies from China.
28 June–4 July	Food strike; attempts to disrupt food supplies from China.
8 July	Second attack on police station at Sha Tau Kok. Five policemen killed, 11 wounded.
9–12 July	Further urban demonstrations.
12 July	Police take offensive action against communists, raiding premises, seizing weapons and detaining suspects.
15 July	Boycott of the port announced.
24 July–15 Sept.	No freight service between China and Hong Kong.

Phase 3	Bomb attacks
August	Random bomb attacks including those in a large shopping centre, a police station, harbour ferries, a tram and the Salvation Army.
August	Rumoured assassination list of well-known Hong Kong senior officials and celebrities, particularly anti-communists.
22 Aug.	Office of British Chargé d'Affaires in Beijing sacked in reprisal for the arrest of Xinhua News Agency reporters and action against communist newspapers.
24 Aug.	Radio commentator, Lam Bun, and his cousin burned to death.
30 Oct.–5 Nov.	Increase in bomb attacks in an attempt to disrupt Hong Kong Week, a promotional display of the territory's products.
Aug.–Dec.	Random bomb attacks. Fifteen killed. A total of 8,074 suspected bombs were found, of which 1,167 were genuine bombs.

Note
1 Adopted from Ian Scott (1989) 98–99 and press coverage at the time. Also see *Hong Kong 1967* (Hong Kong Government Printer, 1968); John Cooper, *Colony in Conflict: The Hong Kong Disturbances, May 1967–Jan. 1968* (Hong Kong: Swindon, 1970).

Table 3 The case of Xi Yang – a time line[1]

27.9.1993	Xi Yang is detained by the Beijing authorities.
7.10.1993	Chinese official arrest of Xi Yang.
28.3.1994	Xi Yang is tried behind closed doors for security reasons for the alleged crime of 'spying and stealing of state secrets'. The verdict is based on Xi's series of news reports on the possible increase of interest rates and a rumour about Chinese gold sales that was published in the *Ming Pao Daily News*. Xi's sister receives a phone call, apparently from the Beijing court, telling her the verdict.
1.4.1994	News of Xi Yang's conviction and 12-year sentence is published in Hong Kong.
4.4. 1994	News of Xi's sentence is confirmed by the Federation of All China Journalists, but not through any legal or formal channels.
5.4.1994	Over 100 journalists take to the streets to protest against China's heavy-handed sentence of Xi Yang.
9.4.1994	Instead of playing the role of reporter, over 150 journalists take to the streets protesting against China's sentence on Xi. *Ming Pao Daily News* staff finish a 72-hour relay hunger strike.
9.4.1994	An open letter signed by more than 1,000 journalists is published in mainstream newspapers in protest at Chinese repression of Xi Yang.
8.4.1994	*Chinese News Services* prints a rebuke aimed at Hong Kong reaction to the Xi case.
11.4.1994	Official version of trial published by *Xinhua (New China) News Agency*.
15.4.1994	Appeal court upholds earlier verdict on Xi Yang.
15.4.1994	Second demonstration and protest by journalists includes *Ming Pao Daily News'* staff and party representatives across political boundaries in Hong Kong.
15.4.1994	*Chinese Central Television (CCTV)* footage shows Xi Yang and Tian Ye, an official of the Bank of China who is alleged to have given state secrets to Xi, appearing in court. Tian Ye, Xi's co-defendant, does not appeal.
16.4.1994	*Ming Pao Daily News* prints a 20-Chinese character editorial: 'Salute to our reporter Xi Yang; in the wake of Chinese oppression we might as well throw our pens away to protest against the Chinese judicial system.' This is a serious condemnatory gesture against Chinese coercion.
17.4.1994	Two-thousand people march to campaign for Xi Yang's early release.
30.4.1994	More than 100 reporters on the China beat[2] issue an open statement: 1. expressing their anger over Xi's case; 2. saying that from that day until the end of May, this group of reporters will boycott China-subsidised trips for publicity and promotional purposes.
11.5.1994	The Hong Kong Legislative Council passes a motion urging China to release Xi Yang and protect Hong Kong's press freedom.
25.1.1997	Xi Yang released on parole. He came back to Hong Kong, and then emigrated to Canada.

Notes
1 Contemporary news reports and *Ming Pao Daily News'* staff writer (1997).
2 China took revenge on this group of reporters a few months later. The Chinese authorities refused permission for them to cover a serious accident in Hangzhou.

Table 4.1 Representation of interviewees within news organisations

Ranking	Numbers	Rejection	Reporters/ editors/ columnist	Senior news executives and proprietors
Senior reporter/columnist/ editorial writer	6	–	6	–
News editor	10	–	10	–
Deputy editor/chief editor	15	–	–	15
Proprietor/publisher	6	1	–	6
Senior news executive (including a chief executive officer and a manager)	3	–	–	3
Broadcasting producer, broadcaster	11	–	–	11
Professor/lecturer in journalism and media and communications who are also columnists	5	–	5	5
Total	–	1	21	40
Grand total	56	–	–	–

Table 4.2 Representation of interviewees across news organisations

Organisation name	Number of interviewees	*Newspaper/ magazine	Broadcasting	Total
Hong Kong Economic Journal	4	4	–	–
Ming Pao Daily News	2	2	–	–
Oriental Daily News	2	2	–	–
South China Morning Post	7	7	–	–
Apple Daily/Next Magazine	7	7	–	–
Sing Tao Daily News	6	6	–	–
Hong Kong Economic Times	3	3	–	–
Wen Wei Po/Ta Kung Pao/Xinhua	3	3	–	–
Metro Broadcast	2	–	2	–
Radio TV Hong Kong	7	–	7	–
TV Broadcast	3	–	3	–
Asia TV	1	–	1	–
Wharf Cable TV	1	–	1	–
Commercial Radio	1	–	1	–
Free Radio Asia	1	–	1	–
Open Magazine	1	1	–	–
Others (academic columnists)	5	5	–	–
Total		40	16	56

Notes

* Many of the interviewees have worked for more than one media organisation, so they were able to provide information not only about their current employer, but also about their previous employers, which in many ways served as a means of cross-checking material.

Table 4.3 Full list of 56 interviewees' names, positions, news organisations and interview details

---

Bale, Cliff. Chief editor, former political editor, *Radio Television Hong Kong (Radio, English channel) (RTHK)*. Former chairperson, Hong Kong Journalists Association (HKJA). Conversation, 2000, 2001 and 2003, London; Interview, 2002, Hong Kong.

Chan, Ida. Executive Producer. *Wharf Cable*. Interview, 2002, Hong Kong.

Chan, Yiu-wah. Head, Radio 2, *RTHK*. Interview, 2002, Hong Kong. Conversation, 2003, London.

Cheng, Albert. Broadcaster, *Commercial Radio*; publisher. Interview, Sept. and Oct. 2002, Hong Kong. Conversation, 2004, London.

Cheng, May. Legal adviser, *Apple Daily*; former senior reporter, *Asia TV (ATV)*, *TV Broadcast (TVB)*. Interview, 2002, Hong Kong.

Cheung, Paul. Former news controller, *Metro Broadcast*. Interview, 2002, Hong Kong.

Chiu, Hsiang-Chung. Retired chief editor, *Hong Kong Economic Journal* 1998–2002; former chief editor/producer, the *BBC World Service* (Chinese). Conversation, 2000, 2003 and 2004, London. Interview, 2002, Hong Kong.

Forsythe, William. Former news editor, *Asia TV*. Written communication, 2003.

Gittings, Danny. Deputy editor, opinion page, *Asian Wall Street Journal (AWSJ)*. Former deputy editor, *South China Morning Post*. Interview, 2002, Hong Kong.

Ho, Andy. Columnist, *Sing Tao Daily News*; former news editor, *SCMP* and *Standard*. Interview, 2002.

Ho, King-Man. Washington D.C. Correspondent, former London correspondent, *Radio Free Asia*. Conversation, 2003, London.

Ho, Man-Hong. Publisher, *Sun*; former news editor, *Oriental Daily News*. Interview, 2002, Hong Kong.

Ip Yat-kin. Publisher, *Apple Daily*, Taiwan and Hong Kong. Former news editor, *Oriental Daily News*. Interview, 2002, Hong Kong.

Jin, Zhong. Publisher, proprietor and chief editor, *Open Monthly Magazine*. Written communication, 2003, 2004.

Kam, Yiu-Yu. Former chief editor, *Hong Kong Wen Wei Po*. Conversation and written communication, 1997 and 1998, Hong Kong and Los Angeles, USA.

Kwan, Bo-Shu. News editor, *Oriental Daily News*. Interview, 2002, Hong Kong.

Kwan, Daniel. Deputy China editor, *South China Morning Post*. Interview, 2002, Hong Kong.

Ma, Eric. Columnist, *Ming Pao Daily News*. Associate Professor, School of Media and Communication, Hong Kong Chinese University. Conversation, 2002, Hong Kong.

Manuel, Gren. Editor (European news), *Dow Jones* (London). Former senior reporter, *AWSJ* (Hong Kong); former senior reporter, *SCMP*. Interview, 2001. Conversation, 2002, 2003, London.

Morarity, Frances. Senior Reporter, *RTHK* (Radio). Executive Committee member, Foreign Correspondents' Club, Hong Kong. Interview, 2002, Hong Kong.

Ng, Ming-Lam. Presenter, *Metro Broadcast*. Founding producer and presenter, *City Forum* and other public affairs programmes, *RTHK*. Interview, 2002, Hong Kong.

Nip, Joyce. Assistant Professor, School of Journalism, Hong Kong Baptist University. Former reporter, *Sunday Morning Post*. Interview, 2002, Hong Kong.

Lai, Ting-yiu. Publisher, *East Weekly Magazine*. Former news editor, *Sing Tao Daily News*. Interview, 2002, Hong Kong.

Lam, Hang-Chi. Publisher, proprietor and columnist, *Hong Kong Economic Journal*. Written communication, 2002 and 2003.

Lam, Man-chung. News editor, *Sing Tao Daily News*; former senior reporter, *Ming Pao Daily News* and *Hong Kong Economic Times*. Interview, 2002, Hong Kong.

continued

Table 4.3 Continued

Lam, Willy. Senior China analyst, *CNN*; former associate editor, China editor, *SCMP*. Interview, 2002, Hong Kong. Conversation 2001, 2003, London.

Lau, Kevin. Deputy editor, *Ming Pao Daily News*. Interview, 2002, Hong Kong.

Law, Ambrose. Chief news producer, *TVB (Satellite)*, London; Former news editor, *Sing Tao Daily News* (European edition). Former producer, Public Affairs, *Wharf Cable TV*. Conversation, 2003, 2004, London.

Lee, Chin-Chuan. Contributor, *Hong Kong Economic Journal*; *China Times* (Taiwan); Professor, University of Minnesota. Head, Department of English and Communication, Hong Kong City University. Conversation, 2002, Hong Kong.

Lee, Tina. Executive producer, Education and Documentary, *RTHK* (TV). Interview and conversation, 2002, London.

Leung, Grace. Lecturer, Hong Kong Chinese University, columnist, *Hong Kong Economic Journal*. Conversation, 2002, Hong Kong.

Leung, Heung-nam. Deputy Editor, *Ming Pao Daily News*. Interview, 2002, Hong Kong.

Leung, Theresa. Former editor, Culture section, *Hong Kong Economic Journal*. Telephone Conversation, 2002, 2003, London.

Li, Daisy. Editor, *Taiwan Apple Daily*. Former chief editor, *Apple Daily* web. Former news editor, *Ming Pao Daily News*. Former chairperson, Hong Kong Journalists Association. Interview, 2002, Hong Kong.

Lin, Diana. Producer, Public Affairs, *TVB* (Pearl Channel). Conversation, 2002, Hong Kong.

Liu, Kin-Ming. Managing editor, Opinion-editorial page; Director, Public Affairs Department, *Apple Daily*. Former manager, *Apple Daily*. Interview, 2002, Hong Kong.

Lo, Chan. News controller, *TVB*. Founding publisher, *Apple Daily*. Interview, 2002, Hong Kong.

Lo, Fu. Former Deputy editor, *Ta Kung Pao*. Former chief editor, the now defunct *New Evening Post*. Interview, 1997 and 2002, Hong Kong.

Lo, Wing-Hung. Chief executive officer, Global China (holding company of *Sing Tao Daily News*). Interview, 2002, Hong Kong.

Shum, Yee-Lan. News editor, *Hong Kong Economic Times*. Former news editor, *Apple Daily*. Interview, 2002, Hong Kong.

Siu, Sai-Wo. Chief editor, *Singtao Daily News*. Interview, 2002, Hong Kong.

Sze, Forever. Spokesman, *RTHK*. Former executive producer, Public Affairs, *RTHK* (TV). Interview, 2002, Hong Kong.

Sze, Li-Yee. Deputy editor, *Hong Kong Economic Journal*. Interview, 2002, Hong Kong.

Szeto, Keung. Retired senior official, *Xinhua News Agency*. Interview, 1997 and 2002, Hong Kong.

Tai, Kin-man. Spokesperson, Director of Education, *RTHK*. Interview, 2002, Hong Kong.

Tsui, Pui-ying. News editor, *TVB*. Former news editor, *ATV*, *Commercial Radio*. Interview, 2002, Hong Kong.

Tung, Chiao. Publisher, *Apple Daily*. Former chief editor, *Ming Pao Daily News*. Interview, 2002, Hong Kong.

Warmington, Charlie. Editor, London *Times*; former editor, *SCMP*. Written communication, 2003.

Wong, Hon-kun. Deputy political editor, *Apple Daily*. Former deputy China editor, *Ming Pao Daily News*. Interview, 2002, Hong Kong.

Wong, Kan-tai. Senior reporter, *Sing Tao Daily News* (European edition). Former photographer, *Yazhou Zhouhan*, *Wen Wei Po*. Conversation 2002 and 2003, London.

To, Yiu-Ming. Columnist, *Ming Pao Daily News*. Assistant Professor, School of Journalism, Hong Kong Baptist University. Interview, 2002, Hong Kong. Conversation and written communication, 2000, 2001, 2003.

Table 4.3 Continued

Tse, Ming-Chong. Former photo editor, *Next Magazine*. Interview and conversation 2003, London.

Yau, Shing-Mu. Deputy editor, *Hong Kong Economic Times*. Former political editor, *Hong Kong Standard*. Interview, 2002, Hong Kong.

Yeung, Chris. Editor-at-large, former political editor, *SCMP*. Interview, 2002, Hong Kong. Written communication 2003.

Yuen, Tai-Ho. Former Chairperson, *RTHK* Trade Union. Retired senior reporter, *RTHK* (Radio). Interview, 2002, Hong Kong.

Zhou, Song-Ming. Former editorial writer, opinion-page editor, *Hong Kong Economic Times, Ming Pao Daily News*. Interview, 2002, Hong Kong.

Table 5.1 Twelve Hong Kong mainstream newspapers[1]

Journal number	Title	Registered date	Launch date
31	*Ta Kung Pao*	4 Aug. 1951	13 Aug. 1938
33	*Wen Wei Po*	11 Sept. 1951	9 Sept. 1948
35	*Sing Pao Daily News*	12 Sept. 1951	1 May 1939
38	*Hong Kong Commercial Daily*	18 Sept. 1951	20 May 1952
78	*Sing Tao Daily News*	11 May 1951	1 Aug. 1938
289	*Ming Pao Daily News*	5 March 1959	20 May 1959
297	*Hong Kong Daily News*	23 Sept. 1959	5 Oct. 1959
318	*Tin Tin Daily News*	10 Oct. 1960	1 Nov. 1960
486	*Oriental Daily News*	21 Jan. 1969	22 Jan. 1969
685	*Hong Kong Economic Journal*	7 June 1973	3 July 1973
1,893	*Hong Kong Economic Times*	20 Nov. 1987	26 Jan. 1988
2,911	*Apple Daily*	27 Jan. 1995	20 June 1995

Note
1 Adopted from Li Kuk-Shing, *A comment on the Press of Hong Kong*: 220.

Table 5.2 Thirty-two Hong Kong political journals between the 1950s and the 1970s[1]

Title	Frequency of publication	Launch year	Closure year
Motherland	Monthly/ weekly	1953	1972
Zhonghua Yue Bao	Monthly	1973	Published in Dec. 1975
Shidai Piping	Weekly	1938	Unknown
Zhanwang	Monthly/ bi-weekly	1958	1983
Zhong guo Pinglun	Weekly	1962	Published in 1969
Minzhu Pinglun	Bi-weekly	1950	Unknown
Xin She Hui	Monthly	1953	Unknown
Xian Dai	Monthly	1965	1968
Ming Pao Monthly	Monthly	1966	Continue to publish
Ren Wu yu Xi Xiang	Monthly	1967	Published in 1972
The Intellectual	Monthly/ bi-weekly	1968	Published in 1972
Pangu	Monthly	1967	Published in 1977
Nan Bei Ji	Monthly/ weekly	1971	1997(?) [*sic*]
The Seventies (*later renamed The Nineties*)	Monthly	1970	1998
The 70s (*not related to 'The Seventies'*)	Bi-weekly	1970	Published in 1978
October Critique	Monthly	1974	Still being published
Zhan Xun	Irregular	1975	Published in 1980
Leftists' new idea	Monthly	1974	Published in 1976
Xinmiao	Unknown	Unknown	Unknown
Ye Chao	Irregular	1971	1977 (merged with the *Yellow River*)
Yellow River	Irregular	1976	1979
Beidou	Monthly	1977	1978
Wide Angle	Monthly	1972	Still being published
West-East Wind	Monthly	1972	1973(?) [*sic*]
South-East Wind	Monthly	1974	Published in 1975
New Observer	Monthly	1977	1978(?) [*sic*]
Observer	Monthly	1977	1981
Zhangming	Monthly	Nov. 1977	Still being published
Dongxiang	Monthly	1987(?)	Closed but re-launched
Mirror	Monthly	1977	Still being published
West and East	Monthly	1979	1981(?) [*sic*]
The Chinese	Monthly	1979	1981(?) [*sic*]

Note
1 Li Kuk-Shing, *A Comment on the Press of Hong Kong*: 250–251.

Table 5.3 Six main evening dailies shut down since the 1980s[1]

Title	Launch year	Closure year
Kung Sheung Evening Post	1930	1984
Hong Kong Standard Evening Post	1986	1987
Wah Kiu Evening Post	1946	1988
Ming Pao Evening News	1969	1988
Sing Tao Evening News	1938	1996
New Evening Post	1950	1997

Note
1 Li Kuk-Shing, *A Comment on the Press of Hong Kong*: 321.

Table 5.4 Daily newspapers shut down since 1980s[1]

Title	Launch year	Closure year
Kung Sheung Daily News	1925	1984
Hong Kong Times	1949	1993
Hong Kong Today	1993	1994
Wah Kiu Yat Pao	1925	1995
TV Daily News	1968	1995
Ching Pao	1956	1991
Hong Kong United Daily	1992	1995
Express News	1993	1995 (28 Oct. 1996 relaunched, 16 Mar. 1998 closed)
Eastern Express (English)	1994	1996
Wah Nam Financial News	1993	1996
Hong Kong Standard (English)	1949	2000

Note
1 Li Kuk-Shing, *A Comment on the Press of Hong Kong*: 322.

Table 5.5 Periodical Titles Shut Down in the 1990s[1]

Title	Closure year
8 Weekly	1998
The Nineties	1998
'Special' Weekly	1998
Youth Bi-weekly	1997
City Weekly	1997
Hong Kong's Window	1996
Ching Sun Weekly	1996
China Times Weekly	1996
Hong Kong TV Weekly	1995

Note
1 Li Kuk-Shing, *A Comment on the Press of Hong Kong*: 323.

Notes

1 Introduction

1 James Curran, 'The New Revisionism in Mass Communication Research: A Reappraisal', *Cultural Studies and Communications*, eds James Curran, David Morley and V. Walkerdine (London: Arnold, 1996) 256–278.
2 Ibid.
3 E.g. Gaye Tuchman, *Making News: A Study in the Construction of Reality* (New York: Free Press, 1978).
4 Todd Gitlin, *Inside Prime Time* (New York: Pantheon, 1983).
5 Todd Gitlin, *Media Unlimited: How the Torrent of Images and Sounds Overwhelms Our Lives* (New York: H. Holt, 2003).
6 For example, Gaye Tuchman, *Making News*.
7 For example, Glasgow University Media Group, *Bad News* (London: Routledge, 1976).
8 Peter Golding, 'The Missing Dimensions: News Media and the Management of Social Change', *Mass Media and Social Change*, eds E. Katz and T. Szecsko (London: Sage, 1981) 63–82.
9 Edward S. Herman and Noam Chomsky, *Manufacturing Consent: The Political Economy of the Mass Media* (New York: Pantheon, 1988); Graham Murdock, 'Large Corporations and the Control of the Communication Industries', *Culture, Society, and the Media*, eds Michael Gurevitch *et al.* (New York: Methuen, 1982) 118–150; Graham Murdock, 'Redrawing the Map of the Communications Industries: Concentration and Ownership in the Era of Privatization', *Public Communication: The New Imperatives*, ed. M. Ferguson (London: Sage, 1990) 1–15.
10 Graham Murdock, 'Large Corporations'.
11 Ibid; James Curran, ed., *Media Organization in Society* (London: Arnold, 2000).
12 James Curran and Jean Seaton, *Power without Responsibility*, 6th edn (London: Routledge, 2003); Harold Evans, *Good Times, Bad Times* (London: Weidenfeld and Nicholson, 1983); Edward S. Herman and Robert McChesney, *The Global Media: The New Missionaries and Corporate Capitalism* (London; Washington, DC: Cassell, 1997).
13 James Curran and Jean Seaton, *Power without Responsibility*.
14 Ben H. Bagdikian, *The Media Monopoly: With a New Preface on the Internet and Communication Cartels* (Boston: Beacon Press, 2000).
15 Herbert Schiller, *Culture Inc.: The Corporate Takeover of Public Expression* (New York; Oxford: Oxford University Press, 1989).
16 Robert W. McChesney, 'The Problem of Journalism', *Journalism Studies* 4(3) (2003) 299–329.
17 Ibid.
18 Graham Murdock (1982).

19 James Curran and Jean Seaton, *Power without Responsibility* 93.
20 Ibid.
21 See James Curran and Jean Seaton, *Power without Responsibility*.
22 Stuart Hall *et al.*, *Policing the Crisis* (London: Macmillan, 1978).
23 Edward S. Herman and Noam Chomsky, *Manufacturing Consent*.
24 For example, Peter Golding and Graham Murdock, 'Culture, Communication and Political Economy', *Mass Media and Society*, eds James Curran and M. Gurevitch (London: Edward Arnold, 1991) 11–30.
25 For example, James Curran *et al.*, 'The Study of the Media: Theoretical Approaches', *Culture, Society and the Media*, eds M. Gurevitch *et al.* (London: Routledge, 1982) 11–29; Hanno Hardt, *Critical Communication Studies* (London: Routledge, 1992).
26 See John Keane, *The Media and Democracy* (Cambridge: Polity Press, 1991); James Curran, 'Mass Media and Democracy Revisited', *Mass Media and Society*, eds James Curran and Michael Gurevitch (London; New York: Arnold, 1996) 81–119.
27 For example, argument advanced by Rupert Murdoch. Rupert Murdoch, *Freedom in Broadcasting* (London: News International, 1989).
28 For example, Michael Schudson and Daniel Hallin.
29 Michael Schudson, 'The Objectivity Norm in American Journalism' *Journalism* 2(2) (2001) 149–170.
30 Ibid. 167.
31 Michael Schudson, 'The Sociology of News Production Revisited', *Mass Media and Society* 3rd edn, eds James Curran and M. Gurevitch (London: Arnold, 2000) 175–200; Michael Schudson, *The Sociology of News* (New York: W. W. Norton, 2003).
32 Daniel Hallin, *We Keep America on Top of the World: TV Journalism and the Public Sphere* (London; New York: Routledge, 1994).
33 Michael Schudson uses this term to refer to agents of source such as public relations firms, public information officers, political spin doctors, and the publicity staffs of a wide variety of institutions, both corporate and non-profit. Michael Schudson, *The Sociology of News* 3.
34 Daniel Hallin, *We Keep America on Top of the World* 4.
35 Ibid. 11.
36 James Curran *et al.*, 'Introduction', *Mass Communication and Society*, eds James Curran *et al.* (London: Edward Arnold, 1977) 9–11.
37 James Curran, Introduction, *Media Organisations in Society*: 9–16.
38 Michael Schudson, *The Sociology of News*; Herbert Gans, *Deciding What's News: A Study of CBS Evening News, NBC Nightly News, 'Newsweek' and 'Time'* (London: Constable, 1980).
39 For example, Robert McChesney.
40 Silvio Waisbord, *Watchdog Journalism in South America: News, Accountability and Democracy* (New York: Columbia University Press, 2000).
41 Zhao Yue-zhi, *Media, Market, and Democracy in China: Between the Party line and Bottom Line* (Urbana: University of Illinois Press, 1998); Hugo de Burgh, *The Chinese Journalist: Mediating Information in the World's Most Populous Country* (London, New York: Routledge, 2003).
42 Joseph M. Chan, 'When Capitalist and Socialist Television Clash: The Impact of Hong Kong TV on Guangzhou Residents', *Power, Money and Media – Communication Patterns and Bureaucratic Control in Cultural China*, ed. Chin-Chuan Lee (Evanston, Illinois: Northwestern University Press, 2000) 245–270.
43 Gaye Tuchman, *Making News*.
44 For example, James Curran *et al.*, 'The Study of the Media'.
45 For example, James Curran, *Media and Power* (London and New York: Routledge, 2002).

46 Gaye Tuchman, *Making News*.

47 Hong Kong is composed of three main parts: Hong Kong island, Kowloon Peninsula and the New Territories. China lost Hong Kong to Britain in three different battles. The result of the negotiation between the Chinese and the British following the British victory in the first Opium War was the Treaty of Nanking, which was signed by the representatives of both sides in Nanking on 29 August 1842. The treaty was ratified in Hong Kong on 26 June 1843, thus formally allowing Hong Kong to become a British crown colony. The Kowloon Peninsula was ceded to Britain after the second Opium War of 1858–1860. China's defeat by Japan in the war of 1894–1895 enabled Britain to demand the lease of the New Territories (which are connected to mainland China) for 99 years. The lease expired in 1997. See Steve Tsang, *A Modern History of Hong Kong* (London: I.B. Tauris, 2004).

48 Norman Miners, *The Government and Politics of Hong Kong* (Hong Kong: Oxford University Press, 1991) 15.

49 Robin Hutcheon, *SCMP: The First Eighty Years* (Hong Kong: South China Morning Post Publishing, 1983); Cheung Kwai-Yeung, *Jin Yong (Louis Cha) and the Press* (Hong Kong [Chinese]: Ming Pao Publishing, 2000) 191 and 391.

50 Cheung Kwai-Yeung, *Jin Yong (Louis Cha) and the Press* 191.

51 For example, Dr Sun Yat-sen, whose revolutionary ideas were said to be partly inspired by his experience of British colonial rule while he studied in Hong Kong at different times. Whilst there, he also tried to mobilise support for his political ends. See Li Kuk-Shing, *A Comment on the Hong Kong Press* (Hong Kong [Chinese]: Ming Pao Publishing, 2000).

52 Ibid.

53 See Chang Kuo-sin, 'Hong Kong', *Newspapers in Asia: Contemporary Trends and Problems 82*, ed. John A. Lend (Hong Kong: Heineman Asia, 1982) 78–82.

54 Lee Chuan-Chin *et al.*, 'Professionalism Among Hong Kong Journalists in Comparative Perspective', *Mass Media in the Asian Pacific*, ed. Bryce T. McIntyre (Philadelphia: Multilingual Matters, 1998) 6.

55 This was also known as the Chinese Publication (Prevention) Ordinance (No. 6 of 1914, repealed by ordinance no. 13 of 1938, the Sedition Ordinance). See Anne Cheung, *Self-censorship and the Struggle for Press Freedom in Hong Kong* (New York: Kluwer Law International, 2003) 71–77. I acknowledge the privilege of having read Cheung's manuscript before it went to print. This section was enhanced by, and benefited from, her legal perspective.

56 Later, the concept of sedition was incorporated into the Crime Ordinance, ordinance no. 60 of 1971, now known as Cap. 200. See Anne Cheung, *Self-censorship and the Struggle for Press Freedom* 71–77.

57 No. 25 of 1927, repealed by ordinance no. 15, the Control of Publications (Consolidation) Ordinance of 1951. The latter was replaced by the Registration of Local Newspapers Ordinance in 1987, ordinance no. 15 of 1987. Ibid.

58 The Licensing Act was repealed due to an intellectual movement that strongly opposed the press licensing system. For a historical account of the development in England, see James Curran and Jean Seaton, *Power without Responsibility* 5th edn (1997) 7.

59 See Tables 5.1 to 5.4 of the Appendix for information about the launch and closure of newspapers over time.

60 No. 8 of 1948, read together with the Emergency Regulations Ordinance of 1922, now becomes Emergency Regulations Ordinance, Cap. 241. See Anne Cheung, *Self-censorship and the Struggle for Press Freedom* 71–77.

61 No. 15 of 1951, later replaced by the Registration of Local Newspapers Ordinance. Now known as Cap 268. Ibid.

62 The ordinances proved to be powerful legal instruments in the oppression of the radical press in the late 1960s. See Chapter 2 for details.

63 Paul S. N. Lee, 'Chinese and Western Press in Hong Kong', *Hong Kong History: New Perspectives*, Vol. 2, ed. Guangwu Wang (Hong Kong [Chinese]: Joint Publishing, 1997) 493–533.

64 *Kung Sheung Daily News* in 1925; *Sing Tao Daily News* in 1938; *Sing Pao Daily News* in 1939; and *Wah Kiu Yat Po* in 1952. *Sing Tao Daily News* and *Sing Pao Daily News* still exist today; while *Kung Sheung* and *Wah Kiu Yat Po* were closed down due to financial reasons in the 1980s and late 1990s, respectively. See Tables 5.1 to 5.4 of Appendix for more detail.

65 Joseph Man Chan, Paul S. N. Lee and Chin-Chuan Lee, *Hong Kong Journalists in Transition* (Hong Kong: Hong Kong Institute of Asia-Pacific Studies, Chinese University Press, 1996).

66 In 1946 there were 14 Chinese papers. A decade after the take-over of mainland China by the CCP there were 49 papers. See Anne Cheung, *Self-censorship and the Struggle for Press Freedom* and Chang Kuo-sin, *A Survey of the Chinese Language Daily Press* (Hong Kong: International Press Institute, 1968).

67 Joseph Man Chan and Chin-Chuan Lee, *Mass Media and Political Transition in Hong Kong: The Hong Kong Press in China's Orbit* (New York: Guilford Press, 1991).

68 Paul S. N. Lee, 'Chinese and Western Press'.

69 Joseph Man Chan and Paul S. N. Lee, 'Communication Indicators in Hong Kong: Conceptual Issues, Findings and Implications', *The Development of Social Indicators Research in Chinese Societies*, eds S. K. Lau *et al.* (Hong Kong: Hong Kong Institute of Asia-Pacific Studies, Chinese University Press, 1996) 175–204; Paul S. N. Lee, 'Chinese and Western Press'.

70 Paul S. N. Lee, 'Chinese and Western Press'.

71 The Nationalist Taiwanese Kuomintang ideological flagship, *Hong Kong Times*, was closed in 1993 and was unable to survive to witness the sovereignty change in 1997.

72 Two second-tier newspapers from the camp, namely *Ching Pao* and *New Evening Post*, shut down in 1991 and 1997, respectively. Only *Ta Kung Pao*, *Wen Wei Po* and *Hong Kong Commercial Daily* managed to survive.

73 Ian Scott, *Political Change and the Crisis of Legitimacy* in Hong Kong (London: Oxford University Press, 1989).

74 See Clement Y. K. So and Joseph Man Chan, 'Research on Press and Politics in Hong Kong: An Overview', *Press and Politics in Hong Kong: Case Studies from 1967 to 1997*, eds Clement Y. K. So and Joseph Man Chan (Hong Kong: Chinese University Press, 1999) 1–32; Lee Chin-Chuan, ed., *Power, Money and Media – Communication Patterns and Bureaucratic Control in Cultural China* (Evanston, Illinois: Northwestern University Press, 2000).

75 The usage of 'left' and 'right' can be confusing in the contemporary context. For example, the politician who is pro-PRC can no longer be clearly defined as 'left-wing', as some of them are already power-holders in the new Hong Kong government. Similarly, pro-PRC newspapers are largely pro-establishment and cannot be classified as progressive. Hence, I prefer to spell out the definition in each of the different stages in the development of the Hong Kong press.

76 The pledge to provide Hong Kong with a high degree of autonomy was made in the Sino-British Joint Declaration agreement and further stipulated in the Hong Kong mini-constitution of the Basic Law. Under the promise of 'one country, two systems', Hong Kong is said to be ruled by Hong Kong people, and allowed to enjoy a high level of autonomy except in relation to foreign and military affairs.

77 Britain and China entered into negotiations regarding the future of Hong Kong in 1982 and reached a joint declaration stipulating that Hong Kong would return to Chinese sovereignty in 1997, with a pledge that Hong Kong would maintain its capitalist style of living and enjoy a high degree of autonomy at least over the next 50 years.

78 See Carol Pui-yee Lai, 'Questionable Beginnings: Hong Kong Press', *Hong Kong after Reunification: Problems and Perspectives*, eds Achim Gussgen, Reimund Seidelmann and Ting Wai (Germany: Nomos Verlagsgesellschaft, Baden-Baden, 2000) 133–144; and Carol Lai and Andy Ho, 'How Free is the Press?' *Hong Kong China: The Red Dawn*, ed. Chris Yeung (Australia: Prentice Hall, 1998) 195–204.

79 Kuan Hsin-chi and Lau Siu-kai, 'Mass Media and Politics in Hong Kong', *Media Asia*, 16 (1989): 185–92, 222.

80 Ibid. 278.

81 Chin-Chuan Lee, 'Partisan Press Coverage of Government News in Hong Kong', *Journalism Quarterly* 62: 770–776.

82 Paul S. N. Lee, 'National Communication and Development: A Comparative Study of Four British Colonies – Nigeria, Guyana, Singapore and Hong Kong', Diss., University of Michigan, 1986.

83 Robert E. Mitchell, 'How Hong Kong Newspapers Have Responded to 15 Years of Rapid Social Change', *Asian Survey* 9 (1969) 669–681.

84 Kuan Hsin-chi and Lau Siu-kai, 'Mass Media and Politics' 277–298.

85 Robert E. Mitchell, 'How Hong Kong Newspapers Have Responded'.

86 Alice Y. L. Lee, 'The Role of Newspapers in the 1967 Riot: A Case Study of the Partisanship of the Hong Kong Press', *Press and Politics in Hong Kong: Case Studies from 1967 to 1997*, eds Clement Y. K. So and Joseph Man Chan (Hong Kong: Hong Kong Institute of Asia-Pacific Studies, Chinese University Press, 1999) 33–66.

87 The case study of 1967 is analysed in Chapter 2.

88 Chin-Chuan Lee, 'The Paradox of Political Economy: Media Structure, Press Freedom, and Regime Change in Hong Kong', *Power, Money and Media – Communication Patterns and Bureaucratic Control in Cultural China*, ed. Chin-Chuan Lee (Evanston, Illinois: Northwestern University Press, 2000) 288–336.

89 This is discussed in more detail in the case study of the late 1960s in Chapter 2.

90 The social reform included the recognition of the Chinese language as the official language, embarking on building housing estates to accommodate the poor and working class people, popularisation of higher education and facilitating better communication with the public at large. See Chapter 2 for more details.

91 'United front work' is a strategy of the Chinese Communist Party that usually involves a variety of tactics to gather support and sympathy from non-party members or even antagonistic factions.

92 Joseph M. Chan, and Chin-Chuan Lee, 'Press Ideology and Organisational Control in Hong Kong', *Communication Research* 15.2 (1988): 185–197; Chin-Chuan Lee, 'Partisan Press Coverage of Government News in Hong Kong'; Joseph M. Chan and Chin-Chuan Lee, 'Journalistic "Paradigms" of Civil Protests: A Case Study in Hong Kong', *The News Media in National and International Conflict*, eds Andrew Arno and Wimal Dissanayake (Boulder and London: Westview Press, 1984) 183–202.

93 Hong Kong Journalists Association and Article 19 (1993–1997). Also see Chin-Chuan Lee, *Power, Money and Media*.

94 *Zhuada fangxiao* – taking a firm grip of the major things and letting the minor ones go free. See Willy Lam, 'Government – Beijing's Hong Kong Policy in the First Year of Transition', *Hong Kong China: The Red Dawn* ed. Chris Yeung (Australia: Prentice Hall, 1998) 22–44.

95 See Annual report on freedom of expression, Article 19 and Hong Kong Journalists Association, 1993–1997. The implications of the Xi Yang case are discussed in Chapter 3.

96 Joseph Man Chan, Paul S. N. Lee and Chin-Chuan Lee, *Hong Kong Journalists in Transition*. Also, see a similar earlier study in the United States, David H. Weaver and G. Cleveland Wilhoit, *The American Journalist: A Portrait of U.S. News People and Their Work* (Bloomington: Indiana University Press, 1986).

97 Clement Y. K. So and Joseph M. Chan, eds *Press and Politics in Hong Kong: Case*

Studies from 1967 to 1997 (Hong Kong: Hong Kong Institute of Asia-Pacific Studies, Chinese University Press, 1999).

98 Chin-Chuan Lee, 'The Paradox of Political Economy: On Media Structure, Press Freedom and Regime Change of Hong Kong', Chin-Chuan Lee, ed. *Power, Money and Media* 288–336.

99 Ibid. 323.

100 Ibid. 323.

101 Paul S. N. Lee and Leonard Chu, 'Inherent Dependence on Power: The Hong Kong Press in Political Transition', *Media, Culture and Society* 20 (1998): 59–77.

2 British policy and the Hong Kong communist press, 1967–1970

102 James T. H. Tang, *Britain's Encounter with Revolutionary China, 1949–54* (Hound-mills, Basingstoke: Macmillan; New York: St. Martin's Press, 1992); James T. H. Tang, 'From Empire Defence to Imperial Retreat: Britain's Postwar China Policy and the Decolonization of Hong Kong', *Modern Asian Studies* 28(2) (1994): 317–337.

103 Sir Alexander Grantham was Governor of Hong Kong from 1948 to 1958. His memoir: Alexander Grantham, *Via Ports: From Hong Kong to Hong Kong* (Hong Kong: Hong Kong University Press, 1965) 164–170.

104 Steve Tsang, *Democracy Shelved: Great Britain, China and Attempts at Constitutional Reform in Hong Kong, 1945–52* (Hong Kong; Oxford: Oxford University Press, 1988); Chan Lau Kit-ching, *China, Britain and Hong Kong 1895–1945* (Hong Kong: Chinese University Press, 1990); James T. H. Tang, 'From Empire Defence to Imperial Retreat'.

105 Chan Lau Kit-ching, *China, Britain and Hong Kong.*

106 D. J. Morgan, *The Official History of Colonial Development, Vol. 5, Guidance towards Self-government in British colonies 1941–71* (Atlantic Highlands, NJ: Humanities Press, 1980).

107 James T. H. Tang, *Britain's Encounter with Revolutionary China.*

108 Ibid.

109 Britain and the United States imposed an embargo on China because of the Korean War.

110 A term used by Alexander Grantham to describe trade with China. See Alexander Grantham, *Via Ports: From Hong Kong to Hong Kong* 164–170.

111 A term which usually appeared in leftist newspapers to describe China's attitude to Britain's presence in Chinese territories in the late 1960s.

112 Lau Siu-Kai, *Society and Politics in Hong Kong* (Hong Kong: Chinese University Press, 1982).

113 Norman Miners, *Hong Kong under Imperial Rule, 1912–1941* (New York: Oxford University Press, 1987).

114 Ibid.

115 Ibid.

116 Unsurprisingly, Steve Tsang notes that there was no 'British-ness' on the whole in Hong Kong society although it had been under British rule for over 150 years. See Steve Tsang, *A Modern History of Hong Kong* (London: I.B. Tauris, 2004).

117 Ngo Tak-wing, 'Colonialism in Hong Kong Revisited', *Hong Kong's History: State and Society under Colonial Rule*, ed. Tak-wing Ngo (London: Routledge, 1999) 1–12.

118 Leonard Chu, 'From British to Chinese "One Country, Two Systems"', *Ming Pao Monthly* May 1997: 30–34.

119 Chan Chong-fung, 'A Study of Hong Kong Press after the Second World War', diss., Beijing University, 1996.

120 See Table 2 for a chronology of events.

121 There is so far no systematic Chinese official analysis concerning the 1967 disturbances in Hong Kong, for example, in the authoritative journal, *File*, one of the
leading publications published by the official Chinese communist history research
team.

122 See Anne Cheung, *Self-censorship and the Struggle for Press Freedom.*

123 Ian Scott, *Political Change* 103–4.

124 FCO 40/113 'Hong Kong: Legal Affairs; Communist press: Action Against'. The
PRO files used in this chapter were largely unpaginated. The page number is stated
accordingly, if available.

125 FCO 40/264 'Briefs for Governor of Hong Kong'.

126 Ibid.

127 Despite the fact that the Chinese capital is widely known as Beijing today, I have
chosen to stick to the term 'Peking' in this chapter in order to reflect the historical
connection. Sometimes, both terms can be used interchangeably.

128 Prior to 1997, a large-scale celebration of Taiwan's national day was usually held on
10 October. KMT members would organise events and decorate certain districts with
KMT flags. On 10 October 1956, there was a clash between KMT and CCP local
members.

129 Chan Chong-fung 'A Study of Hong Kong Press'; Ian Scott, *Political Change.*

130 Chan Chong-fung 'A Study of Hong Kong Press'.

131 Ian Scott, *Political Change.*

132 Ibid.

133 Ibid.

134 FCO 40/113-115 'Hong Kong: Legal Affairs; Communist Press: Action Against'.

135 Ibid.

136 Ibid.

137 In November 1951, a big fire broke out on Tung Tau Estate, Kowloon, which burnt
down hundreds of thousands of squatters' homes, and made more than 16,000
people homeless. A comfort mission was organised from Canton to pay them a visit.
The fact that the Chinese group was prevented from entering Hong Kong territories
by the Hong Kong authorities triggered a protest by hundreds of Chinese who then
clashed with the Hong Kong police. One person died during the riot and the police
arrested around 100 people, with 18 sentenced to prison and 12 deported back to
China. See FCO 40/113: 1h, 13 May 1967.

138 FCO 40/113; 1h.

139 FCO 40/113; see also 'Government Ban on Broadcasts, Move to Stop Specters of
Inflammatory Notice', 25 May 1967, *South China Morning Post* (*SCMP*). News articles in this chapter are cited in relevant PRO files.

140 FCO 40/113: 1e 22 May 1967.

141 Ibid.

142 FCO 40/113: 1g, 13 May 1967.

143 The term Chinese People's Government (CPG) was generally adopted in the
exchanges among British offices in London and in the Far East to refer to the
Chinese Government in Peking.

144 FCO 40/113.

145 See *SCMP* May–Dec. 1967.

146 Here, 'left-wing' refers to communist as stated in the files of both the Colonial
Office and the Foreign and Commonwealth Office.

147 'Governor to Go on Leave', *SCMP* 22 June 1967.

148 FCO 40/113: 2.

149 Ibid.

150 FCO 40/113: 4, 26 July 1967.

151 FCO 40/113: 28, 4 Aug. 1967.

152 FCO 40/113: 58.

153 FCO 40/113: 67.
154 FCO 40/113-115.
155 Ibid.
156 FCO 40/113 'Action Against Communist Press' 1F.
157 Ibid.
158 'Japanese Blamed for Propaganda on Hong Kong Troubles', *SCMP* 6 Aug. 1967, cited in FCO 40/113.
159 FCO 40/113 'Action Against Communist Press' 10, 30 July 1967.
160 FCO 40/113: 22, 1 Aug.1967.
161 Ibid.
162 FCO 40/63 'Hong Kong: Political Affairs (Bilateral) Relations with China' 230.
163 FCO 40/114 'Action against the Communist Press'.
164 Ibid.
165 Ibid.
166 FCO 21/227 'Hong Kong Press: Foreign Journalists', 24 May 1968.
167 Ibid.
168 Ibid.
169 Colonial Office (CO) file 1030/1114 'Relationship of China and Hong Kong (1960–62)' 2.
170 CO 1030/595 'Relation of China and Hong Kong (1957–59)'.
171 CO 1030/ 584 'Chinese Demonstration in Hong Kong (1957–59)'.
172 CO 1030/595.
173 FCO 40/88 'Communist Schools'.
174 Ho Yin, a Chinese businessman and a prominent figure, who acted as a 'go-between' between the Chinese and the Hong Kong government during that critical period. His son, Edmund Ho, became the first Chief Executive of Macau Special Administrative Region in 1999.
175 CO 1030/1114: 145 and 147; see also 'Confusion Reigns Supreme in Theatre Circles', *China Mail* 8 July 1960 as cited in the file.
176 CO 1030/1114 'Relation of China and Hong Kong' 144.
177 CO 1030/1108 'Communist Cultural Activities, Hong Kong' 9.
178 FCO 21/716 'Effect on Hong Kong of Relations between China and Soviet Union'.
179 CO 1030/595 'Relationship of China and Hong Kong 1957–59'.
180 CO 1030/595 'Relationship of China and Hong Kong 1957–59'; see also Reuters dispatch, 6 Sept. 1958 in the file.
181 FCO 40/88 'Communist Schools'.
182 Ibid.
183 'A Blatant Self-exposure', Editorial *SCMP* 29 Nov. 1967; 'Leftist Schools in Protest Closure', *SCMP* 7 Dec. 1967, as cited in FCO 40/88 'Communist Schools'.
184 FCO 40/292 'Diplomatic Reports on Colonial Affairs from Governor of Hong Kong'.
185 FCO 40/292: 17.
186 FCO 40/88 'Communist Schools'.
187 Ibid.
188 CO 1030/1107 'Communism in Schools, Hong Kong 1960–62' 19.
189 Ibid.
190 Ibid.
191 FCO 40/105-106 'Publicity Unit'.
192 Quotes from FCO 40/105–106. The files were withdrawn from public use by the Foreign Office from Jan. 2001.
193 FCO 40/113 'Action against the Communist Press' 2g.
194 Ibid.
195 FCO 40/113.
196 Chan Lau Kit-ching, *China, Britain and Hong Kong*.

197 Kam Yiu-yu, *The Secret of the Chinese Communist Party's Policy on Hong Kong* (Hong Kong [Chinese]: Tien Yuan Publishing, 1998).

198 CO 1030/1114 'Government, Armed Forces and Hospital Chinese Workers' Union' 194.

199 MacLehose succeeded David Trench (1964–1971) as the Hong Kong Governor (1971–1982). He introduced a series of policies to alleviate public resentment. For instance, he started to construct housing estates to accommodate the working class.

200 CO 1030/1114: 13 and 18.

201 CO 21/717 'Approaches Made to the British Trade Commissioner in Hong Kong by Communist United Front Organizations'.

202 FCO 40/264 'Briefs for Governor of Hong Kong'.

203 Ibid.

204 FCO 40/252 'Detainees and Prisoners Convicted for Offences during the Disturbances in 1967/68 in Hong Kong' 7.

205 FCO 40/264.

206 Ibid.

207 CO 21/717.

208 FCO 40/252.

209 FCO 40/253 'Detainees and Prisoners Convicted for Offences during the Disturbances in 1967/68 in Hong Kong' 26.

210 FCO 40/253.

211 Percy Cradock, *Experiences of China* (London: John Murray, 1994) 79–80.

212 Anthony Grey, *Hostage in Peking* (London: Michael Joseph, 1970) 326.

213 'Editor Calls HK's System of Government "an Anachronism"', *SCMP* 6 May 1967, cited in FCO 40/253.

214 Ibid.

215 'Anachronism That Works', *SCMP* 8 May 1967, FCO 40/253.

216 'Newspaper Executive Charged', *SCMP* 10 Aug. 1967, FCO 40/253.

217 'Government Called Too Tolerant Towards Leftist Press', *SCMP* 16 Aug. 1967, FCO40/253.

218 'Suspension of Paper', *SCMP* 18 Aug. 1967, FCO 40/253.

219 John Rear, 'We Run Them In', *Far Eastern Economic Review* (*FEER*) 23 Nov. 1967, FCO 40/253. The Public Order Ordinance was assailed as being badly drafted and as an excessive attack on the fundamental rights of the citizen. John Rear, lecturer in law at the University of Hong Kong, argued that the effects it would have on the rule of law in Hong Kong should be examined.

220 'Rule of Law', Editorial, *SCMP* 19 Aug. 1967, FCO 40/253.

221 Ibid.

222 *The Sunday Post Herald* named *Ming Pao Daily News* as an 'independent' paper to distinguish it from other leftist and rightist newspapers. May–December 1967 *Sunday Post Herald*.

223 Cited in *SCMP*'s press comments, *SCMP* 5 Nov.1967, FCO 40/253.

224 Derek Davis, 'Twisting the Lions' Tails', *Far Eastern Economic Review* (*FEER*) 1 Aug. 1968, FCO 40/253.

225 Ibid.

226 Ibid.

227 'No Retrenchment', *FEER* 22 Aug. 1968, FCO 40/253.

228 *FEER*, Editorial, 21 Sept. 1967, FCO 40/253.

229 Ibid.

230 FCO 40/146 'Hong Kong: Political and Administrative Affairs Internal Disturbances 1967/68'.

231 *The Times* 11 Nov. 1968, FCO 40/146.

232 *The Times* 2 Dec. 1968, FCO 40/146.

233 Andrew Li Kwok-nang, born into an aristocratic family in Hong Kong, received his

early education at St. Paul's Co-educational College, and then at Repton School in Derbyshire, England. After obtaining an M.A. and a LL.B. from the University of Cambridge, he passed his bar finals in 1973 and commenced his practice of law in Hong Kong. He was appointed a Deputy (part time) Judge of the District Court of Hong Kong in 1982. In 1992, he was appointed at-large member of the Executive Council (cabinet) of Chris Patten, last British governor of Hong Kong. In 1997, he was elevated to Chief Justice by Tung Chee-hwa, the first Chief Executive (CE) of Hong Kong.

234 *FEER* 25 July 1968, FCO 40/146.
235 Ibid.
236 This 20-year old was Tsang Tak-sing who became one of the Hong Kong Deputies to the Chinese Parliament, the National People's Congress in the 1990s. He was appointed to be a special adviser to Tung Chee-hwa, the first and second CE of Hong Kong Special Administrative Region, 1997–2002 and 2002–2005.
237 *FEER* 25 July 1968, FCO 40/146.
238 FCO 40/113-115.
239 Kam Yiu-Yu, *The Secret of the Chinese Communist Party's Policy*.
240 FCO 40/149 'Hong Kong: Political and Administrative Affairs; Internal Disturbances 1967/68 Detainees and Prisoners'.
241 Anthony Grey, *Hostage in Peking* 325.
242 Ibid. 328.
243 'Elsie Elliot Speaks, Chinese as Official Language Urged', *SCMP* 15 May 1967; 'Extract from Chinese Press: New Call for Chinese Official Language', *SCMP* 16 Dec. 1967 cited in FCO 40/149.
244 'Reduction of Work Hours, Hong Kong Industrialist Welcomes Lord Shepherd's Proposal, Day Off for Men?' *SCMP* 21 Oct. 1967, FCO 40/149.
245 'New Department Formed to Assess Hong Kong's Progress', *SCMP* 4 Dec. 1967, FCO 40/149.
246 'Demonstrators Being Paid? – $8 for Men and $1 for Children', *SCMP* 19 May 1967, FCO 40/149.

3 Reporting on a jailed journalist

247 In the 1970s, the People's Republic of China (PRC) proposed to the United Nations to exclude Hong Kong from the decolonisation process. The British government did not object to this proposal, so Hong Kong was not involved in the United Nation's decolonisation process. The Hong Kong people were neither given a chance to debate the future of Hong Kong, nor were they allowed representation in the Sino-British negotiations on Hong Kong's future. See Lau Siu-kai, 'Decolonization Without Independence: The Unfinished Political Reform of the Hong Kong Government', Occasional Paper 19 (Hong Kong: Centre for Hong Kong Studies, Institute of Social Studies, Chinese University Press, 1987) and Norman Miners, *The Government and Politics of Hong Kong*, 5th edn, with Post-Handover Update by James T. H. Tang, (Hong Kong: Oxford University Press, 1998).
248 See Lau Siu-kai, 'Decolonization Without Independence'; Norman Miners, *The Government and Politics of Hong Kong*.
249 A Sino-British Joint Declaration. The agreement, which stipulates the arrangement of Hong Kong's political, social and economic system after the handover of Hong Kong sovereignty, was signed by the two governments at the end of the negotiations on Hong Kong's future in 1984.
250 Norman Miners, *The Government and Politics of Hong Kong*.
251 In the early 1980s when the British and the Chinese were negotiating about Hong Kong's future, the island had a population of six million people.
252 The role of the Hong Kong media in the 1989 Tiananmen student movement and its

persistence in reporting on the crackdown and the aftermath had attracted criticism from the Chinese authorities. See Clement So Y. K., and Joseph Man Chan, eds *Press and Politics*. See also Ian Scott, 'Political Transformation in Hong Kong: From Colony to Colony', *Hong Kong-Guangdong Link: Partnership in Flux*, eds Reginald Kwok and Alvin So (Armond, NY: M. E. Sharpe, 1995) 189–223.

253 See Norman Miners, *The Government and Politics of Hong Kong*; Ian Scott, *Political Change*.
254 Wang Gungwu and John Wong, eds *Hong Kong in China: The Challenges of Transition* (Singapore: Times Academic, 1999).
255 The main bulk of the Hong Kong population was, in fact, comprised of Chinese refugees who fled from Canton (in Southern Guangdong province) and the coastal city of Shanghai after the Communist take-over of the mainland. Some arrived following natural or man-made disasters and political purges, e.g. the anti-rightist campaigns and the famine in 1957, and the Proletarian Cultural Revolution in the late 1960s. So the first generation of Hong Kong's population had experience of communist rule and they were anxious about Hong Kong's future after the handover from the British to the Chinese.
256 The Hong Kong government was unable to lead its people out of the shock and sadness following the 1989 Tiananmen massacre, nor to alleviate the uncertainty that existed in anticipation of 1997. Neither could local politicians. For details, see Lau Siu-kai, 'Decolonization Without Independence'
257 The term 'watchdog' adopts the traditional definition that the news media serve as the fourth estate of society to provide checks and balances to the executive administration. See also James Curran's criticisms of this term in James Curran, 'Mass Media and Democracy Revisited', *Mass Media and Society*, eds James Curran and Michael Gurevitch (London; New York: Arnold, 1996) 81–119.
258 The Sino-British Joint Declaration stipulates that Hong Kong could maintain its status and preserve its way of living and civil liberties for 50 years starting from the changeover of 1997. The promise states 'Hong Kong would be given autonomy apart from foreign relationships and defence', 'Hong Kong people ruling Hong Kong' and in short Hong Kong can maintain its former capitalist system under the scheme of 'one country, two systems'.
259 Xu Jiatun, *The Memoirs of Xu Jiatun on Hong Kong* (Taipei [Chinese]: Lian Jing; Hong Kong: *Hong Kong United Daily*, 1993).
260 Ibid.
261 Cited in Wang Gungwu and John Wong, *Hong Kong in China* 46.
262 For example, Louis Kraar, 'The Death of Hong Kong', *Fortune* 26 Feb. 1995.
263 Chris Yeung, 'Hong Kong Media in the Changing Political Landscape', *Harvard Asia Quarterly* (1 Jan. 2002); www.fas.harvard.edu/~asiactr/haq/200201/ accessed 17 Feb. 2005.
264 For instance, C. C. Lee, *Power, Money and Media*.
265 Paul S. N. Lee and Leonard Chu, 'Inherent Dependence on Power' 59–77.
266 See Joseph Man Chan and To Yiu-ming, 'Democratization, Reunification and Press Freedom in Hong Kong: A Critical Event Analysis of the Xi Yang Case', *Press and Politics in Hong Kong: Case Studies from 1967 to 1997*, eds Clement Y. K. So and Joseph M. Chan (Hong Kong Institute of Asia-Pacific Studies, Hong Kong: Chinese University Press, 1999) 465–496.
267 Norman Miners, *The Government and Politics of Hong Kong*.
268 James T. H. Tang, 'The SAR Government and the Changing Political Order in Hong Kong', *The Government and Politics of Hong Kong*, 5th edn, ed. Norman Miners (Hong Kong: Oxford University Press, 1998) 246–270.
269 Lau Siu-kai, *Democratization, Poverty of Political Leaders, and Political Inefficacy in Hong Kong* (Hong Kong: Chinese University Press, 1998).
270 Lui Tai-lok, 'The Hong Kong New Middle Class on the Eve of 1997', *The Other*

Hong Kong Report 1997, ed. Joseph Y. S. Cheng (Hong Kong: Chinese University Press, 1997) 207–225.

271 Ibid.

272 Ibid.

273 See Lee Ming-kwan, 'Hong Kong Identity: Past and Present', *Hong Kong Economy and Society*, eds Wong Siu-lun and T. Maruya (Hong Kong: Centre of Asian Studies, Hong Kong University Press, 1998) 153–175; Lee Ming-kwan, 'Whither Hong Kong's Middle Class?' *Hong Kong in China: The Challenge of Transition*, eds Wang Gungwu and John Wong (Singapore: Times Academia Press, 1999) 231–244.

274 Hong Kong Journalists Association and Article 19. *The Die is Cast, Annual Report on Freedom of Expression*. Hong Kong: Article 19 and HKJA, 1997.

275 Ibid.

276 After the crackdown on the Beijing student movement in 1989, Beijing condemned Hong Kong in general and the Hong Kong press in particular as a 'subversive' base against Chinese authority. Indeed, it imposed a series of rules and regulations on Hong Kong journalists to prevent them from working freely in China. Though some of the regulations have been relaxed over the years, one of the most stringent rules maintains that Hong Kong journalists have to seek official approval for any coverage in mainland China, otherwise Hong Kong journalists could be charged with conducting unlawful activities in China. One of the alleged crimes of Xi Yang, the reporter who was convicted to 12 years' imprisonment, was to cover news without approval there.

277 See Ching Cheong and Willy Lam on the communist policy of Hong Kong. For instance, Ching Cheong, 'China's Administration over Hong Kong – The New China News Agency and the Hong Kong-Macau Affairs Office', *The Other Hong Kong Report 1996*, eds Nyaw Mee-kau and Li Si-ming (Hong Kong: Chinese University Press, 1997) 111–128; Willy Wo-lap Lam, *China after Deng Xiaoping – The Power Struggle in Beijing Since Tiananmen* (New York: John Wiley & Sons, 1995) and Willy Wo-lap Lam, *The Era of Jiang Zemin* (New York: Prentice Hall, 1999).

278 Deng Xiaoping, *Deng Xiaoping Wen Xuan*, Vol. 3 (Beijing [Chinese]: Renmin, 1993); Xu Jiatu, *The Memoirs*; and Kam Yiu-yu, *The Secret of the Chinese Communist Party's Policy*.

279 Hong Kong was one of the main investors in China and Chinese investment/entrepreneurs became dominant and took over the position and role of British *hongs* (big companies) in the run-up to the take-over of Hong Kong. See James T. H. Tang, 'The SAR Government and the Changing Political Order in Hong Kong'.

280 Norman Miners, *The Government and Politics of Hong Kong*.

281 Ibid. 12.

282 Paul S. N. Lee, 'Chinese and Western Press' 493–533.

283 See Chapter 2 for a discussion of Britain's repressive policy and action against the communist press in the late 1960s and early 1970s, and Chapter 6 for the development of journalistic norms.

284 Paul S. N. Lee, 'Chinese and Western Press''.

285 Paul S. N. Lee, 'The Press Response to the Rapid Social Change of Hong Kong in the Past Two Decades', *Asian Journal of Communication* 3(1) (1993): 133–146.

286 For the flourishing of political journals in the 1970s and the 1980s, see Table 5.2 of the Appendix.

287 *MPDN* adopted an 'anti-Chinese Communist Party' (CCP) position in the late 1960s, as discussed in Chapter 2. However, its editorial position started to shift to a pro-PRC one during the transition period. This will be discussed further in later sections.

288 However, as seen from the comparison done by a journalism scholar, To Yiu-ming, the related news stories which the Chinese authorities alleged to be 'state secrets'

were not a scoop. Rather, similar news reports to those written by Xi Yang and sub-sequently published in *MPDN* were, in fact, seen in other Hong Kong newspapers, including the pro-Beijing daily, *Wen Wei Po*. Also see *Ming Pao Daily News*' Staff Writer, *Reflections on Xi Yang's Case* (Hong Kong [Chinese]: *Ming Pao* Publishing, 1997).

289 *MPDN* 30 Apr. and 1 May 1994. All Chinese newspaper articles were retrieved from either the paper's own website or the search server 'Wisenews'. They were unpaginated. Page numbers are given here as reference whenever hard copies could be located.

290 'Heat on Beijing over Xi's Jailing', *South China Morning Post (SCMP)* 18 Apr. 1994, unpaginated. All the news stories of *SCMP* were retrieved from *http://archive.scmp.com/search.php*, accessed 28 Jan. 2005.

291 Ibid.

292 Chris Yeung and Beverly Chau, 'Heat on Beijing over Xi's Jailing', *SCMP* 18 Apr. 1994.

293 It is in particular seen in the Sino-British disagreement with regards to democratic development and other policies affecting the post-1997 situation.

294 A time line of the incident of Xi Yang can be found in Table 3 of the Appendix.

295 See Deacon *et al.*, *Researching Communications: A Practical Guide to Methods in Media and Cultural Analysis* (London: Arnold, 1999); Hansen *et al.*, *Mass Communication Research Methods* (London: Macmillan, 1997).

296 However, there is one critical study of the Xi Yang case. See Joseph Man Chan and To Yiu-ming, 'Democratization, Reunification and Press Freedom in Hong Kong'.

297 'Leftist' has a special meaning in the Hong Kong context, i.e. a tendency to adopt a pro-Beijing position.

298 The *Oriental Daily News* is subject to a slightly different framework for analysis. It is not really part of the western liberal newspaper tradition in the sense that its news, in particular social news, is a mixture of sensationalist and pornographic features and columns. The style and position of this mass circulation paper will be further discussed in the following sections.

299 Apart from the 16 major daily papers, Hong Kong has four commercial TV stations (broadcast and cable) and two commercial radio stations functioning with virtually no government control.

300 According to the circulation figures issued by the newspaper organisation itself in Aug. 2001.

301 Ibid.

302 Lee, Chin-Chuan, 'The Paradox of Political Economy: Media Structure, Press Freedom, and Regime Change in Hong Kong', *Power, Money and Media – Communication Patterns and Bureaucratic Control in Cultural China*, ed., C. C. Lee (Evanston, Illinois: Northwestern University Press, 2000) 288–336.

303 According to the circulation figures issued by the newspaper organisation itself in Aug. 2001.

304 Chris Yeung, Doreen Cheung and Louis Won, 'China Ousts HK Reporter for Spying', *SCMP* 28 Sept. 1993. News articles of the *SCMP* were retrieved from archive.scmp.com/search.php. Accessed 16 Feb. 2005.

305 May Sin-mi Hon, Linda Choy and Wendy Lim Wan-Yee, 'Xi Yang Freed on Parole', *SCMP* 26 Jan.1997.

306 Staff Reporters, '"Repentant" Xi's Jail Term Light, Claims China', *SCMP* 9 Apr. 1994.

307 'Xi Case Raises Fears for Future, Says Patten', *SCMP* 10 Apr. 1994.

308 Ibid.

309 *SCMP* 7 Apr. 1994.

310 *SCMP* 10 Apr. 1994.

311 'Xi Case Raises Fears for Future, Says Patten', *SCMP* 10 Oct. 1993.

312 Chris Yeung and Beverly Chau, 'Heat on Beijing over Xi's Jailing', *SCMP* 6 Apr. 1994.
313 'The Politics of Injustice', *SCMP* 6 Apr. 1994.
314 'Zhu, Qian Deny Role in Case of Reporter', *SCMP* 8 Apr. 1994.
315 'Full Text of Verdict Demanded', *SCMP* 11 Apr. 1994.
316 So Lai-Fun 'Father Sees Little Hope in Appeal', *SCMP* 10 Apr. 1994.
317 'Arrest Reason Unclear', Editorial, *SCMP* 28 Sept. 1993.
318 'Hong Kong Journalists Praise Man of Few Words', *SCMP* 29 Sept. 1993.
319 Chris Yeung, 'Reporter "Stole Interest Rate, Gold Secrets", *SCMP* 8 Oct. 1993.
320 Daniel Kwan, 'Journalist Arrested but Not Charged, Says Editor', *SCMP* 9 Oct. 1993.
321 Political Staff, 'Keep Your Nose Out; Patten Told by Chinese Official', *SCMP* 10 Oct. 1993.
322 Chris Yeung, 'Arrested Reporter May Have Broken Law, Says Ming Pao', *SCMP* 11 Oct. 1993.
323 Ibid.
324 Staff Reporter, 'Shock at Xi's 12-Year Term: Harsh Sentence a "Threat to Press Freedom after 1997"', *SCMP* 5 Apr. 1994.
325 Ibid.
326 Ibid.
327 Chris Yeung, 'Arrested Reporter May Have Broken Law, Says Ming Pao', *SCMP* 11 Oct. 1993.
328 Ibid.
329 Tsui Si-min, a Hong Kong delegate to the Chinese United Front organ, the Chinese Communist Political Consultative Committee, repeatedly told reporters that, according to his sources, the Chinese authorities would release Xi Yang soon.
330 'Xi's Editors in Protest Fast', *SCMP* 7 Apr. 1994.
331 Beverly Chau, 'Fair Chance of Appeal Win', *SCMP* 6 Apr. 1994 and Chan Wai-fong and Beverly Chau, 'Hopes of Finding Private Lawyer', *SCMP* 7 Apr. 1994.
332 'Hopes of Finding Private Lawyer', *SCMP* 7 Apr. 1994.
333 'The Politics of Injustice', *SCMP* 6 Apr. 1994.
334 The writer and China news editor, Willy Lam, was sidelined and forced to resign from the *SCMP* in 2000. For details, see Chapter 5.
335 So Lai Fun, 'Father Sees Little Hope in Appeal', *SCMP* 10 Apr. 1994.
336 'Delegate Offers to Appear in Court for Jailed', *SCMP* 10 Apr. 1994.
337 'Appalled by Journalists' Immature Action', Letter, *SCMP* 11 Apr. 1994.
338 'Xi's Appeal Rejected, Reporter's Jailing Triggers Outcry', *SCMP* 16 Apr. 1994.
339 Beverly Chau and Linda Choy, '400 Newsmen March in Protest Rally', *SCMP* 16 Apr. 1994.
340 'Blow to Confidence', Editorial, *SCMP* 16 Apr. 1994.
341 Ibid.
342 Beverly Chau and Linda Choy, '400 Newsmen March in Protest Rally', *SCMP* 16 Apr. 1994.
343 Ibid.
344 Ibid.
345 Ibid.
346 Emily Lau, 'How the Press is Squeezed by China', *SCMP* 18 Apr. 1994.
347 'Don't Abandon Xi', Letter, *SCMP* 1 May 1994.
348 Glenn Schloss, 'Yellow Ribbon Campaign Pays Off', *SCMP* 26 Jan. 1997.
349 May Sin-mi Hon, Linda Choy and Wendy Lim Wan-yee, 'Xi Yang Freed on Parole', *SCMP* 26 Jan. 1997.
350 Niall Fraser, 'Whereabouts of Jailed Source Unknown', *SCMP* 26 Jan. 1997.
351 Gren Manuel and Quinton Chan, 'Reporters Face Same Risks, Activitists Warn', *SCMP* 27 Jan. 1997.

352 May Si-mi Hon, Linda Choy and Wendy Lim Wan-yee, 'Xi Yang Freed on Parole', *SCMP* 26 Jan. 1997.
353 Chris Yeung, 'Liberation Brings Delight in Days of Doubt', SCMP 26 Jan. 1997. It is interesting to note the shift in the reporter's perspective after 1997. See Chris Yeung, 'Hong Kong Media in the Changing Political Landscape', *Harvard Asia Quarterly* (1 Jan. 2002). www. fas. harvard.edu/~asiactr/haq/200201/. Accessed 17 Feb. 2005.
354 For details see Hong Kong Journalists Association and Article 19, *Urgent Business: Hong Kong, Freedom of Expression and 1997: Joint Report of Article 19 and the HKJA*. London: Article 19, 1993.
355 See Cheung Kwai-yeung, *Jin Yong (Louis Cha) and the Press*; Li Kar-yuen, *On Hong Kong Newspaper History* (Hong Kong: Joint Publishing, 1989).
356 Yu Pun-hoi had used the brand name of *Ming Pao Daily News* to open up a number of media ventures in mainland China. For details, see Lai Pui-yee, 'Investigative Reportage on Yu Pun-hoi', *Hong Kong Economic Times* 10–11 Oct. 1994.
357 For the history and influence of *Ming Pao Daily News* and its founder, Louis Cha, see Cheung Kwai-yeung, *Jin Yong (Louis Cha) and the Press*. For the change in editorial position of *Ming Pao Daily News* and its apparent appeasement of China, see Joseph Kahn, 'Chinese Paper Softens Its Voice', *Asian Wall Street Journal* 22 Apr. 1997.
358 Here 'phasing out' means the daily had been in a process of reducing dissident news by reporting less on them and/or reporting more on non-political issues and event (a way of diluting the concentration of political and dissident news). For the daily's strategy to get rid of news about the dissidents or news that produces dissenting effects, see Joseph Kahn 'Chinese Paper Softens Its Voice'.
359 'Southern Progress', a term used by Hugo de Burgh, *The Chinese Journalist: Mediating Information in the World's Most Populous Country* (London; New York: Routledge, 2003) 21–24. It refers to the late Chinese leader, Deng Xiaoping, reconfirming the economic reform policy by paying a visit to the southern part of China in 1992. China started to adopt an open-door policy in the late 1970s. It suffered a serious setback after the crackdown on the Beijing Student Movement in 1989. Deng, apparently, lent his personal support to the south in order to re-gather the momentum for economic reform in the Special Economic Zones.
360 For the overall policy adopted in the aftermath of 1989, see Willy Wo-lap Lam, *China after Deng Xiaoping*.
361 The Vice-director of the Xinhua News Agency, Zhang Junsheng, had insisted that Xi Yang had done things contradictory to his journalistic duties. Also, a veteran mainland Chinese journalist wrote in the Hong Kong *Open Monthly* magazine suggesting Xi Yang had a double identity and hinting that he was acting as a double agent. See *Open Monthly* Apr. 1994.
362 Xi Yang emigrated to Hong Kong as his grandfather invited him to come and take care of him. He lived in Hong Kong and worked for the *MPDN* before he was jailed. See the column by Xi's father, Xi Lingsheng, 'Grandpa Wants Xi Yang to Emigrate to Hong Kong', *MPDN* 11 Apr. 1994 A2.
363 *MPDN* 28 Sept. 1993 A2.
364 For instance, 'Tam Yiu-chung Hopes that Beijing Handles the Case with Leniency, Zhang Junsheng Said He Would Report Xi Yang Case', *MPDN* 28 Sept. 1993 A2; 'Deputies of the National People's Congress Promise to Find Out from the Chinese Authorities', *MPDN* 1 Oct. 1993: A2.
365 *MPDN* 6 Oct. 1993: A2.
366 *MPDN* 3 Oct. 1993: A2.
367 *MPDN* 8 Oct. 1993: A2.
368 *MPDN* 8 Apr. 1994: A2.
369 *MPDN* 9 Apr. 1994: A2.

370 The paper counted down the days of its reporter's detention until it was suggested that the high-sounding tone of related news stories would only jeopardise Xi's situation. The paper stopped using the countdown graphic; however, its stance, and in turn its strategy of lobbying for Xi's release, was far from consistent.

371 The front page of *MPDN*, as with other Chinese-language daily papers, is usually allocated to a full-page advertisement, so page 2 was usually the first news page.

372 *MPDN* 11 Oct. 1993: A2.

373 Ibid.

374 A senior journalist from *MPDN* interview with the author.

375 Chinese allies include Hong Kong deputies and delegates to Beijing's two main political organs, the National People's Congress (NPC) and the Chinese People's Political Consultative Conference (CPPCC), and local Hong Kong politicians such as pro-China legislators and Hong Kong Affairs Advisers to the Chinese authority.

376 Daisy Li, news editor of *MPDN* and chairperson of the HKJA, made this remark at a journalists' protest gathering.

377 *MPDN* 16 Apr. 1994: A3.

378 *MPDN* translated one tabloid and nine broadsheet editorials and adopted them by printing the gist of them. They were *SCMP*, *Wah Kiu Yat Po* (*Overseas Chinese Daily*), *Sing Tao Daily News*, *Hong Kong Economic Journal*, *Hong Kong Economic Times*, *Hong Kong Daily News*, *Hong Kong Daily*, *Hong Kong Standard*, *Sing Pao* and *Oriental Daily News*. See *MPDN* 16 Apr. 1994.

379 'Xi Yang Comes Back', *MPDN* 26 Jan. 1997: A1.

380 Ibid.

381 Lin Zizhe, 'Reunion of Xi and His Father; Silence is Golden', *MPDN* 27 Jan. 1997: A2.

382 *MPDN* 27 Jan. 1997: A2.

383 'Xi Yang's Parole is in Accordance with Chinese Law', *MPDN* 28 Jan. 1997: A2.

384 *MPDN* 7 Apr. 1994: A2.

385 The HKJA had insisted that Xi Yang was innocent and the trade union had consistently campaigned for an open trial for him.

386 'Is 12-year Sentence a "Lenient Sentence According to Law?"'*MPDN* 9 Apr. 1994: A2.

387 In fact, leaving the editorial blank to express extreme anger was first seen in the Beijing-funded *Wen Wei Po* on the day following the June 4 massacre in 1989.

388 Here it is more a kind of manipulation by the Chinese authorities rather than an over-reaction on the part of the *MPDN* management. Also, many people, in particular Chinese allies played a middle-person's role. Senior journalists at *MPDN* interview with the author.

389 Chan Chong-fung, 'A Study of Hong Kong Press after the Second World War'.

390 Ibid.

391 *ODN* 8 Oct. 1993: 4.

392 Ibid.

393 *ODN* 9 Oct. 1993: 3.

394 *ODN* 10 Oct. 1993: 4 and 17 Apr. 1994: 8.

395 *ODN* 16 Oct. 1993: 3.

396 *ODN* 17 Oct. 1993: 2.

397 *ODN* 28 Oct. 1993: 3.

398 *ODN* 15 Mar. 1994: 3.

399 *ODN* 25 Dec. 1993: 3; 11 Mar. 1994: 3.

400 *ODN* 1 Jan. 1994: 3.

401 *ODN* 18 Mar. 1994: 3.

402 *ODN* 16 Apr. 1994: 3.

403 Ibid.

404 *ODN* 17 Apr. 1994: 8.

405   Ibid.
406   *ODN* 1 May 1994: 3.
407   *ODN* 18 Apr. 1994: 4.
408   *ODN* 17 Apr. 1994: 8.
409   *ODN* 18 Apr. 1994: 4.
410   For instance, *ODN* 5 Apr. 1994: 3; 16 Apr. 1994: 3.
411   For instance, the *ODN* revealed through anonymous sources that the *Ming Pao Daily News'* change of position, open offer of an apology, admission of Xi Yang's alleged crime and rejection of help from the British and Hong Kong governments were in fact suggested by Chinese sources.
412   *ODN* 17 Apr. 1994: 8.
413   'In Order to Prevent Complications in the Xi Yang Incident, Zhang Junsheng [vice-director of the Xinhua News Agency, the de facto Chinese Embassy in Hong Kong] Asks the Hong Kong Government not to Intervene', *ODN* 10 Oct. 1993: 4.
414   *ODN* 12 Oct. 1994: 4.
415   *ODN* 9 Oct. 1993: 3.
416   *ODN* 12 Oct. 1993: 4.
417   *ODN* 16 Apr. 1994: 3.
418   *ODN* 26 Jan. 1997: A15.
419   *ODN* 27 Jan. 1997: 1. The Provisional Legislative Council (PLC) was one of the many representative organisations created by the Chinese authority in order to guarantee a smooth transition of power during the handover. The immediate reason for creating the PLC to replace the incumbent one was because of disagreement between the British and the Chinese governments over the last election of the Hong Kong Legislative Council.
420   The Chinese family name usually precedes the first name.
421   *ODN* 27 Jan. 1997: A1.
422   *ODN* 28 Jan. 1997: A15.
423   Interview with the author.
424   The founder, and father of the current chairman, of the *ODN* group continues to take refuge in Taiwan. This connection may have an effect on the newspaper's position.
425   One of the controversial columns in the *ODN* is 'Kung Fu Tea' which has printed some infamous personal allegations about politicians, including Hong Kong democrats and the last Hong Kong Governor.
426   Chapter 6 contains an analysis of interviews with senior journalists on press freedom.

4   Reporting on the Taiwanese presidential election

427   Colin Sparks with Anna Reading, *Communism, Capitalism and the Mass Media* (London: Sage, 1998).
428   The latest development is that the Chinese President, Jiang Zemin, has announced that entrepreneurs will be allowed to join the Chinese Communist Party. See John Pomfret, 'Rewriting Marx: China Allows Capitalists in on the Party', *International Herald Tribune* 2 July 2001.
429   Deng Xiaoping, *Deng Xiaoping Wen Xuan.*
430   Since 1949, the Chinese people have seen Hong Kong overtake the prosperous city of Shanghai as the major Chinese window on the world.
431   The restrictions relate mainly to the pace of democratic development. See Steve Tsang, *Hong Kong: An Appointment with China* (London: I.B. Tauris, 1997) and Steve Tsang, *A Modern History.*
432   As seen in a series of research projects by Chin-Chuan Lee, Joseph Man Chan and other Hong Kong academics during the transition period.
433   'Doubts held before the transition have lingered too long', Mrs. Anson Chan, the

Chief Secretary of Hong Kong SAR said, adding that the Chinese leadership deserved more credit for 'the light touch they have shown in handling Hong Kong since the handover', in Thomas Crampton, 'Taking a Parting Shot at Hong Kong Powers', *International Herald Tribune* 20 Apr. 2001.

434 The former director of Hong Kong Xinhua News Agency, the de facto Chinese Embassy in Hong Kong, pointed out China's long-term policy of uniting the business community. See Xu Jiatun, *The Memoirs of Xu Jiatun*. The implementation of this policy was discussed by Kam Yiu-yu, the former editor of the leading China-funded newspaper, Hong Kong *Wen Wei Po*. See Kam Yiu-yu, *The Secret of the Chinese Communist Party's Policy*.

435 See Steve Tsang, *An Appointment*; Frank Welsh, *A History of Hong Kong*, rev. edn (London: HarperCollins, 1997).

436 Deng Xiaoping, 'Our Basic Position on the Hong Kong Issue', *Deng Xiaoping Wen Xuan* 12–15.

437 Steve Tsang, *An Appointment*.

438 'Unequal' from the point of view of the Chinese government, which was forced to cede Hong Kong to Britain under the unequal treaties because of the imbalance of power in the nineteenth century. See P. Westley-Smith, *Unequal Treaty 1898–1997* (Oxford: Oxford University Press, 1980).

439 The idea of *fuqiang* ('prosperous and strong') is still commonly associated with Chinese nationalist sentiment today. See Myron L. Cohen, 'Being Chinese: The Peripheralisation of Traditional Identity', *The Living Tree – The Changing Meaning of Beijing Chinese Today*, ed. Tu Wei-ming (U.S.: Stanford University Press, 1994) 101.

440 See Zheng Yongnian, *Discovering Chinese Nationalism in China – Modernisation, Identity and International Relations* (Cambridge, U.K.: Cambridge University Press, 1999); Jonathan Unger, ed. *Chinese Nationalism* (New York: M. E. Sharpe, 1996).

441 The situation in Taiwan is different from that of Hong Kong: first, Taiwan is not a colony. Second, Taiwan is a prosperous territory where democracy has developed rapidly in the past decade and taken root at the end of the last century. Apart from defence and foreign affairs, the Hong Kong SAR administration is allowed to administer local affairs according to its needs. For Taiwan, the Chinese government promises not to station the People's Liberation Army in Taiwan and proposes to give the Taiwanese autonomy to keep its own military force. But the Taiwanese government so far has not committed itself to unification, though it agrees to come back to talks on the Sino-Taiwanese relationship.

442 Deng Xiaoping, *Deng Xiaoping Wen Xuan*.

443 Deng Xiaoping laid down in his speeches the logistics for the administration of the future Hong Kong SAR, such as the formation of the administration and how it would be ruled and regulated by the mini-constitution Basic Law. See ibid.

444 See Jonathan Unger, *Chinese Nationalism*.

445 See C. P. Fitzgerald, *The Birth of Communist China* (England: Penguin, 1964).

446 See Jonathan Unger, *Chinese Nationalism* xiv, xvi.

447 See Myron L. Cohen, 'Being Chinese'.

448 Jonathan Unger, *Chinese Nationalism*.

449 See Deng Xiaoping, *Deng Xiaoping Wen Xuan*.

450 'The Nationless State: The Search for a Nationalism in Modern Chinese Nationalism', *Chinese Nationalism*, ed. Jonathan Unger (New York: M. E. Sharpe, 1996) 84–85.

451 Deng Xiaoping, *Deng Xiaoping Wen Xuan*.

452 George T. Crane, '"Special Things in Special Ways": National Economic Identity and China's Special Economic Zones', *Chinese Nationalism*, ed. Jonathan Unger (New York: M. E. Sharpe, 1996) 148–168.

453   Edward Friedman, 'A Democratic Chinese Nationalism?' *Chinese Nationalism*, ed. Jonathan Unger (New York: M. E. Sharpe, 1996) 169–182.
454   Lucian Pye, 'How China's Nationalism was Shanghaied', *Chinese Nationalism*, ed. Jonathan Unger (New York: M. E. Sharpe, 1996) 86–112.
455   'The Official Discourse of Nationalism: Patriotism and the Constraints of Nationalism', *Discovering Chinese Nationalism in China – Modernisation, Identity and International Relations*, ed. Yongnian Zheng (Cambridge, UK: Cambridge University Press, 1999) 87–95.
456   Deng Xiaoping *Deng Xiaoping Wen Xuan*.
457   For Deng's policy of 'one country, two systems', see ibid. However, the reliance on popular nationalism can be risky: for instance, the Tibetan people asked for a similar relaxation to unification, and turned it into a quest for political independence.
458   Under British rule, the Hong Kong Chinese elite played the role of representing the Chinese. However, they accepted the fact that Hong Kong was deleted from the list of decolonisation when China joined the United Nations in the late 1970s. The British government did not object to the resolution. See Steve Tsang, *An Appointment*; Sze-Yuen Chung, *Hong Kong's Journey to Reunification: Memoirs of Sze-yuen Chung* (Hong Kong: Chinese University Press, 2001).
459   Deng Xiaoping, *Deng Xiaoping Wen Xuan*.
460   Ibid.
461   Ibid.
462   Quote from Lu Ping, Director of Hong Kong and Macau Affairs Office, Chinese State Ministry, in HKJA, *The Die is Cast* 15.
463   HKJA and Article 19, *Patriot Games, Hong Kong's Media Face to Face with the Taiwan Factor, 2000 Annual Report* (Hong Kong: Article 19 and HKJA, 2000).
464   See *2000 Human Rights Report: Hong Kong*, online 26 Feb. 2001. www.usconsulate.org.hk/ushk. Accessed 15 Mar. 2001.
465   Ibid.
466   See HKJA, *Patriot Games* 5–7.
467   HKJA, *Patriot Games*.
468   Ibid.
469   Controversy emerged when the Falun Gong grew rapidly and were able to gather hundreds of adherents to demonstrate outside the headquarters of the Chinese Communist Party (CCP) in the spring of 1999. This alarmed the ruling authority. It was later labeled a 'cult' by the Central Government and a purge of its followers then began. See HKJA and Article 19, *Following The Flag, China's Sensitivities Threaten Freedom of Expression in Hong Kong, 2001 Annual Report* (Hong Kong: Article 19 and HKJA, 2001) 5–8.
470   For a critical narrative on the construction of the identity and image of Falun Gong, see Zhao Yuezhi, 'Falun Gong, Identity and the Struggle over Meaning Inside and Outside China', *Contesting Media Power*, eds Nick Couldry and James Curran (London: Rowman and Littlefield, 2003) 209–226.
471   HKJA, *Following The Flag*.
472   Ibid.
473   See HKJA, *Following The Flag*.
474   HKJA, *Following The Flag* 5–8, 12.
475   May Sin-mi Hon, 'Outgoing Anson Vows Not to Meddle – 'I'm not Lee Kuan Yew … You Owe Your Successor Silence', *SCMP* 28 Apr. 2001.
476   See HKJA, *Following The Flag*.
477   Ibid.
478   In her departing speech, Anson Chan defended her position as being pro-Hong Kong: 'Why do people insist on using terms like pro-China or anti-China? Or even pro-British? Surely we are all pro-Hong Kong!' in Thomas Crampton, 'Taking a Parting Shot at Hong Kong Powers', *International Herald Tribune* 20 Apr. 2001.

479 See HKJA, *The Die is Cast* 54–55.
480 Ibid.
481 See HKJA and Article 19. *Questionable Beginnings, Freedom of Expression in Hong Kong One Year after the Handover to China, 1998 Annual Report* (Hong Kong: Article 19 and HKJA, 1998) 30.
482 Ibid.
483 See HKJA, *Following The Flag* 9.
484 See news report in *Apple Daily* 20 Dec. 2001.
485 Even the media watchdog, the HKJA, acknowledged there was no obvious infringement upon liberty. The Central Government apparently exercised constraint with regard to direct interference in the Hong Kong media. See HKJA and Article 19, *The Ground Rules Change, Freedom of Expression in Hong Kong Two Years after the Handover to China, 1999 Annual Report* (Hong Kong: Article 19 and HKJA, 1999).
486 HKJA, *Following The Flag* 23–25.
487 See HKJA, *The Ground Rules Change* and *Patriot Games*.
488 They are documented in the annual reports of the Hong Kong Journalists Association. See also Yiu-ming To and Tuen-Yu Lau, 'Walking a Tight Rope: Hong Kong's Media Facing Political and Economic Challenges since Sovereignty Transfer 1997–2001', an article presented at the Chinese Communication Association's Annual Meeting, Hong Kong, 3 July 2001. This structural problem will be further discussed in Chapters 5 and 6.
489 HKJA, *Following The Flag*; *2000 Human Rights Report*: Hong Kong.
490 Joyce Y. M. Nip, 'Clash and Compatibility of Journalistic Culture: Mainland China and Hong Kong', *Critical Studies – Communication and Culture: China and the World entering the 21st Century*, eds D. Ray Heisey and Wenxiang Gong (Amsterdam/Atlanta, GA: Editions Rodopi 83–102.
491 See Kam Yiu-yu, *The Secret of the Chinese Communist Party's Policy*. Kam delivered a keynote speech at a conference about the CCP's policy, organised by the HKJA, 1993.
492 There had been rumours about this for some time, and Xu Jiatun later confirmed it. See Xu Jiatun, *The Memoirs of Xu Jiatun* 241, 301.
493 HKJA, *Following The Flag*.
494 In the late 1980s and early 1990s, both the two leading Taiwanese newspapers, the *China Times* and the *United Daily News*, decided to launch a Hong Kong edition to monitor the transition of Hong Kong. However, both of them shut down and withdrew from Hong Kong before 1997, blaming a stringent political atmosphere and a contracting public sphere as the cause. See HKJA, *The Die is Cast*; Clement Y. K. So, 'Pre-1997 Hong Kong Press: Cut-Throat Competition and the Changing Journalistic Paradigm', *The Other Hong Kong Report 1996*, eds Nyaw Mee-kau and Li Si-ming (Hong Kong: Chinese University Press, 1996) 485–506.
495 The *Sing Tao Daily News* erased its historical connection with Taiwan by stopping its previous practice of counting dates according to the Republic of China's calendar from 1 April 1993. See Yau Shing-mu and Cheung Siu-jing, 'Sally Wu – From Pro-Taiwan to Pro-China', *Hong Kong Economic Times* 25 Dec. 1998: A14.
496 These joint ventures included the printing and distribution of the second English-language daily *Hong Kong Standard*, with help from Beijing's official English-language *China Daily*. In the Special Economic Zone of Shenzhen, *Sing Tao* Group published a Chinese *Shenguang Economic Journal* with cooperation from the municipal government of Shenzhen.
497 Robin Hutcheon, *SCMP: The First Eighty Years* (Hong Kong: SCMP, 1983).
498 See HKJA, *The Die is Cast* 52, 54; Jonathan Fenby, *Dealing with the Dragon – a Year in the New Hong Kong* (London: Little, Brown, 2000); Xu Jiatun, *The Memoirs of Xu Jiatun*.
499 See Jonathan Fenby, *Dealing with the Dragon*.

500 Former editor, Jonathan Fenby, helped to defend the paper before 1997. However, after he left the paper, he published a book documenting the pressure put on him by the management after Robert Kuok took over the paper. See Jonathan Fenby, *Dealing with the Dragon*.

501 HKJA, *Following the Flag* 10–12.

502 HKJA, *Following the Flag*; *2000 Human Rights Report: Hong Kong*. Details of the incident will be discussed in Chapter 5 with interview findings from senior journalists.

503 'Interview with Willy Wo-lap Lam', *Apple Daily* 12 Nov. 2000, *Next Magazine* 9 Nov. 2000; Letter, *SCMP* 10 Nov. 2000; Willy Lam, *Asian Wall Street Journal* 10 Nov. 2000.

504 Kuok Hock Nien. 'Speculation'. Letter. *SCMP* 29 June 2000.

505 Jonathan Fenby, *Dealing with the Dragon*.

506 'RTHK: The Government's Broadcaster?' *Media Freedom Watch*, HKJA (Feb. 2001) 5.

507 Jonathan Fenby, *Dealing with the Dragon*.

508 Letter, *SCMP* 10 Nov. 2000.

509 Cheung Kwai-yeung, *Jin Yong (Louis Cha) and the Press*.

510 The majority of media organisations in Hong Kong are owned either wholly or partly by companies or businesspersons with a diverse range of other business interests. This contrasts with the more common situation in Europe, the USA or Australia where media companies specialise in media businesses. HKJA, *The Die is Cast* 51–52.

511 Lee Chin-Chuan, 'The Paradox of Political Economy'.

512 In 1996, *MPDN* was criticised for having terminated outspoken columns. The objectivity of its reports on the would-be Chief Executive, Tung Chee-hwa, was also in question. See Joseph Kahn, 'Chinese Paper Softens Its Line'.

513 See Jesse Wong, 'University Head Adds to Controversy – CUHK Official Denies Paper's Report of Contact with Government – Li later Says He Has No Comment on Article', *Asian Wall Street Journal* 25 July 2000; Jesse Wong, 'Greater China: Newspaper Says Lo Issue was a Threat to Tung – Beijing-funded Daily Supports Chief Executive – Page of Articles Attacks Hong Kong Academics', *Asian Wall Street Journal* 28 July 2000.

514 See Jesse Wong, 'Hong Kong Exerts Persuasive Power with a Quiet Word – Jimmy Lai Loses Advertisement, An Ally Falls From Favor – "You Do as You're Told"', *Asian Wall Street Journal* 21 July 2000.

515 Quotation from Ip Yat-kin, editor, *Apple Daily*. See Carol Pui-yee Lai, 'Interview with Ip Yat-kin', *On the Record* (HKJA 1996).

516 See To Yiu-ming and T. Y. Lau, 'Walking on a Tight Rope'.

517 HKJA, *Following The Flag*.

518 Since the Chinese Communists took over the mainland, China has regarded Taiwan as its renegade province. Although both places across the Taiwan Strait were under authoritarian rule, the political reform in Taiwan has bypassed China and made impressive progress. See Christopher Hughes, *Taiwan and Chinese Nationalism: National Identity and Status in International Society* (London: Routledge, 1997).

520 See Daniel Dayan and Elihu Katz, *Media Events: The Live Broadcasting of History* (Cambridge, MA: Harvard University Press, 1992).

521 Sara Mills elegantly described this idea of contextual constraint on women travel writers and the implicit conflict between colonial discourse and feminist discourse in her textual analysis on women's travel writing. See Sara Mills, *Discourses of Difference: An Analysis of Women's Travel Writing and Colonialism* (London: Routledge, 1991).

522 For instance, Chinese Vice Premier Qing Qichen reportedly set out the limits on Hong Kong reporting after 1997. HKJA, *The Die is Cast*.

523 News organisations, such as *Sing Tao Daily News*, issued political guidelines as regards reporting on China. See HKJA, *The Die is Cast* and *Questionable Beginnings.*

524 This theory of China setting its next goal as 'reunification with Taiwan' was circulated and reported in the Hong Kong press during the Taiwanese election campaign period. Evidence will be shown in the following discussion.

525 Lu Ping, Director of Hong Kong and Macau Affairs Office, Chinese State Council, issued the warning before 1997. See earlier discussion.

526 The Hong Kong Journalists Association emphasised this incident as the main theme of their annual report in 2000, which largely reflects the fact that this remains one of the most contentious issues concerning press freedom in Hong Kong in the post-handover era. See HKJA, *Patriot Games.*

527 'Paper missile' was used as a metaphor for Chinese verbal threats by newspaper reporters.

528 See *Year 2000 Report of Hong Kong Human Rights*, section 2a.

529 *ODN* 13 Mar. 2000: A8 and 18 Mar. 2000: A3 and A23.

530 *ODN* 20 Feb. 2000: A7.

531 *ODN* 21 Feb. 2000: A6.

532 *ODN* 23 Feb. 2000: A8.

533 Ibid.

534 *ODN* 2 Mar. 2000: A7.

535 They were printed on 27, 29 Feb., 4, 7, 11, 14 Mar., with 4 and 7 Mar. carrying two related stories on the same day.

536 *ODN* 27 Feb. 2000: A6.

537 *ODN* 14 Mar. 2000: A9.

538 *ODN* 11 Mar. 2000: A6.

539 *ODN* 14 Mar. 2000: A3.

540 *ODN* 18 Mar. 2000: A3.

541 *ODN* 21 Feb. 2000: A6.

542 *ODN* 22 Feb. 2000: A10.

543 *ODN* 25 Feb. 2000: A9.

544 *ODN* 26 Feb. 2000: A6.

545 *ODN* 27 Feb. 2000: A6.

546 *ODN* 12 Mar. 2000. Unpaginated. www.orientaldaily.com.hk/srh_result/80672_btm.html2000/5/16 and www.orientaldaily.com.hk/srh_result/82185_btm.html2000/5/16. Accessed Sept. 2001.

547 *ODN* 7 Mar. 2000: A6.

548 *ODN* 8 Mar. 2000: A8.

549 *ODN* 11 Mar. 2000: A6.

550 Ibid.

551 *ODN* 14 Mar. 2000: A9.

552 *ODN* 11 Mar. 2000: A6.

553 *ODN* 19 Mar. 2000: A6.

554 Ibid.

555 *ODN* 17 Mar. 2000: A23.

556 *ODN* 18 Mar. 2000: A23.

557 *ODN* 18 Mar. 2000: A3.

558 *ODN* 19 Mar. 2000: A2.

559 *Year 2000 Report on Hong Kong Human Rights.*

560 *MPDN* 6 Mar. 2000:A15.

561 Ibid.

562 Ibid.

563 The column was written under a pen name, Chin Xing.

564 *MPDN* 4 Mar. 2000. Unpaginated. Retrieved via libwisenews.wisers.net. Accessed Sept. 2002.
565 Ibid.
566 The term 'pro-China' here refers to being supportive and sympathetic to the Chinese cause, no matter if it is right or wrong.
567 *MPDN* 8 Mar. 2000: B17.
568 Ibid.
569 *MPDN* 9 Mar. 2000: A2.
570 *MPDN* 16 Mar. 2000: A2.
571 *MPDN* 16 Mar. 2000: A2.
572 *MPDN* 17 Mar. 2000: A2.
573 *MPDN* 24 Feb. 2000: B15.
574 *MPDN* 25 Feb. 2000: A14.
575 *MPDN* 27 Feb. 2000: A10.
576 Ibid.
577 *MPDN* 28 Feb. 2000: A2.
578 *MPDN* 13 Mar. 2000: A2.
579 Ibid.
580 *MPDN* 16 Mar. 2000: A2.
581 *MPDN* 29 Feb. 2000: A27.
582 *MPDN* 10 Mar. 2000: A28 and 27 Mar. 2000: E10.
583 *MPDN* 23 Mar. 2000: F4.
584 Ibid.
585 *MPDN* 22 Mar. 2000: F9.
586 *MPDN* 15 Mar. 2000. Retrieved via /libwisenews.wisers.net. Accessed Sept. 2002.
587 Ibid.
588 *MPDN* 19 Mar. 2000: A2.
589 *MPDN* 20 Mar. 2000: A2.
590 *MPDN* 21 Mar. 2000: A3.
591 *SCMP* 18 Feb. 2000. Unpaginated. News stories of the SCMP in this chapter were retrieved from SCMP archive website archive.scmp.com/showarticles.php.
592 *SCMP* 18 Feb. 2000.
593 *SCMP* 22 Feb. 2000.
594 *SCMP* 23 Feb. 2000.
595 *SCMP* 11 Mar. 2000.
596 *SCMP* 23 Feb. 2000.
597 *SCMP* 24 Mar. 2000.
598 *SCMP* 22 Feb. 2000.
599 *SCMP* 23 Feb. 2000.
600 Ibid.
601 Ibid.
602 *SCMP* 23 Feb. 2000.
603 *SCMP* 28 Feb. 2000.
604 Hong Kong has benefited from indirect trade between Taiwan and mainland China because Taiwan has had rules and regulations restricting the communication, transport and trade between the two places. In 1987 Taiwan lifted martial law and partially relaxed the rule allowing mainlanders to visit Taiwan. In 2002, Taiwan lifted the ban in preparation to entry to international organisations such as the World Trade Organization.
605 *SCMP* 11 Mar. 2000.
606 Ibid.
607 *SCMP* 20 Mar. 2000.
608 Ibid.
609 Ibid.

610 Ibid.
611 Ibid.
612 Ibid.
613 *SCMP* 16 Mar. 2000.
614 *SCMP* 19 Mar. 2000.
615 Chen Shui-bian insisted that the Taiwanese people would not accept the scheme of 'one country, two systems' because they would not like the idea that the Central Government appointed the head of the administration. See *SCMP* 11 Jan. 2002.
616 *SCMP* 14 Mar. 2000.
617 *SCMP* 15 Mar. 2000.
618 *SCMP* 23 Feb. 2000.
619 *SCMP* 16 Mar. 2000.
620 Ibid.
621 Written communication with the author, 12 Jan. 2002.
622 Ibid.
623 Ibid.

5 Regime change and media control

624 HKJA and Article 19, *The Line Hardens – Tougher Stance on Civil Rights Threatens Freedom of Expression in Hong Kong*, (Hong Kong: Article 19 and HKJA, 2002).
625 See Deacon *et al.*, *Researching Communications*; Hansen *et al.*, *Mass Communication Research Methods*.
626 See Jeremy Tunstall, *Television Producers* (London; New York: Routledge, 1993).
627 HKJA, *Urgent Business*.
628 HKJA, *The Die is Cast*.
629 Chinese authorities did not condemn the annual activity to commemorate the anniversary of the crackdown on the 1989 Beijing Student Movement. For instance, in the evening of every 4 June since 1989, Hong Kong democrats and many ordinary people have held an open candlelight vigil in Victoria Park, Hong Kong. See HKJA, *The Die is Cast*. However, that was not the case in Chinese dissident regions.
630 Mao Tse-tung, speech in Yenan, cited in Chang Kuo-sin, *A Survey of the Chinese Language Daily Press*.
631 HKJA, *The Die is Cast*.
632 Ibid.
633 The China Liaison Office in Hong Kong is the office that replaced the Hong Kong branch of the *Xinhua News Agency* as the office representing the central Chinese government after 1997.
634 Mahlon Meyer, 'Muzzling the Press', *Newsweek* 24 Apr. 2000.
635 Reporters Without Borders is an association officially recognised as serving the public interest. According to its web site, Reporters Without Borders is on constant alert via its network of over 100 correspondents, and vigorously condemns any attack on press freedom world-wide by keeping the media and public opinion informed through press releases and public-awareness campaigns. The association defends journalists and other media contributors and professionals who have been imprisoned or persecuted for doing their work. See http://www.rsf.fr/ for more.
636 HKJA, *Questionable Beginnings*.
637 HKJA, *Following The Flag*.
638 According to the mini-constitution of Hong Kong, the Basic Law, the Chief Executive of HKSAR was elected by a selection committee of 400 members in its first term, and 800 members in its second term, respectively. However, the selection committee was not representative and was mainly hand-picked from the pro-China

camp. See Ian Holliday, Ma Ngok and Ray Yep, 'A High Degree of Autonomy? HKSAR, 1997–2002', *Political Quarterly* 73(4) (Oct.–Dec. 2002) 455–465.

639 Column by Lee Yee (of *The Nineties*), *Apple Daily* 29 Apr. 2003.

640 *SCMP* and *Apple Daily,* Jan. 2003.

641 The regulations are the so-called 'Seven Guidelines' laid down by Chinese Vice Premier, Qian Qichen.

642 The worst case in point was that of reporter, Xi Yang, who was sentenced to 12 years' imprisonment. He was released on parole after almost four years in jail, which allegedly signified a friendly gesture on China's part in anticipation of the handover in early 1997. See Chapter 3.

643 This might mean a reporter has written articles in the past that infuriated the Chinese authorities, or simply that reporters were sent to cover events that China thought embarrassing, such as natural catastrophes or man-made disasters.

644 After Beijing's crackdown on the Tiananmen student movement in 1989, the Chinese authorities drew up a list ranking Hong Kong news organisations in several categories ranging from hostile to friendly across the political spectrum. News organisations received different treatment from China depending on their ranking. See HKJA, *Urgent Business.*

645 Jimmy Lai interview with Jonathan Dimbleby, *The Last Hong Kong Governor*, TV documentary, BBC, 1997.

646 HKJA, *The Die is Cast.* There is more about Lai and the Next Group in Chapter 6.

647 Various types of Bauhinia Award were created by the HKSAR government in the post-handover period. They are meant as a substitute for honours granted by the British government in the pre-handover period. See Carrie Chan, 'Honour for Philip Wong Stirs Anger', *SCMP*, 12 Oct. 2003 and Gary Cheung, 'Union's Colourful Past Now on Stage', *SCMP* 20 Aug. 2003.

648 Thomas Abraham, Interview with Qian Qichen, *SCMP* 26 June 2002.

649 Ibid. For counter argument, see Joseph Cheng, 'Duty to Democracy Must be Honoured', *SCMP* 29 June 2002.

650 Interview with the author, Autumn 2002.

651 Interview with the author, 5 Oct. 2002.

652 A senior journalist at *Apple Daily*, interview with the author, 26 Sept. 2002.

653 Examples are seen in the late 1960s in Chapter 2.

654 Interview with the author, autumn 2002.

655 Interview with the author, autumn 2002.

656 See *Sing Tao Daily News*, European edition 29–30 Mar. 2003: A8.

657 Donald Tsang, now as Chief Executive of Hong Kong, is a member of the new elite.

658 The source of information was 'Reporters Sans Frontières' (Reporters Without Borders), *SCMP* 29 Apr. 2003.

659 China has pledged to adopt the principle of 'one country, two systems' to administer Hong Kong after the handover. In other words, Hong Kong has been promised that it will be allowed to retain its capitalist market economy, and continue to enjoy its civil liberties such as freedom of the press, freedom of assembly, freedom of religion and so on.

660 HKJA, *Following The Flag.*

661 Anson Chan, 'Beware of Blurring the Dividing Line', *Financial Times* 1 July 2002 (Hong Kong 3).

662 HKJA, *Following the Flag.*

663 Anson Chan, 'Beware of Blurring the Dividing Line'.

664 HKJA, *Following the Flag.*

665 In Chapter 3, there is a discussion on the restructuring of media organisations and its relation to proprietorial interests in mainland China.

666 For example, *Hong Kong Times* was shut down in the early 1990s. See HKJA, *The Die is Cast.*

667 For example, the two Taiwanese-funded papers, the *Hong Kong United Daily* and the *China Times Weekly*, which originally aimed to cover Hong Kong beyond 1997, were subsequently withdrawn from Hong Kong in the mid-1990s apparently because in the political situation of Hong Kong it was not feasible for the two dailies to continue. See HKJA, *The Die is Cast.*

668 Founding and disillusioned editor, Lo Fu's article on the historical role of *New Evening Post, Ming Pao Monthly* magazine, July 1997

669 There are currently three dailies – *Wen Wei Po, Ta Kung Pao* and *Hong Kong Commercial Daily* – which are funded by mainland China.

670 More details will be discussed in the following section.

671 For more details see Chapter 6.

672 For example in the case of *SCMP* and other Chinese newspapers such as *MPDN*.

673 A description used by a senior editor, interview with the author, 25 Oct. 2002.

674 Hong Kong Audit Bureau of Circulation.

675 HKJA, *The Die is Cast.*

676 Jonathan Fenby, *Dealing with the Dragon.*

677 Nury Vittachi, *North Wind* (Hong Kong: Chameleon, 2001).

678 Interview with the author.

679 HKJA, *Questionable Beginnings.*

680 See 'Rimbunan to Tap Huge Market in China', *The Star* [Malaysia] 30 June 1998; 'Rimbunan Hijau to Develop Industrial Park in Dalian to Form a Joint Venture with Golden Ocean to Develop Property in Malaysia', *The Star* [Malaysia] 3 July 1995.

681 Xu Jiatun, *The Memoirs of Xu Jiatun.*

682 Ibid.

683 Jonathan Fenby, *Dealing with the Dragon.*

684 In his letter to the Editor, Kuok Hock Nien said, 'I refer to Page 18 of the *SCMP*, Wednesday 28 June "Marshalling the SAR's Tycoons". My first reaction to the article is that it is absolute exaggeration and fabrication. Mr. Lam [has a tendency of going overboard]. This time [he] has not only gone overboard, he has fallen into a trap of innuendo that is not supported by the events. The article is full of distortions and speculation. I was present during the meetings 'the SAR's tycoons' had with Planning Chief Mr. Zeng Peiyan, followed by meetings with President Jiang Zemin and later with Prime Minister Zhu Rongji. By the way, the day ended with a banquet given in honor of the visiting 'SAR tycoons' by Vice Premier Mr. Qian Qichen and Mrs. Qian. What a pity Mr. Lam did not further elaborate on other acts of connivance which took place during dinner! The *South China Morning Post* article implies that great conspiracies are afoot and that Hong Kong's businessmen are such idiots and morons that their only way of business survival is to become running dogs of the Chinese Central Government. Could it be that Mr. Lam [has been so steeped during the past few years in the subtle ways of the colonial era that he] can't differentiate between colonial running dogs and ordinary businessmen who conduct their businesses in correct and proper ways. The *SCMP* has more than once published articles written by [in-house] journalists in which manifestations of patriotism to the motherland, especially by natives of Hong Kong, are regarded as something improper or even sinister. Why should this be so?' The words in brackets had been edited by the *Post*'s editorial staff, according to an interviewee. See Kuok Hock Nien, 'Speculation'. Letter. *SCMP* 29 June 2000.

685 Political Desk. 'Tycoon Says *Post* Biased Against Tung', *SCMP* 26 July 2000.

686 Analysis by journalists inside and outside of the *SCMP*, interview with the author, autumn 2002.

687 Interview with the author, 25 Sept. 2002.

688 Robert Keatley, the editor, carried out this duty of vetting Willy Lam's column several times. Interview with the author, autumn 2002 and confidential memo.

689 Interview with the author, autumn 2003.

690 Written communication with the author, Jan. 2003.
691 Interview with the author, autumn 2002.
692 Interview with the author, 25 Sept. 2002.
693 Letter, (by 115 Reporters and Editors) *SCMP* 10 Nov. 2000.
694 Interview with the author, autumn 2002.
695 Written communication with the author, mid-2002.
696 Written communication with the author, early 2003.
697 According to a respondent, Owen Jonathan, having heard about Willy Lam's resigna-
     tion, called and asked what he could do for them. Later, he faxed a letter to the editor
     and it was in turn handed to Robert Keatley. Interview with the author, 25 Sept. 2002.
698 Confidential memo from one of the interviewees.
699 Interview with the author, autumn 2002.
700 Ibid.
701 Since then, Jasper Becker has worked as a China correspondent for the *Independent*
     in London.
702 'Journalists Kow-tow to China or Go', *Australian Financial Review* 1 July 2002;
     'Losing a Voice of Integrity', *Asian Wall Street Journal* 2 May 2002.
703 Staff reporter interview with the author, 7 Oct. 2002.
704 Carina Lai, 'Watching China: A Major Hong Kong Newspaper's Contrasting Views
     of China (1991 and 2001)', Diss. Tufts University (July–Aug. 2002). In her compar-
     ison of the *SCMP*'s reporting in 2001 with that of a decade ago, she found that in
     fact, *SCMP* did not reduce its coverage of China's political news, though more wire
     stories were used.
705 While the political editor, Chris Yeung, was dismissed from his previous duty of
     organising the political desk, he was given another title, 'editor-at-large', in which
     position he could focus on writing a weekly column on top of doing political news
     stories. Interview with the author, Oct. 2002.
706 Interview with the author, Oct. 2002.
707 Ibid.
708 Carina Lai, 'Watching China'.
709 Interview with the author.
710 Ibid.
711 Ibid.
712 HKJA, *Urgent Business*.
713 Interview with the author, Oct. 2002.
714 See Justine Lau and Joe Leahy, 'Hong Kong Chief's Links to Tycoon Raises Eye-
     brows', *Financial Times* 9 Aug. 2003.
715 For example, the grant of a cyber port to Richard Li, the son of Li Ka-shing, without
     allowing an open bid attracted a lot of criticism from both the business community
     and the public at large. See Martin Regg Cohn, 'Li Family Tends to Take Hard Line
     to Get Its Way: Playing Hardball with Air Canada Tycoon Used to Flexing
     Muscles', *Toronto Star [Canada]* 27 Apr. 2004.
716 Simon Pritchard, 'From Rags to Rich Rancour', *SCMP* 1 Sept. 2000. Interview with
     the author, autumn 2002.
717 Interview with the author, autumn 2002.
718 'A Message from the Publisher', *SCMP* 7 Aug. 2002.
719 They included C. K. Lau, the chief news editor, Anthony Lawrence, the managing
     editor. See *SCMP* 16 Aug. 2002.
720 David Armstrong, the new editor, would assume his new post on 1 Apr. 2003.
721 A journalist who has worked at *SCMP* for more than ten years. Interview with the
     author, Oct. 2002. Also see HKJA and Article 19, *False Security: Hong Kong's
     National Security Laws Pose a Grave Threat to Freedom of Expression, 2003
     Annual Report* (Hong Kong: HKJA, 2003).
722 Interview with the author, 16 Oct. 2002.

723 *Sing Tao Daily News*, European edition, 12 July 2002.
724 Interview with the author, autumn 2002.
725 The accusation included several instances of censoring *Metro Broadcast* from broadcasting negative news about the group. See 'Hong Kong's Muzzled Media', *Asian Wall Street Journal*, 23 Aug. 2002. Cheung filed an official complaint to the HKJA. A copy of the confidential letter was obtained from Cheung for the purpose of discussion in this study.
726 Interview with the author.
727 Verdict of the inquiry into Paul Cheung's complaint by an independent panel of HKJA. See 'Report by the Ad Hoc Group to Inquire into the Complaint of Paul Cheung', 11 May 2003. www.freeway.org.hk/hkja/. Accessed 28 Apr. 2004.
728 Interview with the author, 19 Oct. 2002.
729 Written communication with the author, Dec. 2002 – Jan. 2003.
730 Interview with the author, 19 Oct. 2002.
731 For more, see Chapter 6.
732 Jimmy Lai enjoyed particularly positive reportage and commentary by American and British media such as *Asian Wall Street Journal* and *Financial Times*.
733 Interview with the author, Oct. 2002.
734 One media and communication professor noted that even the critical *HKEJ* became less critical of the central Chinese government. He pointed to the change in political parameters as an explanation. Interview with the author, Oct. 2002.
735 For instance, the Chief Executive, Tung Chee-hwa, had on many occasions expressed his wish that the Hong Kong news media should take heed of their 'social responsibility', by which he meant give more positive publicity to both the central as well as the HKSAR government.
736 The apology said: 'Three days before the verdict of a case in which members of Falun Gong were charged with "obstruction", "obstructing the police in the exercise of their official duty" and "assaulting the police", our paper received a request to publish an advertisement about Falun Gong. In consideration of the upcoming verdict and in order to avoid interference with judicial justice, we decided not to accept the advertisement. However, the mass media should shoulder responsibility for social justice and freedom of speech, which override all other concerns. Following internal discussion, we think our decision not to accept that advertisement was wrong. So we apologize to our readers and members of Falun Gong. – The editorial department of the *Apple Daily*, 23 Aug. 2002.' *Apple Daily*, 23 Aug. 2002: A5.
737 Interview with the author, autumn 2002.
738 Interview with the author, 23 Oct. 2002.
739 *HKEJ* 15 Aug. 2002.
740 Interview with the author, 23 Oct. 2002.
741 Ibid.
742 Ibid.
743 Interview with the author, 23 Oct. 2002.
744 Here the chief executive officer was referring to some Hong Kong Chinese-language dailies that have a global distribution and circulation in the major Chinese diaspora cities such as New York, Toronto, Vancouver, San Francisco, London, Amsterdam, Paris and Sydney.
745 Hong Kong was at first criticised by a Chinese official for reporting extensively on the epidemic. Within weeks the official was proved wrong. Hong Kong had done China a favour by reporting relentlessly on the disease, despite China's tight domestic control.
746 Written communication with the author, Jan. 2003.
747 Ibid.
748 Written communication with the author, Jan. 2003; see also Nury Vittachi, *North Wind*.

749 A senior editor used this term to describe the political culture in post-colonial Hong Kong. By coincidence, the term was also used by Joseph Zen, the Roman Catholic Bishop in Hong Kong, to describe the deteriorating cultural and moral standards of the government and elite.
750 See Chapters 1, 3 and 6 for detailed discussion.
751 Written communication with the author, Dec. 2002–Jan. 2003.
752 Ibid.
753 Ibid.
754 Ibid.
755 Andy Ho, 'Mainland Propaganda Mill Wins Ear of Some Local Media', *SCMP* 16 July 2002.
756 Ibid.
757 Joseph Man Chan, 'When Capitalist and Socialist Television Clash: The Impact of Hong Kong TV on Guangzhou Residents', *Power, Money and Media*, ed. Chin-Chuan Lee (Evanston, Illinois: Northwestern University Press, 2000) 245–270.
758 The Chinese Liaison Office in Hong Kong took over the functions of former *Xinhua News Agency*, the de facto Chinese embassy when Hong Kong was under British rule.
759 Interview with the author, June 2003.
760 Written communication and interview with the author, Jan. 2003.
761 Ibid.
762 In 2000, the former Taiwanese president, Lee Teng-hui, stated his 'state-to-state' theory that appeared to be a variation of Taiwan's 'Two China' theory. Lee's rhetoric infuriated the Beijing authorities at the time.
763 Written communication and interview with the author, Jan. 2003.
764 Ibid.
765 Further discussion on the so-called 'wearing of the mountain' – making it easier to effect institutional change by removing heavy-weight journalists – will be discussed in a later section.
766 Mahlon Meyer, 'Muzzling the Press', *Newsweek* 24 Apr. 2000.
767 Interview with the author, 8 Oct. 2002.
768 Interview with the author, autumn 2002.
769 HKJA, *Patriot Games*.
770 Written communication with the author, Jan. 2003.
771 Interview with the author, 26 Oct. 2002.
772 Written communication with the author, Jan. 2003.
773 HKJA, *Patriot Games*.
774 Interview with the author, 8 Oct. 2002.
775 This issue will be discussed further in Chapter 6 when we come to the evolution of the journalistic tradition.
776 See Chapter 6.
777 Written communication with the author, spring 2003.
778 Ibid.
779 Here the analysis of proprietors' views is limited, and based on interviews with one proprietor and several publishers and chief executive officers.

6 Journalistic norms and people power

780 Even the Chief Executive, Tung Chee-hwa, reportedly said that he had had sleepless nights having seen so many Hong Kong people take to the streets to make their voices heard. See HKJA and Article 19, *Beijing Turns the Screws: Freedom of Expression in Hong Kong Under Attack* (Hong Kong: HKJA and Article 19, 2004).
781 The two sacked cabinet ministers were Anthony Leung, the Finance Secretary, and Regina Ip, the Secretary for Security. Before the 1 July march, Tung Chee-hwa had

been reluctant to remove the two cabinet ministers. They were sacked for various reasons, but one thing they had in common was that they were both highly unpopular.

782 According to many sinologists and seasoned China watchers, the protest defied belief. Usually if more than half a million people take to the streets to protest against the head of a government, it would either result in a bloody crackdown or the downfall of the regime. Neither of these things happened in the case of Hong Kong. The threat to China was very real, however. Despite the fact that China prohibited the mass media from reporting on Hong Kong's mass demonstration, the news spread to the mainland through foreign media and Internet transmission. Indeed, what worried China most was that Hong Kong's protestors might set an example to their mainland counterparts in their fight for political concessions there. See Willy Lam, 'One-Country Two-Systems after "7-1"', *Jamestown Journal* 29 July 2003. www.jamestown.org/publications_details.php?volume_id=19&issue_id=680&article_id+4754.

783 Xiao Ping, 'Conspiracy to Subvert SAR's Political System', *China Daily* 14 July 2003.

784 Yum Chi-pang, '60% of Demonstrators are Motivated by Media such as a Newspaper and a Radio Broadcaster', *Hong Kong Wen Wei Po* [Chinese] 15 July 2003. See also 'Joseph Man Chan: Media Role – From Third Party to Advocate', *MPDN* 25 July 2003; 'J. Man Chan: the Bottom Line of Media Politicization', *MPDN* 24 July 2003; 'Mass Media Has Reached its Bottom Line of Getting Involved in Politics', *Apple Daily* 20 July 2003.

785 'Foreign forces' usually means US-based organisations, whereas 'external forces' means Taiwan-related organisations, according to the Chinese Communist Party's traditional definition. See Willy Lam, *Jamestown Journal* 29 July 2003.

786 The *China Daily,* a state-controlled paper, said in its Hong Kong edition that the recent three demonstrations were 'a vehicle for subverting the political system in Hong Kong'. It alleged pro-democracy organisers were 'tricking people into taking part'. *China Daily*, Hong Kong edition, 14 July 2003.

787 See Table 4.3 of the Appendix for a full list of interviewees' names, positions and other details.

788 Liam Fitzpatrick, 'The Long March', *Time Asia Magazine* 14 July 2003, Vol. 161: 27.

789 The Chinese Foreign Minister, Tang Jiaxuan, reportedly said that the enactment of the national security bill was meant to implement the reunification of Hong Kong with China.

790 See also 'Joseph Man Chan: Media Role – From Third Party to Advocate', *MPDN* 25 July 2003; 'Joseph Man Chan: the Bottom Line of Media Politicization', *MPDN* 24 July 2003; 'Mass Media Has Reached its Bottom Line of Getting Involved in Politics', *Apple Daily* 20 July 2003.

791 According to the *Open Monthly*, a Chinese public affairs monthly magazine, Aug. 2003: 7, 27.

792 'Messages from Former Chairmen', *25th Anniversary Bulletin* (Hong Kong: HKJA,1993) 20–23.

793 Ibid.

794 Jack Spackman's article, 'Messages from Former Chairmen' 20.

795 Before the 1980s, many Hong Kong journalists were educated either in Taiwan or in the southern Chinese province of Guangdong as local higher education opportunities were limited. However, since the early 1980s, more and more Hong Kong journalists were educated in the School of Journalism of the Baptist University (then the Baptist College) and the School of Media and Communication at the Chinese University of Hong Kong. See also Clement So and Joseph M. Chan, *Press and Politics in Hong Kong.*

796 Written communication with the author from a journalism professor, 2002 and 2003.
797 Ibid.
798 At that time, the two candidates were Carol P. Lai, deputy chairperson, and the incumbent chairperson Mak Yin-ting.
799 It was noted that 'the HKJA as presently structured suffered from administrative inefficiency caused partly by the voluntary and part-time nature of the organization, and from a lack of independent identity in terms of a location and "home".' Wong Kwok Wah, then newly elected vice-chairman and later chairman (1986–1989), proposed the move from the FCC premises to a local office, as seen in the AGM of HKJA on 25 June 1985 in the Foreign Correspondents' Club (FCC), AGM minutes.
800 'Messages from Former Chairmen' 20–23.
801 Wong Kwok Wah, 'Messages from Former Chairman' 22.
802 Ibid.
803 This section is largely based on Cliff Bale, 'A Brief History of the HKJA's Campaign for Media Law Reform – A Lobby Document' HKJA 2 Dec. 1995; and interviews with Cliff Bale in London and Hong Kong, 2002 and 2003.
804 The HKJA made a formal submission to the government in November 1985 calling for this law to be scrapped. It took the government two years to bring forward a bill to repeal the Control of Publications Consolidation Ordinance, but there was a bitter twist. The ordinance was repealed in March 1987, but a clause was included in the Public Order Ordinance making it an offence to maliciously publish false news. The battle then continued for the repeal of the new section 27 of the Public Order Ordinance, commonly known as the 'false news' provision. The HKJA made personal representations to British leaders and politicians on the issue, and various media organisations in Hong Kong later united in calling for the repeal of section 27. It was repealed in early 1989.
805 Another early example of the same nature was the campaign to amend the Legislative Council (Powers and Privileges) Bill. The bill contained several clauses that posed a direct threat to press freedom. These were dropped following intense lobbying of the Legislative Council's ad hoc group studying the draft legislation. In spite of all the hazards, it was seen as a swift response to the changing political environment of Hong Kong.
806 Interview with an executive committee member of the HKJA. The HKJA met Patten in August 1992, and one month later submitted a list of 17 laws in need of urgent reform. The list included controversial security-related legislation, including the Emergency Regulations Ordinance, the Official Secrets Act, the Crimes Ordinance, the Public Order Ordinance and the Police Force Ordinance.
807 This section is based on Cliff Bale, 'Access to Information – How the Campaign Started', Lobbying Article, HKJA, Feb. 1995.
808 One of the first calls for freedom of information legislation was made in the late 1980s by the Society for Community Organization (SOCO), which was concerned, among other issues, that squatters were being denied information about slope conditions in their neighbourhoods. Initially, the group consisted of the Hong Kong Human Rights Commission, which included SOCO, and Justice (the HK section of the International Commission of Jurists). The environmental organisation, Friends of the Earth, later joined the group. In 1992, a member of the core group, Dr Nihal Jayawickrama, presented a draft access law to a seminar on freedom of information. The bill proposed that individuals should have a general right of access to government documents, except in certain narrowly defined areas. Individuals would also be granted access to records about themselves, plus a right to seek a correction. In July 1993, in a significant boost to the campaign for access legislation, legislative councillor, Christine Loh, expanded the core group, by bringing in more organisations and individuals.
809 In June 1994 the government announced that it would implement an administrative

code of practice, setting out non-binding guidelines for the release of information. It fell far short of the statutory rights sought by the core group and its supporters. A Chinese Foreign Ministry spokesman accused the government of introducing the code without prior consultation and agreement with China. The code came into force in March 1995. The administrative code initially covered nine departments. It now covers all the government.

810 Emily Lau, 'Messages from the Chairmen' 23.

811 Ibid.

812 The chief editor of *MPDN,* Cheung kin-bor, once relayed a question from the *Xinhua News Agency* during an editorial meeting: the *Xinhua* people asked how come so many HKJA core/executive committee members worked for *MPDN?* Indeed, there were several ex-chairpersons/deputy chairpersons who had worked for *MPDN,* e.g. Daisy Li (chair 1992–1994), Ivan Tong (chair 1994–1996), Carol Lai (chair 1997–1998), Kevin Lau (deputy chair), Law Yee-ping (ex committee member). However, most of them have since left *MPDN* and moved on to other news organisations. Interview with the author, autumn 2002.

813 The Johannesburg Principles, National Security, Freedom of Expression and Access to Information, November 1996, No. 3 This paper was originally published in October 1995 following an international consultation convened by Article 19, the International Centre Against Censorship, in collaboration with the Centre for Applied Legal Studies of the University of the Witwatersrand in Johannesburg.

814 Emily Lau, 'Messages from the Chairmen' 23.

815 The seven guidelines to be observed by Hong Kong, Macau and foreign media were announced by Chinese Vice Premier Qian Qichen. See Chapter 5 for more examples of the content of the regulations.

816 See Chapter 3.

817 Ibid.

818 Former executive committee member, HKJA, interview with the author, 10 Oct. 2002.

819 *Dateline,* 1997, the Internet magazine of the Foreign Correspondents' Club, Hong Kong. Accessed Oct. 2003.

820 Former HKJA executive committee members once they were promoted became active members of the News Executives Association and Newspaper Society due to rules and regulations of the HKJA prohibiting those who were in charge of hiring and firing to sit on its board.

821 Thomas Yan (chairman 1977–1978), 'Messages from Former Chairmen' 21.

822 For instance, Paul Cheung said had it not been for economic factors, he would have resigned long before he was sacked. For details, see Chapter 5.

823 The federation, for instance, is not a trade union.

824 The case of Willy Lam can best exemplify this point. See Chapter 5.

825 See Li Kar-yuen, *On Hong Kong Newspaper History*; Cheung Kwai-yeung, *Jin Yong (Louis Cha) and the Press*; Robin Hutcheon, *SCMP: The First Eighty Years*; and Li Kuk-shing, *A Comment on the Hong Kong Press.* Also, Liam Fitzpatrick, 'The Long March'.

826 For example, in the late 1960s, the British government adopted heavy-handed measures to suppress the local Chinese communist press because the government believed that the leftist press posed a threat to its colonial rule. See Chapter 2 for details.

827 See Li Kar-yuen, *On Hong Kong Newspaper History*; Cheung Kwai-yeung, *Jin Yong (Louis Cha) and the Press*; Robin Hutcheon, *SCMP: The First Eighty Years*; and Li Kuk-shing, *A Comment on the Hong Kong Press.*

828 For example, those pro-Taiwan or Taiwan-funded newspapers that used to describe the 'Chinese Communist Party' as 'Zhong Gong' (CCP) and 'Gong Fei' (Communist thief) quietly replaced these terms with 'Central Government'. Besides, those

papers that used to count dates according to the Republic of China's calendar ceased that practice. See Yau Shing-mu and Cheung Siu-jing, 'Sally Aw – From Pro-Taiwan to Pro-China', *Hong Kong Economic Times* 25 Dec. 1998: A14.

829 Andy Ho, 'Teacup in a storm', *MPDN* 23 June 2003: B12.
830 Interview with the author.
831 Andy Ho, 'Teacup in a storm', *MPDN* 23 June 2003: B12; Andy Ho, 'On "Teacup in a Storm"', *Media Digest*, RTHK. July 2003. www.rthk.org.hk/mediadigest/ 20030715_76_90205.html. Accessed 16 Feb. 2004.
832 *Tai-pan* was a term used in the nineteenth century to refer to foreign businessmen doing business in China or Hong Kong. The Chinese term is now used in a more general sense for business executives of any origin. The Chinese term literally means 'big class' which is equivalent to the English term 'big shot'. Hong Kong people like to call Albert Cheng 'Tai-pan' as he was once a senior executive in a publishing business.
833 Interview with the author, 27 Sept. 2002 and Albert Cheng's open talk, University of Hong Kong, 30 Sept. 2002.
834 HKJA, *The Ground Rules Change*.
835 Before Albert Cheng joined Hong Kong Commercial Radio, he was commissioned to act as one of the hosts who chaired a popular TV public affairs programme called 'News Tease' where he became popular. See S. Y. Yue, 'Controversial ATV Show Axed', *SCMP* 16 Nov. 1994; 'Sharpening Up for the Cut and Thrust of TV Debates', *SCMP* 7 Aug. 1994.
836 Interview with the author, 27 Sept. 2002.
837 Interview with the author, 27 Sept. 2002.
838 Letter to George Ho by Selina Chow, 17 Apr. and 27 Apr. 2002 and letter to Selina Chow by George Ho, 22 Apr. 2002. In his letter to Chow, Ho, the chairman and pro-prietor of *Commercial Radio*, said: 'I have referred your letter to our management and the producer of the talk show program.' He thus avoided being accused of inter-ference with editorial independence.
839 As for the cause of the assault, he suspected that it was due to his open support of the government's move to intervene in the stock market. This had, in turn, upset a certain group of people. He once joked with Donald Tsang, the Chief Secretary, that he was the only one who had been badly assaulted because of supporting govern-ment policy.
840 Perry Link, 'More Repression? Beijing's Response to the 21st Century?' Presenta-tion Paper, Conference of University of Hong Kong, June 2003; HKJA, *False Security*.
841 Andy Ho, 'Teacup in a storm', *MPDN* 23 June 2003: B12; Andy Ho, 'On "Teacup in a Storm"', *Media Digest*, RTHK, July 2003. www.rthk.org.hk/mediadigest/ 20030715_76_90205.html. Accessed 16 Feb. 2004.
842 Ibid.
843 Albert Cheng, 'Henry Tang has the responsibility [to make a decision]', *Apple Daily* 21 July 2003.
844 See 'Albert Cheng Won't Resume Hosting the Phone-in Program until The License of the *Commercial Radio* is Renewed', *Apple Daily* 18 July 2003. The report said there were more than 12,000 responses to the Broadcasting Authority regarding the warning issued to *Commercial Radio*.
845 Martin Lee, 'Two Systems, One Destiny', *SCMP* 1 Aug. 2003.
846 Albert Cheng's open talk, 30 Sept. 2002.
847 Lam Hang-chi, publisher, *Hong Kong Economic Journal*, written communication with the author.
848 The other paper concerned was the *Apple Daily*. See Perry Link, 'More Repression?'.
849 Nora Tong, '*Economic Journal* Threatens to Close Down if Security Law Passed', *SCMP* 4 July 2003.

850 Lam Hang-chi, column, *HKEJ* 4 July 2003.
851 For more discussion, see Chapter 5.
852 See Lam Hang-chi, 'Column to Mark the 30th Anniversary of the *HKEJ*', *HKEJ* 3 July 2003.
853 Written communication with the author, Oct. 2002–Jan. 2003. Lam later published his views partially in his column to mark the 30th anniversary of *HKEJ* 3 July 2003.
854 Ibid.
855 Ibid.
856 For *Apple Daily*, the suppression is cruder and more blunt, i.e. there is a blanket ban on it.
857 Written communication with the author, Oct. 2002–Jan. 2003.
858 Written communication with the author. Lam Hang-chi, column, *HKEJ*, 4 July 2003.
859 Ibid.
860 'An Exclusive Interview with Lam Hang-chi', *Shanghai Wen Hui Bao* [Chinese] 12 July 2002, reprinted in Lam's own column, *HKEJ* 22 July 2002.
861 Interview with a founding editor of the *Apple Daily*, autumn 2002; also see Clement So, 'Pre-1997 Hong Kong Press: Cut-throat Competition and the Changing Journalistic Paradigm', *The Other Hong Kong Report 1996*, eds Ngaw Mee-kau and Li Si-ming (Hong Kong: Chinese University Press, 1996) 485–506.
862 See Chapters 3 and 5.
863 The cover picture of *Mad-dog Daily*'s inaugural edition was a flag of the nationalist Taiwanese Kuomintang [KMT] party which was read as posing an open challenge to the Chinese authorities. However, the *Daily*, owned and operated by a political commentator, Raymond Wong, could not survive in Hong Kong's highly competitive media market though it was both outspoken and critical on various controversial issues.
864 Quote from McHugh.
865 Interview with Albert Cheng, Hong Kong, 27 Oct. 2002; Albert Cheng's open talk.
866 A veteran news controller's interview with the author, 25 Oct. 2002. Even more were invited in 2003 when Tung was returned for a second term of office as Chief Executive, for example, the proprietors of *Sing Tao Daily News*, *ODN*, *Hong Kong Economic Times* and *Asia TV* Broadcast. See Chui Siu-ming, 'Media at Last 'Reunified', *HKEJ* 7 Feb. 2003.
867 A veteran news controller's interview with the author, 25 Oct. 2002
868 Fionnuala McHugh, 'The Sensational Jimmy Lai', *Post Magazine*, *Sunday Morning Post* 13 Oct. 2002.
869 Lai appeared to be fond of the foreign media. He turned down most of the Hong Kong Chinese media's requests for an interview. The exception was the *SCMP Sunday* magazine, which made him the cover story prior to the launch of *Apple Daily* in Taiwan. I requested an interview through his chief executive officer. He refused, saying that he needed to consult a dentist. However, a former member of staff on the *Asian Wall Street Journal*, Jesse Wong, is currently in the process of compiling an autobiography of Lai.
870 Clement So, 'Pre-1997 Hong Kong Press'.
871 Interview with the author.
872 Ibid.
873 Ibid.
874 Quote from McHugh.
875 A case in point is his unprecedented tirade regarding the editorial department's rejection of the Falun Gong advertisement, see Chapter 5.
876 Interview with the author, autumn 2002.
877 Ibid.
878 Ibid.
879 Interview with the author, 30 Oct. 2002.
880 Interview with the author, 23 Oct. 2002.

881 The Chief Executive Officer of the *Apple Daily*'s interview with the author, 23 Oct.2002.
882 As mentioned in Chapter 5, Jimmy Lai laid down guidelines for China news, i.e. there would be no 'breaking news' for *Apple Daily*'s China news unless it was attributable. That makes it hard for China desk journalists to write a sensitive news story as there continues to be a blackout in China in terms of press freedom.
883 Frederik Balfour, 'A Thorn in China's Side – Publisher Jimmy Lai is Riding the Wave of Hong Kong Dissent', *Business Week* 28 July 2003.
884 Written communication with the author.
885 Balfour, 'A Thorn in China's Side'.
886 Written communication with the author 2003.
887 Ibid.
888 Quote from McHugh.
889 Ibid.
890 Ibid.
891 According to a member of senior management, they also took heed of the circulation. If they kept on playing up a political issue, the paper's circulation would fall, so it was very important to strike a balance. Interview with the author.
892 See news.bbc.co.uk/1/hi/world/asia-pacific/2577483.stm, accessed Mar. 2004 and *Apple Daily* 16 Dec. 2002. However, Lam Hang-chi and his wife took to the streets for the first time to join hundreds of other journalists and half-a-million Hong Kong people to protest against the enactment of the proposed national security bill on 1 July 2003 to commemorate the sixth anniversary of the establishment of the HKSAR government.
893 news.bbc.co.uk/1/hi/world/asia-pacific/2577483.stm, accessed Mar. 2004.
894 According to Lam's senior editorial staff, they were allowed to hold a different editorial position from Lam's, including in the daily editorial as well. Interview with the author.
895 See Balfour, 'A Thorn in China's Side'.
896 Interview with the author. According to a political editor, at the beginning of the consultation on the national security bill, the majority of the senior editors of the Hong Kong press agreed with the government that there was a need to enact article 23 of the Basic Law. As public sentiment shifted over time, and particularly after the big march on 1 July, the press shifted its position to coincide with public aspirations.
897 A retired founding editor of *RTHK*, Wong Chi-keung, 'The *RTHK* I Know', *MPDN* 24 Apr. 1996; see also Wong Chi-keung, 'A letter to Mr Tung Chee-hwa, Chief Executive of HKSAR', *HKEJ* 10 Mar.1998.
898 Wong Chi-keung, 'The *RTHK* I Know'.
899 Ibid.
900 HKJA, *Following The Flag*: 14.
901 Interview with the author, 2002.
902 The biggest intervention since the handover was the Taiwan Hong Kong Letter by Cheng An-kuo. See Chapter 5 for details.
903 See section on political terminology in Chapter 5. See also HKJA, *The Line Hardens*.
904 Ibid.
905 In another incident, a pro-Beijing legislative councilor, Ng Leung-sing, asked the Chief Executive in October 2000 if he thought *RTHK* should be obliged to help explain government decisions better. Chief Executive Tung Chee-hwa replied ambiguously: 'On the one hand, I hope *RTHK* will help the government; on the other, the government also has the responsibility to do better.' See HKJA, *The Line Hardens*.
906 *RTHK* Framework Agreement with Secretary for Information Technology and Broadcasting, Hong Kong; see also /www.rthk.org.hk/about/about_e.htm for details of producers' guidelines. Accessed Oct. 2003.

907 There were quite a few Directors of Broadcasting seconded from the BBC who headed *RTHK*. Among them were: J. B. Hawthorne, 20 Nov. 1972 to 9 Feb. 1978; D. J. N. Kerr, 1 Jan. 1978 to 14 Nov. 1980; and C. S. Wilkinson, 19 Apr. 1982 to 22 Feb. 1986. This information was provided by a senior member of staff at *RTHK*. Interview with the author, 2002.

908 RTHK spokesman's interview with the author, autumn 2002.

909 Interview with the author, Dec. 2002, London.

910 RTHK Framework Agreement.

911 Chiu Hsiang-zhong, 'On Civilized Institutions', *HKEJ* 3 July 2003.

912 It later emerged that the Chief Executive's senior special assistant, Andrew Lo, had raised doubts about Dr. Chung's polls during a meeting with the university's vice-chancellor, Cheng Yiu-chung. Prof. Cheng had then spoken with pro-vice-chancellor, Wong Siu-lun, who in turn broached the issue with Dr. Chung. See HKJA, *Following The Flag*.

913 The panel said it was sure that the messages were passed to Dr Chung 'as a result of the conversation between Mr Lo and the vice-chancellor' in Jan. 1999. See HKJA, *Following The Flag*.

914 Following the university's inquiry, some (mainly pro-democracy) parties in the Legislative Council called, unsuccessfully, for a formal committee of inquiry to determine whether the Chief Executive himself had been party to the process of exerting pressure on Dr Chung. In the early days of the controversy, Mr Tung denied he had exerted any pressure on the university, but he also turned down a request to testify before the committee of inquiry, leaving observers wondering just what his role in fact was. See HKJA, *Following The Flag*.

915 Written communication with the author, Jan. 2003.

916 Ibid.

917 Ibid.

918 Ibid.

919 See /hkupop.hku.hk/chinese/columns/columns1.html. Accessed Jan. 2003; *Apple Daily*, 13 Jan.2003.

920 'Time for Mr. Tung to Step Up and Sit Back', editorial, *SCMP* 28 Feb. 2003.

921 Tung Chee-hwa stepped down as Chief Executive of Hong Kong in 2005. Donald Tsang is now the new Chief Executive.

922 Apart from leading lawyers, religious leaders, professionals, media publishers and executives, academics also took to the streets to protest. See '15 Academics Take to the Street', *Apple Daily* 15 July 2003.

923 Mainland Chinese might be misled since they mainly rely on official channels for information. 'Mainland Internet Users: Half a Million Taking to the Streets [of Hong Kong] was Mobilized by the West', *MPDN* 8 July 2003.

924 Regarding the Hong Kong rallies in July 2003, the mainland media were not allowed to report, although the Internet edition of the *People's Daily* briefly reported on the sacking of the two Hong Kong cabinet ministers without any reference to the contro-versies surrounding them. See Gabriel Kahn and Kathy Chen, 'Hong Kong Waits for Beijing to Respond to Political Crisis', *Wall Street Journal* 17 July 2003.

925 Martin Lee, 'Two Systems, One Destiny', *SCMP* 1 Aug. 2003.

926 Geoffrey York, 'Chinese Media Blast Bishop – Roman Catholic Leader, 71, is "Sowing the Seed of Discord"', State-run Newspapers Say', *The Globe and Mail* [Canada] 31 July 2003.

927 Keith Bradsher, 'Property Slump Ruins Many in Hong Kong', *The New York Times* 15 Aug. 2003.

928 'Two Major Surveys Show Protestors Well Educated; Ninety Percent of the Half-a-million Marchers Protest Against the National Security Bill', *Apple Daily* 7 July 2003; '500 Journalists Fight for Press Freedom', *HKEJ* 2 July 2003.

929 For instance, Tsang Yok-sing, the chairman of the pro-China political party, the

Democratic Alliance for the Betterment of Hong Kong (DAB), shifted his position by saying that in the wake of the peaceful protest, it might not be a bad idea to consider political reform.

930 Chris Yeung, 'Repairs Needed', *SCMP* 26 May 2003.

931 There was quite a wide range of foreign media interest in the HKSAR administration's consultation on the enactment of Basic Law article 23 and Hong Kong NGOs' protest and campaign against it. See web sites related to controversy over article 23 such as www.article23.com.

932 Many foreign media have played up the notion that the consultation on the proposed enactment of Basic Law article 23 has united both the mainstream and the minority opposition groups for the first time in Hong Kong's history, for instance, the banking community, the American and British Chambers of Commerce, Amnesty International and many other NGOs. See papers such as the *Financial Times, Asian Wall Street Journal*, the *Globe and Mail*, the *Vancouver Sun*, the *Toronto Star* and many more.

933 Bishop Zen was named as the 'conscience' of Hong Kong, an honour previously attributed to the retired Chief Secretary, Anson Chan, by the Anglo-American media, e.g. *Far Eastern Economic Review, Next Magazine*, 13 Mar. 2003.

934 Ian Holliday, Ma Ngok and Ray Yep, 'A High Degree of Autonomy?' 455–465.

7 Conclusion

935 Another example showing that the colonial government suppressed radical groups is the suppression of the 70 Bi-weekly (not the one run by Li Yi but that organised by Mok Chiu Yu etc.) in the early 1970s: written communication with the author, early 2004. However, in fact, the progressive groups were largely prohibited from launching new publications as the registration fee was as high as HK$10,000 in the late 1960s. See Chang Kuo-Sin, *A Survey of the Chinese Language Daily Press*. The registration fee was reduced to an annual fee of HK$785 only in the 1980s. See Li Kuk-Shing.

936 In an editorial in *Ming Pao Daily News* (*MPDN*), it said, 'Frankly speaking, we escaped here because we did not wish to live under Communist rule. ... Hong Kong is ruled by the British ... some people enjoy privileges; some are very rich, and some are very poor. ... Under the present circumstances, although Hong Kong has a thousand disadvantages and 10 thousand bad things, the majority of the population wishes to continue living here.' *MPDN*, 10 May 1967. Quoted in Cheung Kwai-Yeung, *Jin Yong (Louis Cha) and the Press* 150–151.

937 The first journalism department at the official higher education level was founded only when the New Asia College was integrated with two other colleges to form The Chinese University of Hong Kong in the mid-1960s. The Hong Kong Baptist College (which gained university status in the 1990s) also established a department of journalism in the 1960s. The other private higher education institutions offering journalism and communication programmes include Hong Kong Shue Yan College and Chu Hai College. See Clement Y. K. So and Joseph Man Chan, *Press and Politics in Hong Kong*.

938 Kuan Hsin-Chi and Lau Siu-kai, 'Mass Media and Politics in Hong Kong'.

939 Ian Scott.

940 Li Kuk-Shing.

941 See Anne Cheung, *Self-censorship*.

942 At one stage there was a surge in the publication of new political journals, news periodicals and newspapers, however, they dropped off one by one for financial or political reasons as 1997 approached, and in the post-handover period. See Chapters 5 and 6 and the appendix for details.

943 Paradoxically, this political space was in fact enhanced by the lack of democratic

development. The Hong Kong administration started to introduce partially elected members to the legislature only during the last stage of British rule. It was only once the British completed negotiations with the Chinese, and it became clear that Hong Kong would have to return to Chinese rule in 1997, that the British authorities changed their approach. Still, due to Chinese opposition, constitutional reform did not involve universal suffrage, nor did it proceed quickly. In addition, the Hong Kong people were not represented in any kind of Sino-British negotiations on Hong Kong affairs. With a lack of representative government, and fledgling party politics, the press took up a more significant role. See Chapters 3 and 5 for more details.

944 For example, the Beijing-funded *Ta Kung Pao.*
945 An issue that is discussed in more detail in the next section of this chapter.
946 See Chapters 3 and 6 for details.
947 See Chapter 5 for details.
948 Eric Kit-wai Ma, 'Rethinking Media Studies: The Case of China', *De-westernizing Media Studies*, eds James Curran and Myung-Jin Park (London: Routledge, 2000): 21–34.
949 See Chapter 5 for details.
950 For instance, the British continued to attempt to carry out constitutional reform without China's consent. In the meantime the Chinese authorities set up a provisional legislature in the nearby Special Economic Zone of Shenzhen to oversee Hong Kong policy following 1997, and Beijing also claimed that the legislation passed ahead of 1997 would be discarded on the day of the handover.
951 As shown in Chapter 3 in the analysis of the news coverage of the Xi Yang case, the tone of the news media tended to be conciliatory as 1997 approached.
952 For example, pollster-columnist, Dr. Robert Chung, made use of his column in the *SCMP* to expose the pressure from above to stop him from conducting a survey and revealing results unfavourable to the HKSAR administration and the Chief Executive, Tung Chee-wah. There was evidence that pressure was exerted through the Vice-chancellor of the University of Hong Kong. See Chapter 6 for details.
953 In the wake of Donald Tsang becoming Hong Kong Chief Executive in June 2005, following Tung Chee-hwa's resignation in March 2005, there were reports that Donald was asked by Beijing to clean up RTHK, ICAC and the judiciary. The formation of the review committee was secret until the announcement was formally made in January 2006. The committee consists of a seven-member body – chaired by Ray Wong and six others. None has public service broadcasting experience – five have experience in commercial media, one is an artist (Matthias Woo) and one has a business background (Judy Tsui). 'RTHK – History, Struggle for Press Freedom and the Current Government Review', talk by Cliff Bale (acting head, English Newsroom, RTHK), University of Macau, 28 April 2006.
954 For example, Willy Lam joined *CNN* as senior China analyst after resigning from *SCMP*; Danny Gittings moved on to *Asian Wall Street Journal* as deputy opinion-editorial page editor; Jasper Becker joined London *Independent* as Beijing Correspondent. Those less fortunate had to change career, e.g. Paul Cheung began to read for a law degree after being sacked by *Metro Broadcast.*
955 See Chapter 6 for details.
956 For example, in *Apple Daily*'s numerous reports on the movement of mainland Chinese sex workers to Hong Kong and their operations.
957 Article 23 of the mini-constitution of Hong Kong Basic Law stipulates that Hong Kong would enact local law to protect its national security.
958 For example, Willy Lam, former associate editor of *SCMP*, and Paul Cheung, news controller, *Metro Broadcast.*
959 Conversation with Albert Cheng, 5 May 2004, London. Also, see Keith Bradsher, 'Second Hong Kong Democracy Figure Leaves Hastily', *New York Times* 15 May 2004.

960 Albert Cheng, 'Dwindling Freedom of Speech', *SCMP* 17 May 2004.
961 Albert Cheng, 'On the brink of a Dark Age', *SCMP* 24 May 2004. Also see 'HK Radio Hosts Bow to Pressure', *BBC News, Hong Kong* 13 May 2004. news.bbc.co.uk/1/hi/world/asia-pacific/3711747.stm. Accessed 17 May 2004.
962 Albert Cheng and Raymond Wong have now left *Commercial Radio*. See *Annual Report on Freedom of Expression in Hong Kong*, Hong Kong Journalists Association, 2006.
963 News Report, *ODN* 23 May 2004.
964 For example, Colin Sparks, *Communism, Capitalism and the Mass Media*.
965   For example, the collective resignation of six senior producers at *ATV* in protest against management interference with an editorial decision. See Chapters 5 and 6 for a detailed analysis.
966 For example, when *SCMP* attempted to sideline a senior editor, Willy Lam, under the guise of a reorganisation of the newsroom, Lam chose to quit and expose self-censorship within the organisation. However, in another instance, Paul Cheung, news controller of *Metro Broadcast*, informed the author that if it had not been for the economic situation, he would not have put up with the pressure exerted on him. See Chapters 5 and 6 for details.

Bibliography

Primary materials

De-classified files of Colonial Office, Foreign and Commonwealth Office, 1967–1970, Public Record Office, Kew, London

Colonial Office files

CO 21/717
CO 1030/595
CO 1030/584
CO 1030/1107
CO 1030/1108
CO 1030/1114

Foreign and Commonwealth Office files

FCO 21/209
FCO 21/227
FCO 21/716
FCO 40/63
FCO 40/74
FCO 40/75–76
FCO 40/88
FCO 40/105–106
FCO 40/113
FCO 40/113–115
FCO 40/114
FCO 40/146
FCO 40/149
FCO 40/252
FCO 40/253
FCO 40/264
FCO 40/292

Books and articles

'A Brief History of the Hong Kong Journalists Association's (HKJA) Campaign for Media Law Reform – A Lobby Document'. HKJA 2 Dec. 1995.

Anderson, Benedict. *Imagined Communities: Reflections on the Origin and Spread of Nationalism*. Rev. edn. London and New York: Verso, 1983.

Annual General Meeting (AGM) of HKJA on June 25, 1985 in the Foreign Correspondents' Club (FCC), AGM minutes.

Bagdikian, Ben H. *The Media Monopoly; with a New Preface on the Internet and Communication Cartels*. Boston, Mass.: Beacon Press, 2000.

Bale, Cliff. 'Access to Information – How the Campaign Started'. Lobbying Article, Hong Kong Journalists Association, Feb. 1995.

Beja, Jean Philippe. 'Hong Kong Politics One Year On: Worst Case Scenario Fails to Materialise'. *China Perspective* 18 (July/Aug. 1998): 6–11.

Bonavia, David. *Hong Kong 1997*. Bromley, Kent (Britain): Columbus Books, 1984.

Boardman, Robert. *Britain and the People's Republic of China, 1949–1974*. London: Macmillan, 1976.

Bray, Denis. *Hong Kong Metamorphosis*. Hong Kong: Hong Kong UP, 2001.

Brook, Timothy and B. Michael Frolic, eds *Civil Society in China*. New York: M. E. Sharpe, 1997.

Butler, Tim and Mike Savage, eds *Social Change and the Middle Classes*. London: ULC Press, 1995.

Butenhoff, Linda. *Social Movements and Political Reform in Hong Kong*. Westport, CT: Praeger, 1999.

Byrd, Peter, ed. *British Foreign Policy under Thatcher*. Oxford: Philip Allan, 1988.

Cai, Qing. 'Journalism as Politics: Reporting on Hong Kong's Handover in the Chinese Press'. *Journalism Studies* 1.4 (2000): 665–678.

Calhoun, C., ed. *Habermas and the Public Sphere*. Cambridge, MA: MIT Press, 1992.

Chalaby, Jean. 'Journalism as an Anglo-American Invention'. *European Journal of Communication* 11 (1996): 303–326.

Chan, Chong-fung. 'A Study of Hong Kong Press after the Second World War'. Diss. Beijing U. 1996.

Chan, Joseph M. 'Media Internationalization in China: Processes and Tensions'. *Journal of Communication* 44:3 (1994): 70–88.

Chan, Joseph Man. 'When Capitalist and Socialist Television Clash: The Impact of Hong Kong TV on Guangzhou Residents'. *Power, Money and Media*. Ed. Chin-Chuan Lee. Evanston, IL: Northwestern UP, 2000: 245–270.

Chan, Joseph M. and Chin-Chuan Lee. 'Press Ideology and Organisational Control in Hong Kong'. *Communication Research* 15.2 (1988): 185–197.

Chan, Joseph Man and Chin-Chuan Lee. *Mass Media and Political Transition in Hong Kong: The Hong Kong Press in China's Orbit*. New York: Guilford Press, 1991.

Chan, Joseph Man, Paul S. N. Lee and Chin-Chuan Lee. *Hong Kong Journalists in Transition*. Hong Kong: Hong Kong Institute of Asia-Pacific Studies, Chinese UP, 1996.

Chan, Joseph Man, Eric K. W. Ma and Clement Y. K. So. 'Back to the Future: A Retrospect and Prospects for the Hong Kong Mass Media'. *The Other Hong Kong Report 1997*. Ed. Joseph Y. S. Cheng. Hong Kong: Chinese UP, 1997: 455–482.

Chan, Joseph M. and To Yiu-ming. 'Democratization, Reunification and Press Freedom in Hong Kong: A Critical Event Analysis of the Xi Yang Case'. *Press and Politics in*

Hong Kong: Case Studies from 1967 to 1997. Eds Clement Y. K. So and Joseph M. Chan. Hong Kong Institute of Asia-Pacific Studies, Hong Kong: The Chinese UP, 1999: 465–496.

Chan, Lau Kit-ching. *China, Britain and Hong Kong 1895–1945*. Hong Kong: Chinese UP, 1990.

Chan, Lau Kit-ching. *From Nothing to Nothing: the Chinese Communist Movement and Hong Kong, 1921–36*. London: Hurst & Co., 1999.

Chan, Ming K., eds *Precarious Balance: Hong Kong between China and Britain, 1842–1992* (with the collaboration of John D. Young). Armonk, NY: M. E. Sharpe, 1994.

Chan, Ming K. and Tuen-yu Lau. 'Dilemma of the Communist Press in a Pluralistic Society: Hong Kong in the Transition to Chinese Sovereignty'. *Asian Survey* 30.8 (1990): 731–747.

Chan, Wai Kwan. *The Making of Hong Kong Society – 3 Studies of Class Formation in Early Hong Kong*. New York: Oxford UP, 1991.

Chan, Wendy W. Y. 'Home but not Home: A case study of some Canadian Returnees in Hong Kong'. Diss. Hong Kong U. of Science and Technology, 1996.

Chang, Kuo-sin. *A Survey of the Chinese Language Daily Press*. Hong Kong: International Press Institute, 1968.

Chang, Kuo-sin. 'Hong Kong', *Newspapers in Asia: Contemporary Trends and Problems*. Ed. John A. Lend. Hong Kong: Heineman Asia, 1982.

Chang, Kwai-yeung. *Jin Rong (Louis Cha) and The Press*. Hong Kong [Chinese]: Ming Pao Publishing, 2000.

Cheek-Milby, Kathleen. *A Legislature Comes of Age: Hong Kong's Search for Influence and Identity*. Hong Kong: Oxford UP, 1995.

Chen, X. and Shi T. 'Media Effects on Political Confidence and Trust in the People's Republic of China in the Post-Tiananmen Period'. *East Asia* 19.3 (2001): 84–118.

Cheng, Joseph. *Hong Kong: In Search of a Future*. Hong Kong: Oxford University Press, 1984.

Cheung, Anne. *Self-censorship and the Struggle for Press Freedom in Hong Kong*. The Hague, Netherlands; New York: Kluwer Law International, 2003.

Cheung, Anthony B. L. *et al. Class Analysis and Hong Kong*. Hong Kong [Chinese]: Literary Youth Books, 1988.

Cheung, Kar-wai. *Inside Story of 1967 Riot in Hong Kong*. Hong Kong [Chinese]: Pacific Century Press, 2000.

Cheung, Kwai-yeung. *Jin Yong (Louis Cha) and the Press*. Hong Kong [Chinese]: Ming Pao Publishing, 2000.

Ching, Cheong. 'China's Administration over Hong Kong – the New China News Agency and the Hong Kong-Macau Affairs Office'. *The Other Hong Kong Report*. Eds Nyaw Mee-kau and Li Si-ming. Hong Kong: Chinese UP, 1996: 111–128.

Ching, Frank. 'The Hong Kong Press: A Post-1997 Assessment'. *Hong Kong the Super Paradox: Life after Return to China*. Ed. J. C. Hsiung. New York: St. Martin's Press, 2000: 153–170.

Chiu, Stephen W. K., K. C. Ho and Tai-lok Lui. *City-States in the Global Economy: Industrial Restructuring in Hong Kong and Singapore*. Boulder, CO: Westview Press, 1997.

Chiu, Stephen W. K. and Ho-fung Hung. *The Colonial State and Rural Protests in Hong Kong*. Hong Kong: Hong Kong Institute of Asia-Pacific Studies, Chinese UP, 1997.

Chiu, Stephen W. K. and Tai-lok Lui. 'Testing the Global City-social Polarisation Thesis: Hong Kong since the 1990s'. *Urban Studies* 41.10 (Sept. 2004): 1863–1889.

Chomsky, Noam and David Barsmian. *Propaganda and the Public Mind*. London: Pluto, 2001.

Chomsky, Noam and Edward Herman. *Manufacturing Consent: The Political Economy of the Mass Media*. New York: Pantheon, 1988.

Chow, Yi. *A History of Hong Kong Leftist Struggle*. Hong Kong [Chinese]: Leeman, 2002.

Chu, G. C. and Ju, Y. *The Great Wall in Ruins: Communications and Cultural Change in China*. Albany: New York State UP, 1993.

Chu, Leonard L. 'Hong Kong Media System in Transition: A Socio-Cultural Analysis'. *Asian Journal of Communication* 5.2 (1995): 90–107.

Chu, Leonard L. 'From British to Chinese "One Country, Two Systems"'. *Ming Pao Monthly* May 1997: 30–34.

Chu, Leonard L. and Paul S. N. Lee. 'Political Communication in Hong Kong: Transition, Adaptation, and Survival'. *Asian Journal of Communication* 5.2 (1995): 1–17.

Chun, Allen. 'From Nationalism to Nationalizing: Cultural Imagination and State Formation in Post-war Taiwan'. *Chinese Nationalism*. Ed. Jonathan Unger. New York: M. E. Sharpe, 1996: 126–147.

Chung, Sze-yuen. *Hong Kong's Journey to Reunification: Memoirs of Sze-yuen Chung*. Hong Kong: Chinese UP, 2001.

Clayton, David. *Imperialism Revisited: Political and Economic Relations Between Britain and China, 1950–54*. Basingstoke (Britain): Macmillan, in association with King's College London, 1997.

Cohen, Myron L. 'Being Chinese: The Peripheralisation of Traditional Identity'. *The Living Tree – The Changing Meaning of Being Chinese Today*. Ed. Tu Wei-ming. Stanford, CA.: Stanford UP, 1994: 88–108.

Cooper, John. *Colony in Conflict: The Hong Kong Disturbances, May 1967–Jan. 1968*. Hong Kong: Swindon, 1970.

Couldry, Nick. *The Place of Media Power*. London: Routledge, 2000.

Couldry, Nick and James Curran, eds *Contesting Media Power*. London: Rowman and Littlefield, 2003.

Cradock, Percy. *Experiences of China*. London: John Murray, 1994.

Crane, George T. ' "Special Things in Special Ways": National Economic Identity and China's Special Economic Zones'. *Chinese Nationalism*. Ed. Jonathan Unger. Armonk, NY: M. E. Sharpe, 1996: 148–168.

Curran, James. 'Introduction'. *Mass Communication and Society*. eds James Curran *et al.* London: Edward Arnold, 1977: 9–11.

Curran, James. 'Communication, Power and Social Order'. *Culture, Society and the Media*. Eds Michael Gurevitch *et al.* London: Routledge, 1982: 202–235.

Curran, James. 'Mass Media and Democracy Revisited'. *Mass Media and Society*. Eds James Curran and Michael Gurevitch. London; New York: Arnold, 1996: 81–119.

Curran, James, Introduction. *Media Organization in Society*. Ed. James Curran. London: Edward Arnold, 2000: 9–16.

Curran, James. *Media and Power*. London and New York: Routledge, 2002.

Curran, James, Michael Gurevitch and Janet Woollacott. 'The Study of the Media: Theoretical Approaches'. *Culture, Society and the Media*. Eds Michael Gurevitch *et al.* London: Routledge, 1982: 11–29.

Curran, James and Myung-Jin Park. eds *De-westernizing Media Studies*. London: Routledge, 2000.

Curran, James and Jean Seaton. *Power without Responsibility, 6th edition*. London: Routledge, 2003.

Dahlgren, Peter and Colin Sparks, eds *Communication and Citizenship: Journalism and the Public Sphere in the New Media Age*. London: Routledge, 1991.

Dayan, Daniel and Elihu Katz. *Media Events: The Live Broadcasting of History*. Cambridge, Mass.: Harvard University Press, 1992.

De Burgh, Hugo. *The Chinese Journalist: Mediating Information in the World's Most Populous Country*. London; New York, NY Routledge, 2003.

De Burgh, Hugo. 'Great Aspirations and Conventional Repertoires: Chinese Regional Television Journalists and their Work'. *Journalism Studies* 4.2 (2003): 225–238.

Deacon *et al. Researching Communications: A Practical Guide to Methods in Media and Cultural Analysis*. London: Arnold, 1999.

Deng, Xiaoping. *Build Socialism with Chinese Characteristics*. Beijing: Foreign Languages Press, 1985.

Deng, Xiaoping. *Deng Xiaoping Wen Xuan*. Vol. 3. Beijing [Chinese]: Renmin, 1993.

Dittmer, Lowell and Samuel S. Kim. 'In Search of a Theory of National Identity'. *China's Quest for National Identity*. Eds Lowell Dittmer and Samuel S. Kim. Ithaca and London: Cornell UP, 1993: 1–31.

Domes, Jurgen. 'Hong Kong after the Handover to China: Background and Perspectives. A Thematic Survey'. *Hong Kong after Reunification – Problems and Perspectives*. Eds Achim Gussgen, Reimund Seidelmann and Ting Wai. Germany: Nomos Verlagsgesellschaft, Baden-Baden, 2000: 15–24.

Ericson, Richard V., Patricia M. Baranek and Janet B. C. Chan. *Negotiating Control: A Study of News Sources*. Toronto: University of Toronto Press, 1989.

Evans, Harold. *Good Times, Bad Times*. London: Weidenfeld and Nicholson, 1983.

Fenby, Jonathan. *Dealing with the Dragon – a Year in the New Hong Kong*. London: Little, Brown, 2000.

Fitzgerald, C. P. *The Birth of Communist China*. Harmondsworth, England: Penguin, 1964.

Fitzgerald, John. 'The Search for a Nationalism in Modern Chinese Nationalism'. *Chinese Nationalism*. Ed. Jonathan Unger. Armonk, NY: M. E. Sharpe, 1996: 56–85.

Fitzgerald, Stephen. *China and the Overseas Chinese: A Study of Peking's Changing Policy, 1949–70*. Cambridge: Cambridge UP, 1972.

Friedman, Edward. 'A Democratic Chinese Nationalism?' *Chinese Nationalism*. Ed. Jonathan Unger. Armonk, NY: M. E. Sharpe, 1996: 169–182.

Fung, Anthony, Clement So, Joseph Man Chan and Chin Chuan Lee. *Press Freedom and Political Transition in Hong Kong: The Hong Kong Journalist Survey, 1996*. Hong Kong: Hong Kong Institute of Asia-Pacific Studies, Chinese UP, 1997.

Gans, Herbert. *Deciding What's News: A Study of CBS Evening News, NBC Nightly News, 'Newsweek' and 'Time'*. London: Constable, 1980.

Gans, Herbert J. 'Reopening the Black Box: Toward a Limited Effects Theory'. *Journal of Communication* 43 (1993): 32–33.

Gans, Herbert. *Democracy and the News*. New York: Oxford University Press, 2002.

Garnham, Nicholas. *Capitalism and Communism*. London: Sage, 1990.

Ghai, Yash. 'Nationality and Right of Abode'. *The Hong Kong Law Journal* 26.2 (1996): 155–161.

Ghai, Yash. *Hong Kong's New Constitutional Order, The Resumption of Chinese Sovereignty and the Basic Law*. Hong Kong: Hong Kong UP, 1997.

Giddens, Anthony. *The Nation-State and Violence*. Cambridge: Cambridge UP, 1989.

Gitlin, Todd. *The Whole World is Watching*. Berkeley: University of California Press, 1980.

Gitlin, Todd. *Inside Prime Time*. New York: Pantheon, 1983.

Gitlin, Todd. *Media Unlimited: How the Torrent of Images and Sounds Overwhelms Our Lives*. New York: H. Holt, 2003.

Glasgow University Media Group, *Bad News*. London: Routledge, 1976.

Golding, Peter. 'The Missing Dimensions: News Media and the Management of Social Change'. *Mass Media and Social Change*. Eds E. Katz and T. Szecsko. London: Sage, 1981: 63–82.

Golding, Peter and G. Murdock. 'Culture, Communication and Political Economy'. *Mass Media and Society*. Eds J. Curran and M. Gurevitch. London: Edward Arnold, 1996: 11–30.

Grantham, Alexander. *Via Ports: From Hong Kong to Hong Kong*. Hong Kong: Hong Kong UP, 1965.

Graham, Katharine. *Personal History*. New York: Random House, 1997.

Grey, Anthony. *Hostage in Peking*. London: Michael Joseph, 1970.

Habermas, Jürgen. *The Structural Transformation of the Public Sphere*. Cambridge, MA: MIT Press, 1989.

Hall, Stuart, *et al. Policing the Crisis*. London: Macmillan, 1978.

Hallin, Daniel C. *The 'Uncensored War': The Media and Vietnam*. New York: Oxford University Press, 1986.

Hallin, Daniel C. *We Keep America on Top of the World*. London: Routledge, 1994.

Hallin, Daniel. 'Political Clientelism and the Media: Southern Europe and Latin America in Comparative Perspective'. *Media, Culture and Society* 24.2 (2002): 175–195.

Hamilton, Gary G. 'Overseas Chinese Capitalism'. *Confucian Traditions in East Asian Modernity*. Ed. Tu Wei-ming. Cambridge: Harvard UP, 1996: 328–342.

Hansen *et al. Mass Communication Research Methods*. London: Macmillan, 1997.

Hardt, Hanno. *Critical Communication Studies*. London: Routledge, 1992.

Harris, Peter B. *Hong Kong: A Study in Bureaucratic Politics*. Hong Kong: Heinemann Asia, 1976.

Herman, Edward S. and Robert McChesney. *The Global Media: The New Missionaries and Corporate Capitalism*. London; Washington, DC: Cassell, 1997.

Hetherington, Alastair. *News, Newspapers and Television*. Macmillan, 1985.

Ho, Andy. 'On Teacup in a Storm'. *Media Digest*, RTHK. July 2003. www.rthk.org.hk/mediadigest/20030715_76_90205.html. Accessed 16 Feb. 2005.

Hobsbawm, E. J. *Nations and Nationalism since 1780: Programme, Myth, Reality*. Cambridge: Cambridge UP, 1990.

Hoe, Susanna. *The Taking of Hong Kong: Charles and Clara Elliot in China Waters*. Richmond (Britain): Curzon Press, 1999.

Holliday, Ian, Ma Ngok and Ray Yep. 'A High Degree of Autonomy? Hong Kong Special Administrative Region, 1997–2002'. *Political Quarterly* 73.4 (Oct.–Dec. 2002) 455–465.

Hong Kong Journalists Association and Article 19. *Urgent Business: Hong Kong, Freedom of Expression and 1997: Joint Report of Article 19 and the HKJA*. London: Article 19, 1993.

Hong Kong Journalists Association and Article 19. *Freedom of Expression in Hong Kong: 1994 Annual Report*. London: Article 19, International Centre against Censorship, 1994.

Hong Kong Journalists Association and Article 19. *Broken Promises: Freedom of Expression in Hong Kong, 1995 Annual Report*. Hong Kong: Article 19 and HKJA, 1995.

Hong Kong Journalists Association and Article 19. *The Die is Cast: Annual Report on Freedom of Expression*. Hong Kong: Article 19 and HKJA, 1997.

Hong Kong Journalists Association and Article 19. *Questionable Beginnings: Freedom of Expression in Hong Kong One Year After the Handover to China, 1998 Annual Report*. Hong Kong: Article 19 and HKJA, 1998.

Hong Kong Journalists Association and Article 19. *The Ground Rules Change: Freedom of Expression in Hong Kong Two Years After the Handover to China, 1999 Annual Report*. Hong Kong: Article 19 and HKJA, 1999.

Hong Kong Journalists Association and Article 19. *Patriot Games: Hong Kong's Media Face to Face with the Taiwan Factor, 2000 Annual Report*. Hong Kong: Article 19 and HKJA, 2000.

Hong Kong Journalists Association and Article 19. *Following The Flag: China's Sensitivities Threaten Freedom of Expression in Hong Kong, 2001 Annual Report*. Hong Kong: Article 19 and HKJA, 2001.

Hong Kong Journalists Association and Article 19. *The Line Hardens: Tougher Stance on Civil Rights Threatens Freedom of Expression in Hong Kong*. Hong Kong: Article 19 and HKJA, 2002.

Hong Kong Journalists Association and Article 19. *False Security: Hong Kong's National Security Laws Pose a Grave Threat to Freedom of Expression, 2003 Annual Report*. Hong Kong: Article 19 and HKJA, 2003.

Hong Kong Journalists Association and Article 19, *Beijing Turns the Screws: Freedom of Expression in Hong Kong Under Attack*. Hong Kong: HKJA and Article 19, 2004.

Hong Kong Journalists Association. 'Report by the Ad Hoc Group to Inquire into the Complaint of Paul Cheung'. *The Journalist*. HKJA (May 2003): 33–39.

Hong Kong – Report of the Year 1967. Hong Kong Government Press, 1968.

Hughes, Christopher. *Taiwan and Chinese Nationalism: National Identity and Status in International Society*. London: Routledge, 1997.

Hughes, Christopher. 'Post-nationalist Taiwan'. *Asian Nationalism*. Ed. Michael Leifer. London: Routledge, 2000: 63–81.

Hui, Po-keung. 'Comprador Politics and Middleman Capitalism'. *Hong Kong's History – State and Society under Colonial Rule*. Ed. Tak-Wing Ngo. London: Routledge, 1999: 30–45.

Hutcheon, Robin. *SCMP: The First Eighty Years*. Hong Kong: *South China Morning Post*, 1983.

Jain, Jagdish Prasad. *China in World Politics: a Study of Sino-British Relations, 1949–1975*. London: Martin Robertson, 1977.

Johnson, Chalmers A. *Peasant Nationalism and Communist Power: The Emergence of Revolutionary China, 1937–1945*. Stanford: Stanford UP, 1962.

Johannesburg Principles, National Security, Freedom of Expression and Access to Information (Nov. 1996). (This paper was originally published in October 1995 following an international consultation convened by Article 19, the International Centre Against Censorship, in collaboration with the Centre for Applied Legal Studies of the University of the Witwatersrand in Johannesburg).

Kaiser, Wolfram and Gillian Staerck, eds *British Foreign Policy, 1955–1964: Contracting Options*. Basingstoke: Macmillan, in association with the Institute of Contemporary British History, 2000.

Kam, Yiu-yu. *The Secret of the Chinese Communist Party's Policy on Hong Kong*. Hong Kong [Chinese]: Tien Yuan Publishing, 1998.

Kaniss, Phyllis. *Making Local News*. London: Chicago UP, 1991.

Keane, John. *The Media and Democracy*. Cambridge, Mass.: Polity Press, 1991.

Keay, John. *Last Post: The End of Empire in the Far East*. London: John Murray, 1997.

Kee, P. K. and R. Skeldon. 'The Migration and Settlement of Hong Kong Chinese in Australia'. *Reluctant Exiles? Migration from Hong Kong and the New Overseas Chinese*. Ed. R. Skeldon. New York: M. E. Sharpe; and Hong Kong: Hong Kong UP, 1994: 183–196.

Kennedy, Paul M. *The Realities Behind Diplomacy: Background Influences on British External Policy, 1865–1980*. London: Fontana, 1981.

King, Ambrose Y. C. 'The Administrative Absorption of Politics in Hong Kong'. *Asian Survey* 15 (1975) 422–439.

King, Ambrose Yeo-Chi. 'Kuan-hsi and Network Building: A Sociological Interpretation'. Ed. Tu Wei-ming. *The Living Tree – The Changing Meaning of Being Chinese Today*. Stanford, CA: Stanford UP, 1994: 109–126.

Knight, Alan and Yoshiko Nakano, eds *Reporting Hong Kong: Foreign Media and the Handover*. Richmond (Britain): Curzon, 1999.

Kuan, Hsin-chi and Lau Siu-kai. 'Mass Media and Politics in Hong Kong'. *Press and Politics in Hong Kong: Case Studies from 1967 to 1997*. Eds Clement Y. K. So and Joseph M. Chan. Hong Kong Institute of Asia-Pacific Studies, Hong Kong: Chinese UP, 1999: 277–298.

Lai, Carol and Andy Ho. 'How Free is the Press?' *Hong Kong China: the Red Dawn*. Ed. Chris Yeung. Australia: Prentice Hall, 1998: 195–204.

Lai, Carol Pui-yee, 'Interview with Ip Yat-kin'. *On the Record* (HKJA 1996).

Lai, Carol Pui-yee. 'Questionable Beginnings: Hong Kong Press'. *Hong Kong after Reunification – Problems and Perspectives*. Eds Achim Gussgen, Reimund Seidelmann and Ting Wai. Germany: Nomos Verlagsgesellschaft, Baden-Baden, 2000: 133–144.

Lai, Carina. 'Watching China: A Major Hong Kong Newspaper's Contrasting Views of China (1991 and 2001)'. Diss. Tufts University (July–August, 2002).

Lam, Willy Wo-lap. *China after Deng Xiaoping – The Power Struggle in Beijing Since Tiananmen*. New York: John Wiley & Sons, 1995.

Lam, Willy Wo-lap. 'Government – Beijing's Hong Kong Policy in the First Year of Transition'. *Hong Kong China: the Red Dawn*. Ed. Chris Yeung. Australia: Prentice Hall, 1998: 23–44.

Lam, Willy. 'One-Country Two-Systems After "7–1"'. China Brief. *Jamestown Journal* 29 July 2003. www.jamestown.org/publications_details.php?volume_id=19&issue_id =680&article_id+4754.

Lam, Kit Chun and Liu Pak Wai. *Immigration and the Economy of Hong Kong*. Hong Kong: City UP, 1998.

Lam, Kit-chun, Yiu-kwan Fan and Ronald Skeldon. 'The Tendency to Emigrate From Hong Kong'. *Emigration from Hong Kong*. Ed. Ronald Skeldon. Hong Kong: The Chinese UP, 1995: 135–146.

Lane, Kevin P. *Sovereignty and The Status Quo: The Historical Roots of China's Hong Kong Policy*. Boulder: Westview Press, 1990.

Lau, C. K. *Hong Kong's Colonial Legacy – A Hong Kong Chinese's View of the British Heritage*. Hong Kong: Chinese UP, 1997.

Lau, Emily. 'The News Media'. *Hong Kong in Transition*. Ed. Joseph Y. S. Cheng. Hong Kong: Oxford UP, 1986: 420–446.

Lau, Siu-Kai. *Society and Politics in Hong Kong*. Hong Kong: Chinese UP, 1982.

Lau, Siu-kai. 'Social Change, Bureaucratic Rule, and Emergent Political Issues in Hong Kong'. *World Politics* 35.4 (1983): 544–562.

Lau, Siu-kai. 'Decolonization Without Independence'. Occasional Paper 19. Hong Kong: Centre for Hong Kong Studies, Chinese UP, 1987.

Lau, Siu-kai. 'The Unfinished Political Reforms of the Hong Kong Government'. *The Changing Shape of Government in the Asia-Pacific Region*. Eds John Langford and K. Lorne Brownsey. Victoria: The Institute for Research on Public Policy, 1988. 43–82.

Lau, Siu-kai. 'Institutions Without Leaders: Hong Kong Chinese View of Political Leadership'. *Pacific Affairs* 63.2 (1990): 191–209.

Lau, Siu-kai. 'Decolonization Without Independence and the Poverty of Political Leadership in Hong Kong'. Occasional Paper 1. Hong Kong: Hong Kong Institute of Asia-Pacific Studies, Chinese UP, 1990.

Lau, Siu-kai. 'Social Irrelevance of Politics: Hong Kong Chinese Attitudes toward Political Leadership'. *Pacific Affairs* 65.2 (1992): 225–246.

Lau, Siu-kai. 'Public Attitude Toward Political Parties in Hong Kong'. Occasional Paper 11. Hong Kong: Hong Kong Institute of Asia-Pacific Studies, Chinese UP, 1992.

Lau, Siu-kai. 'Public Attitude Toward Political Leadership in Hong Kong: The Formation of Political Leaders'. *Asian Survey* 34.3 (1994): 243–257.

Lau, Siu-kai. 'Hong Kong's Path of Democratization'. *Swiss Asian Studies*, XLIX. 1 (1995): 71–90.

Lau, Siu-kai. 'Democratization and Decline of Trust in Public Institutions in Hong Kong'. *Democratization* 3.2 (1996): 158–180.

Lau, Siu-kai. 'Decolonization à la Hong Kong: Britain's Search for Governability and Exit with Glory in Hong Kong'. *The Journal of Commonwealth and Comparative Politics* 35.2 (1997): 28–54.

Lau, Siu-kai. 'Hongkongese or Chinese: The Problem of Identity on the Eve of Resumption of Chinese Sovereignty over Hong Kong'. Occasional Paper 65. Hong Kong: Hong Kong Institute of Asia-Pacific Studies, Chinese UP, 1997.

Lau, Siu-kai. *Democratization, Poverty of Political Leaders, and Political Inefficacy in Hong Kong*. Hong Kong: Hong Kong Institute of Asia-Pacific Studies, Chinese UP, 1998.

Lau, Siu-kai. 'Government and Political Change in the HKSAR'. *Hong Kong the Super Paradox: Life after Return to China*. Ed. James C. Hsiung. New York: St. Martin's Press, 2000: 35–58.

Lau, Siu-kai. 'The Hong Kong Policy of the People's Republic of China, 1994–1997'. *Journal of Contemporary China* 9.23 (2000): 77–94.

Lau, Siu-kai and Kuan Hsin-chi. *Chinese Bureaucrats in a Modern Colony: The Case of Hong Kong*. Hong Kong: Centre for Hong Kong Studies, Chinese UP, 1986.

Lau, Siu-kai and Kuan Hsin-chi. *The Ethos of Hong Kong Chinese*. Hong Kong: Chinese UP, 1988.

Lau, Siu-kai and Kuan Hsin-chi. 'The Partial Vision of Democracy in Hong Kong: A Survey of Political Opinion'. *China Journal* 34 (July 1995) 239–264.

Lee, Alice Y. L. 'The Role of Newspapers in the 1967 Riot: A Case Study of the Partisanship of the Hong Kong Press'. *Press and Politics in Hong Kong – Case Studies from 1967 to 1997*. Eds Clement Y. K. So and Joseph Man Chan. Hong Kong: Hong Kong Institute of Asia-Pacific Studies, Chinese UP, 1999: 33–66.

Lee, Chin-Chuan. 'Chinese Communication: Prisms, Trajectories, and Modes of Understanding'. *Power, Money and Media: Communication Patterns and Bureaucratic Control in Cultural China*. Ed. C. C. Lee. Evanston, IL: Northwestern UP, 2000: 3–44.

Lee, Chin-Chuan. 'The Paradox of Political Economy: Media Structure, Press Freedom, and Regime Change in Hong Kong'. *Power, Money and Media: Communication Patterns and Bureaucratic Control in Cultural China*. Ed. C. C. Lee. Evanston, IL: Northwestern UP, 2000: 288–336.

Lee, Chin-Chuan. 'China's Journalism: The Emancipatory Potential of Social Theory'. *Journalism Studies* 1.4 (2000): 559–575.

Lee, Chin-Chuan. 'Partisan Press Coverage of Government News in Hong Kong'. *Journalism Quarterly* 62: 770–776.

Lee, Chin-Chuan. 'Liberalization without Full Democracy: Guerrilla Media and Political Movement in Taiwan'. *Contesting Media Power*. Eds Nick Couldry and James Curran. London: Rowman and Littlefield, 2003: 163–176.

Lee, Chin-Chuan, ed. *Chinese Media, Global Contexts*. London: Routledge, 2003.

Lee, Chin-Chuan *et al. Global Media Spectacle: News War Over Hong Kong*. New York: State University of New York, 2002.

Lee, Chin-Chuan, Pan, Z., Chan, J. and So, C. 'Through the Eyes of U.S. Media*'. Journal of Communication* 51.2 (2001): 345–365.

Lee, Francis L. F. 'Radio Phone-in Talk Shows as Politically Significant Infotainment in Hong Kong'. *Harvard International Journal of Press/Politics* 7.4 (2002): 57–79.

Lee, Kar Yuan. *Hong Kong Press History*. Hong Kong [Chinese]: Joint Publishing (H.K.) Co., Ltd.

Lee, Ming-kwan. 'Politicians'. *The Other Hong Kong Report 1990*. Eds Y. C. Wong and Joseph Y. S. Cheng. Hong Kong: Chinese UP, 1990: 113–130.

Lee, Ming-kwan. 'Whither Hong Kong's Middle Class?' *Hong Kong in China: The Challenge of Transition*. Eds Wang Gungwu and John Wong. Singapore: Times Academia Press, 1999: 231–244.

Lee, Ming-kwan. 'Community and Identity in Transition in Hong Kong'. *The Hong Kong-Guangdong Link: Partnership in Flux*. Eds Reginald Kwok and Alvin So. Armonk and London: M. E. Sharpe (1995): 119–134.

Lee, Ming-kwan. 'Hong Kong Identity – Past and Present'. *Hong Kong Economy and Society: Challenges in the New Era*. Eds Wong Siu-lun and T. Maruya. Hong Kong: Centre of Asian Studies, Hong Kong UP, 1998: 153–175.

Lee, Ming-kwan. 'Becoming Chinese Citizens'. *Indicators of Social Development – Hong Kong 1997*. Eds Lau Siu-kai *et al.* Hong Kong: Hong Kong Institute of Asia-Pacific Studies, Chinese UP, 1999: 95–110.

Lee, Ming-kwan and Leung Sai-wing. 'Democracy, Capitalism and National Identity in Public Attitudes'. Occasional Paper 4. Hong Kong: Hong Kong Polytechnic UP, 1995.

Lee, Paul S. N. 'The Press Response to the Rapid Social Change of Hong Kong in the Past Two Decades'. *Asian Journal of Communication* 3:1 (1993): 133–146.

Lee, Paul S. N. 'Chinese and Western Press in Hong Kong'. *Hong Kong History: New Perspectives*. Vol. 2. Ed. Guangwu Wang. Hong Kong [Chinese]: Joint Publishing, 1997: 493–533.

Lee, Paul S. N. 'National Communication and Development: A Comparative Study of Four British Colonies – Nigeria, Guyana, Singapore and Hong Kong'. Diss., U. of Michigan, 1986.

Lee, Paul S. N. and Leonard Chu. 'Inherent Dependence on Power: The Hong Kong Press in Political Transition'. *Media, Culture and Society* 20 (1998): 59–77.

Lee, Rance Pui-Leung and Lau Siu-kai. 'The Birth and Growth of Academic Sociology in Hong Kong'. Occasional Paper 28. Hong Kong: Chinese UP, 1993.

Leifer, Michael, ed. *Asian Nationalism*. London: Routledge, 2000.

Lehmkuhl, Ursula. 'Difficult Challenges: the Far East'. *British Foreign Policy, 1955–64:*

Contracting Options. Eds Wolfram Kaiser and Gillian Staerck. London: Macmillan, 2000: 251–278.

Leung, Benjamin K. P., ed. *Social Issues in Hong Kong.* Hong Kong: Oxford UP, 1990.

Leung, Kar-kuen *et al. An Expose of British Strictly Confidential Files: Secrets of 1967 Disturbance.* Hong Kong [Chinese]: ET Press, 2001.

Leung, Sai-wing. 'The "China Factor" in the 1991 Legislative Council Election: The June 4th Incident and Anti-Communist China Syndrome'. *Hong Kong Tried Democracy: the 1991 Elections in Hong Kong.* Eds S. K. Lau and Louie Kin-shuen. Hong Kong: Hong Kong Institute of Asia-pacific Studies, the Chinese UP, 1993: 187–236.

Leung, Sai-wing. 'Social Construction of Hong Kong Identity: A Partial Account'. *Indicators of Social Development – Hong Kong 1997.* Eds Lau Siu-kai *et al.* Hong Kong: Hong Kong Institute of Asia-Pacific Studies, Chinese UP, 1999: 111–134.

Leung, Wai-yin and Johannes Chan Mun-man, eds *A New Commentary on the Media Laws.* Hong Kong [Chinese]: Commercial Press, 1995.

Li Kar-yuen. *On Hong Kong Newspaper History.* Hong Kong: Joint Publishing, 1989.

Li, Kuk-shing. *A Comment on the Press of HK.* Hong Kong [Chinese]: Ming Pao Publishing, 2000.

Li, Pang-kwong. 'The Democratic Transition of Hong Kong: an Institutional Analysis'. *Hong Kong After Reunification – Problems and Perspectives.* Eds Achim Gussgen, Reimund Seidelmann and Ting Wai. Germany: Nomos Verlagsgesellschaft, Baden-Baden, 2000: 77–94.

Li, Yuet-wah. 'Freedom of the Media'. *From Colony to SAR: Hong Kong's Challenges Ahead.* Eds Joseph Y. S. Cheng and Sonny S. H. Lo. Hong Kong: Chinese UP, 1995: 457–490.

Li, Zhisui. *The Private Life of Chairman Mao.* New York: Random House, 1994.

Liebes, Tamar and James Curran, eds *Media, Ritual and Identity.* London: Routledge, 1998.

Link, Perry. 'The Anaconda in the Chandelier'. *New York Review of Books* XLIX.6 (April 11, 2002): 67–70.

Link, Perry. 'More Repression? Beijing's Response to the 21st Century?' Presentation Paper, Conference of University of Hong Kong, June 2003.

Lo, Shiu-hing. *Political Development in Macau.* Hong Kong: Chinese UP, 1995

Lo, Shiu-hing. 'Hong Kong's Political Influence on South China:

Cross-Border Citizen Participation and Its Impact on the Mainland's Public Maladminis-tration'. Paper presented at an international conference, 'Political Development in Taiwan and Hong Kong'. U. of Hong Kong, 1996 February 8–9.

Lo, Shiu-hing. *The Politics of Democratization in Hong Kong.* London: Macmillan, 1997.

Lu, Ping. 'On the Problem of Reunion of Hong Kong with China'. *Selected Reports of the Central Party School* [Chinese]. 122.6 (6 Oct. 1997): 2–17.

Lui, Tai-lok. 'The Hong Kong New Middle Class on the Eve of 1997'. *The Other Hong Kong Report 1997.* Ed. Joseph Y. S. Cheng. Hong Kong: Chinese UP, 1997: 207–226.

Lui, Tai-lok. 'Social Change – Post-1997 Uneasiness'. *Hong Kong China: the Red Dawn.* Ed. Chris Yeung. Australia: Prentice Hall, 1998: 163–174.

Lui, Tai-lok and Stephen W. K. Chiu. 'Social Movements and Public Discourse on Politics'. *Hong Kong's History – State and Society Under Colonial Rule.* Ed. Tak-Wing Ngo. London: Routledge, 1999: 101–118.

Lui, Tai-lok and Thomas W. P. Wong. 'Chinese Entrepreneurship in Context'. Occasional Paper 38. Hong Kong: Hong Kong Institute of Asia-Pacific Studies, 1994.

Ma, Eric Kit-wai. 'Rethinking Media Studies: The Case of China'. *De-westernizing*

Media Studies. Eds James Curran and Myung-Jin Park. London: Routledge, 2000: 21–34.

Ma, Eric K. W. and Anthony Y. H. Fung. 'Re-sinicization, Nationalism and the Hong Kong Identity'. *Press and Politics in Hong Kong: Case Studies from 1967 to 1997*. Eds Clement Y. K. So and Joseph M. Chan. Hong Kong Institute of Asia-Pacific Studies, Hong Kong: Chinese UP, 1999: 497–528.

Ma, Chung-pak. *A Memoir of the Hong Kong Press*. Hong Kong [Chinese]: the Commercial Press, 2001.

Martin, Helmut. 'Between Local Preservation of Hong Kong Identity and Chinese Self-understanding in Hong Kong Culture'. *Hong Kong After Reunification – Problems and Perspectives*. Eds Achim Gussgen, Reimund Seidelmann and Ting Wai. Germany: Nomos Verlagsgesellschaft, Baden-Baden, 2000: 243–260.

'Messages from Former Chairmen'. *Hong Kong Journalists Association 25th Anniversary* Bulletin. Hong Kong: Hong Kong Journalists Association, 1993: 20–23.

McChesney, Robert. *Rich Media, Poor Democracy*. Urbana: Illinois UP, 1999.

McChesney, Robert W. 'The Problem of Journalism: a Political Economic Contribution to an Explanation of the Crisis in Contemporary US Journalism'. *Journalism Studies* 4.3 (2003): 299–329.

Miliband, Ralph. *Marxism and Politics*. London: Oxford UP, 1978.

Mills, Sara. *Discourses of Difference: an Analysis of Women's Travel Writing and Colonialism*. London: Routledge, 1991.

Miners, Norman. *Hong Kong under Imperial Rule, 1912–1941*. New York: Oxford UP, 1987.

Miners, Norman. *The Government and Politics of Hong Kong*, 5th Ed., with Post-Handover Update by James T. H. Tang. Hong Kong: Oxford UP, 1998.

Ming Pao Daily News' Staff Writer, *Reflections on Xi Yang's Case*. Hong Kong [Chinese]: Ming Pao Publishing, 1997.

Mitchell, Robert E. 'How Hong Kong Newspapers Have Responded to 15 Years of Rapid Social Change'. *Asian Survey* 9 (1969): 669–681.

Moriarty, Francis. 'The Media'. *The Other Hong Kong Report 1994*. Eds Donald H. McMillen and Man Si-wai. Hong Kong: Chinese UP, 1994: 389–414.

Morgan, D. J. *The Official History of Colonial Development vol. 5, Guidance towards Self-government in British Colonies 1941–71*. Atlantic Highlands, NJ: Humanities Press, 1980.

Murdock, Graham. 'Large Corporations and the Control of the Communication Industries'. *Culture, Society and the Media*. Eds Michael Gurevitch *et al*. London: Methuen, 1982: 118–150.

Murdock, Graham. 'Redrawing the Map of the Communications Industries: Concentration and Ownership in the Era of Privatization'. *Public Communication: the New Imperatives*. Ed. M. Ferguson. London: Sage, 1990: 1–15.

Ng, Chi-sum, Jane C. Y. Lee and Alison Ayang Qu. *Nationality and Right of Abode of Hong Kong Residents: Continuity and Change Before and After 1997*. Hong Kong: Centre of Asian Studies, Hong Kong UP, 1997.

Ng, Chun-hung and Thomas W. P. Wong. 'The Ethos of the Hong Kong People: Taking Stock in 1997'. *Indicators of Social Development – Hong Kong 1997*. Eds Lau Siu-kai *et al*. Hong Kong: Hong Kong Institute of Asia-Pacific Studies, Chinese UP, 1999: 233–254.

Ngo, Tak-wing, ed. *Hong Kong's History – State and Society under Colonial Rule*. London: Routledge, 1999.

Ngo, Tak-wing. 'The East Asian Anomaly Revisited: the Politics of Laissez-faire in Hong Kong 1945–1985'. Diss. London U. 1996.

Ngo, Tak-wing. 'Colonialism in Hong Kong Revisited'. *Hong Kong's History – State and Society under Colonial Rule*. Ed. Tak-Wing Ngo. London: Routledge, 1999: 1–12.

Nip, Joyce Y. M. 'Clash and Compatibility of Journalistic Culture: Mainland China and Hong Kong'. *Communication and Culture: China and the World Entering the 21st Century*. Eds D. Ray Heisey and Wenxiang Gong. Amsterdam/Atlanta, GA: Editions Rodopi. (1998) 83–102.

Oksenberg, Michael. 'China's Confident Nationalism', *Foreign Affairs* 65.3 (1987 Special Issue) 501–524.

Ong, Aihwa and Donald Nonini eds *The Cultural Politics of Modern Chinese Transnationalism*. New York: Routledge, 1997.

Pahl, R. and J. Winkler. 'The Economic Elite: Theory and Practice'. *Elites and Power in British Society*. Eds F. Stanworth and Giddens, A. London: Cambridge UP, 1979: 102–122.

Pan, Zhongdang *et al.* 'One Event, Three Stories: Media Narratives from Cultural China of the Handover of Hong Kong'. *Power, Money and Media – Communication Patterns and Bureaucratic Control in Cultural China*. Ed. C. C. Lee. Evanston, IL: Northwestern UP, 2000: 271–287.

Patten, Christopher. *Letters to Hong Kong*. Hong Kong: Information Services Department 1997.

Patten, Chris. *East and West*. London: Macmillan, 1998.

Polumbaum, Judy. 'Professionalism in China's Press Corps'. *China's Crisis of 1989*. Eds R. V. Des Forges, Luo Ning and Wu Yen-bo. Albany: SUNY Press 1993: 295–312.

Postiglione, Gerald A. and James T. H. Tang, eds *Hong Kong's Reunion with China: the Global Dimensions*. Armonk, NY: M. E. Sharpe, 1997.

Pye, Lucian W. 'How China's Nationalism was Shanghaied'. *Chinese Nationalism*. Ed. Jonathan Unger. Armonk, NY: M. E. Sharpe, 1996: 86–112.

Radio TV Hong Kong. 'Framework Agreement with Secretary for Information Technology and Broadcasting'. Hong Kong.

'RTHK: The Government's Broadcaster?' *Media Freedom Watch* HKJA (Feb. 2001).

Roberti, Mark. *The Fall of Hong Kong: Britain's Betrayal and China's Triumph*. New York: John Wiley & Sons, 1994.

Salaff, Janet W. and Wong Siu-lun. 'Exiting Hong Kong'. *Inequalities and Development*. Eds S. K. Lau *et al*. Hong Kong: Hong Kong Institute of Asia-Pacific Studies, Chinese UP, 1994: 205–250.

Salaff, Janet W. and Wong Siu-lun. 'Migration and Identities in Hong Kong's Transition'. Paper presented at the Conference on Hong Kong in Transition, Chatham House, London. 15 Dec. 1997.

Sanders, David. *Losing an Empire, Finding a Role: British Foreign Policy Since 1945*. Basingstoke: Macmillan Education, 1990.

Scannell, Paddy. 'Public Service Broadcasting and Modern Life'. *Media, Culture and Society* 11 (1989): 143–147.

Scannell, Paddy. *Radio, Television, and Modern Life: A Phenomenological Approach*. Oxford, Eng.: Blackwell, 1996.

Schaffer, B. B. 'The Concept of Preparation: Some Questions about the Transfer of Systems of Government'. *World Politics* 18.1 (1965): 42–67.

Schiller, Herbert. *Culture Inc.: the Corporate Takeover of Public Expression*, New York; Oxford: Oxford University Press, 1989.

Schlesinger, Philip. *Putting 'Reality' Together*. Rev. edn. London: Methuen, 1987.

Schlesinger, Philip. 'Rethinking the Sociology of Journalism: Source Strategies and the Limits of Media-Centrism'. *Public Communication*. Ed. Marjorie Ferguson. London: Sage, 1990: 61–83.

Schudson, Michael. *Discovering the News: A Social History of American Newspapers*. New York: Basic Books, 1978.

Schudson, Michael. *The Power of News*. Cambridge, Mass.: Harvard University Press, 1995.

Schudson, Michael. 'The Sociology of News Production Revisited'. *Mass Media and Society*. Eds James Curran and M. Gurevitch. 3rd edn. London: Arnold, 2000: 175–200.

Schudson, Michael. 'The Objectivity Norm in American Journalism'. *Journalism* 2.2 (2001): 149–170.

Schudson, Michael. *The Sociology of News*. New York: W. W. Norton, 2003.

Scott, Ian. *Political Change and the Crisis of Legitimacy in Hong Kong*. London: C. Hurst, 1989.

Scott, Ian. 'Political Transformation in Hong Kong: From Colony to Colony'. *Hong Kong-Guangdong Link: Partnership in Flux*. Eds Reginald Kwok and Alvin So. Armonk, New York: M. E. Sharpe, 1995: 189–223.

Shen, George. 'China's Investment in Hong Kong'. *The Other Hong Kong Report 1993*. Eds Choi Po-king and Ho Lok-sang. Hong Kong: Chinese UP, 1993: 425–454.

Sigal, Leon V. *Reporters and Officials: The Organization and Politics of Newsmaking*. Lexington, MA: D. C. Heath, 1973.

Sigal, Leon V. 'Sources Make the News'. *Reading the News*. Eds Robert K. Manoff and Michael Schudson. New York: Pantheon, 1986: 9–37.

Sinn, Elizabeth. *Power and Charity: The Early History of the Tung Wah Hospital, Hong Kong*. Hong Kong: Oxford UP, 1989.

Sit, Victor F. S. and Siu-lun Wong. *Small and Medium Industries in an Export-Oriental Economy: The Case of Hong Kong*. Hong Kong: Centre of Asian Studies, Hong Kong UP, 1989.

Skeldon, Ronald. 'Hong Kong in an International Migration System'. *Reluctant Exiles? Migration from Hong Kong and the New Overseas Chinese*. Ed. Ronald Skeldon. Hong Kong: Hong Kong UP, 1994: 21–51.

Skeldon, Ronald. 'Emigration from Hong Kong, 1945–94'. *Emigration from Hong Kong*. Ed. Ronald Skeldon. Hong Kong: Chinese UP, 1995: 325–332.

Smart, Josephine. 'Business Immigration to Canada: Deception and Exploitation'. *Reluctant Exiles? Migration from Hong Kong and the New Overseas Chinese*. Ed. Ronald Skeldon. Hong Kong: Hong Kong UP, 1994: 98–119.

Smart, Josephine and Alan Smart. 'Personal Relations and Divergent Economies: A Case Study of Hong Kong Investment in South China'. *International Journal of Urban Regional Research* 15 (1991): 216–233.

Smith, Anthony D. *The Ethnic Revival in the Modern World*. Cambridge: Cambridge UP, 1981.

Smith, Anthony D. *National Identity*. London: Penguin Books, 1991.

Smith, Anthony D. 'Theories of Nationalism – Alternative Models of Nation Formation'. *Asian Nationalism*. Ed. Michael Leifer. London: Routledge, 2000: 1–20.

So, Clement. 'Pre-1997 Hong Kong Press: Cut-throat Competition and the Changing Journalistic Paradigm'. *The Other Hong Kong Report 1996*. Eds Ngaw Mee-kau and Li Si-ming. Hong Kong: Chinese UP, 1996: 485–506.

So, Clement Y. K. and Joseph Man Chan. 'Research on Press and Politics in Hong Kong: An Overview'. *Press and Politics in Hong Kong: Case Studies from 1967 to 1997*. Eds Clement Y. K. So and Joseph M. Chan. Hong Kong: Hong Kong Institute of Asia-Pacific Studies, Chinese UP, 1999: 1–32.

So, Clement Y. K. and Joseph M. Chan, eds *Press and Politics in Hong Kong: Case Studies from 1967 to 1997*. Hong Kong: Hong Kong Institute of Asia-Pacific Studies, Chinese UP, 1999.

Sparks, Colin with Anna Reading. *Communism, Capitalism and the Mass Media*. London: Sage, 1998.

Sparks, Colin and John Tulloch, eds *Tabloid Tales: Global Debates over Media Standards*. Lanham, MD: Rowland and Littlefield, 2000.

Tang, James T. H. *Britain's Encounter with Revolutionary China, 1949–54*. Houndmills, Basingstoke: Macmillan; New York: St. Martin's Press, 1992.

Tang, James T. H. 'From Empire Defence to Imperial Retreat: Britain's Postwar China Policy and the Decolonization of Hong Kong'. *Modern Asian Studies* 28.2 (1994): 317–337.

Tang, James T. H. 'The SAR Government and the Changing Political Order in Hong Kong'. *The Government and Politics of Hong Kong*. 5th edn. Ed. Norman Miners. Hong Kong: OUP, 1998: 246–270.

Thompson, John B. *The Media and Modernity*. Stanford: Stanford UP, 1995.

Tien, Hung-mao, ed. *Mainland China, Taiwan and US Policy*. Cambridge, MA: Oelgeschlager, Gunn and Hain, 1983.

Tien, Hung-mao. *The Great Transition*. Stanford, CA: Hoover Institution, 1989.

Ting, Wai. 'Complex Interdependence and Political Imperatives: the Difficult Relations among Beijing, Taipei, Hong Kong and Washington'. *Hong Kong After Reunification – Problems and Perspectives*. Eds Achim Gussgen, Reimund Seidelmann and Ting Wai. Germany: Nomos Verlagsgesellschaft, Baden-Baden, 2000: 307–326.

To, Yiu-ming. 'Blowing in the Wind: Economic and Political Challenges to the Press in Political Transition'. *The Other Hong Kong Report 1995*. Eds Stephen Y. L. Cheung and Stephen M. H. Sze. Hong Kong: Chinese UP, 1995: 419–438.

To, Yiu-ming, 'Colonial Rule and Press Freedom: Hong Kong's Experience'. *Journalism and Social Change*. Eds Yu Xu, Guo Zhongshe and Huang Yu. Hong Kong [Chinese]: Zhong Hwa, 1999: 281–296.

To, Yiu-ming, 'From Political Institution to Economic Enterprise: China's Political and Economic Changes and Media Commercialisation'. *China: 50 Years in Review, A Hong Kong Perspective*. Ed. Y. C. Wong. Hong Kong: Oxford University Press, 2000: 61–78.

To, Yiu-ming and Tuen-Yu Lau. 'Walking a Tight Rope: Hong Kong's Media Facing Political and Economic Challenges since Sovereignty Transfer 1997–2001'. An Article Presented at the Chinese Communication Association's Annual Meeting, Hong Kong, 3 July 2001.

Townsend, James. 'Chinese Nationalism'. *Chinese Nationalism*. Ed. Jonathan Unger. Armonk, NY: M. E. Sharpe, 1996: 1–30.

Tsang, Steve. *Democracy Shelved: Great Britain, China and Attempts at Constitutional Reform in Hong Kong, 1945–52*. Hong Kong; Oxford: Oxford UP, 1988.

Tsang, Steve. *Hong Kong: An Appointment with China*. London: I. B. Tauris, 1997.

Tsang, Steve. *A Modern History of Hong Kong*. London: I. B. Tauris, 2004.

Tsang, Steve and Hung-mao Tien, eds *Democratization in Taiwan: Implications for China*. Houndsmills, Basingstoke, Hampshire: Macmillan Press, in association St.

Antony's College, Oxford; New York: St. Martin's Press; Hong Kong: Hong Kong U. Press, 1999.

Tu, Wei-ming, ed. *The Living Tree – The Changing Meaning of Being Chinese Today.* Stanford, CA.: Stanford UP, 1994.

Tyrene White, ed. *China Briefing 2000 – The Continuing Transformation.* New York: M. E. Sharpe, 2000.

Tuchman, Gaye. 'Objectivity as Strategic Ritual: An Examination of Newsman's Notion of Objectivity'. *American Journal of Sociology* 77 (1972): 660–679.

Tuchman, Gaye. *Making News: A Study in the Construction of Reality.* New York: Free Press, 1978.

Tumber, Howard, ed. *Media Power, Professionals and Policies.* London: Routledge, 2000.

Tung, Chee Hwa. 'Building Hong Kong for a New Era'. Address. Meeting of Provisional Legislative Council. Hong Kong. 8 Oct. 1997.

Tunstall, Jeremy. *Television Producers.* London; New York: Routledge, 1993.

Tunstall, Jeremy. *Newspaper Power: The New National Press in Britain.* Oxford: OUP, 1996.

Tunstall, Jeremy. *Media Occupations and Professions: A Reader.* New York: OUP, 2001.

Tunstall, Jeremy and David Machin. *The Anglo-American Media Connection.* Oxford: OUP, 1999.

Unger, Jonathan, ed. *Chinese Nationalism.* Armonk, NY: M. E. Sharpe, 1996.

Unger, Jonathan. 'Introduction'. *Chinese Nationalism.* Ed. Jonathan Unger. Armonk, NY: M. E. Sharpe, 1996: xi–xviii.

Vines, Stephen. *Hong Kong: China's New Colony.* London: Orion Business, 1999.

Vittachi, Nury. *North Wind.* Hong Kong: Chameleon, 2001.

Waisbord, Silvio. 'Secular Politics: The Modernization of Argentine Electioneering'. *Politics, Media, and Modern Democracy.* Eds David L. Swanson and Paolo Mancini. New York: Praeger, 1996: 207–226.

Waisbord, Silvio. *Watchdog Journalism in South America: News, Accountability and Democracy.* New York: Columbia UP, 2000.

Waldron, Stephen Edward. 'Fire on the Rim: A Study in Contradictions in Left-Wing Mobilization'. Ph.D. diss., Syracuse U., 1976.

Wang, Gungwu. 'External China as a New Policy Area'. *Pacific Affairs* 58.1(1985): 28–43.

Wang, Gungwu. 'The Study of Chinese Identities in SE Asia'. *Changing identities of the SE Asian Chinese since WWII.* Eds Jennifer Cushman and Wang Gungwu. Hong Kong: Hong Kong UP, 1988: 1–22.

Wang, Gungwu. 'Openness and Nationalism: Outside the Chinese Revolution'. *Chinese Nationalism.* Ed. Jonathan Unger. Armonk, NY: M. E. Sharpe, 1996: 113–125.

Wang, Gungwu and John Wong, eds *Hong Kong in China – The Challenges of Transition.* Singapore: Times Academic, 1999.

Weaver, David H. and G. Cleverland Wilhoit. *The American Journalist: A Portrait of U.S. News People and Their Work.* 2nd edn. Bloomington: Indiana UP, 1991.

Welsh, Frank. *A History of Hong Kong.* Rev. edn. London: HarperCollins, 1997.

Wesley-Smith, Peter. *Unequal Treaty, 1898–1997: China, Great Britain, and Hong Kong's New Territories.* Rev. edn. Hong Kong; New York: Oxford UP, 1998.

White, Tyrene, ed. *China Briefing 2000 – The Continuing Transformation.* New York: M. E. Sharpe, 2000.

Whiting, Allen. 'Assertive Nationalism in Chinese Foreign Policy'. *Asian Survey* 23.8 (1983) 913–933.

Wilson, Dick. *Hong Kong! Hong Kong!* London: Unwin Hyman, 1990.

Won, Ho Chang. *Mass Media in China: The History and the Future*. Ames: Iowa State University Press, 1989.

Wong, Siu-lun. 'Modernization and Chinese Culture in Hong Kong'. *China Quarterly* 106 (1986): 306–325.

Wong, Siu-lun. *Emigrant Entrepreneurs: Shanghai Industrialists in Hong Kong*. Hong Kong: Oxford UP, 1988.

Wong, Siu-lun. 'Migration and Stability in Hong Kong'. *Asian Survey* 32.10 (1992): 918–933.

Wong, Siu-lun. 'Roaming Yuppies: Hong Kong Migration to Australia'. *Asian and Pacific Migration Journal* 3.2–3 (1994): 373–392.

Wong, Siu-lun. 'Political Attitudes and Identity'. *Emigration from Hong Kong*. Ed. Ronald Skeldon. Hong Kong: Chinese UP, 1995: 147–176.

Wong, Siu-lun. 'Business Networks, Cultural Values and the State in Hong Kong and Singapore'. *Chinese Business Enterprise in Asia*. Ed. R. A. Brown. London and New York: Routledge, 1995: 136–153.

Wong Siu-lun and Lee Ming-kwan. *Decline of Authority, Social Conflict, and Social Reintegration in Hong Kong: Patterns of Social Change in the Last Years of British Rule*. Research Report Submitted to the Research Grant Council of the [Hong Kong] Universities Grants Committee, 1997.

Wong Siu-lun and Lee Ming-kwan. 'The Fraying of the Socio-economic Fabric of Hong Kong'. *Pacific Review* 10.3 (1997): 426–441.

Wong, Siu-lun and Janet Salaff. 'Network Capital: Emigration from Hong Kong'. *British Journal of Sociology* 49.3 (1998): 358–374.

Wong, Thomas W. P. and Tai-lok Lui. *From One Brand of Politics to One Brand of Political Culture*. Hong Kong: Chinese UP, Hong Kong Institute of Asia-Pacific Studies, 1992.

Wong, Thomas W. P. and Tai-lok Lui. *Morality, Class and the Hong Kong Way of Life*. Hong Kong: Chinese UP, 1994.

Xu, Jiatun. *The Memoirs of Xu Jiatun on Hong Kong*. Taipei [Chinese]: Lian Jing; Hong Kong: *Hong Kong United Daily*, 1993.

Yahuda, Michael. *Hong Kong: China's Challenge*. London: Routledge, 1995.

Yahuda, Michael. 'The Changing Faces of Chinese Nationalism: the Dimensions of Statehood'. *Asian Nationalism*. Ed. Michael Leifer. London: Routledge, 2000: 21–37.

Yeung, Chris. 'Politics: Change and the Unchanged'. *Hong Kong China: the Red Dawn*. Ed. Chris Yeung. Australia: Prentice Hall, 1998: 1–22.

Yeung, Chris. 'Democracy in Hong Kong?' *Harvard International Review* 22.2 (Summer 2000): 84–86.

Yeung, Chris. 'Hong Kong Media in the Changing Political Landscape'. *Harvard Asia Quarterly* (1 Jan. 2002). www.fas.harvard.edu/~asiactr/haq/200201/. Accessed 17 Feb. 2005.

Yeung, Chris. 'Hong Kong Under One Country Two Systems: Promises and Realities'. CNAPS [Centre for Northeast Asian Policy] Working Paper, Brookings Institution (Spring 2001). www.brookings.edu/fp/cnaps/papers/yeungwp01.pdf-2001-06-22, Accessed 17 Feb. 2005.

Yu, Shiu-wah. 'The Revitalization of Imperial Symbols in the 1997 Reunion of Hong Kong with China'. *Hong Kong Cultural Studies Bulletin* 8–9 (1998): 84–91.

Yu, Xu, Leonard L. Chu and Guo Zhongshi. 'Reform and Challenge – An Analysis of China's Journalism Education under Social Transition'. *Gazette* 64.1: 63–77.

Zhang, Liang. *The Tiananmen Papers: The Chinese Leadership's Decision to Use Force against Their Own People – in Their Own Words*. Eds Andrew J. Nathan and Perry Link; with an afterword by Orville Schell. London: Little, Brown, 2001.

Zhao, Yuezhi. *Media, Market, and Democracy in China: Between the Party Line and the Bottom Line*. Urbana: Illinois UP, 1998.

Zhao, Yuezhi. 'Watchdogs on Party Leashes? Contexts and Implications of Investigative Journalism in Post-Deng China'. *Journalism Studies* 1.4 (2000): 577–597.

Zhao, Yuezhi. 'Falun Gong, Identity and the Struggle over Meaning Inside and Outside China'. *Contesting Media Power*. Eds Nick Couldry and James Curran. London: Rowman and Littlefield, 2003: 209–226.

Zheng, Yongnian. *Discovering Chinese Nationalism in China – Modernisation, Identity and International Relations*. Cambridge, UK: Cambridge UP, 1999.

Zheng, Suisheng. *In Search of a Right Place? – Chinese Nationalism in the Post-Cold War World* (USC Seminar Series 12), Hong Kong Institute of Asia-Pacific Studies, Hong Kong: Chinese UP, 1997.

Newspaper articles

Balfour, Frederik. 'A Thorn in China's Side: Publisher Jimmy Lai is Riding the Wave of Hong Kong Dissent'. *Business Week* 28 July 2003.

'Blow to Confidence'. Editorial. *South China Morning Post* (*SCMP*) 16 Apr. 1994.

Bradsher, Keith. 'Property Slump Ruins Many in Hong Kong'. *New York Times* 15 Aug. 2003.

Bradsher, Keith. 'Second Hong Kong Democracy Figure Leaves Hastily'. *New York Times* 15 May 2004.

Braude, Jonathan. 'Pass for Patten's Benchmark Test'. *SCMP* 30 June 1998.

Cha, Louis. 'Free Press Can Triumph Over China's Influence'. *SCMP* 23 Apr. 1994.

Chan, Carrie. 'Honour for Philip Wong Stirs Anger'. *SCMP* 12 Oct. 2003

Chen, Albert. 'How the Liberals Stopped a Constitutional Crisis'. *SCMP* 8 July 2003.

Cheng, Albert. 'Dwindling Freedom of Speech'. *SCMP* 17 May 2004.

Cheng, Albert. 'On the Brink of a Dark Age'. *SCMP* 24 May 2004.

Cheung, Gary. 'Union's Colourful Past Now on Stage'. *SCMP* 20 Aug. 2003.

Cheung, Jimmy. 'Senior Staff Volunteer to Retire from *RTHK*'. *SCMP* 27 May 2003.

Cohen, Warren I. 'The Cooperative Calm before the Storm'. *Los Angeles Times* 10 Aug. 2003.

Cohn, Martin Regg. 'Li Family Tends to Take Hard Line to Get Its Way: Playing Hardball with Air Canada Tycoon Used to Flexing Muscles'. *Toronto Star [Canada]* 27 Apr. 2004.

Dateline, 1997. [Internet magazine of Foreign Correspondents' Club] Hong Kong.

Davis, Michael. 'Remember, the Basic Law is a Living Document'. *SCMP* 9 Aug. 2003.

'Desperate Remedies: Will Tung Chee-hwa be Next to Go?' *The Economist* 17 July 2003.

Emily Lau. 'How the Press Is Squeezed by China'. *SCMP* 18 Apr. 1994.

'Fair Chance of Appeal Win'. *SCMP* 6 Apr. 1994.

Fitzpatrick, Liam. 'The Long March'. *Time Asia Magazine* 161.27. 14 July 2003.

'500 Journalists Fight for Press Freedom'. *Hong Kong Economic Journal* 2 July 2003.

'400 Newsmen March in Protest Rally'. *SCMP* 16 Apr. 1994.

'Free on Parole'. *SCMP* 26 Jan. 1997.

Gilley, Bruce. 'Asian Millennium – Robert Kuok (1923–) – Father of Industry: The Inexorable Rise of Robert Kuok's Empire Epitomizes the Way Chinese Families Have Shaped Asian Business This Century'. *Far Eastern Economic Review* 25 Nov. 1999.

Gittings, Danny. 'The End of the Tung Era'. *Asian Wall Street Journal (AWSJ)* 8 July 2003.

'Heat on Beijing over Xi's Jailing'. *SCMP* 18 Apr. 1994.

Hogg, Chris. 'HK Warned on Election Abuses'. *BBC News, Hong Kong* 17 May 2004. news.bbc.co.uk/1/hi/world/asia-pacific/3720525.stm 17 May 2004.

'HK Radio Hosts Bow to Pressure'. *BBC News, Hong Kong* 13 May 2004. news.bbc.co.uk/1/hi/world/asia-pacific/3711747.stm 17 May 2004.

Ho, Andy. Column, *SCMP* May 1997.

Ho, Andy. 'Mainland Propaganda Mill Wins Ear of Some Local Media'. *SCMP* 16 July 2002.

Hon, May Sin-mi. 'Outgoing Anson Vows Not to Meddle – "I'm not Lee Kuan Yew . . . You Owe Your Successor Silence"'. *SCMP* 28 Apr. 2001.

'Hopes of Finding Private Lawyer'. *SCMP* 7 Apr. 1994.

'Hong Kong's Muzzled Media'. *AWSJ* 23 Aug. 2002

'Hong Kong's Velvet Revolution'. *Wall Street Journal* 8 July 2003.

Hu, Bei. 'Xinhuaonline Takes on Dotcom Gloom'. *SCMP* 5 July 2001.

'Journalists Kow-tow to China or Go'. *Australian Financial Review*. 1 July 2002.

Kahn, Gabriel and Kathy Chen. 'Hong Kong Waits for Beijing to Respond to Political Crisis'. *Wall Street Journal* 17 July 2003.

Kynge, James and Angela Mackay. 'Beijing's Hong Kong Balancing Act'. *Financial Times* 18 July 2003.

Kahn, Joseph. 'Chinese Paper Soften Its Voice'. *AWSJ* 22 Apr. 1997.

Kahn, Joseph. 'U.S. Panel on Religious Freedom Drops China Visit, Protesting Curbs'. *New York Times* 8 Aug. 2003.

Kahn, Gabriel and Kathy Chen. 'Hong Kong Waits for Beijing to Respond to Political Crisis'. *Wall Street Journal* 17 July 2003.

'Keep Your Nose Out; Patten Told by Chinese Official'. *SCMP* 10 Oct. 1993.

Kong, Lai-fan. 'Tycoon "Committed to HK"'. *SCMP* 31 Aug. 2000.

Kraar, Louis. 'The Death of Hong Kong'. *Fortune* Magazine 26 Feb. 1995.

'Kuok – the Quintessential Asian Tycoon'. *The Star* [Malaysia] 4 June 2001.

Kuok, Hock Nien. 'Speculation'. Letter. *SCMP* 29 June 2000.

Kwong, Kevin. 'Political Monthly Runs Out of Steam'. *Sunday Morning Post* [Hong Kong]. 5 Apr. 1998.

Lam, Willy. *AWSJ* 10 Nov. 2000.

Lam, Willy Wo-lap. 'Marshalling the SAR's Tycoons'. *SCMP* 29 June 2000.

Lee, Martin. 'Two Systems, One Destiny'. *SCMP* 1 Aug. 2003.

Letter. *SCMP* 11 Apr. 1994.

Letter. *SCMP* 1 May 1994.

Leung, Ambrose. 'Shadow Cabinet the Democrats' Goal'. *SCMP* 15 July 2003.

Leung, Ambrose. '*China Daily* Attacks "Political" Bishop Zen'. *SCMP* 26 July 2003.

Lee, Klaudia and Ambrose Leung. 'Don't be a City of Turmoil, Hong Kong Warned'. *SCMP* 7 Aug. 2003.

Lau, Justine and Joe Leahy. 'Hong Kong Chief's Links to Tycoon Raises Eyebrows'. *Financial Times* 9 Aug. 2003.

Letter [by 115 Reporters and Editors]. *SCMP* 10 Nov. 2000.

Lo, Joseph. 'Xinhua Venture Bucks Trend. Global China Technology Group Takes 55pc Stake in Online News Provider'. *SCMP* 20 Jan. 2001.

'Losing a Voice of Integrity'. *AWSJ* 2 May 2002.

Luk, Sidney. 'Jiang Calls for Social Responsibility'. *SCMP* 20 Dec. 2000.

'Mainland Arrest Procedure "Still in Place"'. *SCMP* 27 Jan. 1997.

Marshall, Tyler. 'Hong Kong May Be in the Eye of a Storm'. *Los Angeles Times* 12 Aug. 2003.

McHugh, Fionnuala. 'The Sensational Jimmy Lai'. *Post Magazine, Sunday Morning Post* 13 Oct. 2002.

Meyer, Mahlon. 'Chinese Shadows: Calls to Control the Press are Just the Latest Signs of Hong Kong's Fading Autonomy'. *Newsweek* 6 Sept. 1999.

Meyer, Mahlon. 'Muzzling the Press'. *Newsweek* 24 Apr. 2000.

Open Monthly, Aug. 2003.

'People Power'. *Economist* 7 July 2003.

Political Desk. 'Tycoon Says *Post* Biased Against Tung'. *SCMP* 26 July 2000.

Pritchard, Simon. 'From Rags to Rich Rancour'. *SCMP* 1 Sept. 2000.

'Profile, the Private Life of Robert Kuok'. *Euromoney Magazine* 15 Feb. 1997.

'Rimbunan to Tap Huge Market in China'. *The Star* [Malaysia] 30 June 1998.

'Rimbunan Hijau to Develop Industrial Park in Dalian to Form a Joint Venture with Golden Ocean to Develop Property in Malaysia'. *The Star* [Malaysia] 3 July 1995.

'Ripple Effect: Hong Kong's Turmoil Touches Taiwan'. *Economist* 7 Aug. 2003.

Schloss, Glenn. 'The Real-life Drama of *ATV*: Lim Por-yen Appears to Have Resolved his Dispute at Asia Television, But the Station's Troubles Continue'. *SCMP* 24 Mar. 2000.

Slater, Joanna. 'Listen, It's Our Radio'. *Far Eastern Economic Review* 19 Mar. 1998. 23–24.

Strurman, Mike. 'Mainland Helped Pay for *Post*, Says Kuok'. *Hong Kong Standard.* 23 Oct. 1993.

Staff reporter. '*Radio TV Hong Kong* rush to leave has bosses reeling'. 27 May 2003.

'Should Tung Chee-hwa Fight on? Only He Can Say'. Editorial, *SCMP* 8 July 2003.

Shamdasani, Ravina. 'Tung's Office Points to His Leadership'. *SCMP* 1 Mar. 2003.

'Sharpening up for the Cut and Thrust of TV Debates'. *SCMP* 7 Aug. 1994.

SCMP 28 Sept. 1993.

SCMP 29 Sept. 1993.

SCMP 8 Oct. 1993.

SCMP 9 Oct. 1993.

SCMP 10 Oct. 1993.

SCMP 11 Oct. 1993.

SCMP 5 Apr. 1994.

SCMP 6 Apr. 1994.

SCMP 7 Apr. 1994.

SCMP 8 Apr. 1994.

SCMP 9 Apr. 1994.

SCMP 10 Apr. 1994.

SCMP 11 April 1994.

SCMP 16 Apr. 1994.

SCMP 26 Jan. 1997

'The Politics of Injustice'. *SCMP* 6 Apr. 1994.

'Time for Mr. Tung to Step Up and Sit Back'. Editorial. *SCMP* 28 Feb. 2003.

Tong, Nora. 'Economic Journal Threatens to Close Down if Security Law Passed'. *SCMP* 4 July 2003.

'Two Major Surveys Show Protestors Well Educated; Ninety Percent of the Half-a-million Marchers Protest Against the National Security Bill'. *Apple Daily* 7 July 2003.

Tung, Chee-hwa. 'The Tung Statement'. Editorial *SCMP* 6 July 2003.

Waldron, Arthur. 'China's Choice over Hong Kong'. *Far Eastern Economic Review* 7 Aug. 2003.

'Whereabouts of Jailed Source Unknown'. *SCMP* 26 Jan. 1997.

Wong, Jesse. 'Hong Kong Exerts Persuasive Power with a Quiet World – Jimmy Lai Loses Advertisement, An Ally Falls From Favor – "You do as You're told"'. *AWSJ* 21 July 2000.

Wong, Jesse. 'University Head Adds to Controversy – CUHK Official Denies Paper's Report of Contact with Government – Li later Says He Has No Comment on Article'. *AWSJ* 25 July 2000.

Wong, Jesse. 'Greater China: Newspaper Says Lo Issue was a Threat to Tung – Beijing-funded Daily Supports Chief Executive – Page of Articles Attacks Hong Kong Academics'. *AWSJ* 28 July 2000.

Xiao Ping. 'Conspiracy to Subvert SAR's Political System'. *China Daily* 14 July 2003.

'Xi's Editors in Protest Fast'. *SCMP* 7 Apr. 1994.

'Xi's Appeal Rejected, Reporter's Jailing Triggers Outcry'. *SCMP* 16 Apr. 1994.

Yan, Louisa. 'July 1 Marchers were Well-educated, Says Survey'. *SCMP* 7 July 2003.

'Yellow Ribbon Campaign Pays Off', *SCMP* 26 Jan. 1997

Yeung, Chris. 'Analysis'. *SCMP* 26 Jan. 1997.

Yeung, Chris. 'Tung's Attitude Problem'. *SCMP* 25 Jan. 1998.

Yeung, Chris. 'A Healthy Media'. *SCMP* 2 Apr. 2003.

Yeung, Chris. 'Repairs Needed'. *SCMP* 26 May 2003.

Yeung, Chris, Doreen Cheung and Louis Won. 'China Ousts HK Reporter for Spying', *SCMP* 28 Sept. 1993.

York, Geoffrey. 'Chinese Media Blast Bishop, Roman Catholic Leader, 71, is "Sowing the Seed of Discord," State-run Newspapers Say'. *The Globe and Mail* [Toronto] 31 July 2003.

Yue, S. Y. 'Controversial ATV Show Axed'. *SCMP* 16 Nov. 1994.

Articles in Chinese-language newspapers

'Albert Cheng Won't Resume Hosting the Phone-in Program Until the License of the *Commercial Radio* is Renewed'. *Apple Daily* 18 July 2003.

'An Exclusive Interview with Lam Hang-chi'. *Shanghai Wen Wei Po [Chinese]* 12 July 2002; reprinted in Lam's column, *Hong Kong Economic Journal* (*HKEJ*) 22 July 2002.

Au Wen. 'Catholic Leaders Forsake Altar for Political Stage'. *China Daily* 25 July 2003.

Cha, Louis. 'New Work in Two Societies'. *MPDN* 3 Jan. 2000.

Chan, Anson. 'Beware of Blurring the Dividing Line', *Financial Times* 1 July 2002 (Hong Kong 3).

Cheng, Albert. 'Henry Tang Has the Responsibility [to Make a Decision]'. *Apple Daily* 21 July 2003.

'Chief Executive Tung Chee-hwa's Statement to Media'. *Ta Kung Pao* 18 July 2003.

'China Doesn't Allow 19 Hong Kong Media to Receive Advertising'. *MPDN* 4 June 1993.

Chiu, Hsiang-chung. 'Hong Kong Civilized Institutions are Facing Austere Threat'. In commemoration of 30th anniversary of *Hong Kong Economic Journal*, *HKEJ* 3 July 2003.

Cho, Yan-chiu. 'Column: Diary of an Investor'. *HKEJ* 4 July 2003.

Chu, Leonard. 'Hong Kong Press Freedom: From British to Chinese "One Country, Two Systems"'. *Ming Pao Monthly* May 1997.

Chui, Siu-ming. 'Media at Last "Reunified"'. *HKEJ* 7 Feb. 2003.

'Complaints to Broadcasting Authority Increase to 540'. *Apple Daily* 20 June 2003.

'Deputies of the National People's Congress Promise to Find Out from the Chinese Authorities'. *MPDN* 1 Oct. 1993.

Dong, Chiao. 'Patriotism, Nationalism and Press Freedom'. *Apple Daily* 20 Dec. 1999.

'Fifteen Academics Take to the Street'. *Apple Daily* 15 July 2003.

'Five Hundred Journalists Fight for Press Freedom'. *HKEJ* 2 July 2003.

Ho, Andy. 'Teacup in a Storm'. *MPDN* 23 June 2003.

Hung, Ching-tin. 'The New Space for the *Hong Kong Economic Journal* in the Post-Handover Era'. *HKEJ* 16 July 2003.

'Interview with Willy Wo-lap Lam'. *Apple Daily* 12 Nov. 2000.

'Interview with Willy Wo-lap Lam'. *Next Magazine* [Hong Kong] 9 Nov. 2000.

'In Order to Prevent Complications in Xi Yang's Incident, Zhang Junsheng [vice-director of *Xinhua News Agency*] Asks the Hong Kong Government not to Intervene'. *Oriental Daily News (ODN)* 10 Oct. 1993.

'Is 12-year Sentence a "Lenient Sentence According to Law?"' *MPDN* 9 Apr. 1994.

'Joseph Man Chan: Media Role: From the Third Party to an Advocate'. *MPDN* 25 July 2003.

'Joseph Man Chan: the Bottom Line of Media Politicization'. *MPDN* 24 July 2003.

'Last year Journalists Accused of Being "Naïve", This Year They Are Taught to Recite – President Jiang Supports Tung (Chee-hwa)'. *Apple Daily* 21 Dec. 2001.

Lai, Pui-yee, 'Investigative Reportage on Yu Pun-hoi'. *Hong Kong Economic Times* 10–11 October 1994.

Lai, Carol Pui-yee. 'Emperor Beijing Accused of Treating Clients: Wu Zuguang, Member of the Chinese People's Political Consultative Conference Urges Investigation'. *Hong Kong Economic Times* 10 Mar. 1995.

Lam, Hang-chi. Column. *HKEJ* 22 July 2002.

Lam, Hang-chi. Column. *HKEJ* 16 June 2003.

Lam, Hang-chi. Column. *HKEJ* 2 July 2003.

Lam, Hang-chi. Column. *HKEJ* 4 July 2003.

Lam, Hang-chi. Column. In commemoration of the 30th anniversary of *Hong Kong Economic Journal*. *HKEJ* 3 July 2003.

'Legislation Can Wait'. Editorial, *MPDN*, 8 July 2003.

Lin, Zizhe, 'Reunion of Xi and His Father; Silence is Golden'. *MPDN* 27 Jan. 1997.

Liu, Mei-heung. 'Cho Yan-chiu: His 30 Years of Journalism Fulfil a Dream'. *HKEJ Monthly* 316 (July 2003).

'Mainland Internet Users: the Half a Million Taking to the Streets [of Hong Kong] were Mobilized by the West'. *MPDN* 8 July 2003.

'Mass Media Has Reached its Bottom Line of Getting Involved in Politics'. *Apple Daily* 20 July 2003.

'*Ming Pao Daily News* Studies to Prohibit Staff from Getting Involved in Protest and Signature Campaign'. *HKEJ* 24 June 2003.

Ming Pao Daily News.

28 Sept. 1993.

3 Oct. 1993

6 Oct. 1993.

8 Oct. 1993.
11 Oct. 1993.
7 Apr. 1994.
8 Apr. 1994.
9 Apr. 1994.
11 Apr. 1994.
16 Apr. 1994.
27 Jan. 1997.
Next Magazine 13 Mar. 2003
Open Magazine Aug. 2003.
Oriental Daily News:
8 Oct. 1993.
9 Oct. 1993.
10 Oct. 1993.
12 Oct. 1993.
16 Oct. 1993.
17 Oct. 1993.
28 Oct. 1993.
25 Dec. 1993.
1 Jan. 1994.
11 Mar. 1994.
15 Mar. 1994.
18 Mar. 1994.
5 Apr. 1994.
16 Apr. 1994.
17 Apr. 1994.
18 Apr. 1994.
1 May 1994.
26 Jan. 1997.
27 Jan. 1997
28 Jan. 1997.
'Sally Wu Series'. *Hong Kong Economic Times* 9 Jan. 1999.
'Sally Wu Series'. *Hong Kong Economic Times* 23 Dec. 1998.
'Tam Yiu-chung Hopes That Beijing Handles the Case with Leniency, Zhang Junsheng Said He Would Report Xi Yang Case'. *MPDN* 28 Sept. 1993.
'Two Major Surveys Show Protestors Well Educated; 90% of the Half-a-Million Marchers Protest against the National Security Bill'. *Apple Daily* 7 July 2003.
Tiong, Hiew-hing. 'Operating a Newspaper is for the Goal of Inheriting and Passing on Chinese Cultural Tradition'. *MPDN* 2 Dec. 2002.
'Why I Don't Charge Sally Wu'. *Hong Kong Economic Times* 5 Feb. 1999.
Wong, Chi-keung. 'The *Radio TV Hong Kong* I Know'. *MPDN* 24 Apr. 1996.
Wong Chi-keung. 'A Letter to Mr Tung Chee-hwa, Chief Executive of HKSAR'. *HKEJ* 10 Mar. 1998.
Wong, Chi-keung. 'Give Hong Kong Citizens Freedom of Information: In Commemoration of the 75th Anniversary of Radio TV Hong Kong'. *MPDN* 20 July 2003.
Xi Lingsheng. 'Grandpa Wants Xi Yang to Emigrate to Hong Kong'. *MPDN* 11 Apr. 1994.
'Xi Yang Comes Back'. *MPDN* 26 Jan. 1997.
'Xi Yang's Parole is in Accordance with Chinese Law'. *MPDN* 28 Jan. 1997.

Yau, Shing-mu and Cheung Siu-jing. 'Sally Wu: a Newspaper Proprietor'. *Hong Kong Economic Times* 22 Dec. 1998.

Yau, Shing-mu and Cheung Siu-jing. 'Sally Wu: From Pro-Taiwan to Pro-China'. *Hong Kong Economic Times* 25 Dec. 1998.

Yu, Kam-yin. 'Can *Hong Kong Economic Journal* Survive?' *HKEJ* 4 July 2003.

Yum Chi-pang. '60% of Demonstrators are Motivated by Media such as Newspapers and Radio Broadcasters'. *Wen Wei Po* [Hong Kong] 15 July 2003.

Others

Newspaper Articles For Case study of the 1960s.

Hong Kong Economic Times [Chinese] Dec. 2000.

Far Eastern Economic Review 1967–1968.

SCMP May–Dec. 1967.

MPDN [Chinese] May–Dec. 1967.

Ta Kung Pao English Edn. 1967–1969.

A Draft Agreement between the Government of the United Kingdom of Great Britain and Northern Ireland and the Government of the People's Republic of China on the Future of Hong Kong. London: Her Majesty's Government, 1984.

The Basic Law of the Hong Kong Special Administrative Region of the People's Republic of China. Hong Kong: Consultative Committee for the Basic Law, Apr. 1990.

Index

For Product Safety Concerns and Information please contact our EU
representative GPSR@taylorandfrancis.com
Taylor & Francis Verlag GmbH, Kaufingerstraße 24, 80331 München, Germany